GW01375265

# INTERROGATION AND CONFESSION

for my mother, Mavis
and in memory of my father, Ivan

# Interrogation and Confession
A Study of Progress, Process and Practice

IAN BRYAN
*Department of Law, University of Lancaster, Lancaster*

# Ashgate
**DARTMOUTH**

Aldershot • Brookfield USA • Singapore • Sydney

© Ian Bryan 1997

All rights reserved. No part of this publication may be reproduced, stored in a retrieval system, or transmitted in any form or by any means, electronic, mechanical, photocopying, recording or otherwise without the prior permission of the publisher.

Published by
Dartmouth Publishing Company Limited
Ashgate Publishing Limited
Gower House
Croft Road
Aldershot
Hants GU11 3HR
England

Ashgate Publishing Company
Old Post Road
Brookfield
Vermont 05036
USA

**British Library Cataloguing in Publication Data**
Bryan, Ian
   Interrogation and confession : a study of progress, process and practice
   1.Police questioning  2.Interviewing in law enforcement
   3.Confession (Law)
   I.Title
   363.2'54

**Library of Congress Cataloging-in-Publication Data**
Bryan, Ian.
   Interrogation and confession : a study of progress, process and practice / Ian Bryan.
     p.   cm.
   Includes bibliographical references and index.
   ISBN 1-85521-875-5
   1. Confession (Law)–Great Britain.  2. Police questioning–Great Britain.  I. Title.
   KD8384.B79   1997
   345.41'06–dc21
                                                97-19616
                                                    CIP

ISBN 1 85521 875 5

Printed in Great Britain by The Ipswich Book Company, Suffolk.

# Contents

| | |
|---|---|
| *List of Tables* | *vii* |
| *Acknowledgements* | *viii* |

| | |
|---|---|
| Introduction | 1 |

## PART I: HISTORICAL BACKGROUND

| | | |
|---|---|---|
| 1 | The Evolution of Trial by Jury and the Place of Confession Evidence | 11 |
| 2 | Coerced Confessions and Due Process Reactions | 23 |
| 3 | The Historical Management of Preliminary Procedures | 41 |

## PART II: ENTER THE POLICE

| | | |
|---|---|---|
| 4 | Legitimating Confessions Through 'Voluntariness' | 63 |
| 5 | Accommodating Police Interrogations | 83 |
| 6 | Towards the Regulation of Custodial Interrogations | 105 |
| 7 | Genesis of the Judges' Rules | 125 |

## PART III: IMAGES OF THE POLICE-SUSPECT DYNAMIC

| | | |
|---|---|---|
| 8 | Pre-PACE Images: Detainees | 159 |
| 9 | Pre-PACE Images: The Police | 195 |
| 10 | PACE Images: Detainees | 215 |
| 11 | PACE Images: The Police | 253 |

| | |
|---|---|
| 12  Images of the Police-Suspect Dynamic | 283 |
| 13  Continuity and Change | 297 |
| *Bibliography* | *313* |
| *Index* | *333* |

# List of Tables

| | | |
|---|---|---|
| 1 | Mode of interview record, pre-PACE | 162 |
| 2 | Adviser's attendance at interrogation, pre-PACE | 163 |
| 3 | Mode of interview record, pre-PACE and under PACE | 285 |
| 4 | Use of expletives by detainee, pre-PACE and under PACE | 286 |
| 5 | Use of criminal argot by the police, pre-PACE and under PACE | 286 |
| 6 | Adviser's attendance at interrogation, under PACE | 288 |
| 7 | Police use of leading questions, pre-PACE and under PACE | 289 |
| 8 | Police use of legal closure questions, pre-PACE and under PACE | 290 |

# Acknowledgements

The research and parts of the writing for this book were carried out whilst I was a doctoral student and Teaching Fellow in the School of Law at the University of Warwick. I am grateful to the Economic and Social Research Council (ESRC) for funding the research.

I owe a debt of gratitude to a number of people in writing this book. I thank Jolyon Hall, Law Librarian at the University of Warwick. Grateful thanks are also offered to Mark Charlton and to Francis Halstead of the Computing Services Centre at the University of Warwick. Steve Jenkins and Dave Bleasdale of the Computer Centre at the University of Lancaster are also thanked for helping me prepare camera-ready copy.

I warmly acknowledge the contribution of colleagues, students and friends in Warwick and Lancaster who helped me to clarify my thoughts and encouraged me in other ways. John McEldowney, Joe McCahery and Satnam Choongh have been especially important.

My greatest debt is to Mike McConville. His interest and enthusiasm helped to sustain me through periods of uncertainty. His invaluable comments helped considerably to develop my ideas. Without his support and friendship this book would not have been written.

My promise of complete confidentiality regarding all persons, cases and areas, prevents me from identifying the individuals who gave me access to a great number of their files. However, I take this opportunity to express my gratitude to all concerned.

An incalculable debt is also owed to my greatest and dearest friend, Neda Sadoughi-Nejad. I thank her for her unfailing confidence and enduring support. Her patience, warmth and affection have been a source of inspiration and delight.

Sections of chapter twelve are to appear as 'Shifting Images: Police-Suspect Encounters During Custodial Interrogations', in (1997) *Legal Studies*, 17(2), pp. 215-33, and are reproduced by permission of the Society of Public Teachers of Law.

Finally, many thanks are also due, and offered in full measure, to those I have not mentioned by name. I acknowledge the help they afforded me — whether directly or indirectly, knowingly or unknowingly — in preparing this book.

Ian Bryan
Department of Law
University of Lancaster

# Introduction

The exposure of a succession of high-profile miscarriages of justice during the late 1980s and early 1990s worked to highlight serious failings within successive stages of the criminal justice process, from initial investigation right through to appeal.[1] Of the numerous issues raised by such cases as the 'Guilford Four', the 'Maguire Seven', the 'Birmingham Six', the 'Tottenham Three' the 'Cardiff Three', and, more recently, the 'Bridgewater Four', perhaps the most important relate to the reliance modern procedures place upon confessions as evidence probative of guilt[2] and, in order to procure such evidence, the custodial or extra-judicial interrogation of suspects by the police.[3] The furore which surrounded these and other notorious miscarriages of justice, brought renewed attention to long-standing concerns over police practices within the context of custodial interrogations and over the value accorded to confession evidence which, in the absence of a formal and mandatory corroboration requirement, may lawfully form the sole basis for convictions.[4]

The Police and Criminal Evidence Act 1984 (PACE) which, with its accompanying Codes of Practice, currently regulates police interrogations and the reception in evidence of confessions, attempts to address these concerns.[5] At the same time, however, it effectively ensures that the status traditionally accorded to confession evidence is preserved. The Act, therefore, accepts the long and widely held view that interrogations and their prime object, confessions, are indispensable to the discovery and clearance of criminal offences. As Lord Devlin once put it:

> the accused's statement to the police often plays a great part in the prosecution's case. There can be no doubt of that, and I should emphasise it.... the evidence which ... interrogation produces is often decisive. The high degree of proof which the English legal system requires ... often could not be achieved by the prosecution without the assistance of the accused's own statement.[6]

Whilst there is a strong body of empirical evidence to suggest that the importance of confession evidence, when obtained through police interrogations, has been exaggerated,[7] it continues to be prized as "the clearest evidence of guilt".[8] It is claimed that it works, more than any other item of evidence, to "alleviate doubts" in the minds of police officers, legal advisers, judges and jurors.[9] It is also believed to benefit the confessor since by "purging himself of his guilt, he communicates his desire to make amends to society for his wrongful acts, thereby preparing the way for his return to its good graces".[10] The high proportion of criminal convictions in which confession evidence has played a crucial role would seem to lend support to such claims.[11] The point is that a 'good' confession is commonly seen as providing the most direct and efficient route to conviction. However, whether a confession is 'good' or 'bad', reliable or untrustworthy, will greatly depend on the circumstances in which it was made. The PACE legislation recognises this in placing a mandatory duty on the courts to exclude any confession that was or may have been obtained by oppression or as a result of conduct likely to render the confession unreliable.[12] Nevertheless, the safeguards provided by PACE are by no means infallible.[13]

Given that modern practices respecting the procurement, status and critical role played by the confession may be more fully understood when considered in historical context, this study aims to trace the development, use and regulation of confession evidence from the Middle Ages to the present. Paying particular attention to the pre-trial phase of the criminal process, the study also aims to illuminate the structures and strategies that have evolved to legitimate the extra-judicial interrogation of suspects and to preserve the vitality of the confession as a central item of prosecution evidence. These aims exist at the heart of the study and inform one of its chief concerns: the legitimating forms that, during the history of the criminal justice process, have been utilised to safeguard confessions and to protect the at times covert and more recently increasingly open methods used to secure them.

The second major concern centres on the question of how far images of the police-suspect dynamic as represented in official accounts of PACE-regulated interviews can be said to be distinct in character from images found in authoritative pre-PACE accounts of that dynamic. Images of police-suspect exchanges within the context of custodial interrogations are examined in order to discern the extent to which evidence may be constructed rather than discovered, detected or retrieved. The study also considers the degree to which official accounts of interrogation can be said to be complete, accurate and reliable. The broad object of this part of the study is to assess the apparent impact of PACE on the capacity of the police to generate or utilise particular images of themselves, their work and of suspects. It is also to evaluate the nature, form and content of police-suspect encounters as they appear in cases prepared for prosecution and trial in the period prior to and following the implementation of PACE

The study begins with a consideration of the process under which presenting (or grand) juries and trial (or petit) juries came to displace the older modes of proof in thirteenth century England. It focuses upon the evolution and legitimisation of the criminal jury and, once established, its growing dependence upon evidence presented before it by officials made responsible for getting up the case for the Crown. The early history of the jury is explored in order to explain why confession evidence — which, at the outset, appears to have been of little significance — became a central feature of the administration of justice as the role of the juror took on its modern form.

Chapter two considers the period from the late Middle Ages to the seventeenth century. It examines the inquisitorial measures, including the private application of physical torture, resorted to in order to obtain admissions of guilt to be publicly validated at trial and considers the procedural reforms introduced in response to the hostility the use of such measures engendered. It is here suggested that while the reforms addressed the seventeenth century crisis in criminal procedures, the confession of suspected or accused persons continued to play a pivotal role in the administration of justice. This point is picked up and explored further in chapter three which turns to the pre-trial process as it operated under justices of the peace up to the period when the justices were effectively judicialised and the police began to assume control over the investigation and prosecution of criminal offences.

Procedural reforms introduced in an effort to ensure extra-judicial confessions were not coerced from suspects are discussed in chapter four. A case-based analysis of the emergence and operation of the evidential requirement for 'voluntary' confessions is conducted in this and the following two chapters to highlight the divergence of judicial opinion as to the scope and application of the 'voluntariness' rule during the nineteenth century and early part of the twentieth century. The cases demonstrate that while some judges used the evidential rule to exclude confessions they viewed as involuntary and to express their strong opposition to the unauthorised extra-judicial questioning of suspects by the police, others viewed the practice as a legitimate and indeed vital weapon for crime control and to this end placed a narrow construction on the voluntariness rule — one which was essentially permissive of police interrogations and their evidential fruits.

The next chapter gives consideration to twentieth century developments. It focuses upon the regulatory framework which functioned for much of the century to legitimate the procurement of extra-judicial confessions by the police. In assessing the process through which police interrogations came to be legitimised, the chapter highlights disjunctures between the rhetoric of the law and the reality of police practice. It also discusses the effects of crime control demands for the law to endorse that practice.

The structure and nature of the interrogation process; the police-suspect dynamic within the interrogation process; and images of that dynamic, as seen in cases prepared for prosecution in the period prior to and following the introduction of the PACE legislation, form the subject matter for the remaining chapters. The chapters examine the results of an empirically-based study into the extent to which images of police interrogations can be said to be self-legitimating. The chapters also seek to determine how far and in what ways the capacity of the police to actively construct images of themselves and of suspects has been affected by the introduction of contemporaneous recording systems under the 1984 legislation.[14]

Chapters eight and nine assess and evaluate the form and content of official accounts of interrogations drawn from a randomly selected sample of 400 committal papers relating to contested cases determined in the Crown Court during the period in which the interrogation of suspects by the police was governed by the Judges' Rules.[15] A similar exercise is conducted, in chapters ten and eleven, in respect of a random sample of 283 contested cases determined in the same Crown Court in the period following the implementation of PACE and its Codes of Practice.[16] The following chapter widens the discussion. It takes a broad view of the empirical data and considers the images of the police-suspect dynamic the respective data sets contain.

The concluding chapter reviews the historical and empirical evidence and discusses the themes of continuity and change. These themes are considered with respect both to the role of the confession as a *prima facie* reliable specie of prosecution evidence and to the various legitimating forms that have been utilised in the on-going project to preserve that role.

## Research Methods

The findings presented in the first seven chapters are based on primary and secondary historical sources which were used to identify the significance given to confession evidence in criminal cases and to explain the continuing vitality of the confession as a central item of prosecution evidence. This involved a re-examination of decided cases in which conflict over the legitimate grounds for receiving or excluding extra-judicial confessions in evidence occurred against a background of concern over the relationship between the state and its officials, on the one hand, and the citizen, on the other. These sources provide a valuable standpoint from which to view contemporary developments regarding the place of confession evidence in the criminal process and the forms of regulation that have been applied over police access to suspects.

The methodology used in the remaining chapters involved a close reading of prosecution case papers submitted in evidence to courts of law at two significant periods. The first, at that point in history, prior to the implementation of PACE, when the police enjoyed unmediated control over the way in which police-suspect encounters were represented to courts. This is compared and contrasted with the situation that came into operation during the second period, that is, following the implementation of the 1984 Act and its requirement for official exchanges between suspects and police officers to be recorded contemporaneously.[17]

The overall objective was to establish whether representations of police-suspect encounters had changed and to see whether this provides information about the ways in which confession evidence has been seen to be legitimate. To this end, the pre-PACE and the post-PACE interrogation records collected during the course of the study were subjected to a quantitative analysis, using a coding schedule, and a qualitative analysis, using analytical categories generated by the study and applied consistently across the case papers.

In an attempt to reduce the problem of subjectivity, excerpts from reported or recorded accounts of interrogation have been included in the discussion of the pre-PACE and the post-PACE police-suspect dynamic. The purpose being to illustrate commonly observed features and to buttress the bare classifications applied. However, the names of individuals and of places have been altered in order to protect the anonymity of all persons connected with specific cases.

The methodology used in the empirical sections of this study does not imply or rest upon the premise that the accounts contained in the respective samples faithfully replicate an external reality, nor does it imply that the accounts, even if faithful, comprehensively describe the nature and content of the police-suspect dynamic. It is also acknowledged that the study is subject to the limitation that the cases which make up either the pre-PACE or the PACE sample are not necessarily representative of Crown Court cases heard throughout the country during the period prior to or following the introduction of PACE. Cases were not, however, selected on any basis other than their availability. These limitations notwithstanding, the methodology adopted in the study permitted a systematic documentary and comparative analysis of the value accorded to confession evidence and of the pre-trial process in which that evidence is most commonly secured.

It is intended that by viewing contemporary practices, as reflected in the content and form of records of police interrogations, from a wide historical perspective, the study will contribute to a richer understanding of issues which bear on police-suspect relations within custodial interrogations. The study is also intended as a contribution to debates concerned with the regulation of police powers; the reliability and status of extra-judicial confessions; and, finally, those concerned with miscarriages of justice.

**Notes**

[1] A major inquiry into the operation of the criminal process was set up in 1991 following a string of miscarriages of justice. The Royal Commission on Criminal Justice (RCCJ) was, by its terms of reference, specifically directed to 'examine the criminal justice system from the stage at which the police are investigating an alleged or reported criminal offence right through to the stage at which a defendant who had been found guilty of such an offence has exhausted his or her right of appeal' (RCCJ, *Report*, Cm. 2263, 1993, para. 5, p. 1).

[2] Throughout this study, the term 'confession' is used with reference to statements which are partly or wholly adverse to the maker. It therefore adopts the definition supplied by s. 82 (1) of the 1984 Police and Criminal Evidence Act (PACE).

[3] See McConville, *et al.*, 1991, pp. 50-7; Greer, 1994, p. 110.

[4] See Kaye, 1991; Pattenden, 1991, pp. 321-2; Dennis, 1993, p. 308; Jackson, 1993, p. 821; McConville, 1993; RCCJ, *Report*, 1993, paras. 65-87, pp. 64-8; Leng, 1994, pp. 181-2.

[5] See RCCJ, *Report*, 1993, pp. 58-62.

[6] Devlin, 1960, p. 48. Similar assertions, made without empirical support, are discussed and challenged by Baldwin and McConville, 1980, pp. 2-7. See also Morris, 1980, pp. 12-14.

[7] McConville and Baldwin, 1981, pp. 126-40, 153-4; 1982, pp. 165-9; McConville, 1993, pp. 29, 38-88.

[8] Driver, 1968, p. 42. See also McConville and Baldwin, 1982, p. 169; RCCJ, *Report*, 1993, para. 31, p. 57; paras. 65, 67, p. 64.

[9] Driver, *ibid*. See also McConville and Baldwin, 1982, pp. 169-70; Royal Commission on Criminal Procedure, *Report*, Cmnd. 8092, 1981, para. 4.74.

[10] Driver, *ibid*. See also Morris, 1980, pp. 11-12; Dennis, 1993, p. 305.

[11] See McConville and Baldwin, 1982, p. 166; Kaye, 1991; Rozenberg, 1992; Gudjonsson, 1992, pp. 205-12, 234-40; Maguire and Norris, 1992, p. 1; Dennis, 1993, pp. 291-313; RCCJ, *Report*, 1993, pp. 57, 64.

[12] The duty to exclude a confession for oppression or unreliability is set out at s. 76 of PACE. It is supplemented by s. 78, which gives trial judges a discretion to exclude any evidence that has been obtained unfairly.

[13] See Reiner, 1992, pp. 229-32; RCCJ, *Report*, 1993, pp. 57-68.

[14] PACE, by Code C, para. 11.5, requires custodial interviews to be recorded contemporaneously by verbatim notes. The Code provides that interviews must be accurately recorded irrespective of whether they take place in a police station (para. 11.5 (a)); that, where interviews are not contemporaneously recorded, an accurate record should be made as soon as practicable afterwards (para. 11.7); and that the record must be shown to the suspect for him or her to either sign it as correct or indicate in what respect he or she considers it inaccurate (paras. 11.10 and 11.13). By Code E, para. 3.3, where authority is given for an interviewing officer not to tape record an interview, it is to be recorded in writing and in accordance with Code C.

[15] The Judge's Rules were first formulated in 1912. In 1918 they were increased from four to nine Rules. They were clarified in 1930 (Home Officer Circular 536053/23) and reformulated in 1964 (Home Officer Circular 31/1964). The Rules and their accompanying Administrative Directions (Home Office Circular 89/1978) sought to provide the police with authoritative guidance as to acceptable practice when questioning and taking statements from suspects. The Judge's Rules remained as guides to the police until they were superseded by the provisions of PACE, Code C.

[16] The sample of pre-PACE cases were heard and determined in the Crown Court in 1975 and 1976. The sample of PACE cases were heard and determined in the same Crown Court between 1989 and 1993. Both samples contain records of at least one formal interview of the defendant, as suspect, by the police.

[17] See *supra*., n. 15.

# PART I
# HISTORICAL BACKGROUND

# 1 The Evolution of Trial by Jury and the Place of Confession Evidence

**Introduction**

Confession evidence emerged as a central feature of the administration of justice following the thirteenth century displacement of adjudicative structures which, by and large, relied upon accusatory procedures. Under these procedures a private party would make an accusation and swear an oath to its truth. The accused, in contesting the case, would respond by asserting, also on oath, that the accusation was false.[1] In more serious cases the judgment of God was solicited through the ordeal.[2] Alternatively, the parties in dispute, or parties designated by them, would engage in judicial combat. This was also considered to be a form of ordeal "on the grounds that God would permit the victory only of the party in the right".[3]

The great reliance the 'pre-modern' modes of proof placed upon the judgment of God meant that before the thirteenth century confessions, as evidence sufficient to prove guilt, played only a marginal role in the administration of justice. This chapter will discuss the conditions and events that, firstly, contributed to the displacement of the ancient modes of proof; secondly, that attended the advent of the petit jury mode of trial and with it the need for the adduction of evidence; and, finally, that saw confession evidence become legitimated as "the queen of proofs"[4] in the increasingly specialized machinery of secular justice established following the Norman Conquest.

## Evolution of the Jury of Accusation

Exalted as one of the most fundamental and ideologically important institutions of common law justice,[5] trial by jury has its antecedence in the eleventh century invasion and settlement of England by the Normans.[6] With the Conquest, the Norman kings introduced a centralised system of government, administered by delegates of royal power, which came to displace the disparate arrangement of communal tribunals that employed "irrational" modes of proof and trial.[7] While the precise origins of the jury remains a matter of debate,[8] it is generally accepted that the Normans contributed to the evolution of the English jury with their introduction of the inquest.[9]

The inquisition or *inquisitio* procedure became a regular feature in the administration of the Norman system of central government[10] and evolved to form what is understood to be "the root from which the English jury springs".[11] Also known as the *recognitio*,[12] the Norman inquest was initially a royal device of inquiry used for both fiscal and administrative purposes.[13]

The compulsory *ex officio* oath was central to the operation of the *inquisitio*. With it, Crown officials would command members of the gathered inquisition to answer truly to the questions propounded to them. The inquisitorial oath was seen as a device through which spiritual forces could be employed to meet the temporal requirements of the Crown and was considered to be a strong guarantor of veracity since all who were subject to it were presumed to have material knowledge of the facts in question.[14] Indeed, on their assembly before officers of the King, those who were ignorant of the facts at issue were required by their oaths to say as much and would therefore be excluded from the inquisition.[15]

Under Henry II (1154-1189) the inquisition was extended beyond matters of direct and immediate concern to the administration of government and became a "purchasable favour" granted to prominent or respectable individuals involved in private disputes.[16] It thereby afforded those in receipt of this royal favour a means of avoiding modes of justice which relied upon the transcendental judgment of the spiritual rather than the terrestrial impressions of members of the local community charged by their oaths to surrender pertinent testimony.[17]

In its earliest form the inquest required a body of neighbours summoned from the relevant community to answer — upon their oaths, as witnesses, before officers of the Crown — to questions of a proprietary and fiscal nature. It was later made available to individual litigants to eventually become an established part of the accusatory process.[18]

Largely as a result of the extension of the availability of the inquest during the reign of Henry II, the ancient modes of proof, together with the local tribunals that administered them, began to be "gradually suppressed" as the common law, under the direction of the King and his delegates of itinerant justices, began to be routinely enforced.[19] Though they varied in their application, the ancient methods of proof were almost entirely based upon oaths and ordeals.[20] Paradoxically, under the older modes of trial proof was to follow judgment; the judgment determined which of the parties in dispute was to prove his case, the mode of proof and the consequence of failing to meet the requisite proof.[21] The system of oaths ranged from the single unsupported exculpatory oath of the individual challenged to meet the charge against him, to a procedure which required a certain number of oath-helpers or compurgators to support the oath of the defendant with that of their own.[22]

Maitland (1908) suggests that the system of oaths was restricted to lesser crimes whilst graver charges required a "direct and open appeal to the supernatural" through the ordeal.[23] He describes the four chief forms of ordeal as follows:

> The Ordeal of hot iron: the Accused is required to carry a hot iron in his hand for nine steps, his hand is then sealed up and the seal broken on the third day, if the hand is festered then he is guilty, if not, innocent; the Ordeal of hot water: the accused is required to plunge his hand into hot water, if the Ordeal is simple, to the wrist, if threefold, then to the cubit; the Ordeal of cold water: the accused is thrown into water, if he sinks he is innocent, if he floats he is guilty; the Ordeal of the morsel: a piece of bread or cheese of an ounce in weight is given to the accused, having been solemnly adjured to stick in his throat if he is guilty....[24]

After the Conquest the ordeal — with its reliance upon divine intervention rather than human action for the disposition of cases — was increasingly regarded with scepticism.[25] This scepticism appears to have contributed to the development of the inquisition from a device designed to identify and protect proprietary and fiscal interests, to a means of discovering and suppressing crime,[26] which through the imposition of fines and forfeitures was also a source of royal revenue.[27]

The Assize of Clarendon (1166),[28] later buttressed by the Assize of Northampton (1176),[29] formally incorporated the *inquisitio* into the increasingly systematized machinery of criminal justice.[30] It required that inquiry be made in every county, hundred and vill of twelve lawful men or knights representing the community. The twelve were charged by their oaths to 'present', before the itinerant justices of the King, any accused or notorious criminals or harbourers of them. Those accused in this manner were to be put to trial by ordeal.[31]

Thus by the Assize of Clarendon and that of Northampton, the Crown formally institutionalized the jury of presentment which, as the grand jury, survived in its basic form until the twentieth century.[32] By placing the community under an obligation to present suspected persons before its officials, the Crown was no longer entirely dependent upon the initiative of private individuals to mount an appeal. Indeed, Maitland (1908)[33] suggests that the appeal system — once the principal method of initiating proceedings[34] — began to be threatened from the late twelfth century as appellees increasingly sought and gained from the Crown the privilege of answering appeals instituted against them through the common voice of their neighbours, the presentment or inquest jury.

The evolution of the inquest into the jury of final decision, however, resulted from the demise of the ordeal in the thirteenth century. This effectively deprived the prevailing adjudicative structures of a means of trying persons accused of crime.

## The Emergence and Legitimisation of the Petit Jury

The petit jury appears to have developed as an expedient means of ascertaining the truth of an accusation in the face of the gradual de-legitimisation of the ordeal which, during the thirteenth century, had become discredited and had fallen into disuse.[35] Instrumental in the demise of the ordeal was a decree issued by the Fourth Lateran Council in 1215. This prohibited the performance of religious ceremonies by members of the clergy in connection with the ordeal, in all jurisdictions where the authority of the Council was recognized.

The decree effectively abolished the ordeal as a regular means of trial since the procedure was thereby deprived of the requisite religious sanction that gave it its validity.[36] This, Foster (1979) declares, "threatened to cast the entire English criminal justice system into confusion".[37] Indeed, the repudiation of trial by ordeal meant that in practice an accusation by the presenting jury became "practically equivalent to a conviction".[38] It is not clear whether in these circumstances presenting juries became loath to indict suspects in the absence of formal trial procedures. However, it was in direct response to the prevailing uncertainty that Henry III (1216-72) issued the following writ to his justices in 1219:

> Because it was in doubt and not definitely settled before the beginning of your eyre, with what trial those are to be judged who are accused of robbery, murder, arson, and similar crimes, since the trial by fire and water has been prohibited by the Roman Church, it has been provided by our council that, at present, in this eyre of yours, it shall be done thus with those accused of excesses of this kind; To wit, that those who are accused of the aforesaid greater crimes, and of whom suspicion is held that they are guilty of what whereof they are accused, of whom also, in case they were permitted to abjure the realm, still there would be suspicion that afterwards they would do evil, they shall be kept in our prison and safeguarded, yet so that they do not incur danger of life or limb on our account. But those who are accused of medium crimes, and to whom would be assigned the ordeal by fire or water, if it had not been prohibited, and of whom, if they should abjure the realm there would be no suspicion of their doing evil afterwards, they may abjure our realm. But those who are accused of lesser crimes, and of whom there would be no suspicion of evil, let them find safe and sure pledges of fidelity and of keeping our peace, and then they may be released in our land.... We have left to your discretion the observance of this aforesaid order ... according to your own discretion and conscience.[39]

This response to the crisis brought about by the repudiation of the ordeal makes clear that proof of guilt was to be abandoned. The justices were to be guided by their own discretion in deciding whether the accused should be imprisoned, exiled or bound over. Posited upon a presumption of guilt, the order merely required the justices of the Crown to determine the appropriate punishment, without testing the accusation.

Several other attempts were made to fill the void left by the demise of the ordeal. However, by a gradual and piecemeal process, the petit jury, an excrescence of the presenting jury,[40] became the predominant determinative institution in cases of serious crime.[41] "By its intrinsic fairness", comments Thayer (1898), "as contrasted with older modes, and by the favour of the Crown and the judges, it grew fast to be regarded as the one regular common-law mode of trial, always to be had when no other was fixed".[42] Nevertheless, the consent of the accused was required to legitimate the operation of this novel method of trial.[43] The case against the accused could not proceed without it. Furthermore, it seems that a defendant's refusal to 'put himself upon his country', could not be construed as amounting to a confession of guilt.[44] This is noteworthy because it implies that confessions from persons accused of involvement in criminal activity played only a limited role in circumstances which saw the petit jury struggle against older modes of trial for legitimacy.

The procedures of the ordeal were not dependent upon the confession of the accused since the verdict was left to the divine judgment of the supernatural. For this reason the Crown may have been reluctant to convict accused persons without some legitimate form of trial, even where the accused confessed his guilt. Only by gaining the consent of the accused could the officially sanctioned form of trial be fully legitimated. However, the imposition of trial by jury was frequently resisted by those who objected to being condemned merely by the general suspicions of their neighbours.[45] Thus, as the ordeal had fallen into disuse, it became necessary to introduce an element of coercion to secure that consent.[46]

The accused who accepted trial by jury would be confronted with a body composed of his neighbours, often drawn from the very presenting jury that had indicted him. He had no power to object to the presence of neighbours who might be hostile to him.[47] And while jurors were selected on the basis of their character as witnesses, in many cases they were prejudiced witnesses.[48] Also, if convicted of a felony, the accused would effectively disinherit his family since his land would escheat to his lord and his chattels would be forfeited by the King.[49] If convicted as a traitor, the accused was considered to have broken his obligation of allegiance to the Crown. His goods, land, profits, life interests and estates in fee simple would, therefore, be forfeited by the Crown.[50] Such considerations appear to have caused large numbers of accused persons to reject the new method of trial.[51]

The problem posed by recalcitrant suspects refusing to submit to the new means of trial occasioned the introduction of the first Statute of Westminster (1275). The statute provides:

> that notorious felons who are openly of evil fame and who refuse to put themselves upon inquest of felony at the suit of the King before his justices, shall be remanded to a hard and strong prison [*en le prison forte et dure*] as befits those who refuse to abide by the common law of the land; but this is not to be understood of persons who are taken upon light suspicion.[52]

In its subversion of the requirement of consent, the statute reflects the

Crown's determination to control criminal activity, particularly that of convicted felons, and to ensure that those suspected or accused of involvement in crime were convicted by petit jury trial. Though it specifically excludes from its ambit those who attract only "light suspicion", it nonetheless, requires all other suspected felons to be subject to a form of preventive detention prior to their trial.

This sanction was designed to coerce suspects into submitting to petit jury trial and to further legitimate trial by jury as part of "the common law of the land". However, it is not clear whether this method of compulsion was restricted to eliciting the consent of accused persons, or whether it was also used to coerce confessions from those to whom great suspicion attached in order to confirm or substantiate the "truth" of that suspicion.

For Ratushny (1979), there is a close relationship between this form of coercion, as it later developed, and that of torture:

> ... the words 'prison forte et dure' by some unaccountable means became transformed into 'peine forte et dure', and finally into a form of torture which, by the sixteenth century, took the barbarous form of placing the accused between two boards and piling weights upon him until he accepted trial by jury or expired....[53]

The view that *prison forte et dure* was corrupted into a form of torture is supported by Summerson (1983).[54] His study of *peine forte et dure* suggests that a refusal by the accused to submit to the common law absolved the officials having charge of him of any responsibility should their prisoner perish in custody. In these circumstances Medieval gaolers were given "an almost entirely free hand in any future treatment of him they felt inclined to apply".[55] The officials were, therefore, free to compel their prisoner to disclose information which would facilitate the process of prosecution and conviction. As their practices were shielded from external scrutiny, the precise nature of their treatment of suspects must remain largely unknown. Nonetheless, the *peine forte et dure*, described by Lord MacDermott (1957) as "an act of torture",[56] may be seen as a clear manifestation of the capacity of the Crown, through its agents, to impose its will.

*Peine forte et dure* may indeed be regarded as a form of torture since its purpose was to coerce the accused into acquiescence. Certainly, judicial torture had, by about this time, become widespread in Continental Europe[57] and instances of its use in England have been documented by Jardine (1837)[58] and by Langbein (1977).[59]

Langbein contends that while the torture of suspects became a common characteristic of the Roman cannon law requirement of proof as practiced on the Continent, the development of the jury system in England precluded any systematic reliance on judicial torture. This is because the English system relied on a process of persuasion, rather than on a formal system of accumulated proofs. "To this day", he maintains, "an English jury can convict a defendant on less evidence than was required as a mere precondition for interrogation under torture on the Continent".[60]

Langbein finds a "crucial distinction" between torture and *peine forte et dure*. In the latter case "coercion was not being used to extract information, to gather evidence", rather it was used to extort a plea. Therefore, *peine forte et dure* is "best regarded as a special kind of guilty plea".[61] Torture, on the other hand, presupposes a legal system based upon "rational" procedures geared to the discovery of "the truth". Torture is to be seen within these procedures as a tool in the fact-finding process; it existed as a "means of regulated coercion".[62]

The distinction drawn by this argument is extremely slight, if not illusory. It may be conceded that in its original form *peine forte et dure*, which thrived from the late thirteenth century and was not abolished until 1772,[63] was used to coerce pleas. However, while the official use of torture did not become a routinised aspect of English criminal procedure,[64] *peine forte et dure* may have been employed to elicit confessions, to secure convictions and to underpin the legitimation of the petty jury mode of trial.

The treatment suspected felons received under *peine forte et dure* was, Levy (1968) believes, an "undoubted form of torture".[65] The important point here is that *peine forte et dure* and judicial torture both rest on the physical coercion of individuals in a manner intended to extract material detrimental to their interests.

The use of torture to secure confessions of guilt may not have been as widespread in England as it was on the Continent, however, its utility in obtaining confessions, in legitimating the public aspects of petit jury trial and in authenticating criminal convictions was not lost on the Crown. The high value placed on confession evidence by English criminal procedures was later acknowledged by Staunford (1607). He made clear that confessions provide "the best and surest answer that can be made in our law for quieting the conscience of the judge and for making it a good and firm condemnation".[66]

The historical evidence suggests that the presenting jury evolved from the *inquisitio* procedures introduced by the Normans. The trial of criminal matters by petit jury, a scion of the jury of presentment, developed in direct response to the decline of the ordeal. It was imposed on unwilling individuals — as a matter of expedience rather than of principle — by means of physical coercion. It was a device which gave the Crown direct influence over the collection of evidence, the prosecution process and thus convictions. In its early form, the petit jury method of trial did not contemplate protections for the individual but, instead, significantly advantaged the Crown. Its imposition, rather than creating valuable rights for the accused, was seen as depriving the accused of the valuable right to be tried by the older modes of trial.[67] The ancient modes of proof and trial were displaced by procedures controlled by the Crown. These procedures were such that the individual, without the aid of witnesses or of counsel, could be accused and condemned by his neighbours on the basis of their assessment of his character.

Confessions had an important structural function in legitimating the petit jury mode of trial. With the repudiation of the ordeal and the demise of communal tribunals, the jury of presentment — whose members were, in effect, to operate as informants — condemned the accused since, in the absence of alternative trial procedures, its indictments sufficed to secure convictions.[68] As a result, confessions grew in functional importance. Under the ancient modes of trial, the condemned were given an opportunity to atone for their sins and redeem themselves for the edification of the community in a purgatorial exercise of contrition. Under the centralizing policies of the Crown, the confession was transformed into an instrument with which to legitimate the punishment of the 'guilty'. The determination of guilt by jury enhanced the utility of confessions which, as evidence probative of guilt, were frequently extorted to legitimate the "good and firm"[69] conviction of accused persons.

Under early Anglo-Saxon criminal procedures the role of the court was limited to determine the mode of trial, rather than to determine guilt or innocence. It was not dependent upon the presentation of evidence. Verdicts centered on the intervention of the divine. "The judges or doomsmen were merely guardians of a ritual performance, who at most decided by which of a number of mechanical means the defendant should try and clear himself."[70] In the operation of these ancient procedures, therefore, there was no reliance upon self-incriminatory admissions from accused persons and no special necessity to obtain them. The development of trial by jury increased the need for the criminal justice process to acquire evidence suitable for use at trial. It therefore evolved procedures geared to the acquisition of such evidence. Confession evidence was particularly prized.[71] Put shortly, the advent of the petit jury mode of trial worked to elevate the confession into its position of decisive importance within the machinery of criminal justice.

**Notes**

[1] Either party to the dispute might support their own oath with those of oath-helpers or compurgators, persons willing to testify to a person's good character rather than to any fact at issue. See Jenks, 1912, p. 9; Peters, 1985, pp. 41-2. For a discussion of this form of trial see Thayer, 1898, pp. 24-34.
[2] Thayer, 1898, pp. 34-9.
[3] Peters, 1985, p. 42. See also Thayer, 1898, pp. 39-46.
[4] Peters, 1985, p. 41.
[5] See 3 Blackstone, 1768, p. 379; 4 Blackstone, 1769, pp. 342-44; 1 Pollock and Maitland, 1898, p. 140. See also Devlin, 1956, p. 164, where he argues that 'trial by jury is more than an instrument of justice and more than one wheel of the constitution: it is the lamp that shows that freedom lives'. Also see Plucknett, 1956, p. 107; Van Caenegem, 1973, p. 73. And see Hay, 1988, pp. 305-357.
[6] Thayer, 1898, p. 49; 1 Holdsworth, 1956, p. 312; Foster, 1979, pp. 281-3.
[7] Thayer, 1898, p. 49; 1 Holdsworth, 1956, p. 312; Harding, 1966, pp. 21-4; Van Caenegem, 1973, pp. 63-3, 67.
[8] See Deosaran, 1985, pp. 9-10; Foster, 1979, pp. 281-2; Harding, 1973, pp. 29, 30-41
[9] Harding, 1966, p. 38; Foster, 1979, p. 282.
[10] Thayer, 1898, p. 46; 1 Pollock and Maitland, 1899, pp. 141-5; Maitland, 1908, pp. 120-6; Plucknett, 1956, pp. 106-38; Van Caenegem, 1973, p. 73.
[11] 1 Holdsworth, 1956, p. 312. See also 1 Pollock and Maitland, 1898, p. 140.
[12] Van Caenegem, 1973, p. 133, n.30.
[13] Plucknett, 1956, pp. 110-11; Harding, 1966, p. 38. The compilation of the Domesday Book (1085-6) is a most conspicuous example of this, see Douglas, 1964, pp. 347-54; Baker, 1966, pp. 183-5; Finn, 1973, pp. 5-24.
[14] Devlin, 1956, pp. 6-8; Harding, 1966, p. 24.
[15] 1 Stephen, 1883, pp. 255-6. See also Thayer, 1898, pp. 50-1; 1 Pollock and Maitland, 1898, p. 141; Maitland, 1908, pp. 12-16, 121-5; 1 Holdsworth, 1956, p. 313; Plucknett, 1956, pp. 110-14; Van Caenegem, 1973, p. 73.
[16] Maitland, 1908, pp. 121-5; Harding, 1966. p. 39.
[17] Maitland, 1908, pp. 10-11, 121; 1 Holdsworth, 1956, p. 313.
[18] 2 Pollock and Maitland, 1898, p. 602; 1 Holdsworth, 1956, p. 314.
[19] Maitland, 1908, pp. 12-13, 115, 126.

[20] *Ibid.*, p. 115. 'The oath, the corner-stone of medieval judicial procedure, was, in some sense, an ordeal, but one which relied upon God's eventual rather than his immediate judgement' (Bartlett, 1986, p. 30).
[21] Maitland, *Ibid.*; Levy, 1968, p. 5.
[22] Maitland, 1908, p. 115-17; Bartlett, 1986, p. 30.
[23] Maitland, 1908, pp. 119-22; see also Levy, 1968, p. 6.
[24] Maitland, 1908, p. 119.
[25] Thayer, 1898, p. 38; Foster, 1979, p. 285; see also Bartlett, 1986, pp. 71-2, 75-7.
[26] Maitland, 1908, p. 127.
[27] 2 Pollock and Maitland, 1898, p. 153; Plucknett, 1956, p. 112; Levy, 1968, p. 8.
[28] Reproduced in Stephenson and Marcham, 1937, pp. 76-80.
[29] *Ibid.*, pp. 80-2
[30] 1 Stephen, 1883, pp. 250-2; Thayer, 1899, p. 55; Maitland, 1908, p. 128; 8 Wigmore, 1961, pp. 270-3; Plucknett, 1956, p. 112; Devlin, 1956, pp. 1-6.
[31] 1 Stephen, 1883, p. 251; 2 Pollock and Maitland, 1898, p. 152; Harding, 1966, pp. 39-40.
[32] The Grand Jury was abolished by s. 1(1) of the Administration of Justice (Miscellaneous Provisions) Act, 1933 and the Criminal Justice Act, 1948.
[33] Maitland, 1908, p. 129. See also 1 Stephen, 1883, p. 254.
[34] Thayer, 1898, p. 245.
[35] 1 Stephen, 1883, p. 253.
[36] Thayer, 1898, pp. 68-9; 1 Holdsworth, 1956, pp. 321-2; Plucknett, 1956, pp. 118-9; Devlin, 1956, p. 9; Foster, 1979, p. 288.
[37] Foster, 1979, p. 288.
[38] 1 Stephen, 1883, p. 254; see also Wells, 1911, p. 358; Levy, 1968, pp. 15-6; Groot, 1988, pp. 21-35.
[39] Reproduced in Plucknett, 1956, p. 119; see also 1 Holdsworth, 1956, p. 323.
[40] Wells, 1911, p. 348.
[41] 1 Holdsworth, 1956, p. 324; Plucknett, 1956, pp. 119-26; Devlin, 1956, p. 10; Langbein, 1974, p. 75; and see Groot, 1988, pp. 3-35.
[42] Thayer, 1898, p. 60.
[43] Thayer, 1898, p. 73; Wells, 1911, p. 353; Foster, 1979, pp. 291-3.
[44] Thayer, 1898, p. 73.
[45] Foster, 1979, p. 291.
[46] Maitland, 1908, p. 129; Plucknett, 1956, p. 120; Levy, 1968, p. 17; Foster, 1979, 291.
[47] It was not until the statute 25 Edw. 3, 5., c.3. (1350) that the accused became entitled to challenge any member of the trial jury who had previously served on the presentment jury.
[48] Wells, 1911, p. 352.
[49] Foster, 1979, p. 293.

[50] Veall, 1970, p. 3.
[51] Wells, 1911, p. 353.
[52] 1 Statute of Westminster, 3 Edw. 1, c.12 (1275)
[53] Ratushny, 1979, p. 126.
[54] Summerson, 1983, pp. 117-25.
[55] *Ibid.*, p. 122
[56] MacDermott, 1957, p. 17; see also Williams, 1963, pp. 12-3.
[57] See Peters, 1985, pp. 47-60, 90-1.
[58] Jardine, 1837, pp. 13-4, 16, 52-3.
[59] Langbein, 1977, pp. 81-129.
[60] *Ibid.*, p. 78; see also 4 Holdsworth, 1945, p. 528.
[61] Langbein, 1977, p. 77.
[62] *Ibid.*
[63] 12 Geo. 3, c.20, S.1 (1772). This statute provided that an accused standing mute to an indictment of felony could be convicted by verdict or confession. It was not until an enactment of 1828 (7 & 8 Geo. 4, c.28) that the courts were directed to enter a plea of not guilty for the accused who stood "moot of malice".
[64] Langbein, 1977, p. 80.
[65] Levy, 1968, p. 33.
[66] Staunford, 1607, 11 c.51.
[67] 1 Holdsworth, 1956, p. 296; Foster, 1979, p. 296.
[68] Wells, 1911, p. 354.
[69] *Supra.*, n. 66.
[70] Harding, 1973, p. 16.
[71] Levy, 1968, pp. 7-10; Berger, 1980, pp. 4-5.

# 2 Coerced Confessions and Due Process Reactions

**Introduction**

Confessions came to play a vital instrumental and legitimating role within the adjudicative structures introduced by the Normans. They were also of pivotal importance for institutions, established to preserve the orthodoxies of Church and State, operating largely outside the common law. These institutions employed *inquisitio* methods which negatived formal accusatory and trial procedures as required by the common law.

Later, under the rigorous law enforcement policies of the Tudor state, inquisitorial methods were employed to suppress religious and political offences. With the continuing spread of political and constitutional dissent, the prerogative government of the Stuart state further extended the use of inquisitorial procedures. Such procedures became routine features of Church and Crown justice. They were designed to secure confessions from those suspected or accused of infringing the prevailing socio-political order and were frequently made use of both internally and extraneously to the common law.[1]

By the beginning of the seventeenth century the use of inquisitorial methods and the power of the Crown to authorise the use of torture, were increasingly vilified as being in contravention of the principles of common law. Opposition to the inquisitorial practices of the prerogative courts developed into popular discontent which began to articulate itself in a concerted movement for reform. During the course of the century this movement led to the formal denunciation of inquisitorial methods, to the abolition of courts employing these methods and to the strengthening of common law accusatory and trial procedures.

However, common law procedures also became the subject of popular disquiet. Thus, while the common law courts had begun, from the mid-1600s, to accord defendants a right not to incriminate themselves under judicial questioning — and in so doing acknowledged that the inquisitorial examination of defendants was incompatible with the reconstruction of judges as disinterested umpires — the common law pre-trial process continued to facilitate the construction of cases against suspected or accused persons based upon evidence acquired under compulsory interrogations conducted by partisan state agents. Therefore, while challenges to the legitimacy of convictions founded upon confessions elicited from defendants by judges would ultimately lead to the repudiation of compulsory judicial examinations, the growing reliance on confessions extracted from suspected and accused persons prior to trial would place new and increasing strains upon the on-going project to preserve the role of confessions as sufficient evidence of guilt and to legitimate structures specifically designed to secure them.

## Inquisition and Accusation

William I (1066-87) had brought an end to the pre-Conquest practice which permitted bishops to sit in a judicial capacity in local courts.[2] As a result, the bishops were required to confine their judicial activities to ecclesiastical matters in accordance with canonical laws. Consequently, there "sprang up a separate system and a double judicature".[3]

With respect to church courts, the Fourth Lateran Council (1215), which had effectively rendered the ordeal redundant, also handed down details for the introduction of *inquisitio* procedures in those jurisdictions, including England, taking cognizance of its ecclesiastical authority.[4] Trial by ordeal was losing its status as the primary mode of reaching final decisions and trial by compurgation oath was "already little better than a farce".[5] The *inquisitio* and the *ex officio* oath were introduced into ecclesiastical practice so as to replace the previously prevailing methods of church trial.[6]

The procedures of the ecclesiastical *inquisitio* diverged with common law practice. The latter incorporated within its formal procedures the requirement of a specific accusation in cases of serious crime either by an individual, by appeal of felony, or by the community as represented by the jury of presentment. Trial by a jury of neighbours was, by this stage, also beginning to be established as a key element of common law criminal justice procedures. *Inquistio* procedures, by contrast, allowed church officials to inquire into the particulars of the offence through the *ex officio* oath which was used to compel those suspected of violating canonical order to testify their guilt.

Wigmore (1902) considered the path taken by the ecclesiastical courts to be "an epochal difference of method", and found that, "the radical part played, for the progress of English procedure, by the new jury trial in the 1200s and early 1300s, was paralleled, in a near degree, for ecclesiastical procedure, by the inquisitional oath in the 1200s".[7] By the middle of the thirteenth century, the divergent methods of investigation and trial had brought the Church into jurisdictional conflict with the Crown.[8]

The Crown, by the statute *Articuli Cleri* (1315-16),[9] sought to place definite limits on the jurisdiction of ecclesiastical officials. The statute restricted the authority of the church to conduct investigations or examinations of laymen under the inquisitional oath to matrimonial and testamentary matters. This action may not have been inspired solely by the complaints voiced by the community in opposition to the use made by the ecclesiastical courts of the *ex officio* oath procedure. Wigmore (1902) suggests the Crown was rather more concerned to strengthen its own authority and to circumscribe the extensive jurisdiction church officials sought for themselves.[10]

Evidence affording support to this argument is provided by Leadam and Baldwin (1918).[11] Their work reveals that during the period under discussion the King's Council was using similar inquisitorial methods in respect of cases brought before it for adjudication. Under its procedures the accused was required to appear before the council in person and without legal representation to:

> answer the charges, which were most likely not known to him in advance.... If he did not immediately confess or satisfactorily explain the charges, he was put to the method known as the interrogatory examination.... It was a method that was creeping into secular practice, in the courts of King's bench and common pleas, as early as the reign of Edward I.... As practically administered the examinations were of several kinds or degrees, according to the nature of the case and the advancement of the art of questioning.[12]

The statute *Articuli Cleri* notwithstanding, the House of Commons found it necessary to protest against the forced subjection of accused and suspected persons to the inquisitorial procedures of the ecclesiastical courts and those of the King's Council. Edward III (1327-77), responded with an assurance that the practice would be discontinued, unless there were sufficient grounds with which to justify its use.[13] The protestations, it would seem, continued since, some four years later, a statute was passed which invoked the Magna Carta and provided that "from henceforth none should be taken by petition or suggestion made to our Lord the King, or his Council, unless it be by the indictment or presentation of good and lawful people of the same neighbourhood ... in due manner, or by process made by writ original at the common law".[14]

The objections to which this statute was addressed appear to have been based not on the application of the inquisitional oath but rather on its use without the common law prerequisite of a specific accusation.[15] Inquisitorial methods were not eliminated however; they continued to be employed by the ecclesiastical courts, and they were to re-emerge within the Crown's prerogative courts, they were also to appear within common law procedures.[16] This would seem to indicate a cleavage between the rhetoric of the ordinances promulgated by the Crown and day-to-day reality. "Legal niceties, procedural regularities, and forms of law", Levy (1868) observes, "counted for little when the objective was to obtain a conviction at any cost".[17]

During the fifteenth century the ecclesiastical courts worked in close co-operation with the Crown, its Council and increasingly with the common law courts.[18] In the absence of enforceable common law accusatory procedures within the conciliar and ecclesiastical courts, the *inquisitio*, with its compulsory inquisitorial oath, developed to become a weapon of political and religious suppression.[19] The procedures utilized by these courts were such that suspects could be tried and convicted by secret examination before officials of the Church and Crown. Suspects were examined without prior knowledge of the charges against them, of the nature of the evidence or of their accusers, in a manner designed to extort evidence and confessions of guilt. Later, confessions were increasingly being extracted by means of torture. Confessions obtained in this manner served to furnish the authorities with virtually unassailable material with which to legitimate convictions. Once compelled to confess, accused persons would be required to 'freely' repeat their confession in open court. Failure to do so would frequently attract further coercive measures to secure compliance.[20] The appearance of spontaneous avowals of guilt behind the private application of direct physical compulsion, gave the public proceedings a veneer of legitimacy to both sanitise those proceedings and to authenticate the punishments meted out by the courts.

The inquisitorial procedures of the ecclesiastical courts, and those of the conciliar courts, were again to become the object of popular disquiet in the early sixteenth century.[21] During the reign of Henry VIII (1509-47), the Crown once again responded to widespread public opposition to the inquisitorial oath procedure derived from the canon law of papal Rome and the civil law of imperial Rome.[22] In 1533 an Act for the punishment of heresy insisted that every person presented or indicted of any heresy or duly accused by two lawful witnesses, "shall and may after every suche accusacion or presentment and none otherwyse nor by any other meanes be cited convented arrested taken or apprehended ..." be committed to answer, "in open Courte ... to their accusation and presentmentis".[23]

The statute seems to have again intended that any persons suspected or accused of heresy should be convicted only after the prosecution had negotiated the common law due process procedures of formal accusation and public trial. However, Mary I (1553-58) repealed the 1533 statute,[24] reviving the jurisdiction of the ecclesiastical courts. In the first year of the reign of Elizabeth I (1558-1603) the measures that had been introduced by Mary I in her response to the Henrician Reformation and to the Protestantism of Edward VI (1547-53), were themselves repealed by the Act of Supremacy, 1558.[25] The Act restored to the Crown jurisdiction over the ecclesiastical, spiritual and secular state, "abolyshing all Forreine Power repugnant to the same". It also reserved to the Queen the power by letters patent to authorise her Commissioners to investigate, "correct and amend all such errors, heresies scisms abuses offences contempts and enormities" by means of inquisitorial procedures designed to obtain confessions and to secure convictions.[26] The statute, therefore, formally transferred from the ecclesiastical courts to the Crown, the administration of the religious inquisition.[27]

The *ex officio* oath procedure became a characteristic feature of the investigations conducted by the Commissioners. This was expressly authorised by the Crown. Under the supervision of the Privy Council, the Commissioners formed the tribunal which became known as the Court of High Commission.[28] Though concerned primarily with heresy, the Court of High Commission began to extend its jurisdiction to other matters of ecclesiastical concern.[29]

The Court was empowered by fiat of the royal prerogative to inflict torture upon witnesses and accused persons to extract confessions.[30] The use of torture could only be authorised by the express written sanction of the sovereign or Privy Council.[31] An individual brought before the Court was not entitled to be informed of the source, nature or strength of the allegations made against him.[32] The High Commission Court was not governed by common law procedures;[33] it examined suspected and accused persons in secret under the *ex officio* oath. Those aspects of its operation open to the public, normally sentencing and punishment, served to publicise and, therefore, to legitimise the correctness of its judgements. *Ex officio* oath examinations might be undertaken before specific charges had been preferred. This permitted the Court to construct its case against the suspect on the basis of its examination and to convict the suspect on the basis of his forced and uncorroborated confession.[34]

Refusal to answer *ex officio* oath interrogatories rendered suspects liable either to severe sanctions since "it was considered that an innocent man had no reason to refuse and was guilty of contempt of court".[35] Returned to prison, the Court could then seek from the Crown and its Council authorisation to employ torture. Indeed, the obstinate suspect could be examined before torture, under torture, between torture and after torture.[36] Adverting to the Elizabethan recourse to torture, Jardine (1837) comments that:

> Among other instruments of power which prerogative had placed at the disposal of the Sovereign, the torture was one peculiarly applicable to the discovery of the real or supposed treasons of religious fanatics; and ... there is no period of our history at which this instrument was used more frequently and mercilessly....[37]

The Crown could not be required to justify its imposition of torture.[38] Its use, however, was denounced as being illegal and in contravention of the principles of common law. On this basis, various legal commentators, such as Sir John Fortescue, in the fifteenth century, Sir Thomas Smith in the reign of Elizabeth I and Sir Edward Coke, opposed the administering of torture.[39]

## The Legality of Torture Questioned

It was not until the early part of the seventeenth century that the legality of torture became the subject of judicial appraisal. At his trial in 1628, for the murder of the Duke of Buckingham, John Felton[40] confessed his guilt. The court nonetheless pressed him further to "confess who set him to work to do such a bloody act". Felton maintained he acted alone. He was told that if he did not confess he would be sent to torture by the rack. The case report relates that Felton replied:

if it must be so he could not tell whom he might nominate in the extremity of torture, and if what he should say then must go for truth, he could not tell whether his lordship (meaning the Bishop of London) or which of their lordships he might name, for torture might draw unexpected things from him: after this he was asked no more questions, but sent back to prison.[41]

The King, who was present at the trial, sought the opinion of the Lord Chief Justice and all other judges as to the legality of the use of torture under the common law. The judges returned their unanimous opinion that Felton "ought not by the law to be tortured by the rack, for no such punishment is known or allowed by our law".[42] Evidently the King chose not to authorise the application of torture in this instance. Felton was subsequently tried, convicted and sentenced to death.

While not used in Felton's case, the royal prerogative continued to sanction the use of torture through to the middle of the seventeenth century.[43] Confessions thus obtained were admitted "evidentially without scruple".[44]

## Star Chamber

The royal prerogative also legitimated the use of torture in a tribunal of "an almost indistinguishable character" to that of the High Commission: the Court of Star Chamber.[45] This prerogative court developed as the judicial limb of the Privy Council, composed of the highest ranking noble and clerical officers of state.[46] It sat at Westminster in the "Starred Chambre", a room with its ceiling ornamented with stars, from which it may have derived its name.[47] The origins of the Court, however, have also been attributed to the *Pro Camera Stellata* Act of 1487.[48]

Under Elizabeth I this Court became active as a political institution.[49] It replicated the inquisitorial procedures of the ecclesiastical courts to enhance the authority of the Crown.[50] Like the Court of High Commission, it was also empowered to subpoena any witnesses or suspect, for interrogation under the *ex officio* oath, to determine guilt without a jury of accusation or of trial and to convict persons by their coerced and uncorroborated confessions as if they had been condemned at common law.[51] Its largely unspecified jurisdiction,[52] included the hearing of minor offences or misdemeanours,[53] contempt of other courts, the punishment of common law jurors who handed down verdicts considered perverse,[54] and the preliminary examination of suspects, often by means of torture.[55] Under its inquisitorial procedures, the accused was presumed guilty and carried the burden of proving his innocence.[56]

The Star Chamber, like its ecclesiastical counterpart, invariably delivered its verdicts in public. While this served to legitimise its punishments, the crucial stages prior to conviction and sentence were conducted in private.[57] Nevertheless, there is some evidence to suggest that until the last decade of its existence, the Star Chamber was held in high esteem. For example, Coke, in a comment made sometime before his death in 1634, regarded this instrument of Crown policy as "the most honourable court (our Parliament excepted) that is in the Christian world".[58] Its advantage to the Crown lay in its procedures through which it could get convictions "more effectually" than the ordinary common law courts.[59] However, it was these very procedures that would, by the middle of the seventeenth century, arouse sufficient enmity as to cause the abolition of the Court and secure its place of notoriety in history as an instrument of Stuart despotism.[60]

In the aftermath of the dynastic disputes associated with the protracted Wars of the Roses, Tudor authorities sought to strengthen the machinery of centralised government. To achieve this objective the Crown increased the severity of the criminal law and established new courts to operate alongside the traditional common law courts.[61] Under this policy courts of a similar nature to that of the Star Chamber came into existence in strategic parts of the Kingdom.[62] These courts followed the inquisitorial practices of the High Commission and Star Chamber courts.[63] They were, in effect, instruments of central authority expressed through the agency of the Privy Council, which by the sixteenth century had become, "the most important organ of the State".[64] The regional courts were staffed by officers of the Crown enjoined to enforce its policies rather than by judges directed to administer the common law.[65] These officers, acting in the inquisitorial manner as both prosecutor and judge, could fortify their impressions of guilt by employing coercive measures to force the vital confession.[66] The investigative methods employed by these courts indicate that the law of this period had no hesitation in resorting to extreme measures of coercion, including torture, to extract confessions when the exigencies of criminal procedure required it.[67] The essentially extra-common law procedures commissioned by the Crown in these courts had a "decidedly inquisitorial cast".[68] Such procedures were of immense benefit to governmental and law enforcement policies pursued by the Crown. In supplementing the common law, these inquisitional methods were "simpler, speedier, and cheaper than in the common law courts". The power of the Crown, therefore, to influence prosecutions and to secure convictions was heightened by its use of prerogative courts where "technicalities were less important, examination of witnesses was more efficient and there was no jury".[69]

## The Common Law Courts

The power and influence of the Crown over the criminal process as manifest within the prerogative courts, was also evident within common law criminal procedures.[70] The common law also displayed inquisitorial characteristics in spite of the due process requirements of specific accusation, indictment and public trial.

Common law procedures were such that a person accused of felony, when apprehended, was confined to prison until his trial. Bail was seldom granted. Once detained the accused was closely examined, incommunicado, on all aspects of the case against him. The answers to his preliminary interrogation were written down to construct the case for trial. This examination would be conducted in the inquisitorial manner. The examiner did not act as an impartial or disinterested arbiter of the evidence against the presumptively innocent. Rather, he acted as a partisan detective committed to assembling an impregnable case against the accused.

The purpose of the examination was to expose a man assumed to be guilty. A confession of guilt was, therefore, vital for the affirmation of this presumed guilt. The confession was decisive since alone, without corroboration, it sufficed to secure a conviction. If a confession was not obtained during the pre-trial examination, the prisoner would be further examined by the trial judge who would base his "bullying" interrogation upon the depositions received from the preliminary examination.[71]

As Veall (1970) observes, "the odds were heavily weighted against the accused and the trial was regarded as a conflict between the State and its enemies rather than an impartial inquiry into the guilt or innocence of the accused".[72] It is clear that this conflict was not an adversarial encounter between comparable forces before an impartial and disinterested judge.[73] Rather, it was a conflict between the unaided individual and the unequalled power of the Crown.

The inquisitorial procedures that obtained under the prerogative courts and the common law, revolved around and depended upon confessions which were crucial for the affirmation of actual or supposed guilt. The common law, in parallel with the prerogative courts, evolved interrogatory practices for the principal purpose of eliciting required confessions. The examination was, for that reason, the essence of the criminal justice process. It was, as Sir Francis Bacon argued in 1673,[74] considered to be the point at which justice enters into criminal causes.

## Inquisition Under Attack

By the end of the sixteenth century, mounting public disaffection with the procedures and jurisdictional excesses of the conciliar courts were increasingly supported by common law lawyers.[75] Consequently, the lawyers of the common law courts began to articulate their opposition to the procedures of their jurisdictional rivals by granting writs of prohibition.[76] These writs, often directed against the administration of the *ex officio* oath, frequently invoked the statue *Articuli Cleri* (1315-16) which had attempted to restrain the ecclesiastical courts to matrimonial and testamentary causes.[77]

By the beginning of the seventeenth century the maxim: *memo tenetur produre seipsum* had emerged, as a product of the Puritan campaign against inquisitorial methods, to convey the principle that no one should be compelled to accuse themselves.[78] The maxim was employed by common lawyers and religious non-conformists against the practice of subjecting suspects to inquisitional-oath interrogatories, without first formally charging them with a specific offence.[79] The precise source and meaning of the Latin maxim is obscure,[80] though in his assessment Morgan (1949) concludes:

> All that can be safely asserted is that the common lawyers both in the second half of the 13th and all of the 14th century and under Henry VIII and Elizabeth resisted the inquisitorial procedure of the spiritual courts, whether Romish or English, and under Elizabeth began to base their opposition chiefly upon the principle that a person could not be compelled to furnish under oath answers to charges which had not been formally made and disclosed to him, except in causes testamentary and matrimonial. No doubt there was some confusion between the attack and the power of the spiritual courts even to entertain certain causes and its power to institute proceedings by the ex-officio oath. But there can equally be no doubt that to the common lawyers a system which required a person to furnish his own indictment from his own lips under oath was repugnant to the law of the land.[81]

This statement indicates that the common lawyers objected to compelling individuals to answer examinations under oath and implies that were individuals to be examined after a formal accusation, and without the inquisitorial oath, this would comply with prevailing common law procedures. Supposing this construction to be so, there would appear to be an element of insincerity in the claim of the common lawyers since, at this time, their preliminary procedures did not meet this standard. Though the *ex officio* oath may not have been required at common law, individuals were examined in secret without first being duly accused.[82] This permits the conclusion that the objections of the common lawyers were not based upon the inquisitorial practices of the prerogative courts alone; they may also have been aimed at the jurisdictional incursions made by these rival courts into common law matters.[83]

## John Lilburn's Case

Beginning in 1637, the trial of the Puritan, John Lilburn,[84] focused the discontent of the non-conformists and the public at large upon the imposition of the inquisitorial oath. The trial precipitated the abolition of all courts employing the *ex officio* oath to coerce suspected persons to confess their supposed guilt.[85] The opposition had, by the time of this trial, reached such proportions that Charles I (1625-49) was moved to write to the High Commission insisting on the continued validity of inquisitorial methods. The letter, dated February 4, 1637,[86] required that those non-conformists who had "Withdrawn themselves from their obedience to our ecclesiastical law, into several ways of Separation, sects, schisms and heresies", and who had, "grown to that obstinacy - that some of them refuse to take their oaths, and others being sworn, refuse to answer", should be compelled, "to answer upon their oath in causes against themselves". Such people, the letter continues, should be "enjoined to take their corporal oaths and by virtue thereof, to answer to such articles and interrogatories as shall be objected against them". Where these people refuse to be so sworn or being sworn then refuse to answer, the letter obliged the Commission to declare them "'pro confesso' - held and had as confessed and convicted legally".

Lilburn had been remanded in prison by the Court of Star Chamber after having been charged with printing and importing into England, heretical and seditious material. At his subsequent examination before the Attorney General, Lilburn was questioned upon his relationship with other suspects. When his examination turned to the nature of his acquaintance with Warton, the co-accused, Lilburn reports himself as objecting "... why do you ask me all these questions? these are beside the matter of any imprisonment; I pray come to the thing for which I am accused and imprisoned".[87] On being further pressed he replied:

> ... I am not imprisoned for knowing and talking with such and such men, but for sending over Books; and therefore I am not willing to answer you any more of these questions, because I see you go about by this to ensnare me for seeing the things for which I am imprisoned cannot be proved against me, you will get other matter out of my examination: and therefore if you will not ask me about the thing laid to my charge, I shall answer no more.[88]

He refused to submit to the *ex officio* oath and relates that:

> ... some of the clerks began to reason with me, and told me every one took that oath: and should I be wiser than all other men? I told them, it made no matter to me what other men do; but before I swear, I will know better grounds and reasons than other men's practice, to convince me of the lawfulness of such an oath, to swear I do not know to what.[89]

He was then examined as to the basis of his refusal. He maintained that he perceived "the oath to be an oath of inquiry ... and of the same nature as the High Commission Oath", which he considered unlawful.[90]

The Court found Lilburn and Warton "guilty of a very high contempt" and condemned them to be fined, whipped and pilloried for their "presumptuous boldness in refusing to take a legal oath; without which many great and exorbitant offences, to the prejudice and danger of his majesty, his Kingdoms, and loving subjects, might go away undiscovered, and unpunished".[91] The sentence of the Court was carried out in April, 1638.

In November, 1640, Lilburn petitioned the House of Commons which, on May 4, 1641, voted the sentence of the Star Chamber "illegal and against the liberty of the subject".[92] He also petitioned the House of Lords. The Lords ordered the sentence to be "totally vacated, obliterated and taken off the file in all courts ... as illegal".[93]

In March, 1641, against a background of much public attention which accompanied Lilburn's case,[94] two bills were introduced to the Long Parliament to abolish the Courts of Star Chamber, High Commission and all courts exercising like jurisdiction. The bills were passed into law in July of that year.[95] The second of these statutory measures also prohibited any ecclesiastical tribunal or official from administering the *ex officio* oath for the purpose of obliging anyone charged "to confess or accuse himself or herself of any crime, offence, delinquency or misdemeanour", which may expose them "to any censure, pain, penalty or punishment whatsoever".[96]

Following the 1641 Acts a case was heard in December of that year where the privilege against compulsory self-incrimination was asserted and appears to have been judicially acknowledged. In the *Twelve Bishops' Trial* (1641)[97] the defendants — who had been charged with high treason by the House of Commons in its capacity as the "grand jury of the nation" and who had been brought before the House of Lords, which sat as judge and jury — refused to answer on their oaths whether they had subscribed to a treasonable petition on the ground that they were not "bound to accuse themselves".[98] The case suggests that the Acts prohibiting the inquisitional oath were construed restrictively as applying only to ecclesiastical courts and their officials. Thus, in 1662, it was necessary to further enact that "no one shall administer to any person whatsoever the oath usually called 'ex officio', or any other oath, whereby such persons may be charged or compelled to confess any criminal matter".[99]

Upon the mid-seventeenth century relinquishment of official torture,[100] the abolition of the prerogative courts through which torture was most frequently administered and with them the inquisitorial oath, the common law, its jurisdiction and its procedures — which formally eschewed the compulsory self-incriminatory oath — gained greater legitimacy.[101] However, common law preliminary and trial procedures were such that suspected and accused persons continued to be compelled to answer self-incriminatory questions, albeit without the operation of the *ex officio* oath.[102]

Barnes (1977) argues that the "triumph of the common law" in the seventeenth century, coupled with the Glorious Revolution of 1688, "substantially dismantled the vigorous, inquisitive, interfering government of the Tudor and early Stuart monarchs".[103] Nevertheless, while compulsory interrogations under the *ex officio* oath were formally repudiated, the judicial practice of subjecting defendants to searching interrogatories at their common law trial persisted through to the early eighteenth century.[104] Indeed, in the absence of a sophisticated corpus of evidential rules within the common law, a defendant could still be convicted on the basis of the impression the petit jury derived from his bearing under stringent judicial examination.[105] However, this practice appears to have been so closely associated in the public mind with the inquisitorial procedures of the prerogative courts that pressing judicial interrogatories of defendants gradually died out. The development of rules of evidence, from the eighteenth century, underscored this movement and transformed it into a practice which — as a matter of common law, rather than any statutory measure — prohibited the judicial interrogation of defendants at their trial.[106]

Opposition to the inquisitional oath, to the use of torture and to the conciliar courts that relied upon inquisitorial methods appears, therefore, to have brought about the gradual elimination of coercive judicial questioning at common law trial. As a direct consequence, by the early eighteenth century, defendants were accorded a 'right' to remain silent at their trial.[107] However, while the judicial interrogation of defendants under the inquisitorial oath was eschewed, inquisitorial interrogations were to continue at a location which remained almost entirely immune from the reforms instituted at the public trial phase of the common law criminal process. Two statutes from the middle of the sixteenth century authorised justices of the peace to 'examine' suspected felons. The statutes governed the crucial pre-trial process until their abrogation in the middle of the nineteenth century.[108] The preliminary examination of suspects sanctioned by these statutes was designed to extort confessions of guilt from suspects or enough damaging admissions to ensure a successful prosecution. Such examinations had the effect of countering developments made at the trial stage of criminal proceedings. Specifically, they worked to ensure that the a defendant's 'right' to remain silent at his trial was effectively undermined prior to trial.

The role assigned to justices of the peace, and later the police, in the evolving pre-trial structures, which were modelled to furnish the courts with confession evidence, are subjects discussed in the following chapter.

## Notes

[1] Levy, 1968, pp. 34, 39; Veall, 1970, p. 25.
[2] Wigmore, 1902, p. 611; Harding, 1966, p. 35.
[3] Wigmore, 1902, p. 611; see also 1 Pollock and Maitland, 1898, pp. 66-7, 432. This was to become a source of a prolonged jurisdictional conflict over the delimitation of papal and regal power, see Wigmore, 1902, pp. 611-25; Harding, 1966, pp. 35-6.
[4] Ratushny, 1979, p. 161; see also Wigmore, 1902, pp. 613-16.
[5] Thayer, 1898, p. 37.

[6] Wigmore, 1902, pp. 614-5.
[7] Wigmore, 1902, p. 615.
[8] See Morgan, 1949, pp. 1-3.
[9] 9 Edw. 2 (1315-16). Wigmore (1892, pp. 74-5) regarded this statute as the source of the modern privilege against self-incrimination. It was, he argues "the earliest legal opposition" that was made to combat the imposition of the inquisitorial oath.
[10] Wigmore, 1902, pp. 612-3. See also Levy, 1968, p. 44.
[11] *Select Cases Before the King's Council, 1243-1482,* Vol. 35.
[12] *Ibid.,* p. xiii; see also Morgan, 1949, p. 4.
[13] 11 *Rotuli Parliamentorum* 168, item 28 (1347); see Morgan, 1949, p. 4.
[14] 1 Statutes of the Realm (iv), pp. 319-21 (1351); see also Morgan, 1949, p. 4.
[15] Ratushny, 1979, p. 167.
[16] *Ibid.,* p. 166.
[17] Levy, 1968, p. 26.
[18] Morgan, 1947, p. 6.
[19] Ratushny, 1979, p. 163.
[20] Levy, 1968, pp. 26-30.
[21] Beard, 1904, pp. 114-17; Morgan, 1947, p. 6; Langbein, 1974 pp. 71-4; Bellamy, 1984, pp. 30-1.
[22] Morgan, 1947, p. 6; Levy, 1968, pp. 45-82; Veall, 1970, p. 11.
[23] 25 Hen. 8, c. 14 (1553).
[24] 1 & 2 Phil. and Mar., c.6 (1554).
[25] 1 Eliz., c.1 (1558).
[26] *Ibid.* See Levy, 1968, p. 76.
[27] Ratushny, 1979, p. 165.
[28] Morgan, 1947, p. 7; Veall, 1970, p. 12.
[29] Veall, 1970, p. 10.
[30] Levy, 1968, pp. 83-103.
[31] Jardine, 1837, p. 67. See also Levy, 1968, pp. 83-103.
[32] Veall, 1970, p. 25; Levy, 1968, pp. 126-7.
[33] Veall, 1970, p. 23.
[34] Lowell, 1897-8, p. 293; Veall, 1970, p. 26.
[35] Veall, 1970, p. 23.
[36] Morgan, 1949, pp. 14-5; Veall, 1970, p. 26.
[37] Jardine, 1837, p. 26.
[38] *Ibid.,* pp. 66-9; Langbein, 1977, pp. 129-31.
[39] Jardine, 1837, pp. 6-10. See also Veall, 1970, p. 25.
[40] *Felton's Case* (1628) 3 Cobb. St. Tr. 368. See also Jardine, 1837, pp. 6-12.
[41] *Felton's Case, Ibid.*
[42] *Ibid.*
[43] Jardine, 1837, pp. 58-9; Anon., 1964, pp. 1036-7.

## Interrogation and Confession

[44] 3 Wigmore, 1970, p. 294; see also Jardine, 1837, pp. 67-8; Langbein, 1977, pp. 129-31.
[45] 1 Holdsworth, 1956, p. 505.
[46] Morgan, 1949, pp. 14-15; Harding, 1966, p. 151.
[47] Maitland, 1908, p. 261; Levy, 1968, pp. 49, 100; Walker, 1976, p. 12.
[48] 3 Hen. 7, c. 1 (1487). See Harding, 1966, p. 158. Barnes argues that a new conciliar court was indeed established by the 1487 Act. However, he suggests that by the early sixteenth century its composition so resembled that of the King's Council that "administrative convenience" necessitated its absorption into the council sitting in the Star Chamber (Barnes, 1977, p. 318).
[49] Wigmore, 1902, p. 619; Phillips, 1939, p. 115.
[50] Levy, 1968, pp. 49-50; Veall, 1970, p. 10.
[51] Bellamy, 1984, p. 17.
[52] Maitland, 1908, p. 263; Phillips, 1939, p. 117; Barnes, 1977, p. 317.
[53] 1 Stephen, 1883, p. 337; see also Harding, 1966, pp. 75, 159-54.
[54] Maitland, 1908, p. 263.
[55] Lowell, 1897-8, p. 294.
[56] Veall, 1970, p. 22.
[57] *Ibid*.
[58] 4 Coke, 1797, p. 65, referred to in 1 Holdsworth, 1956, pp. 505-6. See also Veall, 1970, p. 10; Phillips, 1939, p. 107.
[59] 1 Holdsworth, 1956, p. 505.
[60] Phillips, 1939, pp. 107, 124-31; Veall, 1970, p. 10.
[61] Veall, 1970, pp. 1, 10.
[62] The Council of the North which sat at York and the Council in the Marches of Wales are two examples. See Maitland, 1908, pp. 263-4.
[63] Wigmore, 1902, p. 619.
[64] 4 Holdsworth, 1945, p. 57.
[65] Maitland, 1908, p. 263.
[66] Lowell, 1897-8, p. 293-4.
[67] *Ibid.*, p. 290. See also 9 Holdsworth, 1944, pp. 198-9; Horowitz, 1958, pp. 129-31; Levy, 1968, p. 26.
[68] Lowell, 1897-8, p. 294.
[69] Veall, 1970, p. 37. See also Cheyney, 1913, p. 746; Phillips, 1939, pp. 107, 123, 128; Levy, 1968, pp. 270-71; Ratushny, 1979, p. 170; Berger, 1980, pp. 12-14.
[70] Ratushny, 1979, p. 116.
[71] 1 Stephen, 1883, pp. 216, 221, 357-68; Kauper, 1931-2, pp. 1232-34; 1 Holdsworth, 1956, p. 296; 8 Wigmore, 1961, pp. 327-29; Levy, 1968, pp. 325-6; Veall, 1970, pp. 17-20; Berger, 1980, p. 101.
[72] Veall, 1970, p. 20.
[73] Harding, 1966, pp. 129-32.
[74] *Countess of Shrewsbury's Case* (1613) 2 Cobb. St. Tr. 770, p. 778.

75 Wigmore, 1902, pp. 620-24; Morgan, 1949, pp. 6-10; Ratushny, 1979, pp. 168-74.
76 Levy, 1968, pp. 42, 220-8.
77 9 Edw. 2 (1315-6). See Levy, 1968, pp. 227-8; Ratushny, 1979, pp. 168-9.
78 Lowell, 1897-8, p. 296; 9 Holdsworth, 1944, p. 199; Ratushny, 1979, p. 169.
79 Lowell, *ibid.*; Morgan, 1949, p. 8. The opposition to inquisitorial procedures seems to have become pronounced when the common law courts began to recognise the increasingly insistent claims for the privilege against compulsory self-incrimination. See Pittman, 1935, p. 769; Moreland, 1956, p. 272; Levy, 1968, p. 220.
80 Horowitz, 1958, pp. 130-6; Ratushny, 1979, pp. 169, 173.
81 Morgan, 1949, p. 9. Horowitz (1958, pp. 131-8) however, suggests that the maxim *nemo tenetur produre seipsum* was first translated into a firm common law doctrine by Lord Coke, when acting as counsel, in *Collier's Case* (1590) 4 Leo. 194. See also 9 Holdsworth, 1944, p. 200.
82 Lowell, 1897-8, p. 294.
83 The objections of the common lawyers drew a large measure of support from Puritans and Separatists who were also hostile to the inquisitorial methods of the High Commission and Star Chamber courts (see Wigmore, 1902, pp. 610-12; Horowitz, 1958, pp. 136-8; Pittman, 1935, pp. 769-70).
84 *The Trial of John Lilburn and John Warton* (1637) 3 Cobb. St. Tr. 1315. It should be noted that the case report consists of Lilburn's own account of his trial. This raises questions as to the report's objectivity. However, in providing a sketch of seventeenth-century criminal justice practice, it remains valuable.
85 Wigmore, 1902, p. 264; Pittman, 1935, p. 770; Morgan, 1949, p. 9; Levy, 1968, pp. 271-2; Ratushny, 1979, p. 171.
86 'King Charles 1. Letters to the High Commission Court' (1637) Hazard, 1 State Papers, p. 428. This letter is reproduced in Pittman, 1935, pp. 770-1.
87 *Supra.*, n. 84, p. 1317.
88 *Ibid.*, p. 1318.
89 *Ibid.*, p. 1320.
90 *Ibid.*, p. 1332.
91 *Ibid.*, p. 1327.
92 *Ibid.*, p. 1342.
93 *Ibid.*, p. 1348.
94 Wigmore, 1902, pp. 625-6.
95 16 Car. 1, c. 10 and c. 11 (1641).
96 16 Car. 1, c. 11, s. 4(2).
97 *Twelve Bishops' Trial* (1641) 4 Cobb. St. Tr. 63.
98 *Ibid.*, p. 76; see also Wigmore, 1902, p. 633; Levy, 1968, pp. 284-5.
99 13 Car. 2, c. 12 (1662); see Wigmore, 1892, p. 82.
100 See Jardine (1837, pp. 16, 45, 68-70) and Langbein (1977, pp. 134-9) who agree that the last recorded torture warrant was issued in 1640. However, the

unofficial use of torture may have continued beyond this date. Certainly there is evidence to suggest that the threat of torture was used to coerce confessions for some time after 1640. See, for example, *Tonge's Case* (1662) 6 How. St. Tr. 225, p. 259.

[101] Wigmore, 1902, p. 619; Horowitz, 1958, pp. 123-4. See also Stephen, 1877, p. 748; Levy, 1968, p. 324.

[102] Wigmore, 1902, pp. 627-9; Ratushny, 1979, p. 171.

[103] Barnes, 1977, p. 322; see also 4 Holdsworth, 1945, p. 70; 5 Holdsworth, 1945, p. 433; 9 Holdsworth, 1949, p. 209. The collapse of prerogative government in the seventeenth century and the abolition of courts employing the inquisitorial oath had a decisive impact upon common law procedures. It was from about this period that defendants began to be regarded as being incompetent and non-compellable to testify on oath at their trial. This developed as a result of common law judges' increasing acceptance of the principle that defendants should not be compelled to incriminate themselves (Morgan, 1949, p. 12; Levy, 1968, pp. 322-5). Defendants were permitted to make unsworn statements on their own behalf but this was of limited probative value as unsworn statements were not subject to cross-examination (see *Dyer* (1844) 1 Cox C.C. 133, *per* Alderson, B; 1 Stephen, 1883, p. 441; Nobel, 1970, pp. 252-3; Heydon, 1976, p. 376). By the beginning of the nineteenth century, the practice which worked to render the accused non-compellable and incompetent to give evidence on oath — seen by some commentators as a 'right' not to give evidence on oath, or as the 'right to silence' at trial, and as an expression the privilege against compulsory self incrimination — became the subject of intense debate. It was a result of this debate that moves were made, from 1843, through a number of statutes, to render the accused 'oath-worthy'. The movement culminated in 1898 with the Criminal Evidence Act which made defendants competent, though not compellable, to give evidence on oath in their defence (see Nobel, 1970, pp. 254-61; Parker, 1984, pp. 162-72).

[104] See Wigmore, 1902, p. 635; Levy, 1968, p. 263. Stephen, however, suggests the practice of pressing defendants with interrogatories 'died out soon after the Revolution of 1688' (1 Stephen, 1883, p. 440).

[105] 1 Stephen, 1883, pp. 336-7.

[106] Stephen, 1877, pp. 749-52; see also Pittman, 1968, p. 774.

[107] *Supra.*, n. 103.

[108] The statutes: 1 & 2 Phil. and Mar. c.13 (1554); 2 & 3 Phil. and Mar. c.10 (1555), and their import are discussed in chapter 3.

# 3 The Historical Management of Preliminary Procedures

**Introduction**

It has been seen that following the Conquest, local communities were placed under an obligation to apprehend and 'present' for trial all suspects they, as represented by the jury of presentment, accused of crime.[1] Under these arrangements, it was assumed that the presenting jury — being composed of the accused's neighbours — was sufficiently well informed to duly indict suspected offenders for trial. However, with the emergence and establishment of the petit jury mode of trial, an effective official means of supervising the arrest, detention and presentment of accused persons became vital to the capacity of the prosecution process to generate evidence capable of facilitating secure convictions. Accordingly, it became necessary to supplement the information upon which the largely self-informed presentment and petit jury could base its decisions.

With the gradual erosion of feudalistic social structures, jurors gradually became less reliant upon their own inherent knowledge of suspected individuals. An official element was, therefore, required to ensure presenting juries indicted and petit juries convicted accused persons. The collapse of the self-informing jury fostered the need for a process of official evidence-gathering. Increasingly, juries were to be persuaded of the correctness of their decisions to indict and to convict on the basis of the evidence presented before them, rather than on their personal impressions of their accused neighbour. The office of justice of the peace evolved to perform this vital evidence-gathering function. Through this office the Crown created an official agent with authority to manage the operation of the preliminary phase of the criminal process.

A key feature in the evolution of English criminal procedures, therefore, was the gradual contraction of jury members reliant upon their own first-hand knowledge of the issues upon which they were to indict and convict. The preservation of the peace occasioned and justified the progressive displacement of community-based responsibility for arrest, accusation and prosecution.[2] Under the justices, the community-based prosecution process was reconstructed to permit the officially sanctioned modes for procuring testimony from witnesses and confession evidence from suspects to prevail.

Over time, the Crown vested the justices with powers with which to summarily convict and punish suspected wrongdoers. Elevated into the status of "intermediate judges",[3] justices also acquired control over preliminary examinations and, thereby, governed the flow to the courts of evidence indicative of guilt — particularly confession evidence as irrefutable proof of guilt. It was, therefore, at the crucial pre-trial stage of the criminal process that inquisitorial interrogatories were received by the common law.[4]

## The Early Justices

The origin of the office of justice of the peace has been traced to its twelfth century ancestors, knights appointed to perform local administrative, military and policing functions attendant to their general duty to keep the King's peace.[5] As part of the extension of royal power through the progressively centralized legal system, an Act of 1237[6] required good and lawful knights of each county to be "assigned to keep the peace". By the mid-thirteenth century, such functions as making arrests and the hearing of inquests came to be regularly invested in the office of the Keeper.[7] In 1285 the Statute of Westminster provided for the presentment of breaches of the King's peace to be made before these custodians of the peace.[8]

In the mid-fourteenth century an attempt was made to restrict the quasi-judicial authority enjoyed by the keepers and to subordinate their duties more directly to the jurisdiction of centrally commissioned circuit justices. The House of Commons, in which the interests of the local gentry were championed, resisted these efforts and under Edward III (1327-77) secured for the keepers, powers to hear and determine petty offences.[9] It was also through their representatives in the Commons that the keepers succeeded in acquiring responsibility for administering the economic legislation passed in response to the ravages wrought by the Black Death of 1349 which had depleted the work force. This, combined with the Peasants' Revolt of 1381, created "special and urgent reasons for social control".[10] The Crown responded by augmenting the responsibilities of the justices to include the acceptance of presentments and the power to do justice summarily — that is, in the absence of a trial jury — in respect of lesser offences known as trespasses against the peace, or later as misdemeanours.[11]

The title 'justice of the peace' appeared in statute for the first time in 1360-61 and may have derived from common parlance descriptions of the office.[12] Subsequent developments enabled the justices to emerge, from the late fourteenth century, supreme among the local representatives of Crown authority in the administration of common law preliminary procedures.[13] Beard (1904) argues, the desire of the Crown to extend and consolidate its central power obliged it to promote the royal office of justice of the peace since: "Only by concentrating power in the hands of the strong middle class gentry independent of the great lords, could the Crown hope to crush the turbulent elements in the Kingdom".[14] Indeed, in its development of the office, the Crown had created a "convenient and effective" agent for extending to the localities its social and crime control policies.[15]

**Examining Justices**

The statutory source of justices' powers respecting pre-trial examinations of suspects and of summary trial has been ascribed to the labour legislation of the mid-fourteenth century.[16] One such statute required labourers, by their oaths, to conform to fixed rates of pay. Those who were suspected of receiving more than the fixed rate were to be summoned to answer before justices who were authorized to fine or imprison suspected offenders until they gave sureties to observe the employment regulations.[17] It appears that suspects were to be examined by the justices as a means of providing supplementary information upon which the presenting jury was to frame its indictment. It was not, therefore, designed as an alternative to jury of presentment indictments.[18]

This legislation represents an early illustration of the growing primacy of social and crime control considerations over those of due process.[19] The accusatory procedure — which was grounded on the initiative of the local community and systematised in the twelfth century by the Assizes of Clarendon and Northampton — was effectively relegated by the legislation's infusion of official actors instructed to enforce the law. The introduction of an official element into the underlying community-based prosecution process meant that convictions were no longer wholly dependent upon the due process requirement that the community suspected, presented and indicted individuals on the basis of its collective knowledge of the issues. Under its provisions this statute supplemented this arrangement by authorising Crown officials to initiate proceedings on the basis of their own suspicions.

The increasingly transient populace of the formerly fixed hierarchical structure of feudal society may have been instrumental in the decay of the community-based system of denunciation. However, it has been suggested that at this early stage in its development, the jury of presentment was regarded by the Crown and governing classes with some degree of distrust. "It was probably felt", Bellamy (1984) argues, "that out of sympathy with the would-be employee [members of the local community] might refuse to report offences".[20]

The breakdown of the system of prosecutions founded upon neighbours exhorted to inform agents of the Crown of trespasses against its peace, coupled with the dominating social and crime control interests of the powerful, appears then to have been at the root of "the birth of summary justice of an every day nature under the common law".[21] In other words, early conceptions of local justice which had assumed an identity of interest between the rulers and the ruled began to collapse as the rulers lost confidence in the ruled. This created the need for new forms of social and crime control.

Such considerations emerge as key themes pervading the early statutes empowering justices to examine suspects and to deliver summary justice. Initially restricted to minor offences, the progressive infusion of an official dimension into the prosecution process ensured that the repression of conduct stigmatised as criminal was not impeded either by a reluctance on the part of individuals to institute proceedings, or by the perceived shortcomings of the presentment jury.

In 1383, the Crown again sanctioned the examination of suspects as an investigative technique under the justices.[22] This statute enjoined justices to take sureties for good behaviour from vagabonds, or to imprison them until the next gaol delivery where they failed to find the required sureties. The justices were authorized to conduct their inquiries on the basis of their examination of the suspect.[23] It is not clear whether evidence elicited from such examinations was intended to furnish the presenting jury with ancillary information with which to indict the suspect, or whether the evidence was used as an alternative to the indictment of the presenting jury. It may be assumed that this would depend on the extent to which such examinations yielded confessions of guilt capable of rendering the traditional inquiry before the presenting jury unnecessary and, therefore, to enable a prosecution to proceed to conviction.

Bellamy (1984) suggests that recourse to the pre-trial examination procedure resulted, in this instance, from the recognition that suspects were often unknown to the community in which they were apprehended and thus, unknown to members of the presenting jury.[24] The degeneration of the rigid structures of feudal society may have necessitated this deviation from the process of due accusation required by the Assizes of Clarendon and Northampton. However, social and crime control considerations also informed the extension throughout the following centuries, of the power of justices to proceed by examination to summary conviction in respect of a growing number of misdemeanours. The inability of the Crown to initiate criminal proceedings was thereby tempered by the activities of its intermediary who was authorized to arrest individuals on the basis of his own suspicions, rather than on the accusation of neighbours, and to test those suspicions through extra-judicial interrogations.

The Crown's social and crime control agenda is also evidenced in its facilitation of convictions in the event that its officers witnessed an offence against its peace. In such circumstances the justice of the peace was required to certify the details of the incident. The certificate had the force of a jury of presentment indictment. Those accused in this manner could be required to answer *ex officio* oath interrogatories before the Star Chamber or one of its associated tribunals.[25] The effect of such procedures was to gradually shift from the community responsibility for investigating and prosecuting offenders and to vest those responsibilities in Crown officials.

In 1414 the justices were authorized to examine suspects to discover whether any servant was receiving, and any master giving, excessive wages.[26] The examination was to be conducted upon the oath of the suspect, who, upon his confession, was to be punished as though he had been convicted by jury trial.[27] In legitimating procedures designed to procure confessions and in circumventing the indictment of the presenting jury,[28] the statute demonstrates that the common law had no hesitation in resorting to the very methods it would later denounce as being "repugnant to the law of the land" where the imperatives of crime control demanded them.[29]

In his discussion of this enactment Bellamy (1984) suggests that in the event that a confession was not extracted, the traditional presentment procedure would be activated.[30] However, under *ex officio* oath examination, confessions of guilt or other incriminatory admissions would seem probable. Furthermore, in the event that a full confession was not forthcoming, justices may well have been reluctant to invoke the presentment procedure which Bellamy himself acknowledges was regarded with uncertainty by those most interested in securing convictions.[31] Were the 'normal' common law process of presentment and trial to be engaged, however, incriminatory evidence elicited during pre-trial examination may have been adduced for the Crown against the defendant — a practice that was to become increasingly common.[32]

The Statute of 1414 was supplemented by one of the similar nature. This empowered justices to summarily confine to gaol, for a period of one month, suspects considered by the justices to be guilty, irrespective of whether a confession of guilt had been elicited.[33] Enacted to suppress excessive wage demands, the provisions of this statute mark the further extension of powers of examination and summary conviction under the justices, displacing the juries of a presentment and of trial. From this period such powers began to appear in numerous enactments aimed at an increasing array of minor offences.[34] In one example, justices were authorized to avoid awaiting presentments, to regard suspects they examined as having been duly indicted and to fine those they determined were guilty.[35]

The growth in the employment of examination and summary trial — with its concomitant marginalization of features associated with due process, namely, the common law procedures of presentment and trial by jury — is of itself an articulation of the dominant social and crime control values of the Crown. Under Henry VII (1485-1509) the examination and summary conviction competence of justices were again extended.[36] Bellamy (1984) has located no less then ten statutes from this reign commanding the employment of these "truncated procedures"[37] and a similar number from the reign of Henry VIII (1509-47).[38]

The frequent recourse to summary trial conducted by examination accompanied the increasing utilisation of such methods within the prerogative courts of the Tudor period which administered summary justice "without any pretence of a jury trial".[39] Indeed, the practices that prevailed at the preliminary phase of common law criminal justice worked in conjunction with the procedures of the prerogative courts and, to a large extent, shared their *modus operandi*; each employing inquisitorial methods geared to the procurement of confessions.[40] These methods were essentially sympathetic to the interests of crime control and antagonistic to the formal due process requirements of the common law.

The social and crime control oriented legislation of the Tudor period, which rested upon inquisitorial powers of examination and of summary conviction, was of itself a product of prevailing social and economic developments. The Wars of the Roses had had a disintegrating effect upon centralized government.[41] The Reformation had transferred many ecclesiastical concerns to the State and its organs of local government. The problem of discharged soldiers and wandering vagrants had become a matter of acute concern. This problem was compounded by the onset and rapid development of the enclosure movement. The increasingly mobile and largely unpoliced population perturbed the ruling classes. These considerations necessitated "a complete system of state control".[42] As Beard (1904) observes, the "landed and commercial middle classes were anxious for internal order and willing to pay almost any price for it".[43] The consequent policing legislation expanded the criminal law and employed the justices of the peace to enforce it. Tudor government, through the King's Council and locally-based justices, ensured criminalised activities were "discovered and checked in their incipiency".[44]

The King's Council supervised the judicial and administrative duties of the justices. The Crown was, therefore, able to keep "a firm grasp upon the whole system of local government and to maintain a penetrating and constant surveillance over the whole Kingdom".[45] The Council, on behalf of the Crown, appointed justices from the ranks of the most loyal and stable elements of the local gentry. Such individuals satisfied "the requirements of the central autocracy" since they were seen as possessing sufficient knowledge of local conditions to facilitate the efficient administration in the localities of central government policies.[46] The justices, armed with stringent powers of social control, also carried the support of the landed and commercial middle classes. In an age of unprecedented social, commercial and industrial transformation their demands for the rigorous suppression of domestic disorder were acknowledged in the crime control legislation which emanated from the centre and was enforced in the localities by the justices.[47]

Thus, by a series of thirty or so enactments — dating from the mid-fourteenth to the mid-sixteenth centuries — the justice of the peace acquired authority to issue warrants of arrest; to examine suspects; to bail or take recognizances from suspects; to summarily convict in minor offences; and had almost complete charge of the preliminary phase of criminal prosecutions.[48] Under these measures justices did not, however, enjoy powers to convict or discharge persons suspected of felony. Here, petit jury trial was preserved. Thus, in 'serious cases' justices could only conditionally release the suspect on bail or imprison him until the next gaol delivery.[49]

The use of examination and summary conviction procedures at common law, displacing the juries of presentment and of trial in cases of misdemeanour was prompted, argues Bellamy (1973), by a perceived failure of grand juries to indict persons suspected of involvement in crime.[50] This assessment accords with that made earlier by Beard (1904) who found: "Complaints were continually made about the difficulty of securing impartial verdicts from jurors on account of their fear or favouritism".[51] Such complaints guided the passing of statutes explicitly devised to confront the problem. For example, in 1495 a statute[52] recites that owing to the corruption of jurors, it had been impossible in many cases to obtain indictments from juries of inquest. The statute provided that justices of the peace, upon information made before them for the King, be authorized to hear and determine, without indictment from juries, offences and contempts committed by any person, saving treason, murder and felony.

Measures such as this may also have been a response to the increasingly mobile population which was expanding at an unaccustomed rate, bringing with it the gradual disintegration of Medieval self-informing juries — which were being transformed into passive court-room triers largely ignorant of the facts at issue. The process which operated to denude jurors of their character as witnesses who, based on their own first-hand knowledge, could be expected to accuse and convict suspects, was complete by the beginning of the sixteenth century. From about this time jurors began to be required to act only upon the evidence laid before them by officers of the Crown.[53]

It was the justices of the peace who performed the vital evidence-gathering function fostered by the gradual metamorphosis of the jury. The legislation authorizing summary trial by examination was an attempt to confront the declining confidence in the competence of jurors. This enabled the Crown, through its agents, to circumvent the presenting and trial juries and to legitimate this departure from traditional due process requirement on the basis of extorted confessions. The point is that it allowed the Crown, by way of its officers, to supervise the construction of cases against individuals and the collation of incriminatory evidence upon which criminal convictions could be founded.

## The Marian Statutes

Until the middle of the sixteenth century the examination and summary trial statutes were largely concerned with lesser offences. For cases of serious crime the presentment, indictment and trial by jury procedure was preserved. Langbein (1974) suggests this prevented the further extension of summary procedures. However, he also states that "the clumsiness of jury proceedings as a system of detection and denunciation was perpetually felt".[54] During the brief reign of Mary I (1553-8), a major step was taken to address the perceived weaknesses of the community-based process for the detection, presentment and trial of serious cases. Two statutes, of fundamental structural importance, remodelled common law preliminary proceedings and further elevated the justice as the central figure in the management of pre-trial criminal procedures geared to eliciting and to utilizing confessions. Drawing on the examination procedures of their statutory forebears, these enactments of 1554[55] and 1555[56] effectively rationalised and formalised preliminary procedures behind an underlying rationale that accorded primacy to the values of crime control. They represent the culmination of a trend which progressively interposed an official prosecutorial dimension into a system that retained its formal reliance upon the due process requisites of presentment, indictment and trial by jury in cases of serious crime.

The 1554 'bail statute' was enacted to regulate the bailment powers of justices in respect of suspected felons. To combat the problem of improper or collusive bailing of suspects, in which single justices would sign each others bailments, the statute prescribed that at least two justices — one of whom was to be of the *quorum* and therefore "skilled in the law" — act simultaneously in the granting of bail.[57] It also required the justices to make a written record of the evidence against the accused. This account was to be scrutinised by the trial court to thereby bring the propriety of the bailment practices of justices under judicial supervision.[58] The judges were empowered by the statute to fine those justices who had breached its provisions.[59] This gave the Crown effective control over the duties of its justices.[60]

Langbein (1974) argues that the documentary account of examination was intended only to provide the supervising judges with a means of evaluating the propriety of bailments and not to supply the prosecution with information upon which to structure its case.[61] The apparent absence of similar procedures applicable to suspects denied bail would seem to support this view. However, should a conditionally released suspect honour his obligation to appear for trial, the documentation relating to his examination would, presumably, have been available to the court as a source of evidence against the accused.

Holdsworth (1945) confirms that the provisions of the 1554 Act "applied only when the prisoner was bailed",[62] suggesting that the chief object was to rationalise bailment procedures. However, he goes on to argue that it was soon recognised "that some preliminary examination was quite useful when the prisoner was committed on a charge of manslaughter or felony as when he was bailed".[63] The 1555 'committal statute', therefore, extended the procedures of the 'bail statute' to incorporate cases in which bail had been denied to those suspected of felony and prescribed:

> ... from henceforth such Justices or Justice before whom any person shall be brought for Manslaughter or Felony, or for suspicion thereof, before he or they shall commit or send such Prisoner to Ward, shall take the examination of such Prisoner, and information of those that bring him, of the fact and circumstance thereof, and the same or as much thereof as shall be material to prove the Felony shall [be] put in writing, within two days after the said examination, and the same shall certify in such manner and form and at such time as they should and ought to do if such Prisoner so committed or sent to Ward had been bailed or let to Mainprise, upon such pain as in the [1554] Act....

The Act not only required examining justices to provide a written account of their interrogation of those suspected or accused and their accusers for the trial court, they were also authorized to "bind all such by Recognizance or Obligation, as do declare anything material to prove the said Manslaughter or Felony, against such prisoner as shall be so committed to ward, to appear at the next general Gaol Delivery ... to give evidence against the party". The taking of recognizances also had to be certified in the manner of the bail statute to ensure that the binding over of witnesses was similarly subject to judicial supervision.

By its measures, the 'committal statute' formerly instructed justices of the peace to manage the collection of evidence *against* the accused and hence *for* the prosecution. Fashioned to secure and exploit confessions, this statute established a regime in which:

> All suspects were to go on to trial, and the magistrates' task was to ensure that they got there and that the strongest evidence of their guilt would be contained

in the depositions and examination that they were required to send in to the court.[64]

While the criminal process retained some reliance on the initiative of the private victim-prosecutors, the 'committal statute', in placing justices at the centre of pre-trial structures, represents a "decisive step in the crystallisation of the public prosecutorial function for cases of serious crime".[65] Its provisions charged justices to "assemble a prosecuting brief that would stiffen and supplement the case presented orally by the victim-prosecutor in court".[66] However, in the absence of surviving aggrieved or interested citizens who could be compelled to prosecute, or in circumstances where their evidence was considered insufficient to secure a conviction, the statute worked to allow material preserved in the examination document to have a forensic role.

Although oral evidence was preferred, the absence of evidential rules excluding hearsay evidence from trial juries meant that deficiencies in the case for the prosecution might be made good by pre-trial examinations conducted and recorded by justices.[67] The records of such examinations functioned "like the notes a modern policeman uses to refresh his memory".[68] The justices, therefore, served the Crown as "back up prosecutors" at the trial of those accused of felony.[69]

The 'committal statute', in formalising the questioning of suspected and accused persons and in conferring a prosecuting brief upon justices, may be properly regarded as laying the foundations of the public prosecutor at common law.[70]

The examinations prescribed by the statute may not have been intended to have direct evidentiary use since the 'committal statute' expressly allowed justices to delay, for up to two days, their transcription of statements made by the accused, accusers and witnesses. It seems that initially the written examination was not adduced in evidence but used as an *aide-memoire* by the justice.[71] By dint of subsequent practice, however, the written examination came to acquire direct evidentiary force, facilitating the admission of confessions in evidence elicited from suspected and accused persons under their examination before the justices.[72]

It was not until the early eighteenth century that the status of such extra-judicial confessions began to receive judicial rather than statutory re-evaluation. This was a consequence of the seventeenth century judicial acceptance of the 'right' of defendants to remain silent at their trial. Thus, long after the 'right to silence' had emerged at the trial phase of the criminal process, attention began to focus on the pre-trial phase. It was here that individuals could be isolated and subjected to coercive, extra-judicial questioning; it was here where the privilege against compulsory self-incrimination had yet to intrude.[73]

The historical evidence, then, indicates that while the use of torture was to be repudiated,[74] the organisation and consolidation of Tudor and early Stuart social and crime control values meant that:

> A complete national system from the humblest office of the parish to the Star Chamber and Privy Council was built up, and in this carefully articulated hierarchy, the justices of the peace were the important connecting link between the Crown and the community.[75]

Under this regime the common law use of confessions elicited under pre-trial examination, served to re-constitute the petit jury which had largely ceased to be self-informing triers of issues. The evidence-gathering role of the justices ensured the regular flow of information to that jury and worked to reinforce its role as trier-of-fact.[76] Thus, the Marian scheme "became the very core of the law of criminal evidence" in the respect that its examination procedures "secreted the law of evidence" as the investigative and accusatory functions of the presenting jury shifted to the justices.[77] Exclusionary rules of evidence were later to develop with the extensive incursion of lawyers into the criminal justice process.[78] The view that it was the Marian legislation which laid the foundations for this incursion would seem, therefore, to run counter to the assumption that the laws of evidence are "the child of the jury".[79]

It is clear that the preliminary examination process systematised and made mandatory by the Marian legislation constitutes "a development of decisive importance in the history of English criminal procedures and the enforcement of the criminal law".[80] Justified as being necessary "to secure the observance of the law and protect the state from its enemies",[81] these procedures continued to govern pre-trial investigations and prosecutions until the middle of the nineteenth century.

The preliminary examination was crucial to the ability of the prosecution to construct its case against the accused. It did not contemplate an impartial preliminary inquiry into the suspicions or allegations relevant to the case.[82] The 'committal statute' is silent in respect of the basis upon which justices were to satisfy themselves of the degree of suspicion necessary to justify the detention and examination of individuals. It follows, therefore, that this was left to the discretion of individual justices, thereby, providing them with considerable latitude within which to conduct their inquiries.[83] Indeed, it was not until 1826 that magistrates were expressly enjoined by statute to discharge prisoners for want of a *prima facie* case.[84]

The preliminary examination "fitted a particular form and conception of [the accused's] trial in which it was believed that the truth would be most clearly revealed if the prisoner was confronted with the evidence only in the courtroom so that the jury could judge the quality of his immediate, unprepared response".[85] Such features can be properly regarded as expressions of the predominant considerations of crime control which worked to produce a criminal justice process that afforded the suspected individual only a nominal ability to oppose the capacity of the Crown to obtain convictions.

While confessions were not a *sine qua non* for convictions, they were, nevertheless, an important objective of pre-trial examinations since they were conducive to the successful prosecution to conviction of suspected offenders. The suspect could be drawn into the examination process merely on the basis of the suspicions justices entertained, that is, in the absence of a due and specific accusation. Once within the process systematised by the Marian statutes, the suspect would be subjected to interrogatories specifically designed "to wring out of him a confession of his guilt, unsworn, or enough damaging testimony to put him on trial for a crime".[86] The coercive pressures the suspect was exposed to and the central role confessions played in the criminal justice process are related by Levy (1968) in the following comment:

> Secret examinations characterized by bullying and incriminatory interrogatories were common practice. Justices of the peace were prosecutors and policemen as well as magistrates. Any admissions which they might extort from a suspect could be introduced against him as evidence at his trial ... an actual confession was as good as his plea of guilt.[87]

The inherent presumption of guilt within the common law criminal process resembled the investigative and prosecutorial practices of the prerogative courts of Star Chamber and High Commission. Indeed, under the common law machinery of criminal justice the suspect "gained no greater advantages ... and in this preliminary inquisition remained virtually gagged and bound until the nineteenth century".[88]

## Conclusion

The interrogation of suspects was a central feature of the procedures of the discredited prerogative courts. It remained a crucial aspect of the common law process of criminal justice. That social and crime control considerations continued to prevail over the interests of individuals brought into that process was adverted to by Stephen (1883), who remarked:

> I do not think any part of the old procedure operated more harshly upon prisoners than the summary and secret way in which justices of the peace, acting frequently the part of detective officers, took their examinations and committed them for trial....[89]

Examination and prosecutorial responsibilities, vested in the single office of the justice by the Marian statutes, had the gradual effect, during the ensuing centuries, of absorbing the functions of the presentment or grand jury. This was a consequence of the "efficient and regular" inquiries justices made, leaving "little for the grand jury to do" since "it was really the justices who decided whether the accused should stand his trial".[90] The grand jury inquiry was rendered superfluous "for it merely duplicated the formal inquiry that was being conducted by the justices".[91] The grand was effectively left to perform a largely ceremonial role until it was formally abolished in the twentieth century.[92]

The disintegration of pre-trial investigations by the populace, as represented by the grand or presenting jury, was accompanied by the gradual transformation of preliminary examinations from an inquisitorial process into a judicial inquiry, with justices acting in an increasingly judicial capacity.[93] By the middle of the nineteenth century this alignment had received statutory recognition.[94]

These developments occurred against a background which saw the formal creation and establishment of professional police forces from 1829, allowing the formerly pre-eminent position of the justice of the peace in the English prosecution process to be reconfigured.[95] This new organ of social and crime control came to acquire competence over investigative and prosecutorial functions previously conducted by the justices within a system that, in form, remained based on the prosecutorial initiative of private citizens.[96] The state, in the 'new' police, thereby added a novel dimension to the officialised and progressively bureaucratised system of criminal justice. This meant that the focal point of the process under which individuals could be arrested, detained and examined in custody, shifted from formal judicialized committal proceedings to informal and for some time unregulated, interrogative practices of the police.[97]

Such practices were largely unaffected by the reforms, dating from the Parliamentary conflicts with the prerogative governments of the Crown, which purported to ameliorate the position of the suspect in relation to the State at both the trial and later committal phases of the prosecution process. These reforms — together with the abolition of the inquisitional oath, the courts of Star Chamber and High Commission, the disuse of torture to coerce confessions — included the state conceding to suspects the right to legal representation, to inspect depositions taken against them and the right to be present when prosecution witnesses were examined.[98] These and other related reforms were, to a great extent, set in motion by the movement that led to the judicial recognition of the privilege against compulsory self-incrimination from the late seventeenth and early eighteenth centuries.[99]

The principle that individuals should not be compelled to incriminate themselves at trial began to impact upon pre-trial procedures during the eighteenth and early nineteenth centuries. As a result, it was established that when tendered for admission at trial, extra-judicial confessions should, as a precondition to admission, be shown to have been freely and voluntarily made.[100] The nascent rules governing the admissibility of criminal evidence, therefore, began to address concerns not only for the circumstances in which incriminatory admissions and confessions were obtained but also for the status and reliability of confession evidence. Coerced confessions as evidence capable of validating conviction were to be re-legitimated behind the emerging judge-made and somewhat protean 'voluntariness rule'.

**Notes**

[1] Baker, 1977, p. 15; Harding, 1966, pp. 26-7.
[2] 4 Holdsworth, 1945, p. 528; Devlin, 1960, pp. 3-11; Baker, 1977, pp. 16-17.
[3] 1 Stephen, 1883, p. 233; see also Devlin, 1960, pp. 3-5.
[4] Beard, 1904, pp. 55-8; 4 Holdsworth, 1945, p. 528; Levy, 1968, p. 35; Walker, 1976, p. 15.
[5] Beard, 1904, pp. 17-28; Kiralfy, 1962, p. 227; Bellamy, 1973, pp. 94-5; Walker, 1976, p. 15.
[6] 1 Edw. 3, c. 16 (1237). See Beard, 1904, pp. 35-44.
[7] 1 Stephen, 1883, p. 112; Beard, 1904, pp. 28-32; Moir, 1969, p. 16; Powell, 1989, p. 15.
[8] 13 Edw. 1, c. 6 (1285)

56  *Interrogation and Confession*

[9] Beard, 1904, pp. 42-4; Harding, 1966, p. 71; Moir, 1969, pp. 17-9; Powell, 1989, pp. 15-20.
[10] Allen, 1953, pp. 132, 136; see also Beard, 1904, pp. 49, 59-60; Harding, 1966, pp. 71-2; Moir, 1969, p. 18; Skyrine, 1979, p. 2.
[11] Lee, 1901, pp. 44-6; Beard, 1904, pp. 47, 55-7; Moir, 1969, p. 19; Bellamy, 1973, pp. 89-98; Walker, 1976, p. 10.
[12] 34 Edw. 3, c. 1 (1360-61). See Beard, 1904, pp. 38-42; Kiralfy, 1962, p. 228; Harding, 1966, p. 71; Langbein, 1974, p. 5.
[13] Moir, 1969, p. 19; Langbein, 1974, p. 66.
[14] Beard, 1904, p. 40.
[15] *Ibid.*, p. 19; see also 4 Holdsworth, pp. 529-30.
[16] Beard, 1904, pp. 32-5, 58-64; Allen, 1953, p. 136; Walker, 1976, p. 11; Bellamy, 1984, pp. 8-9.
[17] 23 Edw. 3, cc. 1-7 (1351)
[18] Bellamy, 1984, p. 9.
[19] *Ibid.*
[20] Bellamy, 1984, p. 9; see also Beard, 1904, pp. 101-2.
[21] Bellamy, 1984, p. 9.
[22] 7 Rich. 2, c. 5 (1383).
[23] See Langbein, 1974, p. 68; Bellamy, 1984, p. 10.
[24] Bellamy, 1984, p. 10.
[25] Harding, 1966, pp. 77-8; Bellamy, 1984, pp. 10-11.
[26] 2 Hen. 5, c.4 (1414).
[27] Langbein, 1974, p. 68. On the complaints made regarding the corruption of presenting jurors see Bellamy, 1984, pp. 101-2. The statute of 1414 appears to be the first and only such statute to require justices to compel suspects to answer interrogatories under oath, see Langbein, *ibid.*
[28] See Langbein, 1974, p. 68; Bellamy, 1984, p. 12.
[29] Jardine, 1837, p. 6; Morgan, 1949, p. 9; Baker, 1986, p. 267.
[30] Bellamy, 1984, pp. 9, 11-12.
[31] Bellamy, 1984, p. 9; see also Beard, 1904, pp. 101-2.
[32] Langbein, 1974, pp. 118-125.
[33] 2 Hen. 6, c. 18; see Bellamy, 1984, pp. 12-13.
[34] Beard, 1904, pp. 58-71; Langbein, 1974, pp. 68-9; Bellamy, 1984, pp. 13-15.
[35] 8 Hen. 6, c. 4 (1429); see Langbein, 1974, pp. 68-9; Bellamy, 1984, pp. 14-15.
[36] Langbein, 1974, pp. 69-75; Bellamy, 1984, p. 15.
[37] Bellamy, 1984, pp. 15-19.
[38] *Ibid.*, pp. 19-22.
[39] Beard, 1904, p. 117.
[40] Beard, 1904, pp. 114-17; Morgan, 1947, p. 6; Langbein, 1974, pp. 71, 73-4, 80; Bellamy, 1984, pp. 30-1.
[41] Veall, 1970, pp. 1-10. See also Harding, 1966, p. 72.
[42] Beard, 1904, p. 72; see also pp. 85-93, 98-100; Bellamy, 1973, p. 102.

[43] Beard, 1904, p. 74.
[44] Beard, 1904, p. 73. See also 4 Holdsworth, 1945, pp. 529-30; Harding, 1966, pp. 86-7.
[45] Beard, 1904, p. 118; see also Harding, 1966, p. 144.
[46] Beard, 1904, pp. 70-71; see also Harding, 1966, pp. 72-3.
[47] Harding, 1966, pp. 244, 269; see also Beard, 1904, pp. 59, 61-4; Kauper, 1932, p. 1233.
[48] 4 Holdsworth, 1945, p. 173; Langbein, 1973, p. 319; 1974, pp. 63-6.
[49] Langbein, 1974, p. 7.
[50] Bellamy, 1973, pp. 158-61; 1984, p. 5.
[51] Beard, 1904, p. 101.
[52] 11 Hen. 6, c. 3 (1495).
[53] Thayer, 1898, pp. 90-136; Beard, 1904, p. 19; 4 Holdsworth, 1945, pp. 529-30; Devlin, 1956, pp. 4-10; Levy, 1968, p. 35; Langbein, 1973, pp. 314-15; 1974, pp. 118-25.
[54] Langbein, 1974, p. 75.
[55] 1 & 2 Phil. and Mar. c.13 (1554).
[56] 2 & 3 Phil. and Mar. c.10 (1555).
[57] See the judgment of Grose, J in *Lambe* (1791) 2 Leach. 552, pp. 555-57. See also 1 Stephen, 1883, pp. 219, 236-38.
[58] Langbein, 1973, p. 320; 1974, pp. 8-10.
[59] 4 Holdsworth, 1945, pp. 527-28.
[60] Beard, 1904, p. 77. The Act appears to have been a second attempt to exercise stricter control over the bailment practices of the justices. The first, 3 Hen. 7, c. 3 (1487), seems to have proved ineffectual. See 4 Holdsworth, 1945, p. 527.
[61] Langbein, 1974, p. 11.
[62] 4 Holdsworth, 1945, p. 529.
[63] *Ibid.*
[64] Beattie, 1986, p. 271. See also Langbein, 1973, pp. 322-3; Glazebrook, 1977, p. 584.
[65] Langbein, 1974, p. 34. See Stephen, who erroneously claimed that the statutes gave 'legal sanction to a practice which had grown up without statutory authority' (1 Stephen, 1883, p. 219).
[66] Beattie, 1986, p. 271.
[67] 1 Chitty, 1816, pp. 585-9; 1Stephen, 1883, pp. 399-401; 9 Holdsworth, 1944, p. 229; Glazebrook, 1977, p. 584; Beattie, 1986, p. 271.
[68] Langbein, 1974, p. 35.
[69] 1 Stephen, 1883, pp. 222-3. By its express terms the 'committal statute' applied only to persons suspected or accused of 'manslaughter or felony'. However, justices soon began to extend its operation to cover both minor and serious offences. See Glazebrook, 1977, p. 585.
[70] See Langbein, 1973, pp. 313-14; 1974, pp. 23-4; Bellamy, 1984, pp. 40-1. Langbein contends that justices acted as public prosecutors in cases of serious

crime and that this development occurred as jurors lost their self-informing character. The Marian solution was to place a high degree of responsibility for the investigation and prosecution of crime in the office of justice of the peace (Langbein, 1973, pp. 313-35; 1974, pp. 23-4, 34-54). Although Hay and Snyder (1989, pp. 3-52) take issue with Langbein's thesis, they accept that justices regularly assisted private prosecutors in bringing individuals before the courts (*ibid.*, p. 18). Stephen goes further, he argues that 'the justice who had got up the case was the principal witness against the prisoner, and detailed at length the steps he had taken to apprehend him' (1 Stephen, 1883, pp. 222-23). See also Glazebrook, 1977, p. 584 and Beattie, 1986, p. 271.

[71] Langbein, 1974, p. 24; Beattie, 1986, p. 270.

[72] Langbein, 1974, pp. 27-9, 39-54, 118-25. Once apprehended suspects were invariably remanded in custody until trial. Bail was seldom granted (Hale, 1678, p. 98; 1 Stephen, 1883, p. 225; Veall, 1970, p. 17; Langbein, 1974, p. 7; Beattie, 1986, pp. 271, 282). In detention, the suspect would be closely examined by the justices (1 Chitty, 1816, p. 72; 1 Stephen, 1883, p. 221; 1 Holdsworth, 1856, p. 296; 9 Holdsworth, 1844, pp. 224, 232-3; Beattie, 1986, p. 271). There was no conception of the suspect being considered innocent until proved guilty (Glazebrook, 1977, p. 587). And there appears to have been no limit to the length of time in which the suspect could be detained and interrogated. Chitty notes 'many instances of prisoners being detained much more than twenty days, between their being first brought before a justice, and their commitment for trial, and being brought up for examination several different days during the interval' (1 Chitty, 1816, p. 73).

[73] Beattie, 1986, p. 271. See also 1 Stephen, 1883, pp. 336-7; Wigmore, 1902, p. 635; Morgan, 1949, p. 12; 3 Wigmore, 1970, p. 514; Levy, 1968, pp. 263, 322-25. The inquisitorial features of the 'committal statute' are reminiscent of the inquisitorial procedures of the prerogative courts. It is not clear whether or to what extent the statute borrowed its inquisitorial aspects from those extra-common law courts (Kauper, 1932, p. 1232). However, the thirty or so statutes which predate the Marian legislation and which authorize justices to proceed by examination, indicate a degree of evolution that was indigenous to the common law. Indeed, virtually every feature of the committal statute can be located in the pre-Marian legislation (Langbein, 1974, pp. 65-77; Bellamy, 1984, pp. 8-53). A point that appears to have been overlooked by Stephen, who concluded that: 'Whatever may have been the reason, the fact is certain that no allusion is made to the holding of any sort of preliminary inquiry by justices before the statutes of Philip and Mary...' (1 Stephen, 1883, p. 219.)

[74] Jardine, 1837, pp. 6-10; Veall, 1970, p. 25. See also *Felton's Case* (1628) 3 Cobb. St. Tr. 368.

[75] Beard, 1904, p. 85. See also 4 Holdsworth, 1945, p. 137; Devlin, 1960, p. 4.

[76] Langbein, 1974, pp. 118-25.

[77] Langbein, 1974, p. 119. See also Maitland, 1885, p. 133; Kauper, 1932, p. 1233.
[78] Langbein, 1978, p. 306.
[79] Thayer, 1898, p. 47.
[80] Glazebrook, 1977, p. 582.
[81] 4 Holdsworth, 1945, p. 529.
[82] 4 Holdsworth, 1945, p. 529; 1 Holdsworth, 1956, pp. 295-6; Veall, 1970, p. 17; Beattie, 1986, p. 271.
[83] The prisoner was prohibited from consulting a lawyer prior to his trial and denied legal representation at his trial. The check against legal representation was relaxed only when it was deemed a point of law arose. The prohibition was legitimated under the contention that proof of guilt would be so manifest that no lawyer could argue against it. It was also felt that legal representation was unnecessary as the trial judge would act as counsel for the prisoner to safeguard his interests (Levy, 1968, p. 322; Veall, 1970, p. 18; Baker, 1977, pp. 36-8). Prisoners had no notice before trial of the evidence collated against them (1 Stephen, 1883, p. 398). Evidence from prosecution witnesses was recorded in private and in the absence of the accused. He, therefore, was not given an opportunity to challenge witnesses before trial. He was also denied a copy of the depositions. Indeed, he was not allowed even to see them (1 Stephen, 1883, p. 221. See also 1 Chitty, 1816, p. 83; Devlin, 1960, pp. 5-6). The accused was also denied a copy of the indictment since, it was felt, a copy would enable him to take advantage of any technical errors in the case for the prosecution (3 Holdsworth, 1944, p. 615; Veall, 1970, p. 17; see also Emlyn, 1730, p. xxxi; Beattie, 1986, pp. 271-77). That case could be proved on the basis of the depositions taken from the accused and his accusers, though passages of those depositions which were favourable to the accused were frequently suppressed (Veall, 1970, p. 19).
[84] 7 Geo. 4, c. 64 (1826). And see 1 Chitty, 1816, p. 89; Devlin, 1960, p. 6; Glazebrook, 1977, pp. 585-6; Beattie, 1986, pp. 274-9.
[85] Beattie, 1986, p. 271.
[86] Levy, 1968, p. 325.
[87] *Ibid.*
[88] Allen, A. K., 1953, p. 149.
[89] 1 Stephen, 1883, p. 225.
[90] Devlin, 1960, p. 5. See also Maitland, 1885, p. 132.
[91] Devlin, 1960, p. 7. See also Baker, 1977, p. 20.
[92] See both the Administration of Justice (Miscellaneous Provisions) Act, 1933, and the Criminal Justice Act, 1948, which finally abolished the grand jury.
[93] 1 Stephen, 1883, p. 221; Kauper, 1932, pp. 1234-5; 1 Holdsworth, 1956, p. 297; Devlin, 1960, pp. 7-9; Baker, 1977, pp. 16-17.
[94] 11 & 12 Vict. c.42 (1848).

## 60  Interrogation and Confession

[95] Lord Devlin suggests that the judicialization of justices 'would not have been possible' without the creation of another organ of criminal inquiry: the police. (Devlin, 1960, p. 7.) See also Plucknett, 1956, p. 432.

[96] Hay, 1983, pp. 167-86; Hay and Snyder, 1989, pp. 26-27; Cornish and Clark, 1989, p. 554.

[97] Baker, 1977, pp. 16-17.

[98] 1 Holdsworth, 1956, p. 297.

[99] 1 Stephen, 1883, pp. 749-52; Wigmore, 1902, pp. 627-36; Mirfield, 1985, pp. 43-7.

[100] 1 Chitty, 1836, p. 83; Kauper, 1932, pp. 1233-4.

# PART II
# ENTER THE POLICE

## PART II
## ENTER THE POLICE

# 4 Legitimating Confessions Through 'Voluntariness'

**Introduction**

The statutory measures which authorised the pre-trial interrogation of suspects by justices survived both the collapse of prerogative government in the seventeenth century and the erosion of "unduly harsh" inquisitorial forms of investigation and trial associated with the prerogative courts.[1] Thus, while "humaner methods" of common law trial were to prevail,[2] the inquisitorial character of common law pre-trial investigations was left, to a substantial extent, intact.

Magistrates retained extensive powers with which to prepare the case against the accused right up to the mid-nineteenth century when their power to interrogate was severely restricted by statute. By this time, however, the 'new' professionalised police had — without statutory licence — assimilated that power.[3]

The case law surrounding the period when the 'new' police began to supersede the justices in the crucial pre-trial phase of criminal investigations yields important information regarding judicial attitudes to the reception in evidence of incriminatory admissions made to law enforcement officials. The case law also brings into sharp relief, concerns over the adequacy of legal principles protecting accused persons from being compelled to answer questions inviting incriminatory replies; the acceptable limits of pre-trial questioning; and, finally, the propriety of police interrogations.

During the period which saw the development of the pre-trial expression of the privilege against compulsory self-incrimination in the form of the evidential requirement for statements to be given freely and voluntarily, such questions would be addressed in ways which would ensure the continued centrality of the confession as sufficient evidence of guilt. Indeed, while the 'voluntariness requirement' worked to exclude extra-judicial admissions extorted from suspects by persons in authority through the use of 'improper' inducements, conflicting judicial decisions respecting the requirement would effectively serve to legitimate the power state officials exercised over suspects in the pre-trial process to obtain confession evidence.

## The Privilege Against Self-Incrimination and the Evidential Requirement of Voluntariness

As part of the struggle to entrench common law procedures, judges began, from the middle of the seventeenth century, to permit witnesses for the accused to give unsworn evidence at trial.[4] This practice was subject to the discretion of individual judges. Even when granted, the unsworn testimony of witnesses for the defendant was of limited value. This was a consequence of the pre-seventeenth century prohibition against witnesses for the accused giving evidence, on their oaths, against the cause of the Crown.[5] "The disadvantage to the accused", Levy (1968) explains, "was evident from the fact that unsworn testimony did not carry the same weight as testimony given under oath, a fact that judges as well as prosecutors pointed out to juries".[6] Before the end of the seventeenth century, however, judges began to admit both witnesses and counsel for defendants.[7]

The 1696 Treason Act[8] brought consistency to what hitherto had been a matter of judicial discretion. The Act permitted defendants to subpoena witnesses to appear to give their evidence on oath.[9] The Act also provided for persons accused of treason to be presented with a copy of the indictment at least five days before trial. It thereby unseated a pre-existing practice which appears to have been a rigidly enforced principle of law.[10] The accused, under the same Act, also became entitled to make his "full defence by counsel learned in the law". Legal representation in criminal matters had been strongly resisted. It was seen as running counter to the legal theory that held that it was for the court, in matters of law as distinct from matters of fact, to act as counsel for the defendant.[11] However, as the prohibition against counsel was being relaxed — for those defendants who could afford their services — in minor cases,[12] the legal theory opposing legal representation became difficult to sustain.[13] Thus, by the end of the seventeenth century:

> A practice had sprung up ... by which counsel were allowed to do everything for prisoners accused of felony except addressing the jury for them....[14]

This practice did not receive statutory force until 1836[15] and it seems that suspects detained in custody for pre-trial examination were not entitled, as of right, to engage a person skilled in law at any stage of the preliminary investigation.[16] Thus, in the period following the acute political and constitutional turmoils of the seventeenth century, the introduction of "humaner methods" at common law trials[17] appear to have had little immediate impact on the inquisitorial procedures that obtained at the pre-trial phase of the criminal process.[18] Indeed, the pre-trial process was affected, and then only indirectly, some time after the privilege against compulsory self-incrimination had received judicial recognition.

The principle that a defendant ought not to be compelled to answer questions that tended to incriminate him had been widely acknowledged by the courts from the middle of the seventeenth century. However, the piecemeal development of the privilege was noted by Wigmore (1961) who found that the judicial "habit of questioning and urging the accused died hard — did not disappear, indeed, until the 1700s had begun".[19] Levy (1968) points out that the principle of disqualification for interest, coupled with the privilege, contributed to the final demise of the practice of judges interrogating accused persons at their trial.[20] This principle, which originated in civil cases, was based on the assumption that an individual who had a personal and direct interest in the verdict of the court was "so irresistibly tempted to perjury that his testimony was regarded as untrustworthy".[21] By the early eighteenth century, the privilege against self-incrimination, which protected the accused from judicial questions which would require him to condemn himself out of his own mouth, had combined with the principle of disqualification for interest to ensure that the accused was in effect excluded from his own trial.

Thus, procedural reforms conceded by judges and later endorsed by statute, eventually made it possible for defendants to present their defence through counsel and witnesses. The defendant retained the right to make an unsworn statement to the court in answer to the charge but the development of the privilege, while protecting him from exposure to pressing interrogatories, also rendered him incompetent to testify an oath at his own trial.[22]

The desuetude of official torture had, also by the early eighteenth century, become a source of common law pride as demonstrated by the comment that:

> In other countries, Racks and instruments of torture are applied to force from the prisoner a confession, sometimes of more than is true; but this is a practice which Englishmen are happily unacquainted with, enjoying the benefit of that just and reasonable maxim, "Nemo teneture accusarer seipsum".[23]

The establishment of the privilege against self-incrimination was, therefore, closely linked both conceptually and historically with the repudiation of torture. Indeed, the emergence and acceptance of the freedom from the compulsion of questions designed to incriminate the accused coexisted with and contributed to the demise of official torture. As Moreland (1956) points out, the absence of the privilege conduces its inevitable concomitant, namely, torture.[24] To put it in the words of Levy (1968): "Where there is a right against self-incrimination, there is necessarily a right against torture".[25]

The threat of torture, however, continued for some time to be employed to exert a coercive influence over suspects to compel information, admissions and confessions. For example, in *Tonge's Case* (1662)[26] the defendant, indicted for high treason, was apprised by the court of the evidence against him which included his own confession. To this the defendant replied: "I confess I did confess it in the tower, being threatened with the rack".[27] The allegation made by the defendant was not investigated by the court which, in admitting the confession, concluded that a confession made "before him that hath power to take an examination" is admissible in evidence providing it be "voluntarily made without torture".[28]

This case permits the conclusion that while the court sought reliable evidence, if such evidence was to have that quality it ought to be voluntarily given. However, it seems that rather than establish a rule capable of excluding confession evidence of doubtful reliability, the judges intended to guide the practices of those authorised to conduct extra-judicial examinations. Nevertheless, the ruling of the court in *Tonge* suggests a movement towards the formulation of an exclusionary rule — with reliability through voluntariness as its primary rationale — well before the end of the seventeenth century.[29]

Before the turn of the century, considered legal opinion had begun to conflate the *nemo tenetur seipsum accusare* maxim (that no one should be compelled to incriminate themselves) both with the illegitimacy of torture and with the requirement that confessions be free from any form of coercion if they were to be considered reliable. For instance, Gilbert, LCB, in his work published posthumously in 1754, commented that although a confession under the common law is to be regarded as the best evidence of guilt:

> this confession must be voluntary and without Compulsion; for our Law in this ... will not force any Man to accuse himself; and in this we do certainly follow that Law of Nature, which commands every Man to endeavour his own Preservation; and therefore Pain and Force may compel men to Confess what is not the truth of facts, and consequently such extorted Confessions are not to be depended on.[30]

That the voluntariness principle and the privilege against compulsory self-incrimination had become inextricably linked is illustrated by the observation that "the general maxim that confessions ought to be voluntary is historically the old rule that torture for the purpose of obtaining confessions is, and long has been, illegal in England".[31] For Wigmore (1970), however, the law against the reception in evidence of involuntary confessions and the privilege against self-incrimination have been erroneously confused both in history and in practice. He contends that "the history of the two principles is wide apart, differing by one hundred years in origin, and derived through separate lines of precedents".[32]

Nevertheless, while the historical evidence supports the view that the privilege was "fully established by 1680"[33], it does not of necessity follow that the development of the exclusionary rule by the end of the eighteenth century was entirely independent of privilege. There is, in short, at least one respect in which the two principles have been conceptually connected, namely, in the protection they purport to afford the accused from being compelled to acknowledge his own guilt. Essentially, therefore, 'voluntariness' is a requirement common to both principles.[34]

## An Exclusionary Rule of Law

The earliest indication that the voluntariness principle had become one capable of acting as a precondition to the admissibility of extra-judicial confessions is found in *White's Case* (1741).[35] White had been charged with murdering a "gentleman of distinction". The prosecution sought to prove his guilt with a confession White had made before the examining justice. White's counsel asked the court to inquire whether the confession was voluntarily made "[f]or if it was not ... it ought not to be read". The Recorder considered this to be "an improper question" since the prisoner had not "made it a part of his case, that his confession was extorted by threats, or drawn from him by promises". Had he done so "it would have been proper for us to enquire by what means the confession was procured: but as the prisoner alleges nothing of that kind, I will not suffer a question to be asked ... which carries in it a reflection on the magistrate before whom the Examination was taken...."[36] The confession was received in evidence. White was convicted and sentenced to death. Nevertheless, the Recorder's comments suggest that the voluntariness principle had, by this date, formed a basis upon which to exclude evidence deemed to have been extracted under the compulsion of threats or promises. However, it would seem that the principle had yet to become a firm rule of law.

Wigmore (1970), in his survey of the early development of the exclusionary rule, found no indication of its existence in the "treatise of Hale and Butler [published in the 1680s] where the doctrine would naturally be mentioned".[37] Mirfield (1985), placing his review of the early development of the doctrine more closely to the decision in *White*, found it "surprising that both Bacon and Nelson writing in the mid-1730s, offer no hint of any such exclusionary principle".[38] The Recorder in *White*, therefore, may be taken to have stated what was then a judicially approved principle that had yet to acquire full exclusionary force. *Rudd's Case*,[39] however, indicates that by 1775 the principle may have been employed on a regular basis to exclude coerced confessions from criminal proceedings. As the presiding judge, Mansfield LCJ, observed:

> The instance has frequently happened, of persons having made confessions under threats or promises: the consequence as frequently has been, that such examinations and confessions have not been made use of against them on their trial.[40]

This *dictum* is ambiguous as it may refer to the practice of trial judges or, indeed, that of examining justices who, as prosecutors, may have been reluctant to employ coerced confessions when the courts were becoming increasingly hostile to their use as evidence of guilt.[41]

In *Warickshall* (1783),[42] decided eight years after *Rudd*, it became clear that the voluntariness principle had finally become a firm exclusionary rule of law. Jane Warickshall was charged with and confessed to having received stolen goods. As a result of this confession the goods were found concealed in her bed. At her trial the confession was ruled inadmissible "having been obtained by promises of favour". Her counsel argued that "as the fact of finding the stolen property had been obtained through means of an inadmissible confession, the proof of the fact ought also be rejected". The judges rejected this contention arguing that:

> it is a mistaken notion, that the evidence of confessions and facts which have been obtained from prisoners by promises or threats, is to be rejected from a regard to public faith: no such rule ever prevailed ... confessions are received in evidence, or rejected as inadmissible, under a consideration whether they are or are not entitled to credit. A free and voluntary confession is deserving of the highest credit, because it is presumed to flow from the strongest sense of guilt.[43]

The court ruled that "although confessions improperly obtained cannot be received in evidence," this principle had "no application whatever as to the admission or rejection of facts" obtained in consequence of such confessions.[44] However, the court also confirmed that:

> a confession forced from the mind by the flattery of hope, or by the torture of fear, comes in so questionable a shape when it is to be considered as evidence of guilt, that no credit ought to be given to it; and therefore it is rejected.[45]

The exclusionary rule, as expounded in *Warickshall* (1783), *Thompson* (1783)[46] and in *Cass* (1784),[47] appears to have been limited in application to coerced confessions rendered unreliable by threats or promises. The cases make no explicit reference to whether incriminatory replies made to extra-judicial questions might be treated as *per se* involuntary admissions and thus be subject to the exclusionary rule. These cases were, apparently, more concerned to decide whether there had been *any* threats or promises which would impair the voluntariness of statements made in the extra-judicial context and adduced in evidence against their author.[48]

Wigmore (1970) argues that from the formation of the exclusionary rule in the latter part of the eighteenth century, the subsequent "history of the doctrine is merely a matter of the narrowness or broadness of the exclusionary rule".[49] He suggests that from the outset confessions were declared inadmissible in evidence only when promises or threats worked to raise questions concerning the reliability of the ensuing confession.[50] He also suggests that from its inception, the exclusionary rule was so narrow in scope that "[i]t was for a long time the clear unquestioned law in England that the mere circumstances of arrest, *even when combined with the circumstance that the confession was made in answer to questions put by the custodian*, did not exclude the confession",[51] since "there was no general sentiment against them — no 'prima facie' doubt of their propriety".[52]

Wigmore relies on the case of *Lambe* (1791)[53] to demonstrate his point. The accused in this case was indicted for breaking and entering a house where he "feloniously and burglariously" removed certain goods. When apprehended he was taken before a magistrate for examination in accordance with the Marian statutes.[54] The examination contained the "full and voluntary confession" of the prisoner who declined to endorse it with his signature. The magistrate also neglected to sign the examination. Counsel for the prisoner argued that the governing statute required the examination to be authenticated by the signatures of the prisoner and examining magistrate and that if these ceremonies were omitted the confession could not be received against the prisoner.[55] Wilson, J admitted the examination. The prisoner was found guilty. The case was, however, respited for the opinion of the Judges. The Judges, led by Grose, J ruled that the examination was "well received in evidence".

Wigmore draws attention to that part of the judgment which states that:

> Confessions of guilt made by a prisoner to any person at any moment of time, and at any place, subsequent to the perpetration of the crime and previous to his examination before the magistrate, are at common law admissible in evidence as the highest and most satisfactory proof of guilt, because it is fairly presumed that no man would make such a confession against himself if the facts confessed were not true.[56]

This statement would seem to lend support to the thesis advanced by Wigmore. However, the ruling also makes clear that only a:

free and voluntary confession made by a person accused of an offence is receivable in evidence against him, whether such confession be made at the moment he is apprehended, or while those who have him in custody are conducting him to the magistrates, or even after he has entered the house of the magistrate for the purpose of undergoing his examination.[57]

The decision does not, therefore, support the contention that the presumption in favour of 'voluntariness' was vitiated *only* when the courts found promises or threats had operated to induce the accused to confess. The ruling makes no mention of the scope of the voluntariness test as it might relate to the reliability of confessions resulting from extra-judicial questions put to suspects by individuals interested in securing convictions.

The requirement of voluntariness, as articulated in cases decided before the end of the eighteenth century — suggesting that *any* threat or promise could impair the voluntariness of a confession — did not exclude the possibility of extra-judicial questions being viewed as capable of subverting the privilege against compulsory self-incrimination so as to render confessions involuntary and accordingly inadmissible. Thus, in so far as the argument presented by Wigmore constitutes an attempt to identify a clear pre-nineteenth century trend in favour of the reception of confession evidence, irrespective of the extra-judicial context in which that evidence was obtained (providing the confession did not flow from specific threats or promises), the argument has not been satisfactorily made.

This notwithstanding, the view advanced by Wigmore (1970) enabled him to characterise the period beginning from the early nineteenth century through to the decision in *Baldry* (1852),[58] as one giving the "appearance of sentimental irrationality".[59] He claims that from the beginning of this period "the whole attitude of judges changed". They developed "a general suspicion of all confessions, a prejudice against them ... and an inclination to repudiate them upon the slightest pretext".[60] Mirfield (1985) agrees that "during the period from 1800 to 1852, judges seem, for the most part, to have been keen to exclude confessions".[61]

Such comments carry the unstated assumption that judges co-operated or conspired with each other as a unitary body to reject confessions out of some weak and misplaced sentimentalism held towards defendants.[62] Wigmore refers to judicial decisions he considered "almost incredible" to support his proposition. Without citing the source of the authorities in question, he argues that the decisions meant that:

a confession could be excluded because it was made upon a promise to give a glass of gin; because the prosecutor said "if the prisoner would only give him his money, he might go to the devil if he pleased"; because a handbill, offering a few pounds' reward for evidence, was posted in the magistrate's office; because the prisoner was told that "what he said would be used against him".[63]

Wigmore felt that such rulings "disfigured the law of the admissibility of confessions".[64] However, a wider, less selective examination of the case law from the period under consideration reveals a number of inconsistent and contradictory rulings by individual and semi-autonomous judges — rather than a simple lineal predilection on the part of a corporate or collaborative body of judges to exclude confession evidence upon insubstantial grounds.

The case concerning the promise of gin, for instance, was decided in the early part of the nineteenth century.[65] The accused, who was suspected of burglary, had told the constable having charge of him that he was prepared to reveal his part in the offence if given a glass of gin. He was given *two* glasses of gin after which he made a confession. The trial judge refused to receive the confession in evidence since it had been "very improperly obtained by the officer". Best, J added that police officers "must not be permitted to tamper with prisoners to induce them to make confessions".[66] He also suggested that:

> Had the magistrate known that the officer had given the prisoner gin, he would, no doubt, have told the prisoner that what he had already said could not be given in evidence against him; and it was for him to consider whether he would make a second confession.[67]

The judge argued that as the prisoner had not been so cautioned, he might have signed the confession under the impression "that he could not make his case worse than he had already made it". Turning to the conduct of the police officer, Best, J then stated:

> If a confession so obtained were allowed to be proved at the trial of the prisoner, however careful a magistrate might be that a prisoner should not be entrapped into a confession, an over zealous constable might defeat the humane provisions of the law, by so practising on the hopes and fears of the prisoner ... to make him, when before the magistrate, appear to make an uninfluenced and voluntary confession, when every sort of trick had been made use of. I will not on this ground allow this confession to be read ... and I hope that I shall not

find a police officer again employed in preparing, either the depositions of witnesses or the confessions of prisoners.[68]

Best, J was here concerned not only with the voluntariness of the confession being impaired by the inducements of threats or of promises but also — under a wider aspect of the voluntariness requirement than advocated by Wigmore — to regulate the investigative conduct of police officers where it encroached upon the protections the courts afforded suspected persons.[69]

Contrary to the assumption that the first half of the nineteenth century was a period of sentimental excess,[70] throughout the whole of the nineteenth century the 'voluntariness rule' was extended by individual judges to address the treatment of the accused before trial either at the hands of magistrates or, as the century progressed, of the police. Many of the nineteenth century authorities covering the admissibility of confession evidence, therefore, reveal an inter-judicial dialogue which concerned the capacity of the exclusionary rule to govern the conduct of criminal investigations.

Further evidence of this is found in *Wilson* (1817).[71] In this case the prosecution produced the examination of the accused, taken before the committing magistrate, to confirm the testimony of an accomplice. Giving evidence at the trial, the magistrate stated that while he had examined the accused "at a considerable extent" he nonetheless "held out no hopes or inducement to the prisoner, employed no threats" and had not put the prisoner on oath. Richards, LCB, in refusing to permit the examination to be read in evidence, said:

> No matter whether a prisoner be sworn or not. An examination of itself imposes an obligation to speak the truth. If a prisoner will confess, let him do so voluntarily.[72]

Here the judge utilised the voluntariness rule to govern admissibility and implied that the right of the prisoner not to answer judicial interrogatories must be respected and protected at the pre-trial phase of the prosecution process if it is not to be undermined. Although the decision was overruled in 1826,[73] it demonstrates that when the voluntariness requirement was given a wide construction it was not done, as Wigmore (1970) suggests, on pretexts that were "trivial and irrational".[74] Rather the broad interpretation was used as a means to control the extra-judicial investigative process and to ensure that confessions were not obtained under the inherently coercive pressures of interrogatories carried out by those having authority over the liberty of the suspect. This would indicate that some judges were prepared to consider the force of pressures beyond specific threats or promises that may induce an involuntary confession.[75]

There are a number of judicial decisions which appear to contradict the period of "sentimental excess"[76] thesis. One such is *Lloyd* (1834).[77] The accused and his wife were detained in police custody, in separate rooms, charged with receiving stolen property. Lloyd was told by a constable: "if you tell where the property is; you shall see your wife". The evidence of what the prisoner had said in response to this incentive to confess was received in evidence. Another is *Spilsbury* (1835).[78] In this case the prisoner made a statement to the constable who had him in custody. However, the prisoner "was drunk at the time; and it was imputed that the constable had given him liquor to cause him to be so". Coleridge, J, placing a narrow construction upon the evidential requirement that a confession be a free and voluntary expression of guilt, found that the statement the prisoner made was admissible in evidence against him. He stated that "to render a confession inadmissible, it must either be obtained by hope or fear".[79]

These and other such cases[80] suggest that some judges adopted a restrictive interpretation of the exclusionary rule, basing their reception of incriminatory statements on the ground that only the hope of promises or the fear of threats could, but would not invariably, disable the reliability of a confession. These authorities serve to undermine the proposition that the attitude of judges towards confessions was one of a general suspicion that articulated itself in a prejudice against the admission in evidence of all extra-judicial confessions.[81] It is, therefore, misleading to assume that the law governing the admissibility of confessions in the first half of the nineteenth century had become "very rigid and unable to adapt to the circumstances of the individual case"[82] and to suggest that this supposed inflexibility meant that:

> It became settled that any statement to the accused to the effect that he had better confess or that it would be better for him to confess would render his confession inadmissible.[83]

Wigmore (1970) reasons that this "unnatural development" was a product of "absurd and dangerous sentimentalities" which inclined judges — in view of the unfairness of a criminal justice system that had rendered the accused incompetent to testify and denied him the assistance of counsel

— to exclude confessions and disfigure the law.[84] The force of this reasoning is, however, diluted by the observation that a practice of permitting the accused to make his defence through counsel began to emerge almost a century before the Prisoners' Counsel Act of 1836.[85] In respect of the testimonial incompetency of accused persons, the prolonged debate that preceded the 1898 Criminal Evidence Act, suggests that much legal opinion considered the law preventing defendants from giving evidence on oath to be a distinct advantage to the delivery of an effective defence through counsel.[86] Furthermore, the cases in which judges ruled in favour of excluding confessions tended to be based not upon judicial sentimentalities but rather upon legalistic applications of the exclusionary rule. These rulings indicate a close judicial assessment of the probative value of extra-judicial confessions when obtained under conditions that might weaken their authenticity. They also indicate a readiness to exclude confessions that were not shown to be spontaneous, unreserved and voluntary avowals of guilt made willingly by free-acting individuals, unbidden by either physical or mental inducements.

It was the exclusionary rule, rather than any fixed irrational judicial sentiment, that was employed by some judges who, throughout the nineteenth century, seem to have considered that the nature of the prosecution process — whether as a result of the unsupervised practices of prosecuting agents or the pressures inherent in criminal investigations — could of itself actuate involuntary and unreliable confessions from citizens who were to be afforded the right not to be compelled to incriminate themselves. Contrary to the suggestion of a 'period of sentimental irrationally', the nineteenth century authorities betray conflicting judicial views as to the precise meaning and application of the voluntariness test.

## Conclusion

A review of the relevant case law suggests that commentators such as Wigmore, (1970),[87] Kaufman (1985)[88] and Mirfield (1985),[89] misunderstand or misrepresent judicial attitudes of the first half of the nineteenth century towards confessions as founded on sentimental excess. The decisions of the period point to a legalistic implementation of the exclusionary rule grounded on conceptions of the voluntariness principle as understood by individual, relatively autonomous, judges and as ratified by their insistence that suspects be properly cautioned. That caution was to be issued to suspects to inform them that — as in open court, so in pre-trial criminal investigations — they were not obliged to answer questions which invite them to incriminate themselves. Before an extra-judicial confession can be received "it must be seen that the prisoner's mind is free from any false hope or fear".[90] Investigative agents ought not to solicit incriminatory statements from suspects who had not been so cautioned since some judges would not receive the evidence — irrespective of its actual reliability — as being free and voluntary.[91]

The decisions of individual judges, rather than resulting from any supposed sentiment in favour of accused persons,[92] seems to have been an uncoordinated attempt to employ the voluntariness requirement as a check upon the extra-judicial excesses of magistrates and police officers. This approach worked to generate a number of conflicting rulings. Some of these decided in favour of the admission of incriminatory statements in evidence with judges placing a narrow construction on the requirement of voluntariness.[93] In other cases the judges rejected them under an extended interpretation of the voluntariness test.[94] These cases suggest that the voluntariness requirement was not to be circumscribed by narrow conceptions of the effects of specific threats or promises. They also suggest a judicial preparedness to infuse a 'disciplinary principle' into the voluntariness test, to discourage impropriety on the part of investigative and prosecution agents. Law enforcement officers were to understand that extra-judicial confessions must be shown to be entirely voluntary if they were to be accepted as flowing from "the strongest sense of guilt" and, therefore, as "deserving of the highest credit".[95]

The conflicting authorities, therefore, militate against the assumption that judges, in the period between 1800 and 1852, uniformly engaged in a "habit of seizing upon the slightest pretext in order to exclude a confession".[96] Moreover, the relevant authorities do not appear to support the argument that the circumstances attending the arrest and detention of suspects and the possibility that a confession was involuntarily made in answer to incriminatory questions, were not bases upon which judges invoked the exclusionary rule.[97] In short, the authorities indicate that there was not a collective or marked shift in judicial opinion mid-way through the century away from an interpretation of the evidential requirement of voluntariness that was unduly favourable to accused persons. Indeed, the case law discussed in the next chapter suggests that judicial attitudes regarding extra-judicial confessions and the role played by the police in

*Legitimating Confessions Through 'Voluntariness'* 77

their acquisition remained, to a great extent, inconsistent throughout the nineteenth century and the early years of the twentieth century.

## Notes

1. 9 Holdsworth, 1944, pp. 230-1; Levy, 1968, pp. 323-4.
2. 1 Stephen, 1883, p. 385; see also 9 Holdsworth, 1944, pp. 230-1; Levy, 1968, pp. 320-1.
3. Section 18 of the Indictable Offences Act, 1848, required magistrates to inform suspects that they were not obliged to answer questions put to them during preliminary examination. See *Pettit* (1850) 4 Cox C.C. 164, where it was argued that magistrates could not ask the accused any question bearing on the offence charged.
4. 9 Holdsworth, 1944, p. 230.
5. See, for example, *Hullet's Trial* (1660) 5 Cobb. St. Tr. 1185, p. 1192.
6. Levy, 1968, p. 321; see also *Hullet's Trial*, (1660) *ibid.*, pp. 1191-2.
7. Again, this appears to have been an entirely non-statutory initiative. See *Roswell's Case* (1684) 10 Cob. St. Tr. 147, *per* Jeffreys, LCJ, p. 267.
8. 7 Will. 3, c. 3.
9. See Parker, 1984, p. 158; see also 1 Stephen, 1883, p. 416; Thayer, 1898, p. 161. This right was extended to all felony cases under 2 Anne., c. 12 (1701). See also 1 Anne., c. 9 (1702).
10. In *Colledge's Case* (1681) 8 Cobb. St. Tr. 541, p. 570, North, LCJ declared: 'No man can have a copy of the indictment in law'. And in *Rosewell's Case* (1684) 10 Cobb. St. Tr. 147, p. 268, Jeffreys, LCJ remarked that: 'the practice has been always to deny a copy of the indictment. And, therefore, if you ask me as a judge, to have a copy of the indictment ... I must answer you, Shew me any precedents where it was done....'
11. For example in *Twyn's Case* (1663) 6 Cobb. St. Tr. 513, pp. 516-17, Hyde, CJ responded to a request for counsel with the remark: 'I will tell you, we are bound to be counsel with you in point of law; that is, the court, my brethren and myself, are to see that you suffer nothing for your want of knowledge in matter of law ... in this case the law does not allow you counsel to plead for you; but in matter of law we are counsel for you, and it shall be our care to see that you have no wrong done you'. See also *Colledge's Case*, (1681) *ibid.*
12. See *Roswell's Case* (1684) 10 Cob. St. Tr. 147, p. 267.
13. Levy, 1968, p. 322. This notwithstanding, the defendant was normally forced to make his own defence, unassisted by counsel (Levy, *Ibid.*; Beattie, 1986, p. 352; 1 Stephen, 1883, pp. 336-7; 9 Holdsworth, 1944, p. 229).
14. 1 Stephen, 1883, p. 424; see also Langbein, 1978, pp. 307-16; Beattie, 1986, pp. 356-62.
15. Prisoners' Counsel Act, 6, 7 Will. 4, c. 114 (1836).
16. See *Cox v. Coleridge* (1822) 1 Barn. & Cress. 37.

78  *Interrogation and Confession*

[17] See 9 Holdsworth, 1944, pp. 230-35.
[18] See Levy, 1968, p. 325.
[19] 8 Wigmore, 1961, p. 291.
[20] Levy, 1968, p. 324.
[21] *Ibid.*
[22] The accused finally became competent, though non-compellable, to give evidence on oath under the 1898 Criminal Evidence Act.
[23] Emlyn, 1730, p. xxv.
[24] Moreland, 1956, pp. 270, 275.
[25] Levy, 1968, p. 324.
[26] *Tonge's Case* (1662) 6 How. St. Tr. 225.
[27] *Ibid.*, p. 259.
[28] *Ibid.*, p. 228, n. 2. The illegitimacy of involuntary confessions in such cases received statutory recognition under the 1696 Treason Act (7 Will. 3, c. 3) which required indictments for high treason to be based upon the testimony of two lawful witnesses 'unless the party indicted and arraigned or tried shall willingly without violence in open court confess ....'
[29] See Mirfield, 1985, pp. 45-6.
[30] Gilbert, 1754, quoted in Levy, 1968, p. 327. Gilbert died in 1726. The second edition of his work, *The Law of Evidence*, appeared in 1760 where the view above was repeated (at p. 140).
[31] 1 Stephen, 1883, p. 441.
[32] 8 Wigmore, 1970, p. 401.
[33] *Ibid.*
[34] See Levy, 1968, pp. 495-7.
[35] *White's Case* (1741) 17 How. St. Tr. 1079.
[36] *Ibid.*, p. 1085.
[37] 8 Wigmore, 1970, pp. 295-6.
[38] Mirfield, 1985, pp. 42-3.
[39] *Rudd* (1775) 1 Leach. 115.
[40] *Ibid.*, p. 118.
[41] See 8 Wigmore, 1970, p. 297; Mirfield, 1985, p. 47.
[42] *Warickshall* (1783) 1 Leach. 263.
[43] *Ibid.*
[44] *Ibid.*, p. 264.
[45] *Ibid.* As the report of the case does not reveal the character of the favour promised to the accused, it may be assumed that in basing its decision to exclude the involuntary confession on its questionable reliability, the court was not concerned to assess the precise causal effect of the promise upon the veracity of the confession or, indeed, to leave that assessment to the jury. See Mirfield, 1985, p. 48.
[46] *Thompson* (1783) 1 Leach. 291. The accused was questioned by the Receiver-General for Somerset in connection with the theft of a £30 bank note. The

accused's explanation was not accepted by the Receiver-General who told the him that unless he gave a more satisfactory account he would be taken before a magistrate. The prisoner confessed. At the trial, it was contended that the actions of the Receiver-General 'amounted to a threat'. The court was invited to exclude the confession since even 'if it was not considered as a threat, it was certainly a promise, by implication, and indirectly, that if he did give a more satisfactory account he should not be taken before a Magistrate'. Hotham, B felt that it was 'almost impossible to be too careful upon this subject'. He did not accept that the prisoner was subjected to what could be considered a threat, however, he agreed that the 'prisoner was hardly a free agent at the time' at which he was under 'a strong invitation' to confess. The judge was not concerned with the specific question of whether the inducement stemmed from a threat or a promise. The key to his decision to exclude the confession lay in his assessment of its voluntariness. He stated that he did 'not like to admit confessions, unless they appear to have been made voluntarily, and without any inducement. Too great a chastity cannot be preserved on this subject, and I am of the opinion, that under the present circumstances the prisoner's confession, if it was one, ought not to be received'.

[47] *Cass* (1784) 1 Leach. 293, n. (a), where a person, suspected of theft, was promised favourable treatment if he confessed. At the trial Gould, J instructed the jury to 'acquit the prisoner; for that the slightest hopes of mercy held out to a prisoner to induce him to disclose the fact, was sufficient to invalidate a confession'.
[48] See Mirfield, 1985, pp. 47-49.
[49] 3 Wigmore, 1970, p. 297.
[50] *Ibid.*
[51] *Ibid.*, p. 502 (my emphasis).
[52] *Ibid.*, p. 297.
[53] *Lambe* (1791) 2 Leach. 552.
[54] 1 & 2 Phil. and Mar. c. 13 (1554); 2 & 3 Phil. and Mar. c. 10 (1555).
[55] *Lambe* (1791) 2 Leach. 552, pp. 552-3.
[56] *Ibid.*, pp. 554-5. See 3 Wigmore, 1970, pp. 297, 502, 510-11.
[57] *Lambe* (1791), *ibid.*, p. 554.
[58] *Baldry* (1852) 2 Den. 430.
[59] 3 Wigmore, 1970, p. 298.
[60] *Ibid.*, p. 297. See also 1 Stephen, 1883, p. 447.
[61] Mirfield, 1985, p. 50.
[62] See 3 Wigmore, 1970, p. 298.
[63] *Ibid.*, p. 297.
[64] *Ibid.*, p. 298.
[65] The case of *Sexton*, decided in 1823, is reported in Burn (1823) *The Justice of the Peace and Parish Officer*, in the section entitled *Chewynd's Supplement*, at pp. 103-4.

80  *Interrogation and Confession*

[66] *Ibid.*, p. 103.
[67] *Ibid.*
[68] *Ibid.*, pp. 103-4.
[69] It has been suggested that Wigmore, 'being totally committed to an unreliability basis for the exclusionary rule', could not support any judicial decision that excluded evidence in order to discourage improper police methods (Mirfield, 1985, p. 52).
[70] 3 Wigmore, 1970, pp. 298-301.
[71] *Wilson* (1817) Holt. 597.
[72] *Ibid.*
[73] *Ellis* (1826) Ry. & M. 432.
[74] 3 Wigmore, 1970, p. 299.
[75] *Thornton* (1824) 1 Moo. 27, constitutes a direct challenge to the thesis advanced by Wigmore. Here it was held that a confession, obtained from a boy of fourteen who had been detained in police custody without food and water, had been 'rightly received' by the trial judge, 'on the ground that no threat or promise had been used'. In this instance the voluntariness rule was given a restrictive interpretation in the so called 'period of sentimental excess'. See, also example, *Enoch and Pulley* (1835) 5 C. & P. 538; and *Croyden* (1846) 2 Cox C. C. 67.
[76] See 3 Wigmore, 1970, pp. 298-308; Mirfield, 1985, pp. 50-3.
[77] *Lloyd* (1834) 6 Car. & P. 398.
[78] *Spilsbury* (1835) 7 Car. & P. 187.
[79] *Ibid.*, p. 188.
[80] See, for example, *Richards* (1852) Car. & P. 318, and compare *Doherty* (1784) 13 Cox C.C. 23. See also *Thorton* (1824) 1 Moo. 27; *Long* (1833) 6 Car. & P 179; *Thomas* (1836) 7 Car. & P. 345; *Court* (1836) 7 Car. & P. 487; *Sleeman* (1853) 6 Cox. C. C. 245.
[81] Wigmore, 1970, p. 297.
[82] Mirfield, 1985, p. 51. See also 1 Stephen, 1883, p. 447.
[83] Mirfield, 1985, *ibid.*
[84] 3 Wigmore, 1970, pp. 298-301; see also MacDonald and Hart, 1947, pp. 824-28; Kaufman, 1979, pp. 20-21.
[85] 6, 7 Will. 4, c. 114 (1836). See 1 Stephen, 1883, p. 424; Langbein, 1978, pp. 307-16; Beattie, 1986, pp. 356-62.
[86] See Noble, 1970, pp. 249-66; Parker, 1984, pp. 156-75.
[87] 3 Wigmore, 1970, pp. 297-301; see also MacDonald and Hart, 1947, p. 826.
[88] Kaufman, 1979, pp. 20-1.
[89] Mirfield, 1985, pp. 50-3.
[90] *Morton* (1843) 2 M. & Rob. 514, *per* Coleridge, J.
[91] See, for example, *Swatkins* (1831) 4 Car. & P. 548; *Green* (1832) 5 Car. & P. 312; *Arnold* (1838) 8 Car. & P. 621; *Drew* (1838) 8 Car. & P. 140; *Morton* (1843) 2 M. & Rob. 514; *Furley* (1844) 1 Cox. C. C. 76.

[92] See 3 Wigmore, 1970, p. 297;; Mirfield, 1985, pp. 50-3.
[93] See, for example, *Lambe* (1791) 2 Leach. 552; *Thornton* (1824) 1 Moo. 27; *Richards* (1832) 5 Car. & P. 318; *Long* (1833) 6 Car. & P. 179; *Lloyd* (1834) 6 Car. & P. 393; *Spilsbury* (1835) 7 Car. & P. 187; *Wild* (1835) 1 Moo. 452; *Thomas* (1836) 7 Car. & P. 345; *Court* (1836) 7 Car. & P. 487; *Kerr* (1837) 8 Car. & P. 177.
[94] See, for example, *Thompson* (1783) 1 Leach. 291; *Cass* (1784) 1 Leach. 293; *Wilson* (1817) Holt. 597; *Sexton* (1823) *supra.*, n. 65; *Kingston* (1830) 4 Car. & P. 387; *Dunn* (1831) 4 Car. & P. 543; *Slaugter* (1831) 4 Car. & P. 544; *Shephard* (1836) 7 Car & P. 579; *Furley* (1844) 1 Cox. C. C. 76; *Harris* (1844) 1 Cox. C. C. 106; *Drew* (1838) 8 Car. & P. 140.
[95] *Warickshall* (1783) 1 Leach. 263, p. 264.
[96] Kaufman, 1979, p. 21.
[97] 3 Wigmore, 1970, p. 502.

# 5 Accommodating Police Interrogations

The case of *Baldry* (1852)[1] is widely regarded as marking the end of the period of judicial 'sentimental excess' and the point at which the courts curtailed or corrected a supposed trend in favour of excluding confession evidence.[2] Again, however, a close examination of the authorities suggests a more problematic picture. This picture is influenced by the consideration that, by the mid-nineteenth century, various features of the investigative and prosecution process stood out in profound contrast with that which had been routinized under the Marian legislation.[3] Chief amongst these features is the emergence and institutionalisation of professional police forces.

**The 'New' Police in the Nineteenth-Century Prosecution Process**

The period in which modern forms of policing emerged may be dated from the 1829 Metropolitan Police Act, which introduced the 'new' police, to the 1856 County and Borough Police Act, which obliged all local authorities to set up and maintain 'new' police forces on the Metropolitan Police model. These major Acts marked the unprecedented formation and spread throughout England and Wales of unified, bureaucratic, semi-military bodies, employing full-time, uniformed civilians for the prevention and detection of crime.[4] Under the measures that appeared between these dates,[5] the 'new' police gradually displaced the traditional modes of policing and prosecution which were largely victim-based, reactive and heavily dependent upon parish constables, watchmen, private associations, thief-takers and the investigative-prosecutorial powers of magistrates.[6]

As a centrally directed and regionally-stationed institution,[7] specifically designed to occupy a social space "midway between an outside military force and the group of people to be controlled",[8] the 'new' police — in their policing of the lower orders, who were being disciplined in the developing modes of production necessitated by industrial capitalism — worked in the social and crime control interests of the governing classes.[9] Indeed, during the course of the first half of the nineteenth century, the police came to acquire a key role in the maintenance of stable capitalistic social relations.[10]

At the outset the architects of the 'new' police had placed emphasis upon preventive policing of a pro-active, rather than reactive, nature. Instead of conducting detective investigations into offences after the fact, the police were to prevent crime through a system of surveillance and highly visible patrols.[11] In practice, however, this conception of policing[12] began to erode as the police assimilated and utilised powers not only to arrest, detain, interrogate and take incriminatory statements from suspects, but also to institute criminal proceedings against them.[13] Indeed, by as early as the middle of the century the police had become "convenient substitutes for private prosecutors".[14]

The emergence of the 'new' police as an unparalleled organ of social and crime control, not only added a novel official dimension to the prosecution process it also contributed to the gradual shift away from Marian-style preliminary examinations before justices toward an increasingly open quasi-judicial inquiry into cases prepared for prosecution.[15] Midway through the nineteenth century this shift found statutory expression in the 1848 Indictable Offences Act.[16]

The Act, which was designed to codify prevailing practice,[17] formally empowered justices to conduct public hearings into cases being prepared for trial by the prosecution and, after being satisfied of *prima facie* case, to commit the accused for trial.[18] Should the prosecution fail to so satisfy the justices, the accused was to be discharged.[19] The statute also imposed a formal duty on justices, following the examination of prosecution witnesses, firstly, to caution the accused that he was not obliged to answer the charge and, secondly, to give the accused to understand "that he has nothing to hope from any promise of favour, and nothing to fear from any threat which may have been holden out to him to induce him to make any admission or confession of his guilt".[20]

Thus, by the middle of the nineteenth century, with the effective judicialisation of the justices, the active investigation and prosecution of crime passed to the 'new' police.[21] And while statute governed the taking of statements from suspects by justices, it was left to the courts[22] to develop rules which would control and ultimately legitimate the extra-judicial questioning of suspects by the police.

## Voluntariness and Police Questioning

At the outset the caution, as to suspects' pre-trial right to silence and as required by the 1848 Act,[23] was considered to be a condition precedent to the admission of confession evidence.[24] Thus, it was argued in *Pettit* (1850)[25] that the magistrate "had no right, under any circumstances, to put questions to a prisoner". It was further contended that the position of authority enjoyed by magistrates would of itself necessarily exercise undue force over prisoners to compel them to answer and, therefore, render their statements involuntary. The trial judge was invited to rule the examination record inadmissible on the basis that the prisoner had not been cautioned in accordance with the 1848 Act. Wild, CJ rejected the evidence "upon the general ground that magistrates have no right to put questions to a prisoner with reference to any matters having bearing upon the charge upon which he is brought before them".[26] In short, the judge confirmed that the caution limited the role of magistrates to inviting the suspect to respond, if he so elects, to the case presented against him at his preliminary examination. Presumptively innocent suspects should be left free to exercise their right to remain silent and oblige the state — should the magistrates accept that a *prima facie* case had been established — to prove its case before judge and jury at trial where, according to the rhetoric of the law, the defendant is again to be presumed innocent and is again afforded a right to remain silent.

As stated earlier, it has been argued that *Baldry*, (1852)[27] brought to an end a trend, covering the first half of the nineteenth century, which was "completely in favour of the accused".[28] The case is also widely seen as having stemmed the high tide of judicial sentiment in favour of the exclusion of incriminatory admissions made extra-judicially by accused persons.[29]

The accused in *Baldry* was indicted for administering poison with intent to murder. It appeared in evidence that the constable who had apprehended the prisoner informed him that he need not say anything to incriminate himself but "what he did say would be taken down and used as evidence against him". Thereupon, the prisoner made an immediate confession. The first instance judge admitted the evidence as a voluntary confession of guilt even though the caution given by the constable differed from that directed by the 1848 Act in that the constable had suggested that the accused *would* rather than *might* be prosecuted. The judge thought that this departure from the Act did not operate as a promise or threat to induce the prisoner either to confess or to say anything untrue. However, on the ground that doubts had been entertained by judges as to the admissibility of confessions obtained after similarly worded cautions, Campbell, LCJ reserved the question for the Court for Crown Cases Reserved.[30] The Court, comprising five judges, unanimously affirmed the decision of Campbell, LCJ.

Certain *dicta* from the case are often referred to as evidence of a judicial desire to return to an orthodox or narrow interpretation of the voluntariness test.[31] That test, according to Wigmore (1970), was to ask whether the inducements, if any, were of themselves capable, in the specific circumstances, of producing a false or unreliable confession.[32] While it has not been demonstrated that a single or orthodox test of voluntariness had ever prevailed in the nineteenth century, *dicta* from the decision lends support to the view that the Court was concerned to rationalise the disparate precedents and establish a more attenuated interpretation of what may constitute an inducement having the capacity to render a confession involuntary and inadmissible. For example, Park, B thought that the authorities exhibited "too much tenderness towards prisoners in this matter". He went on to confess that he could not "look at the decisions without some shame" when he considered "what objections have prevailed to prevent the reception of confessions in evidence". He felt that the exclusionary rule had "been extended quite too far, and that justice and common sense [had], too frequently, been sacrificed at the shrine of mercy".[33] For Erle, J confessions were "the best evidence that can be produced" and the "many cases where confessions have been excluded, justice and common sense [had] been sacrificed, not at the shrine of mercy, but at the shrine of guilt".[34]

Other less frequently cited *dicta* from the case indicate a degree of ambivalence in the attitude of the Court in respect of the operation of the exclusionary rule, the caution and therefore, the legitimate practices of law enforcement officers. Campbell, LCJ stressed "that if there be any worldly advantage held out, or any harm threatened, the confession must be excluded".[35] He added that suspected or accused persons "are not to be interrogated. By the law of Scotland they may be; but by the law of England they cannot".[36] Park, B confirmed that in order to render a confession admissible in evidence it must be "perfectly voluntary". He was in "no doubt that any inducement in the nature of a promise or threat held out by a person in authority, vitiates a [voluntary] confession".[37] Finally, Pollock, CB argued that it should be "left to the prisoner a matter of perfect indifference whether he should open his mouth or not".[38]

The Court, therefore, was not concerned simply to place restrictions on judicial interpretations of the voluntariness rule. The Court also seems to have been anxious to arrest what it appears to have perceived as a recent trend — exhibited by some individual and largely independent judges of the lower courts — to project too stringent a construction of the voluntariness test onto the required caution.[39] In this respect the Court expressed its difficulty in appreciating "how it could be argued that any advantage is offered to a prisoner by being told that what he says will be used in evidence against him".[40] However, the Court also confirmed that a caution was required to remind the suspect "that he need not say anything, but if he says anything let it be true".[41]

Thus, a close examination of the decision in *Baldry* reveals that far from propounding an unambiguous direction to the lower courts intended to restrict the scope of the exclusionary rule and to prevent "almost anything being treated as an inducement to confess",[42] the Court reaffirmed the status and validity of the voluntariness test and the attendant caution. The decision of the Court, therefore, can be seen as an attempt on the part of a convocation of senior judges to provide guidance both to the lower courts and lesser law enforcement officials — chiefly magistrates but also police officers — in respect of the acquisition and reception in evidence of 'voluntary' avowals of guilt.

Essentially, *Baldry* stands as an authority for the contention that while suspects were to be cautioned not to incriminate themselves,[43] the words of the caution should not be 'tortured' by judges in their assessment of its effects as a possible inducement upon the mind of the accused. The caution should be taken at its 'natural' and 'obvious' meaning. So that while "[i]t is proper that a prisoner should be cautioned", what that prisoner might say following the caution "ought to be advanced either as evidence of guilt or as evidence in his favour", providing it be voluntarily given. As such the word *will* instead of *may* in the caution cannot act as an inducement capable of vitiating the voluntariness of a confession.[44]

In respect of the interrogation of suspects, however, the judges in *Baldry* did not modify the basic principle prohibiting both magistrates and the police from questioning the suspect in relation to the offence upon which that suspect had been arrested or detained. Indeed, Campbell, LCJ confirmed that under the common law both the judicial and extra-judicial interrogation of prisoners was absolutely prohibited.[45] He thereby indicated that an invasion on an individual's right not to respond to questions inviting incriminatory replies remained a legitimate ground upon which judges might exclude confession evidence.

It has been argued that *Baldry* "considerably modified" the law respecting the exclusion of confessions with the result that the judicial trend in favour of "almost anything" being treated as an inducement to confess was, from the middle of the nineteenth century, reversed.[46] However, the extra-judicial questioning of suspects in custody and the use of confessions obtained in consequence of this proscribed practice continued to provoke judicial hostility which was frequently articulated through the medium of the exclusionary rule.

In *Berriman* (1854),[47] the accused, at her preliminary examination, had been cautioned, after which she stated that she had nothing to say in answer to the charge. The presiding magistrate, before committing the prisoner, asked her a question to which she gave an incriminatory reply. The trial judge refused to receive the statement in evidence on the ground that it had been "so irregularly elicited" following a question that "ought never have been put".[48]

The case also afforded the judge an opportunity to censure the police. The suspect had been apprehended and charged by a police officer who questioned her on the basis of rumours he had received suggesting she had concealed the birth of her child. There was no other evidence against the prisoner who made a statement in response to the questions put to her by the officer. In ruling the statement inadmissible the judge declared:

> I very much disapprove of this proceeding. By the law of this country no person ought to be made to criminate himself, and no police officer has any right; until there is clear proof of a crime having been committed, to put searching question to a person for the purpose of eliciting from him whether an offence has been perpetrated or not. If there is evidence of an offence, a police officer is justified, after a proper caution, in putting to a suspected person interrogatories with a view to ascertaining whether or not there are fair and reasonable grounds for apprehending him. Even this course should be very sparingly resorted to.[49]

This statement suggests that the judge accepted that the extra-judicial questioning of suspects by the police would undermine the privilege against compulsory self-incrimination afforded to individuals suspected or accused of crime. However, the judge appears to depart from the common law proscription against the interrogation of suspects in his intimation that such questioning would be acceptable provided, firstly, that it was based upon material evidence that an offence had been committed, secondly, that the questions were limited to establishing whether there were grounds for arrest and, finally, that such questions were preceded by a proper caution. The remarks the judge made in respect of police questioning of suspects may, therefore, be regarded as ambiguous and essentially permissive.

The hostility some judges evinced towards the 'new' police and their investigative practices was not, it would seem, entirely shared by the judge who tempered his condemnation of the police with the remark that in his view "[w]hat was done here I have every reason to believe was done for no improper motive. It was doubtless, an error of judgement".[50] Presumably, had the judge found that the actions of the officer in question been borne of 'improper' motives, he would have adopted a less favourable view. Nevertheless, it is difficult to appreciate in what respect the motive or intention of the officer could be of relevance to the issue of whether the evidence had been obtained, firstly, in contravention of the prohibition against any questioning of suspects and, secondly, in violation of a voluntariness test that required judges to assess the likely effect any inducement might have had on the presumptively uninhibited mind of the accused.[51] In excluding the evidence in this case, the judge seems to have appreciated this and have intended that the police also acknowledge the point since he felt it necessary to add:

> I wish it to go forth amongst those who are inferior officers in the administration of justice, that such a practice is entirely opposed to the spirit of the law.[52]

Nonetheless, eight years later, in *Cheverton* (1862)[53] the same judge ruled that a failure on the part of the police to issue a caution to suspects would not necessarily result in the exclusion of confession evidence. Thus, illustrating that the caution was not to be regarded as a *sin qua non* to admissibility.

Much of the case law from the period following *Baldry* suggests an increasing acceptance of the police and of police interrogations. These cases also indicate that the caution was gradually relegated from what appeared to be a condition precedent to the admissibility of confession evidence to become a means of authenticating the evidential products of custodial interrogations conducted by the police. As long as the caution was issued, such interrogations — the probity of which remained debatable — were progressively legitimised behind rulings that purported to focus upon the issue of voluntariness. Yet where the caution was omitted, incriminatory admissions made by suspects could, under this judicial interpretation of the voluntariness test, still be admitted in evidence against the defendant. Some judges, however, frequently reproached the police for engaging in 'improper' investigatory practices though, with few exceptions, tended not to invoke the 'disciplinary principle' to exclude evidence so obtained.[54]

In *Mick* (1863),[55] for example, the suspect, while in police custody in connection with a wounding offence, was invited by an officer to make "a different statement" to that which he made (denying any involvement in the offence) when first taken into custody. The prisoner replied: "Yes sir, I will tell the truth". At this point the prisoner was interrupted and cautioned before he continued to make his confession. Mellor, J addressed the police officer in the following terms:

> I think the course you pursued in questioning the prisoner was exceedingly improper. I have considered the matter very much: many judges would not receive such evidence. The law does not intend you, as a policeman, to investigate cases in that way. I entirely disapprove of the system of police officers examining prisoners. The law has surrounded prisoners with great precautions to prevent confessions being extorted from them, and the magistrates are not allowed to question prisoners, or to ask them what they have to say; and it is not for policemen to do these things. It is assuming the functions of the magistrate without those precautions which the magistrates are required by the law to use, and assuming functions which are entrusted to the magistrates and to them only.[56]

This forthright judicial condemnation in defence of the rule of law and in favour of the rights the law extends to individuals suspected of involvement in criminal activity, serves to make clear that judicial opinion was divided as to whether such questioning should render subsequently obtained confessions inadmissible. In this instance, while Mellor, J disapproved of the questioning of prisoners to extract confessions by police officers — a practice denied to both magistrates and to judges — he ruled the evidence admissible. The decision suggests a fissure between the due process rhetoric of the law and the crime control practice of the law. Thus, while some judges took exception to the interrogation of suspects by the police, this practice would not invariably render confessions so obtained inadmissible.

## The Crown Against Johnston

Twelve years after *Baldry* (1852), the law and the conflicting authorities pertaining to the admission of confession evidence, the legal delineation of the concept of voluntariness and the scope of the exclusionary rule as it related to police interrogations, were comprehensively considered by senior members of the Irish judiciary. The case is significant not only because of its status as an authority widely cited in English courts during the nineteenth and early twentieth centuries but also because of the insight it affords to contemporary thinking as to the admissibility of confessions and because of its recognition of the problems raised by the psychology of confessions and police interrogations.

The case of *Johnston* (1864)[57] was reserved for the opinion of eleven judges in the Court for Crown Cases Reserved on the question of the admissibility of confession evidence made in the following circumstances. The accused, Mary Johnston, was suspected, having been followed by two police officers, of having stolen a number of boots from a shop. The plain-clothed officers, apprehended the suspect at a railway station where they identified themselves and proceeded to question her in respect of a parcel she was carrying. It was stated in evidence that the officers did not caution the suspect or inform her that had she attempted to leave her captors, she would have been prevented from doing so. During the course of the interrogation, the parcel was taken from the prisoner after which she admitted that she had taken the boots from the shop. It was at this point that the prisoner was cautioned as to her right to silence. Subsequently, she was formally arrested and taken to a police station.

The eleven judges agreed that the 'voluntariness rule' governed the admissibility of extra-judicial confessions and, by a majority of eight to three, held that, under this test, the confession had been properly received in evidence. The point of interest here, however, is that while the judges' opinions are couched in terms of the voluntariness rule, they are diametrically opposed in respect to the application of that rule, with the majority applying it restrictively.[58]

On the basis of his understanding of the voluntariness test, Deasy, B could find no legal objection to the admission of the confession. Furthermore, regarding the proposition that any statements made by an accused person in answer to police questions are not, on that ground alone, receivable in evidence, he found that:

The fact that the statement was elicited by questions so put, may be an element in leading to the conclusion that it was made under the influence of fear or hope excited by a person in authority, but we could not decide that it was *per se* sufficient to cause the rejection of the statement, without overruling the numerous cases in which such statements have been received in evidence against prisoners both in England and Ireland.[59]

Deasy, B referred to the Act which then regulated the manner in which voluntary admissions should be taken in proceedings before magistrates.[60] It had been contended that as this Act precluded magistrates from interrogating prisoners, it would be 'unreasonable' to allow police officers to do so.[61] However, the judge argued that the proviso to section 18 of the Act[62] made clear that the law had not been altered by the Act in the respect that it could not affect the admissibility of statements made to police constables any more than it could affect those made to any other person. He cited *Lambe's Case* (1791)[63] in support of his opinion that the law did not prevent the admission of such statements and that in the seventy-three years following *Lambe's Case* the law had not been changed.[64] He then observed that:

If the objection that the statement of the accused were made in answer to questions put by policemen were to prevail, that objection would apply still more strongly to answers made to questions by a magistrate, since his authority, and consequently his influence over the accused, considerably exceeds that of the policeman, yet it has been held, more than once, that answers to questions so put are admissible against the prisoner.[65]

That some of the decided cases had ruled in favour of the admission of such evidence cannot be disputed. However, it seems that Deasy, B so misunderstood the section 18 proviso and *Lambe's Case* as to distort his interpretation of the voluntariness requirement. A close reading reveals that neither the section 18 proviso nor the decision in *Lambe* are authorities in favour of the admissibility of statements made *in answer to police questions*. Rather, they hold for the proposition that pre-trial incriminatory admissions, when voluntarily made by the suspect, whether to police officers, to magistrates or to witness-prosecutors, may be received in evidence against their author. Deasy, B apparently, failed to appreciate that the Act gave statutory force to the voluntariness requirement and limited the power magistrates had enjoyed — under the Marian legislation of the mid-sixteenth century — to question suspects brought before them.[66] It would seem, therefore, that the judge did not adequately address the suggestion that it was "unreasonable to allow the constable to interrogate the prisoner, while the Magistrate, before whom it is the duty of the constable to bring him, is precluded from doing so".[67] Indeed, Deasy, B expressed his reluctance to give an opinion as to any distinction between incriminatory statements made in answer to questions and those made without the instrumentality of questions,[68] preferring to be guided by the decision of *Hughes*.[69] In that case Crampton, J is reported to have said:

> The confession of a man, to be admitted, is not to be extorted by fear or induced by flattery; but when a person voluntarily gives it, it may be received, whether the questions be put to him by an authorised or unauthorised person; wherever the declaration is voluntary he would receive it....[70]

Thus, for Deasy, B the questioning of suspects was not necessarily proscribed by law and was not of itself destructive of the requirement of voluntariness.

For Ball, J the conflicting authorities established that statements made by a prisoner in answer to questions put by a police officer, without a caution, are admissible in evidence "provided there has been no threat or inducement held out calculated to influence him to make the statement".[71] Ball, J was satisfied that the caution was irrelevant to the issue of voluntariness and thus to the admissibility of confession evidence. The voluntariness rule was limited to the issue of whether admissions obtained from prisoners through the instrumentality of police questions, even in the absence of a caution, were free from the operation of explicit hopes or threats on the mind of the prisoner.[72] Therefore, the legality of the police practice of questioning suspects to obtain admissions was, on this view, irrelevant to the judicial determination of whether those admissions were involuntary or improperly induced by threats or promises.

Monahan, CJ considered it unnecessary to attempt to reconcile the "absolutely irreconcilable" authorities which failed to provide clear guidance for the purposes of the present case.[73] He argued, nonetheless, that the highest of those authorities clearly established "that the fact of a confession having been made by a prisoner in custody, to a constable in whose custody he is, does not render the confession inadmissible".[74] Thus, "after giving the matter the most full consideration", he concluded that the mere asking of questions by a policeman was not "calculated to convey to the prisoner either hope of benefit or threat of injury".[75] He added that it was difficult to sustain an objection to the admissibility of confession evidence merely on the ground that it resulted from police questions.

The dissenting judges also considered the central issue to be the voluntariness of the confession evidence. However, they inclined to a less narrow view of the application of the voluntariness test. O'Brien, J was satisfied that the accused considered herself to be in custody when questioned by the police. He argued that the officer who asked questions of the accused, did so to elicit answers that would establish her guilt. "Having attained his object", the judge remarked, "he then goes through the mockery of giving her a caution".[76]

For this judge, the caution required by statute to be issued by magistrates demonstrated "that the intention of the Legislature was to give the prisoner an opportunity of making any statement he desired; but not to allow the Magistrate to interrogate him, save by asking him, in general terms, if he desired to say anything in answer to the charge".[77] Should a magistrate transgress his duty and interrogate the prisoner, the answers to such interrogatories would not be receivable in evidence. The Act was framed for the purpose of ensuring that confession evidence was voluntary; not extracted by questions; and made after the prisoner was apprised of the effect his statement might have. The reception in evidence of confessions obtained in contravention of the Act would "frustrate the policy of the Act, and render the securities thereby provided with regard to the prisoner's statement of little or no value".[78]

In the view of O'Brien, J, quite apart from the provisions of the statute, answers given by a prisoner to questions put to him by those who have him in custody could not be considered as voluntary statements, unless the prisoner is first informed that he is not obliged to answer the questions and that any answer given may be used against him at his trial. He insisted that:

> The very fact of these questions being put by a person, unaccompanied by any such caution, conveys to the prisoner's mind the idea of some obligation on his part to answer them, and deprives the statement of that voluntary character which is essential to admissibility.[79]

Under his examination of the case law O'Brien, J acknowledged that there appeared to be "a conflict of authority" on the question of the admissibility of statements elicited by extra-judicial questions. He was of the opinion, however, that "the preponderance of authority is against the reception of the evidence".[80]

In concluding that the evidence in the present case was improperly received, the judge suggested that the police should be deterred from adopting a 'system' of questioning which exploited the apprehensions of prisoners. However, O'Brien, J seems to have considered an absolute prohibition of the practice to be unattainable since he felt that it would "be far better for the administration of justice, to hold that the police should be at liberty, without the risk of censure, to question a prisoner".[81] Though he suggested that such questioning should be limited so as to guide police investigations for the discovery of other evidence. He also felt that the answers to police questions should not be adduced in evidence against a prisoner at his trial.

Lefroy, CJ also found that earlier rulings had generated "a mass of varying and somewhat contradictory authority". He considered it the object of the Court to extract from those rulings a clear and common principle to guide magistrates and policemen in the exercise of their duties.[82] He argued that it was a "great mistake" to confine the Court's inquiry to the sole issue of whether threats or promises had induced the confession. For a confession may be made under circumstances where there had been no specific inducements and yet be made involuntarily.[83]

In his suggestion of an extended definition of voluntariness, Lefroy, CJ shifted the inquiry from the question of threats or promises to the psychological and emotional pressures attending arrest, detention and interrogation. The caution was required to ensure, firstly, that suspects were not entrapped and, secondly, to inform them that their statements would be taken down in writing and might be used against them. He argued that questioning by the police should be limited to justifying themselves to the individual under suspicion but officers should not "be privileged to give in evidence the answers they may receive to those questions".[84] In respect of the present case, he found that the police, by questioning the suspect without a caution, had employed "an ingenious stratagem, which had the effect of making [the suspect] the deluded instrument of her own conviction".[85] Thus, the statement obtained from her was not made freely and voluntarily.

For Pigot, CB it was "undeniable" that there had been a "diversity of practice" among judges as to the reception of confession evidence. He also felt that the "great preponderance of authority" had been against its reception.[86] He too drew a distinction between the investigative and prosecutorial functions of the police, arguing that questions may be put to determine whether there were reasonable grounds for arresting a suspect but "answers elicited by interrogations put with a view to establish the guilt of the prisoner in custody, and thus to make him, while a prisoner, his own accuser", should not be received in evidence against him at his trial.[87]

Pigot, CB felt that, even after a caution has been administered, when a police officer puts a series of searching interrogatories to a suspect "he virtually, and I think, actually and in effect, abandons the caution, and announces, by the very course of interrogation which he applies, that it is better for the prisoner to answer than be silent".[88] He suggested that it was for this reason magistrates were prohibited from questioning suspects except to ask whether they wished to reply to the charge. The 1848 Act,[89] he argued, recognised that:

> The process of question[ing] impresses, on the mind of the greater part of mankind, the belief that silence will be taken as an assent to what the questions imply. The very necessity which that impression suggests, of answering the question in *some* way, deprives the prisoner of his free agency; and impels him to answer, from fear of the consequences of declining to do so. Daily experience shows that witnesses, having deposed to the strict truth, become, on a severe or artful cross-examination, involved in contradictions and excuses, destructive of their credit and of their direct testimony. A prisoner is still more liable to make statements of that character, under the pressure of interrogatories urged by the person who holds him in custody; and thus truth, the object of the evidence of admissions so elicited, is defeated by the very method ostensibly used to attain it.[90]

Thus, the very circumstances in which a police officer has custody of a suspect — by virtue of their relative positions of power — negatives the capacity of the prisoner to act as a free agent. It would seem that Pigot, CB was suggesting that confessions made under such conditions could not be presumed to be voluntary. Indeed, he intimated that such circumstances furnish the "strongest presumption" that any statement so elicited, was not voluntary since the interrogation environment is of itself "calculated" to cause any answers given to be influenced by hope *and* fear.[91]

The view of the scope and operation of the exclusionary rule advanced by Hayes, J represents a compromise between the broad approach of the minority judges and the narrow approach adopted by the majority.[92] For him, the law regarding the admissibility of confessions depended upon which of the three primary phases of the prosecution process they were made. As to a confession made in open court, the trial judge is to satisfy himself that it is made freely and voluntarily before it can be received in place of a conviction by a jury. Secondly, as to a confession made before a committing magistrate, this may be received only if it is shown that the accused was duly cautioned to make a voluntary statement.[93]

Of the pre-trial investigative phase, Hayes, J observed that the admissibility of a confession made at any time after the commission of the offence until the accused is brought up for trial was "not regulated by any statutory enactments but [was] governed wholly by the principles of Common Law, as enunciated in the maxim *nemo teneture prodere seipsum*, and by judicial decision in elucidation of that maxim".[94] The common law required this class of confession to made voluntarily. "But that word is to be understood in a wide sense, as requiring not only that the prisoner should have free will and power to speak, or refrain from speaking, as he may think right, but also that his will should not be warped by any unfair, dishonest, or fraudulent practices, to induce a confession."[95] So that while judges have refused to receive confessions in evidence that have been either certainly or probably elicited by promises or threats, confessions may also be rejected if it appears that they have been extracted by:

> the presumed pressure and obligation of an oath, or by pestering interrogatories, or ... by the party to rid himself of importunity, or ... by subtle and ensnaring questions, as those which are framed to conceal their drift or object, he has been taken at a disadvantage, and thus entrapped into a statement which, if left to himself, and in the full freedom of volition, he would not have made.[96]

These the judge instanced as "several ways in which a confession may be unfairly and improperly procured, so as to deprive it of the character of being voluntary".[97] This attitude suggests that the practice of police officers putting questions to suspects held in custody was not to be prohibited. Judges were to place emphasis instead upon the nature and circumstances of that questioning to determine whether the confession elicited was voluntarily given. Only where police investigative methods generated confession evidence that could not be deemed 'voluntary' would it be excluded. As Hayes, J put it:

> Whether a confession be or be not voluntary, is a question altogether for the judge to decide, when all the circumstances have been laid before him in evidence; and if he, in the sound exercise of his understanding, be well satisfied that it is the voluntary and unbiased effusion of the mind of the criminal, though it may have been elicited by questions, he will be bound to receive it in

evidence; as otherwise he would be unwarrantably contracting, if not wholly stopping up, one of the avenues of justice.[98]

The judge accepted that suspects should be cautioned against giving involuntary confessions but argued that police officers issued such a caution only as a matter of practice, not as a result of any common law or statutory rules. He also recognised that a suspect may be susceptible "to every influence that addresses itself to his hopes and fears".[99] He maintained, however, that it was for the purpose of counteracting such influences that the police followed the practice of cautioning suspects "the better to ensure a voluntary confession, but not ... in all cases essential to it".

For Hayes, J, therefore, the voluntariness test should be applied, under the discretion of trial judges, with reference to the due process protections afforded to suspects but also with reference to considerations of crime control. However, the latter demanded that the ability of the police to conduct criminal investigations and to obtain confessions from those they 'reasonably' suspect, should not be unduly inhibited. The activities of the police with respect to the procurement of confessions are reviewable by trial judges in their *post hoc* assessment of a confession's 'voluntariness'. In the instant case, the confession was properly received since it was not obtained by any threat, promise or other undue or unfair means and was "made at a time when the party neither was a prisoner, nor felt or supposed herself to be a prisoner".[100]

The judge did not accept the contention that Johnston was, in effect, in police custody when she answered the questions put to her. Yet, somewhat paradoxically, he argued that "had she felt herself to be in custody on the criminal charge, then her statements, in answer to the questions would not have been receivable, unless prefaced with a caution" since she would not have been at liberty to speak or to refrain from speaking but bound to account for herself.[101]

## Conclusion

The conflicting judicial opinions given in *Johnston* are illustrative of the imprecise nature of the law in the second half of the nineteenth century respecting the admissibility of confession evidence as it related to the growing police practice of interrogating suspects. Although considerations of crime control and of due process are exhibited by all the judges, those in favour of a broad application of the voluntariness rule appear to incline towards a due process stance, while the majority seem disposed to one of crime control. For the majority judges, crime control considerations predominated so that for them the act of questioning a suspect to obtain a statement could not of itself render that statement inadmissible. The voluntariness test merely required judges to determine whether the specific inducements of threats or promises had been held out. In the absence of such inducements the statement, notwithstanding that it was obtained by police questions, would be admissible against the accused.

For the dissenting members of the court, in assessing the admissibility of confession evidence under the voluntariness rule, judges should presume that statements made by persons in police custody — without such persons being previously cautioned — to have been made involuntarily. Under this view, evidence suggesting that confessions were elicited by the instrumentality of police questions should buttress the presumption against voluntariness. Thus, the voluntariness rule should be given an extended meaning to effectuate the due process rhetoric of the law which purports to be opposed to making suspects the deluded instruments of their own conviction[102] and to be "against anything that could be calculated to excite the prisoner to confess".[103]

Nevertheless, both majority and dissenting judges seem to have regarded the custodial interrogation of suspects either as of great utility to the investigation of crime and the conviction of the guilty, or as a regrettable but unavoidable investigative technique that would generate potentially unreliable confessions which should not be received in evidence. This permits the conclusion that by the mid-nineteenth century there were the beginnings of a shift in judicial attitude. This attitude moved away from one of hostility to *any* police questioning as to the guilt of the suspect (a form of questioning that might be viewed as usurping the functions of the court), to one more acquiescent towards the investigative practices of the police, underpinned by necessarily *post hoc* judicial efforts to ensure police prosecutions did not benefit from confessions obtained through 'improper' means.

In short, while *Johnston* reveals that neither English nor Irish judges were in complete agreement as to the scope and application of the voluntariness rule, the authorities cited and opinions delivered in the case indicate, firstly, that confessions made in an extra-judicial context were considered by judges to be legitimate when shown to have been made freely and voluntarily; and, secondly, that confessions were viewed as such even when obtained by police questioning, provided the questions put did not involve explicit threats or promises. The case also serves to illuminate the essentially crime control view that was beginning to prevail amongst the judiciary in the latter half of the nineteenth century respecting the contours of the relationship that was being established between suspected persons and law enforcement personnel to question such persons before formal trial. It will be seen in the following chapters that this view provided the political space for the police to assume control over the detention and pre-trial interrogation of suspects. While this development would continue to excite judicial opposition, by the early part of the present century the custodial interrogation of suspects by the police, for the purpose of securing incriminatory statements and the admission of those statements in evidence, would be progressively legitimised by an increasingly corporatised judiciary.

## Notes

[1] *Baldry* (1852) 2 Den. 430.
[2] 1 Stephen, 1883, p. 447; 3 Wigmore, 1970, p. 298; Kaufman, 1979, p. 21; MacDonald and Hart, 1949, p. 826; see also Mirfield, 1985, pp. 50-6.
[3] 1 & 2 Phil. and Mar. c. 13 (1554); 2 & 3 Phil. and Mar. c. 10 (1555).
[4] See Miller, 1977, p. 2; Cornish, 1978a, pp. 305, 308, 314; Jefferson and Grimshaw, 1984, p. 28; Emsley, 1987, p. 171; Hay and Snyder, 1989, pp. 4-5.
[5] For a discussion of the series of legislative measures that appeared between 1829 and 1856 providing for the creation of 'new' police forces, see Lee, 1901, pp. 262-308; 14 Holdsworth, 1964, pp. 208-9, 235; Hart, 1978, pp. 181-200; Jefferson and Grimshaw, 1984, pp. 28-34; Cornish and Clark, 1989, pp. 587-95.
[6] See Miller, 1977, pp. 74, 82; Cornish, 1978a, pp. 305-6, 308; Emsley, 1987, pp. 148-50; Cornish and Clark, 1989, pp. 551-7; Hay and Snyder, 1989, p. 5. The condemnation of pre-industrial forms of policing (as uncoordinated, corrupt, inadequate and ineffectual) not only contributed to the development of professional policing it also helped to legitimate it. See 10 Holdsworth, 1938, pp. 143-6; Phillips, 1977, p. 61; Bunyan, 1977, pp. 58-60; Ascoli, 1979, pp. 93-5; Brogden, 1982, pp. 52-6; Reiner, 1985, pp. 10-11, 22-3, 27-8; Peters, 1985, p. 110; Emsley, 1987, pp. 171, 174; Cornish and Clark, 1989, pp. 552, 554-5; Hay and Snyder, 1989, pp. 5-9, 15, 37; Emsley, 1991, pp. 56-61.
[7] 14 Holdsworth, 1964, p. 94; Gatrell, 1990, pp. 260-2.
[8] Monkkonen, 1981, p. 39. See also Gatrell, 1990, pp. 249-61, 266-7, 277-9.

[9] Silver, 1967, pp. 3-5, 7-15, 20-2; Storch, 1975, p. 61-90; Storch, 1976, pp. 481-509; Bunyan, 1977, pp. 63-4, 66; Miller, 1977, pp. 5-10, 106-11; Cohen, P., 1979, pp. 120-8.

[10] Miller, 1977, pp. 104-39; Brogden, 1982, pp. 49-71, 184; Hay and Snyder, 1989, p. 8; Gatrell, 1990, pp. 260-2.

[11] See Bunyard, 1978, p. 10; Stead, 1985, p. 51; Scraton, 1985, p. 20; Reiner, 1985, pp. 14, 58-9; Emsley, 1991, p. 24; Weinberger, 1991, pp. 78-9.

[12] A conception that served to legitimate the notion that the police were no more than citizens in uniform and, as such, equally subject to the rule of law. See Lee, 1901, pp. 214, 228-32, 240-1; Miller, 1977, pp. 15-6, 47; Monkkonen, 1981, p. 39; Reiner, 1985, pp. 53-4; Hay and Snyder, 1989, p. 39; Gatrell, 1990, p. 274.

[13] See Miller, 1977, pp. 74-5; Cornish, 1978b, p. 60.

[14] Hay and Snyder, 1989, p. 37. See also Devlin, 1960, pp. 7-25; Jackson, 1972, p. 155; Miller, 1977, pp. 74, 82, 84-5, 107-8; Cornish and Clark, 1989, p. 554.

[15] See Freestone and Richardson, 1980, pp. 9-16; Cornish, 1978b, pp. 60-1.

[16] 11 & 12 Vict., c. 42 (1848). This was one four Acts collectively known as Jervis' Acts after the then Attorney-General, Sir John Jervis (1802-56). The remaining Acts were: 11 & 12 Vict., cc. 43, 44 (1848); 12 & 13 Vict., c. 18 (1949).

[17] *Parliamentary Debates* (Commons), vol. 96 col. 6; Osborne, 1960, pp. 224, 226; Freestone and Richardson, 1980, pp. 10-16; Cornish, 1978a, pp. 310-11.

[18] According to 11 & 12 Vict., c .43, s.12: 'the room or place in which justices shall sit to hear any complaint or information shall be deemed an open and public place to which the public generally may have access'. This, in the view of Osborne (1960, p. 226), was a revolutionary development; one that made clear that justice was not to be secured behind 'the closed doors of a Justice's parlour'.

[19] 11 & 12 Vict., c. 42, s. 25.

[20] *Ibid.*, s. 18.

[21] Cornish, 1978b, p. 60.

[22] *Ibid.*, p. 61.

[23] Indictable Offences Act, 1848, s. 18.

[24] See *Kimber* (1849) 3 Cox. C. C. 223; *Higson* (1849) 2 C. & K. 769; compare *Samsome* (1850) 4 Cox. C. C. 203.

[25] *Pettit* (1850) 4 Cox. C. C. 164.

[26] *Ibid.*, p. 165.

[27] *Baldry* (1852) 2 Den. 430.

[28] Kaufman, 1979, p. 20.

[29] MacDonald and Hart, 1947, pp. 826-7.

[30] This court was established under 11 & 12 Vict., c. 78, 1848.

[31] See, for example, Mirfield, 1985, p. 54.

[32] 3 Wigmore, 1970, pp. 497-8.

[33] *Baldry* (1852) 2 Den. 430, p. 445.
[34] *Ibid.*, p. 446.
[35] *Ibid.*
[36] *Ibid.*, p. 442.
[37] *Ibid.*, pp. 444-5.
[38] *Ibid.*, p. 442.
[39] See *ibid.*, p. 445, *per* Park, B.
[40] *Ibid.*
[41] *Ibid.*, p. 442, *per* Pollock, CB.
[42] 1 Stephen, 1883, p. 447.
[43] Indictable Offences Act, 1848, s. 18.
[44] *Baldry* (1852) 2 Den. 430, *per* Pollock, CB, pp. 443-4 and Park, B, p. 444.
[45] *Ibid.*, p. 442.
[46] 1 Stephen, 1883, p. 447.
[47] *Berriman* (1854) 6 Cox C.C. 388, p. 389.
[48] *Ibid.*, p. 389, *per* Erle, J.
[49] *Ibid.*, pp. 388-89.
[50] *Ibid.*, p. 389.
[51] See *Jarvis* (1867) 10 Cox. C.C. 57.
[52] *Berriman* (1854) *supra.*, n. 47, p. 389.
[53] *Cheverton* (1862) 2 F. & F. 833, p. 835, where Erle, J observed that to put questions to the suspect 'without any caution was most improper especially since the prisoner does not seem to have to have been aware of their drift or object'.
[54] See, for example, *Reason* (1872) 12 Cox C.C. 228; *Brackenbury* (1893) 17 Cox C.C. 628; *Miller* (1895) 18 Cox C.C. 54; *Hirst* (1896) 18 Cox C.C. 122; *Best* (1909) 1 KB 692; compare *Bodkin* (1863) 9 Cox C.C. 403; *Gavin* (1885) 15 Cox C.C. 656; *Male and Cooper* (1893) 17 Cox C.C. 689; *Histed* (1898) 19 Cox C.C. 16.
[55] *Mick* (1863) 3 F. & F. 322.
[56] *Ibid.*
[57] *Johnston* (1864) 15 ICLR. 60.
[58] The majority comprised: Deasy, B; Fitzgerald, J; Keogh, J; Hughes, B; Fitzgerald, B; Monahan, CJ; Ball, J; and Hayes, J.
[59] *Supra.*, n. 57, p. 80.
[60] 12 & 13 Vict. c. 69 (1849). This Act replicated for Ireland the English Act, 11 & 12 Vict., c. 42 (1848). Its provisions regarding the examination of suspects, were incorporated into The Petty Sessions (Ireland) Act, 1851 (14 & 15 Vict. c. 93).
[61] *Supra.*, n. 57, p. 77.
[62] The proviso to s. 18 of the 1849 Act duplicates the same in s. 18 of the English Act (*supra.*, n. 60). The proviso states 'that nothing herein enacted or contained shall prevent the Prosecutor in any Case from giving in Evidence any

[63] *Lambe's Case* (1791) 2 Leach. 552.
[64] *Supra.*, n. 57, p. 77.
[65] *Ibid.* pp. 77-8.
[66] *Ibid.* p. 90, *per* O'Brien, J: 'It appears to me that such proviso refers to voluntary statements, made by the prisoner of his own accord, but not to answers given by him, while in custody, to questions put by a magistrate or policeman'.
[67] *Ibid.*, p. 77.
[68] *Ibid.*, p. 79.
[69] Reported in *Joy on Confessions* (1842), p. 39.
[70] Quoted in *Johnston* (1864), *supra.*, n. 57, pp. 79-80.
[71] *Ibid.*, p. 106.
[72] *Ibid.*, pp. 109-10.
[73] *Ibid.*, pp. 124-5.
[74] *Ibid.*, p. 125.
[75] *Ibid.*, p. 127.
[76] *Ibid.*, p. 88.
[77] *Ibid.*, p. 89.
[78] *Ibid.*
[79] *Ibid.*, p. 90. The judge also stated that: 'A prisoner ... cannot be interrogated as to any matter whatever; and I trust the practice prevailing in other countries will never be legalized here' (*ibid.*, p. 88). He considered the case of *Wilson* (1817) 1 Holt. 597 (which concerned the examination of a prisoner by a magistrate and in which Richards, CB observed that 'an examination, of itself, imposes an obligation to speak the truth') to be equally applicable to cases where the prisoner is examined by police officers (*ibid.*, p. 94).
[80] *Ibid.*, p. 105.
[81] *Ibid.*
[82] *Ibid.*, p. 130.
[83] *Ibid.*, pp. 130, 133.
[84] *Ibid.*, p. 133.
[85] *Ibid.*
[86] *Ibid.*, p. 118; see also p. 119.
[87] *Ibid.*, p. 121. This judge also considered the likely effects on suspects of the psychological pressures associated with criminal investigations. He argued that apart from direct promises or threats, a suspect may be 'actuated by hope that his answers will lead to his liberation, or fear that his answers may cause his detention in custody ... Manner may menace and cause fear as much as words. Manner may insinuate hope as well as verbal assurances. The very fact of questioning is in itself an indication that the questioner will or may liberate the

answerer if the answers are satisfactory, and detain him if they are not'(*ibid.*, p. 122).
88 *Ibid.*
89 11 & 12 Vict. c. 42, s. 18; see also its Irish equivalent, 12 & 13 Vict. c. 69, s. 18.
90 *Johnston* (1864), *supra.*, n. 57, p. 122.
91 *Ibid.* See also *Wilson* (1817) 1 Holt. 597.
92 Jackson, 1985, p. 214.
93 *Johnston* (1864), *supra.*, n.57, pp. 82-3; compare *Stripp* (1856) 1 Dears. 648.
94 *Johnston* (1864), *ibid.*, p. 83.
95 *Ibid.*
96 *Ibid.*, p. 84.
97 *Ibid.*, p. 84.
98 *Ibid.*, pp. 84-5.
99 *Ibid.*, p.84
100 *Ibid.*, pp. 86-7.
101 *Ibid.*, p. 87.
102 *Ibid.*, *per* Lefroy, CJ, pp. 131, 134.
103 *Ibid.*, p. 66.

# 6 Towards the Regulation of Custodial Interrogations

**Introduction**

The division of learned opinion voiced by the judges in *Johnston* (1864),[1] finds expression in the English decisions of the late nineteenth and early twentieth centuries. Indeed, in spite of the decision's persuasive force in favour of admitting the accused's statement as a voluntary, non-induced, response to police questions, English law remained unsettled and continued to generate contradictory case law. This suggests a degree of ambivalence on the part of individual judges, firstly, in respect of the custodial questioning of suspects by the police and, secondly, in regard to the admissibility of evidence obtained by such questioning. The greater number of cases, however, indicate that most judges considered the interrogation of suspects in police custody to be objectionable but not of itself sufficient to exclude confession statements which, in all other respects, appeared to have been made voluntarily.[2]

In some of these cases the caution seems to have been viewed as an essential precondition to the reception of extra-judicial confessions. Thus, should it be asserted that the accused, while in police custody, was apprised of his or her right to remain silent and nonetheless went on to make an incriminatory statement, that statement would generally be received in evidence as being free from coercion and voluntarily made. However, a number of decisions from the period suggest that judges increasingly admitted confessions as 'voluntary' expressions of guilt, even where the accused had not been formally cautioned. Such cases reveal that a narrow interpretation of the voluntariness rule, as advocated by the majority judges in *Johnston*, was generally followed by the English courts.[3]

## Facilitating Custodial Interrogations

Although the exclusionary rule, as articulated in *Warickshall* (1783), is said to be based upon the 'reliability principle',[4] Taylor (1864) maintained that the disciplinary aspect of the voluntariness requirement was "a more sensible reason" for excluding improperly obtained confession evidence.[5] That is, the evidential requirement for 'voluntary' confessions should be used not only to ensure the courts received reliable avowals of guilt but also to discourage impropriety on the part of police officers.

Counsel for the prisoner in the case of *Reason* (1872)[6] drew the presiding judge's attention to this authority. Sarah Reason had been indicted for the murder of her child. Prior to her formal arrest, a police officer had put questions to, and obtained incriminating statements from, her. The judge did not respond to the direct invitation to invoke the 'disciplinary principle' however, in referring to the inquisitorial role played by the police officer, he remarked that:

> It is the duty of the police-constable to hear what the prisoner has voluntarily to say, but after the prisoner is taken into custody it is not the duty of the constable to ask any questions. So, when the police-constable has reason to suppose that the person will be taken into custody, it is his duty to be very careful and cautious in asking questions.[7]

At a glance this statement would seem to clarify the scope of the police power to question suspects. However, closer consideration exposes its equivocality. The judge implies that the police might receive admissions voluntarily made by suspects not in custody but should not ask questions of such suspects. He then suggests that suspects may not be questioned once taken into custody. In doing so, however, he contradicts his earlier suggestion by allowing the inference that the pre-custodial questioning of suspects, without a caution, is permissible. He then suggests that the questioning of suspects detained in police custody may be sanctioned if conducted in a 'careful and cautious' manner. Finally, the ambiguity is compounded by the failure of the judge to indicate whether the act of subjecting a suspect to interrogatories may of itself constitute wrongful custodial questioning.[8]

The judge's attitude in *Reason* as to the custodial interrogation of suspects by the police runs counter to that expressed by Cockburn, LCJ who, in the *Yeovil Murder Case* (1877),[9] unambiguously re-affirmed that:

the law did not allow a man under suspicion and about to be apprehended to be interrogated at all.[10]

He further pointed out that as a "judge, magistrate or jury could not do it" it was a "great mistake" for the police to presume to do so.[11] In spite of this emphatic assertion of due process values, the courts continued to rule in favour of the reception in evidence of confessions obtained under police interrogations and, as such, continued to exhibit a largely uncritical acceptance of the police practice of putting questions designed to invite incriminatory replies from suspects.[12]

For example, in *Miller* (1895)[13] it was proved that a detective inspector had said to the suspect: "I am going to ask you some questions on a very serious matter, and you had better be careful how you answer". The suspect's resulting statement was admitted in evidence by Hawkins, J who found "that no inducement was held out to the prisoner to make any admission". In concluding that the statement was voluntary and admissible, the judge added that:

> It was impossible to discover the facts of a crime without asking questions, and these questions were properly put.[14]

In *Rogers v. Hawkin* (1898)[15] the accused was charged with permitting a horse to be worked while in an unfit state. It was proved in evidence that the accused's servant, when questioned by a police officer, made a statement implicating his master. Later, the accused was questioned "without any warning or caution". This appears to have been considered immaterial to Russell, LCJ who found that when the accused was questioned upon the incriminatory statement of his servant he "had the opportunity of either declining to reply or making an answer to it".[16] The accused's confession was held to have been properly received in evidence.

It is clear from these and many similar cases from the period that the caution had been transformed from being considered a condition precedent to admissibility, to become a mere factor which some judges considered as conducive to the admission of confession evidence. The case law also suggests that the issue of whether the suspect was actually in custody at the time in which the questions were put was increasingly used, under the discretion of individual judges,[17] to distinguish impermissible interrogations from extra-judicial questioning as that contemplated by the 1848 Indictable Offences Act. This distinction meant that the exclusion of custodial admissions made under police interrogatories depended either upon a judge accepting the suspect was indeed in custody, so as to attract judicial censure under the disciplinary principle, or upon a judge ruling that confessions made in such conditions are invariably involuntary.[18] In short, the narrow interpretation of 'voluntariness' and of 'custody' operated to create a two-tier obstacle *against* the exclusion of confessions made under police questioning.

In this regard the case of *Booth and Jones* (1910)[19] is instructive. This was an appeal against conviction, heard in the then recently constituted Court of Criminal Appeal,[20] on the ground that a confession, the only evidence against the appellant, had been forced from the accused by a series of questions put to him while he was detained in custody. Counsel for the appellant submitted that the confession should have been ruled inadmissible as it was not made freely and voluntarily. Counsel also pointed out that it had been conceded that the accused was indeed practically in custody at the time of the interview and would not have been allowed to leave. To this Lawrance, J observed that "[a] policeman's eye is not custody". Darling, J added:

> If this sort of investigation were not allowed very few crimes would ever be discovered.[21]

Delivering the judgment of the court, Darling, J found that the accused was given a "definite option either to speak or not to speak" when he was cautioned. The judge held that there had been no infraction of the exclusionary rule. The evidence was rightly admitted since the trial judge "came to the conclusion that there was no evidence to justify him in holding the interrogator had already determined to take [the accused] into custody or that he was then practically in custody".[22]

Evidently, neither the trial judge nor the judges in the Court of Appeal accepted that the police had acknowledged that the accused was practically in custody during the interview. Yet it is clear from the judgment of Darling, J that "physical custody is not necessary to make such evidence inadmissible".[23] It would seem that had 'custody' been ascribed by the judge to the circumstances in which the interrogation had taken place, the confession, irrespective of its reliability, would have been excluded.[24]

Such cases notwithstanding, that the extra-judicial questioning of suspects by the police might meet with strong judicial disapproval is demonstrated by a case heard in 1912 at the Marlborough Street Police

Court.[25] In this case a magistrate had cause to reprimand a police inspector for questioning, at the rear of the court, a prisoner who had previously been arrested and was awaiting hearing. It was accepted on behalf of the police, that "once a man was in custody he should not be questioned in any form by a police officer". It was then argued "in extenuation" that the information the inspector had gained from the interrogation proved to be advantageous to the prisoner. The magistrate was then invited to "modify the strictures he passed on the inspector, who had absolutely no *mala fides* in putting the questions".[26] The magistrate observed that he found having to reproach the police "an unpleasant duty" and while he did not impute any *mala fides* to the inspector "it was the disregard of the general rule by an officer of position that caused him to make some grave remarks, and the fact that he felt that undue laxity was prevailing after he had occasion to make similar observations rather frequently".[27] Finally, in alluding to the privilege afforded to prisoners against compulsory self-incrimination, the magistrate trusted that it would not be necessary for him to so admonish the police again.[28]

Of those nineteenth century decisions that evinced a narrow conception of 'voluntariness' within the exclusionary rule, considerations of crime control are generally given primacy over those of due process. The practical effect of these decisions was to progressively legitimate the practice and utility of police interrogations. Confessions obtained under police questioning would generally be admitted in evidence even where the accused held in custody had not been cautioned of his right to remain silent. These authorities suggest that only when the fears or hopes of the accused had been excited by a person in authority using inducements to secure admissions would the evidence be excluded.

As originally conceived, the exclusionary rule could not have anticipated the key role the bureaucratised police were to acquire in the prosecution process. Furthermore, the statutory caution was directed to suspects brought before magistrates.[29] It did not directly address the police practice of detaining and interrogating suspects in order to construct and prosecute cases through to trial.

## Due Process Values Upheld

The cases dating from the second half of the nineteenth century in which judges ruled against the reception of confessions obtained through the extra-judicial interrogation of suspects by the police, though less numerous than those that ruled in favour of their reception,[30] suggest that some judges were prepared to accept that police interrogations were inherently coercive upon detained suspects.[31] In these cases judges frequently referred to the prohibition against the questioning of suspects, the privilege against compulsory self-incrimination, the right of the accused not to testify at trial and the related right of the suspect to refuse to answer police questions.[32] Confessions obtained in consequence of improper extra-judicial questioning conducted by persons having authority over the suspect would, therefore, be excluded as being involuntary. Alternatively, the judge's discretion would be exercised under the 'disciplinary principle', to deny prosecutors the use of such evidence in order to deter them from engaging in unacceptable investigatory practices in the future.[33]

These cases reveal that some judges attempted to constrain the police questioning of suspects to that necessary to guide their legitimate investigations. Permissible police questioning was to be distinguished from police interrogations which aimed to extract incriminatory evidence from suspects and to implicate them in their own conviction. Nonetheless, the case law suggests that this demarcation was, firstly, inadequately drawn and enforced and, secondly, inadequately understood (or indeed actively exploited) by the police whose drive for convictions, under the imperatives of crime control, conflated the theoretically distinct investigative and prosecutorial aspects of the criminal justice process.

One case in which due process considerations appear to have prevailed over those of crime control is that of *Bodkin* (1863).[34] In this case the court excluded evidence of what a prisoner had said in reply to questions put by the arresting police officer. The officer had, before questioning the prisoner, issued the "usual and proper caution". The court, nevertheless, ruled that "where a constable arrests a party he ought to abstain from asking questions".[35] The court appears to have invoked the 'disciplinary principle' implicit in the exclusionary rule,[36] by making clear that police officers had no authority to question suspects in custody. The police "ought to leave that duty to the magistrate, who alone has the power to reduce to writing what is said by the prisoner".[37] The judgment demonstrates that the acquisition by the police of competence over the interrogation of detained suspects met with a protracted resistance from some members of the judiciary.[38]

In *Gavin* (1885)[39] the accused, while in police custody, made a statement admitting his own guilt and implicating two others. When the others were taken into custody they denied all knowledge of the offence. Subsequently they were confronted with Gavin and his statement was read over to them, whereupon they made incriminatory statements. Smith, J refused to receive Gavin's statement against the two prisoners saying:

> When a prisoner is in custody the police have no right to ask him questions. Reading a statement over, and then saying to him 'What have you to say?' is cross-examining the prisoner and therefore I shut it out. A prisoner's mouth is closed after he is once given in charge, and he ought not to be asked anything. A constable has no more right to ask a question than a judge to cross-examine.... Before the prisoner is charged or is in custody he may be asked what he has to say in explanation or in answer to the charge.[40]

This comment suggests that for Smith, J the protection afforded to suspects against compulsory self-incrimination was not to be infringed by questions put to them by any officer of state interested in the criminal process, including the lesser office of police constable, once the suspect is charged or taken into custody. An element of ambiguity, however, arises in the paradoxical suggestion that a suspect might be properly questioned by the police after he has been charged.[41]

In *Brackenbury* (1893)[42] Day, J expressly dissented from the decision in *Gavin* when he admitted statements made by the accused in answer to police questions which were made prior to the accused being taken into formal custody.[43] This again permits the conclusion that the judiciary did not share a unitary attitude either to the scope and function of the exclusionary rule, or to the role and influence of the police in taking confession statements from suspects.

Thus, in *Thompson* (1893),[44] after having affirmed that it was the duty of the prosecution to show that confessions adduced in evidence were free and voluntary, Cave, J expressed a distrust of confessions supposed to have been the offspring of free will and yet were repudiated by the prisoner at his trial. As he put it:

> It is remarkable that it is of very rare occurrence for evidence of a confession to be given when the proof of the prisoner's guilt is otherwise clear and

satisfactory; but when it is not clear and satisfactory the prisoner is not infrequently alleged to have been seized with a desire born of penitence and remorse, to supplement it with a confession, and this desire again vanishes as soon as he appears in a court of justice.[45]

That Cave, J was critical of any invasion upon the privilege against compulsory self-incrimination and of the police practice of interrogating suspects in custody was confirmed in *Male and Cooper* (1893).[46] In this case a witness for the prosecution stated that she had been told by a police inspector that she had better tell the truth and that if she did not, she would be prosecuted in connection with an illegal operation said to have been performed upon her. Cooper was subsequently arrested under a warrant relating to a similar charge. While being taken into police custody, Cooper was informed of the statement made by the witness. At Cooper's request, the statement was read over to her. Cave, J considered Cooper's reply to be inadmissible on the ground that "the police had no right to ask questions, or to seek to manufacture evidence".[47] The judge observed that it was "quite right" for the police, when taking a person into custody, to charge them "but the prisoner should be previously cautioned, because the very fact of charging induces a prisoner to make a statement and he should have been informed that such a statement may be used against him".[48]

Cave, J seems, therefore, to have considered that while the voluntariness rule presupposes the free will of the suspect, custodial questioning, without a caution, constitutes such an impairment of mental freedom that ensuing statements could not be regarded as voluntary.[49] It may be doubted whether the caution actually had the properties he and other judges ascribed to it.[50] However, his judgment, as his concluding remarks indicate, was also couched in terms intended to discipline the police:

> The law does not allow the judge or jury to put questions in open court to prisoners; and it would be monstrous if the law permitted a police officer to go, without anyone being present to see how the matter was conducted, and put a prisoner through an examination, and then produce the effects of that examination against him. Under these circumstances, a policeman should keep his mouth shut and his ears open. He is not bound to stop a prisoner in making a statement; his duty is to listen and report, but it is quite another matter that he should put questions to prisoners.... It is no business of a policeman to put questions, which may lead a prisoner to give answers on the spur of the

moment, thinking perhaps he may get himself out of a difficulty by telling lies. I do not intend these remarks to apply only to this case.[51]

Russell, CJ, in *Rogers* v. *Hawkin* (1898),[52] felt it necessary to correct any impression that Cave, J might have given to suggest that, as a general proposition of law, a statement made to a policeman by a suspect who has not been previously cautioned and who has not been induced to make that statement by threats or promises, is legally inadmissible.[53] In the opinion of the judge there was "no rule of law excluding statements made under such circumstances, and such a rule would be most mischievous and a hardship upon a falsely accused person. The statement of an innocent person may be most valuable to exculpate him".[54]

Although the observations of Russell, CJ are articulated in terms which appear to display concern for the falsely accused, the import of his remarks implicitly shifts the assessment of a suspect's culpability from the courts to the investigative stage of the prosecution process. Thus, his attempt to circumscribe the interpretation of voluntariness suggested by Cave, J in *Male and Cooper*, and to re-impose a narrow definition of the voluntariness requirement, worked to give legitimacy to the crime control mandate of police investigations.

The criticism of *Male and Cooper* by Russell, CJ illustrates that throughout the nineteenth century some judges felt obliged to counter what may have been perceived as the unorthodox rulings of some of their incorrigible colleagues. Nonetheless, the polarity of judicial opinion respecting the function of the voluntariness rule was a result of views held by individual members of an, as yet, relatively unincorporated and unintegrated judiciary. This in turn led to decisions which suggested that the exclusionary rule, itself posited upon a vaguely defined legal conception of voluntariness, was of questionable applicability to the progressive encroachment of the 'new' police in the prosecution process.

The exclusionary rule was formulated towards the end of the eighteenth century[55] and the leading decision of *Ibrahim* (1914)[56] re-affirmed the narrow legal concept of voluntariness as its underlying rationale. However, from its inception, before the development of modern professional police forces,[57] through to the early twentieth century, the requirement of voluntariness — in spite of that aspect of its historical origins that related to the protection of individual citizens from the power of state organs to compel individuals to incriminate themselves — failed to adequately address the investigative methods of the 'new' police. Consequently, some judges, either in the exercise of their discretion or by extending the voluntariness rule, excluded evidence obtained by what was considered to be unacceptable police practices.[58] Thus, in the case of *Histed* (1898),[59] where the prisoner, held in police custody, was questioned without being cautioned, Hawkins, J instantly rejected the confession evidence, saying:

> It is a matter on which I hold a strong opinion. No one, either policeman or anyone else, has a right to put questions to a prisoner for the purpose of entrapping him into making admissions. A prisoner must be fairly dealt with.... In my opinion, when a prisoner is once taken into custody, a policeman should ask no questions at all without administering previously the usual caution.[60]

As Hawkins, J implied that such questioning could be legitimately conducted if it followed a caution, it may be concluded that by the end of the nineteenth century the police, and police interrogations, had acquired a greater, though perhaps qualified, degree of legitimacy in the eyes of even their strongest judicial opponents.

A note to the case states that when the decisions of *Gavin* (1885)[61] and *Brackenbury* (1893)[62] were subsequently brought to the attention of Hawkins, J he said: "I entirely agree with the ruling of Smith, J in *Reg.* v. *Gavin*. Cross-examination of a prisoner by a policeman should not be permitted, and in my discretion I should exclude evidence obtained in that way. The case I have just tried shows exactly the danger of allowing such evidence to be given."[63] It is noteworthy that Hawkins, J elected to exercise his discretion to exclude the evidence, rather than to attempt to extend that conception of the voluntariness rule, as defined by the leading authority of *Baldry* (1852),[64] which suggested that a judge might exclude confession evidence only when promises or threats had been used to procure it.

This judicial discretion was also employed to exclude technically admissible confession evidence — under the narrowly drawn voluntariness test — in the case of *Knight and Thayre* (1905).[65] A detective had questioned the two prisoners, after cautioning them, for some six hours during which time, the detective admitted, he would not allow Knight to leave the room alone. He also stated that he did not have sufficient evidence for a prosecution at the beginning of the interview, though he did not necessarily intend to obtain a confession. It was shown that after two hours of questioning, Knight began to make "compromising statements" which the prosecution sought to submit in evidence. It was objected that the "protracted cross-examination" brought such pressure to bear on the mind of the accused that his statements could not be regarded as being voluntary. Channell, J in excluding the evidence, appears to have vacillated between whether he should base his decision on the ground that the prolonged questioning had impaired the voluntariness of the statement or to exclude the evidence in the exercise of his discretion. He found that it was "not easy to extract from the cases what is the guiding principle underlying the matter". However, he felt that the authorities indicated that a law enforcement officer "may question persons most likely to able to give him information" whether or not such persons are suspected, provided he has not already determined to take them into custody. Once the officer has decided to charge and take a person into custody, he should not question the prisoner.[66] Channell, J then observed that:

> A magistrate or judge cannot do it, and a police officer certainly has no more right to do so.[67]

The judge accepted the rule that a confession must be shown to have been given voluntarily before it could be received in evidence, though he was not prepared to accept it as a "universal rule" since the admissibility of a confession "must to some extent depend on the facts of the particular case".[68] He then adverted to his discretion to exclude otherwise admissible evidence, saying:

> I am not aware of any distinct rule of evidence that if ... improper questions are asked the answers to them are inadmissible, but there is clear authority for saying that the judge at trial may in his discretion refuse to allow the answer to be given in evidence and in my opinion that is the right course to pursue.[69]

In indicating that the distinction the recent authorities had erected — between the unsanctioned custodial interrogation of suspects as to their guilt and the permissible non-custodial questioning of individuals who might provide information to guide criminal investigations — was so tenuous as to leave the police free to interrogate suspected persons before they had been cautioned, arrested, and taken into formal custody, Channell, J also stated:

> I cannot help thinking that in the case of a person not already a prisoner, or at any rate accused, there must something which might possibly induce him to

make an untrue confession, otherwise it is difficult to see any satisfactory reason for rejecting the evidence.[70]

It seems, therefore, that for Channell, J the judicial discretion to exclude confession evidence was to be activated where technically admissible evidence (that is, evidence not induced by specific promises or threats) was obtained in violation of the proscription against any questioning designed to extract self-incriminatory admissions, irrespective of the location of that questioning.

## Shaping principles and practice

It is clear that many of the decisions from the late eighteenth through to the beginning of the present century conflict with respect to the scope and application of the voluntariness rule, and thus the admissibility of extra-judicial confessions.[71] The contrasting decisions may be understood as indicative of an absence of judicial consensus as to the exclusionary rule's ambit.

As the judicial practice of rejecting confessions when deemed involuntary hardened into a firm rule of law,[72] and as that rule operated throughout the nineteenth century, two competing interpretations of the evidential requirement of voluntariness vied for ascendancy. The two opposing conceptions of voluntariness were brought into particularly sharp focus with the growth of the police practice of obtaining confessions from suspects detained in custody.[73] The two interpretations can be readily distinguished on the basis that one pressed for a broad understanding of voluntariness, while the other inclined towards a narrow interpretation of the concept.

Under the broad interpretation, consideration was to be given to circumstances, beyond the force of threats and promises, which might work to render an extra-judicial confession involuntary. Thus, such factors as the effect on the accused of the inherently compelling pressures of criminal investigations, the strength of mind of the accused and the legality of questions inviting incriminatory replies, were immediately relevant to the crucial issue of whether the mental freedom of the accused to volunteer a confession was impaired.[74] The determination of whether an extra-judicial confession had been made voluntarily was not, therefore, to be limited to the issue of whether specific threats or promises had been employed.[75]

Fry (1938)[76] argues that decisions which suggest a contrary view are founded upon a misrepresentation of *Warickshall* (1783),[77] where it was established that 'a confession forced from the mind by the flattery of hope, or by the torture of fear is rejected'.[78] He maintains that a "heresy" evolved in subsequent cases when the phrase 'flattery of hope' was translated into 'promises' and the phrase 'torture of fear' was interpreted as referring to 'threats'. As a result, extra-judicial confessions came to be viewed, by some judges, as voluntary unless there was evidence to suggest that they had been elicited by the action of express threats or promises.[79]

It may be objected that the source of the heresy, which Fry suggests evolved to challenge the "pristine purity" of the voluntariness rule,[80] can be found within the *Warickshall* ruling.[81] The point is that the case failed to make clear that other factors, including the extra-judicial questioning of suspects by persons in authority, may engender the flattery of hope or the torture of fear so as to render a confession involuntary.[82] This failure enabled the proponents of a narrow voluntariness rule to construe what is generally agreed to be the first case to lay down the contours of the exclusionary rule[83] as an authority for the proposition that where threats or promises are not used to obtain extra-judicial confessions, the evidence must be treated as being voluntary and, therefore, admissible.

Implicit in the narrow construction of the test is the assumption that a person in a position of authority, such as a police officer, must act in some overt way to induce an involuntary confession.[84] This assumption worked to support the contention that an assessment of whether influences other than patent threats or promises had acted to impair the mental freedom of the accused, could not be legitimately made within the strict terms of the voluntariness rule as outlined by the majority judges in *Johnston* (1864).[85] It also meant that the prohibition against the interrogation of suspects by the police could be made subsidiary to the overriding question of whether any resulting confession had been obtained in breach of the voluntariness rule.

However, the case law indicates that some judges continued to give the concept of voluntariness an extended meaning.[86] Increasingly, as the narrow interpretation of voluntariness came into prominence,[87] these judges marked their disapproval of police interrogations by exercising their discretion in favour of excluding otherwise admissible confession evidence.[88] This is not to suggest that these judges were actuated by "absurd or dangerous sentimentalities",[89] rather their broad yet legalistic interpretation of the voluntariness rule drew upon the principle, enshrined in the maxim *nemo tenetur prodere seipsum*, that no one should be compelled to incriminate himself.[90] It follows from this that no confession may be considered 'free and voluntary' if the will of the accused to remain silent has been in any way overborne.[91]

That the privilege against compulsory self-incrimination necessarily extended beyond judicial proceedings to the extra-judicial level of the criminal justice process, as a safeguard against involuntary and unreliable confessions, was acknowledged by Wigmore (1961) when he explained that:

> The real objection is that any system of administration which permits the prosecution to trust habitually to compulsory self-disclosure as a source of proof must itself suffer morally thereby. The inclination develops to rely mainly upon such evidence, and to be satisfied with an incomplete investigation of the other sources. The exercise of the power to extract answers begets a forgetfulness of the just limitations of that power. The simple and peaceful process of questioning breeds readiness to resort to bullying and to physical force and torture. If there is a right to an answer, there soon seems to be a right to the expected answer — that is, to a confession of guilt. Thus the legitimate use grows into the unjust abuse; ultimately the innocent are jeopardized by the encroachments of a bad system.[92]

The broad construction some judges were prepared to place upon the voluntariness rule — a construction which suggested threats and promises were but illustrations of the kinds of inducement which would result in the exclusion of extra-judicial confessions — would appear to rest upon similar concerns. Nevertheless, it was the narrow interpretation of the voluntariness rule which, by the beginning of the present century, prevailed.[93] This interpretation of the evidential rule inclined to the position that the questioning of suspects by the police could not, without some evidence of threats or promises having been held out, lead to the exclusion confession evidence on the ground that it had been made involuntarily.[94] It was as a consequence of this approach to the voluntariness rule that a dissonance between the rhetoric of the law and the practice of the law emerged.

The rhetoric of the law pursuant to the exclusionary rule suggests a postulate of free will[95] and appears to require a judicial assessment of all potentially coercive factors attending the pre-trial phase of the criminal justice process. In practice, however, the concept of voluntariness, as understood by "the balance of decided authority",[96] shifted from one which laid stress upon a pre-trial articulation of the privilege against compulsory self-incrimination (the right to silence) as the fundamental consideration against which the voluntariness of a confession should be tested,[97] to one which provided a niche in which the police practice of interrogating suspects in custody could develop during the twentieth century.

## Notes

[1] *Johnston* (1864) 15 ICLR 60.
[2] See *Ibrahim* (1914) AC 599, *per* Lord Sumner, pp. 609-14. See also Leigh, 1974, p. 144.
[3] For two examples, see *Jarvis* (1867) 10 Cox C.C. 574 and *Regan* (1867) 17 LT 325.
[4] See *Warickshall* (1783) 1 Leach. 263, see pp. 263-4; 3 Wigmore, 1970, p. 246; Williams, 1983, pp. 224, 251; Mirfield, 1985, pp. 48, 61-5.
[5] *Treatise on the Law of Evidence*, 4th edn., 1864, pp. 754-5.
[6] *Reason* (1872) 12 Cox C.C. 228.
[7] *Ibid.*
[8] See *Booth and Jones* (1910) 5 Cr.App.R. 177, where it is suggested that the issue as to what may constitute custody is a question for the judge.
[9] *Yeovil Murder Case* (1877) 41 JP 187.
[10] *Ibid.*
[11] *Ibid.*
[12] See, for example, *Brackenbury* (1893) 17 Cox C.C. 628; *Miller* (1895) 18 Cox C.C. 54; *Hirst* (1896) 18 Cox C.C. 374; 60 JP 491; *Rogers* v. *Hawken* (1898) 19 Cox C.C. 122; 62 JP 279; *Best* (1909) 1 KB 692; 25 TLR 280; *Booth and Jones* (1910) 74 JP 475; 5 Cr.App.R. 177; and *Lewis* v. *Harris* (1913) 30 LTR 109; 78 JP 68.
[13] *Miller* (1895) 18 Cox C.C. 54.
[14] *Ibid.*, p. 55. See also *Hirst* (1896) 18 Cox C.C. 374.
[15] *Rogers* v. *Hawkin* (1898) 62 JP 279.
[16] *Ibid.*
[17] See Brownlie, 1960, pp. 301-2.
[18] See *Knight and Thayre* (1905) 20 Cox C.C. 711.
[19] *Booth and Jones* (1910) 5 Cr.App.R. 177.
[20] Formally constituted under the Criminal Appeal Act, s. 1 (1907), the Court of Criminal Appeal superseded the Court for Crown Cases Reserved.
[21] *Booth and Jones* (1910) 5 Cr.App.R. 177, p. 179.
[22] *Ibid.*, p. 180.
[23] *Ibid.*
[24] This view seems to have been adopted by Darling, J himself in *Lewis* v. *Harris* (1913) 30 LTR 109, p. 110, where the judge states that it 'had never been laid down that a constable was bound to caution every one to whom he spoke.... It

## Interrogation and Confession

was another matter if a constable had made up his mind to take the person into custody; then he should give the caution. And if this rule were infringed the judge might reject the evidence'.

[25] This unnamed case is recorded in 76 JP, 1912, p. 187.
[26] Ibid.
[27] Ibid.
[28] Ibid.
[29] Indictable Offences Act, 1848, s. 18.
[30] See *Ibrahim* (1914) AC 599, pp. 609-14.
[31] Rothblat and Rothblat, 1960, pp. 63-4.
[32] Cross, 1970, p. 67; Neasey, 1977 p. 360.
[33] See *Ibrahim* (1914) AC 599, pp. 611-12; Oaks, 1970, p. 722; Mirfield, 1985, pp. 70-4.
[34] *Bodkin* (1863) 9 Cox C.C. 403.
[35] Ibid.
[36] MacDonald and Hart, 1947, pp. 825-6.
[37] *Bodkin* (1863) 9 Cox C.C. 403.
[38] See also *Hassett* (1861) 8 Cox C.C. 511.
[39] *Gavin* (1885) 15 Cox C.C. 656.
[40] Ibid., p. 657.
[41] See *Wong Chiu Kwai* (1909) 3 HKLR 89, pp. 94-5. A note to the case report of *Gavin* observes that the decision conflicts with leading authorities on the reception of confessions obtained in answer to questions. It points out that on those authorities, only inducements relating to the immediate charge could prevent a confession from being admitted in evidence against its author. However, the note is clear in its conclusion that 'the judges are by no means unanimous in their decisions and all of them express disapproval of the practice while admitting its technical accuracy' (*Gavin* (1885) 15 Cox C.C. 656, p. 657). In this regard see, for example, *Thornton* (1824) 1 Moo. 27; *Wild* (1835) 1 Moo. 452; *Kerr* (1837) 8 C. & P. 177. The note also counsels that *Gavin* 'must be taken to be a considered opinion, as affording guidance for the future' (*Gavin* (1885) *ibid*). That guidance was, presumably, intended to inform the police of what the courts regarded as the border between acceptable and improper questioning and to give notice of a judicial preparedness to reinforce that guidance by excluding evidence obtained in contravention of it.
[42] *Brackenbury* (1893) 17 Cox C.C. 628.
[43] See also *Best* (1909) 1 KB 692, where the contention that prisoners should not be questioned in custody was rejected by Alverstone, CJ, sitting with Channell and Walton, JJ, who suggested that a 'prisoner is *entitled* to give an explanation' (my emphasis) and that such questioning might afford the prisoner an opportunity to do so. The judges felt that *Gavin* was 'not a good decision' and that its statement of the law was too wide.
[44] *Thompson* (1893) 17 Cox C.C. 641.

45 *Ibid.*, p. 674.
46 *Male and Cooper* (1893) 17 Cox C.C. 689. See also the judgment of Cave, J in *Morgan* (1895) 59 JP 827.
47 *Male and Cooper* (1893) *ibid.*, p. 690.
48 *Ibid.*
49 Compare the ruling of Hawkins, J in *Miller* (1895) 18 Cox C.C. 54, p. 55.
50 See Brownlie, 1960, p. 307; Williams, G., 1961, p. 50.
51 *Male and Cooper* (1893) 17 Cox C.C. 689, p. 690.
52 *Rogers* v. *Hawken* (1898) 62 JP 279.
53 *Ibid.*, p. 280.
54 *Ibid*; 67 LJQB 526, p. 527.
55 See *White's Case* (1741) 17 How. St. Tr. 1079; *Rudd* (1775) 1 Leach. 115; *Warickshall* (1783) 1 Leach. 263; *Cass* (1784) 1 Leach. 293.
56 *Ibrahim* (1914) AC 599.
57 See Neasey, (1977, p. 362) who argues that by as late as '1832 the police force as we know it was in swaddling clothes'.
58 See Neasey, *ibid.*, who asserts that even after '120 years or so of experience of questioning of suspects by the police [the common law has not been able] in its pragmatic way to produce any coherent body of law which attempts to regulate police investigatory power, but only a formless and somewhat imprecise combination of rules'.
59 *Histed* (1898) 19 Cox C.C. 16.
60 *Ibid.*, p. 17.
61 16 Cox C.C. 656.
62 17 Cox C.C. 628, which expressly dissented from *Gavin*.
63 *Histed* (1898) 19 Cox C.C. 16, p. 17.
64 *Baldry* (1852) 2 Den. 430, p. 443.
65 *Knight and Thayre* (1905) 20 Cox C.C. 711.
66 *Ibid.*, p. 713.
67 *Ibid.*
68 *Ibid.*
69 *Ibid.*
70 *Ibid.*, pp. 713-4. See also *Wong Chiu Kwai* (1908) 3 HKLR 89.
71 *Wong Chiu Kwai* (1908) 3 HKLR 89, *per* Alverstone, LCJ and Compertz, J.
72 See *Rudd* (1775) 1 Leach 115; *Warickshall* (1783) 1 Leach 263; *Thompson* (1783) 1 Leach 291; and *Cass* (1784) 1 Leach 263.
73 *Ibrahim* (1914) AC 599, *per* Lord Sumner, p. 610.
74 *Green* (1832) 5 Car. & P 312, *per* Gurney, B. See also *Morton* (1843) 2 M & Rob. 514, p. 515, *per* Coleridge CJ: 'The prisoner's mind must be left entirely free'; *Garbet* (1847) 1 Den. 236, p. 257 where Alderson, B suggested that evidence of an accused's confession must be excluded where 'his liberty of refusing to say anything on the subject has been infringed'. Also see *Baldry*

122    *Interrogation and Confession*

(1852) 2 Den. 430, p. 442, *per* Pollock, CB: 'it is left to the prisoner a matter of perfect indifference whether he should open his mouth or not'. Park, B in the same case (*ibid.,* p. 444) stated that 'in order to render a confession admissible in evidence it must be perfectly voluntary'. It should be noted that for some time it was felt that to caution a suspect that anything he or she might 'freely' say whilst *would* be used in evidence, raised the possibility of the suspect's mind being 'improperly induced'. See *Wild* (1835) 1 Moo. 452, p. 455; *Arnold* (1838) 8 Car. & P. 621. See also *Morton* (1843) 2 M & Rob. 514, p. 515 and *Furley* (1844) 1 Cox C.C. 76. See also *Baldry* (1852) 2 Den. 430, particularly the arguments of counsel for the prisoner, and *Reason* (1872) 12 Cox C.C. 228, p. 229, *per* Keating, J.

[75] See, for example, *Moore* (1852) 2 Den. 522, p. 527, *per* Park, B: 'Perhaps it would have been better to have held (when it was determined that the Judge was to decide whether the confession was voluntary), that in all cases he was to decide that point upon his own view of all the circumstances, including the nature of the threat or inducement, and the character of the person holding it out.... But a rule has been laid down in different precedents by which we are bound, and that is, that if the threat or inducement is held out actually or constructively by a person in authority, [the confession] cannot be received'.

[76] Fry, 1938, p. 429.

[77] *Warickshall* (1783) 1 Leach. 263.

[78] *Ibid.*, p. 264.

[79] Fry, 1938, p. 429. See, for example, *Thornton* (1824) 1 Moo. 27, p. 28; *Spilsbury* (1835) 7 Car. & P 187, p. 188, *per* Coleridge, J: 'to render a confession inadmissible, it must either be obtained by hope or fear'; *Scott* (1856) 1 D. & B. 47, p. 58, *per* Campbell, LCJ: 'It is a trite maxim that the confession of a crime, to be admissible against the party confessing, must be voluntary; but this only means that it shall not be induced by improper threats or promises'; *Jarvis* (1867) 10 Cox C.C. 574, p. 576, *per* Kelly, CB: 'we ought to see that no one is induced, either by a threat or a promise, to say anything of a incriminatory character against himself'. See also *Regan* (1867) 17 LT 325 and *Miller* (1895) 18 Cox C.C. 54, p. 55.

[80] Fry, 1938, p. 429.

[81] It is noteworthy that while the court in *Warickshall* (1783) 1 Leach 263, used language that appears to restrict the classification of improper inducements to threats and promises, in *Thompson* (1783) 1 Leach 291, Hotham, B suggested that the exclusionary rule required judges to reject confessions 'unless they appear to have been made voluntarily and without *any* inducement'(p. 293, my emphasis). See also *Moore* (1852) 2 Den. 522, pp. 526-7, *per* Park, B.

[82] See, for instance, *Wilson* (1817) Holt. 597; *Tool* (1856) 7 Cox C.C. 244, *per* Richards, B: 'From the mere circumstances of being in custody, the prisoner [is] not on equal terms with her interrogator'; *Johnston* (1864) 15 ICLR 60, p. 90, *per* O'Brien, J: 'The very fact of ... questions being put ... conveys to the

prisoner's mind the idea of some obligation ... to answer them, and deprives the statement of that voluntary character which is essential to admissibility'. *Per* Hayes, J (*ibid.*, p. 80): 'the prisoner should have free will and power to speak, or refrain from speaking ... his will should not be warped by any unfair, dishonest, or fraudulent practices, to induce a confession'. See also *Male and Cooper* (1893) 17 Cox C.C. 689, p. 690, *per* Cave, J: 'the very fact of charging induces a prisoner to make a statement'.

[83] Kaufman, 1979, p. 18.
[84] Ratushny, 1979, p. 454.
[85] 15 ICLR 60. See, for example, *Reason* (1872) 12 Cox C.C. 228, p. 228 where Keating, J states that: 'The real question is whether there has been any threat or promise of such a nature that the prisoner would be likely to tell an untruth'. See also *Ibrahim* (1914) AC 599, p. 611.
[86] See *Gavin* (1885) 15 Cox C.C. 656; *Male and Cooper* (1893) 17 Cox C.C. 689; *Histed* (1898) 19 Cox C.C. 16; *Wong Chiu Kwai* (1908) 3 HKLR 89, p. 100.
[87] See *Brackenbury* (1893) 17 Cox C.C. 628; *Rogers v. Hawken* (1898) 19 Cox C.C. 122; *Booth and Jones* (1910) 74 JP 475; *Ibrahim* (1914) AC 599.
[88] See, for example, *Histed* (1898) 19 Cox C.C. 16; *Knight and Thayre* (1905) 20 Cox C.C. 711. See also *Ibrahim* (1914) AC 599, p. 614, *per* Lord Sumner: 'Many judges, in their discretion, exclude such evidence, for they fear that nothing less than the exclusion of all such statements can prevent improper questioning of prisoners by removing the inducement to resort to it'.
[89] 3 Wigmore, 1970, pp. 298-301.
[90] The point being that the rule excluding involuntary confessions 'grew out of' and extends the privilege against compulsory self-incrimination to the pre-trial phase of the criminal process (Levy, 1968, p. 495). See also Lidstone and Early, 1982, p. 501.
[91] See Fry, 1938, p. 431; *Gavin* (1885) 15 Cox C.C. 656; *Male and Cooper* (1893) 17 Cox C.C. 698; *Thompson* (1893) 2 QB 12; 17 Cox C.C. 641; *Histed* (1898) 19 Cox C.C. 16; *Knight and Thayre* (1905) 20 Cox C.C. 711; *Wong Chiu Kwai* (1908) 3 HKLR 89.
[92] 8 Wigmore, 1961, p. 296, n. 1. Wigmore's comment would seem to militate against his own contention that the exclusionary rule and the privilege are separate and independent in both origin and function (8 Wigmore, 1961, pp. 400-2; 3 Wigmore, 1970, p. 338). For the view that these principles are indissolubly linked, see McCormick, 1938, pp. 452-5; Levy, 1968, pp. 327-8, 495-7.
[93] See *Ibrahim* (1914) AC 599, pp. 609-14.
[94] 3 Wigmore, 1970, p. 502; *Johnston* (1864) 15 ICLR 60, pp. 84-5, *per* Hayes, J; *Jarvis* (1867) 10 Cox C.C. 574, p. 576; *Regan* (1867) 17 LT 325; *Brackenbury* (1893) 17 Cox C.C. 628; *Hirst* (1896) 18 Cox C.C. 374; *Rogers v. Hawken*

(1898) 19 Cox C.C. 122; *Booth and Jones* (1910) 5 Cr.App.R. 177. See also *Ibrahim* (1914) AC 599, p. 609, *per* Lord Sumner.

[95] See *Wilson* (1817) Holt. 597, *per* Richards, LCB; *Morton* (1843) 2 M & Rob. 514, p. 515, *per* Coleridge, CJ; *Pettit* (1850) 4 Cox C.C. 164, p. 165, *per* Wild, CJ; *Baldry* (1852) 2 Den. 430, p. 446, *per* Campbell, LCJ; *Mick* (1863) 3 F & F 322, *per* Mellor, J; *Jarvis* (1867) 10 Cox C.C. 574, p. 576, *per* Kelly, CB; *Histed* (1898) 19 Cox C.C. 16, p. 17, *per* Hawkins, J. See also Grano, 1979, p. 879.

[96] *Ibrahim* (1914) AC 599, p. 614, *per* Lord Sumner.

[97] See, for example, *Green* (1832) 5 Car. & P 312, *per* Gurney, B; *Johnston* (1864) 15 ICLR 60, p. 83, *per* Hayes, J; *Jarvis* (1864) 10 Cox C.C. 574, p. 576, *per* Kelly, CB; *Gavin* (1885) 15 Cox C.C. 656, p. 657, *per* Smith, J; *Histed* (1898) 19 Cox C.C. 16, p. 17, *per* Hawkins, J.

# 7  Genesis of the Judges' Rules

It has been shown that judges were by no means unanimous in their decisions on the exclusionary rule's purview, or on the question of whether the interrogation of suspects by the police was itself a sufficient ground to justify excluding extra-judicial confessions. That said, the general principle to emerge from the nineteenth-century case law is that the courts would not receive any confession that appeared untrustworthy and a confession would be considered as such if it had been induced by the flattery of hope or by the torture of fear.[1]

Elliott (1987) accepts that, with the emergence of the exclusionary rule and its attendant requirement of voluntariness, confessions were rejected when of doubtful reliability.[2] He adds, however, that by the end of the nineteenth century "it became recognised that the real reason was to restrain the activities of the police in the questioning of suspects in custody".[3] This observation would appear to gain support from the consideration that while the rhetoric of the exclusionary rule indicates a concern for the reliability of confession evidence, in practice, the rule was incapable of ensuring reliable confessions were received and untrustworthy confessions excluded.[4]

Despite this, the exclusionary rule afforded judges a limited means with which to supervise the largely unregulated and unspecified investigatory powers of the 'new' police. That some judges were rather more concerned than others to scrutinise police practices is demonstrated in a number of rulings from the period.[5] As a consequence, the attitude of the judiciary in regard to the propriety of questioning suspects in custody, the increasing use of police stations for interrogations,[6] the role of the caution and the ambit of the exclusionary rule,[7] lacked uniformity, clarity and precision.[8]

In 1882, however, an attempt was made to provide the police with authoritative guidance as to their investigatory powers and the position they could expect the courts to adopt in respect of confession evidence obtained in the exercise of that power. This guidance was delivered by Lord Brampton,[9] who stated that:

there is no objection to you making enquiries of, or putting questions to, any person from whom you think you can obtain useful information. It is your duty to discover the criminal if you can, and to do this you must make such inquiries; and in the course of them should you chance to interrogate and to receive answers from a man who turns out to be the criminal himself, and who inculpates himself by these answers, they are nevertheless admissible in evidence, and may be used against him.

By this part of his advice to the police Lord Brampton suggests the courts would receive confessions obtained by the police through their questioning of individuals not accused of crime. The statement appears to accord with the common law position as to the police questioning of individuals who have not been arrested or detained in custody. However, it fails to make clear that, also under the common law, the police could not oblige an individual to respond to their questions or to otherwise assist them in their investigations.[10] The address continues, however, by drawing a distinction between persons at liberty and those detained in police custody. It states that:

When ... a constable has a warrant to arrest, or is about to arrest a person on his own authority, or has a person in custody for a crime, it is wrong to question such person touching the crime of which he is accused. Neither judge magistrate nor juryman, can interrogate an accused person — unless he tenders himself as a witness — or require him to answer questions tending to incriminate himself. Much less, then, ought a constable to do so whose duty as regards that person is simply to arrest and detain him in safe custody.... For a constable to press any accused person to say anything with reference to the crime of which he is accused is very wrong.

The guidance points out that an extra-judicial confession, when made in consequence of any promise or threat, cannot be used against the person making it. It concludes:

There is, however, no objection to a constable listening to any mere voluntary statement which the prisoner desires to make, and repeating such statement in evidence; nor is there any objection to his repeating in evidence any conversation he may have heard between the prisoner and any other person. But he ought not, by anything he says or does, to invite or encourage an accused person to make any statement without first cautioning him.... Perhaps the best maxim for a constable to bear in mind with respect to an accused person is, 'keep your eyes and your ears open, and your mouth shut.' ... Never act unfairly to a prisoner by coaxing him by word or conduct to divulge anything. If you do, you will assuredly be severely handled at the trial, and it is not unlikely that your evidence will be disbelieved.

Three years after its appearance in a leading manual directed to the police and their duties, the approach advocated by Lord Brampton was emphatically endorsed by Smith, J in *Gavin* (1885).[11] However, the decision in *Best* (1909),[12] disapproving of *Gavin*, suggests other judges felt it necessary to counter the assumption that any statement made in reply to questions put by persons in authority such as police officers should *ipso facto* be deemed involuntary and therefore inadmissible.

Judicial views, however, remained inconsistent and contradictory. Although it seems to have been accepted that the police could ask questions of a person not in custody,[13] some judges continued to condemn the questioning of suspects detained in custody.[14] Furthermore, it was felt that the caution — originally designed to inform suspects of their legal right to remain silent — had, under the police, become a device with which "to make it easy and simple for the prosecution to discharge the burden of proving that the confession was voluntary".[15]

It was against this background of conflicting judicial authorities that the Chief Constable of Birmingham wrote, in 1906, to the Lord Chief Justice, Lord Alverstone, requesting guidance respecting the taking of statements from individuals by the police.[16] Pursuant to this correspondence, and at the request of the Home Secretary,[17] further directions for the guidance of the police were issued in 1912 in the form of four principles which became known as the Judges' Rules.[18]

The Rules were not widely disseminated and the outbreak of war in 1914 further postponed their subjection to critical evaluation.[19] In 1918, however, in two decisions heard before the then recently established Court of Criminal Appeal,[20] the Judges' Rules were considered judicially for the first time.[21] Later in the same year the four 1912 Rules were increased to nine.[22] In 1930, after the Royal Commission on Police Powers and Procedure revealed differences of opinion and practice among police officers,[23] an attempt was made to clarify the Rules through a Home Office circular, issued with the approval of the judges.[24] Aside from the appearance of another circular in 1947, directed to supplementary rules of procedure,[25] the Judges' Rules stood unaltered until they were revised in

1964.[26] In 1986 this version was superseded by the coming into force of the 1984 Police and Criminal Evidence Act.

**The 1912 and 1918 Judges' Rules**

For McCormick (1946), the Judges' Rules represented a "strange extension of the judicial function".[27] Certainly, the Rules were not the product of any *ratio decidendi* and cannot be described as *obiter dicta*.[28] Further, as guidance for police officers — drawn up extra-judicially by a convocation of senior judges, with the apparently private cooperation of the executive and without the express participation of Parliament[29] — the Rules were not intended to be legislative in either form or effect, to be enforceable in court or, indeed, to have the force of law.[30]

In terms recalling the advice written by Lord Brampton, the Rules constituted the considered view of senior members of the judiciary respecting the overriding common law requirement that extra-judicial statements, to be received in evidence against accused persons, must be shown by the prosecution to have been made 'voluntarily'.[31] When the Rules were framed the prevailing view of the exclusionary rule held that, irrespective of the administration of a caution, whether a confession was obtained under custodial interrogation or not it could be excluded only if threats or promises were held out to induce an otherwise voluntary confession.[32] Although this view of voluntariness conflicted with the broad view that had in the preceding century been espoused by other judges,[33] it nevertheless reflected the balance of common law authority.[34]

While the case law, as it obtained at the beginning of the present century, was "still unsettled",[35] it seems clear that the Rules were intended to reflect common law rulings which, on the one hand, did not prohibit the police from asking questions of any person not yet charged,[36] or taken into custody,[37] and, on the other, made clear that once a person was in custody, the police had no authority to interrogate him.[38]

In embracing the common law requirement of voluntariness, as understood by the judges of the Kings' Bench,[39] the Rules also recognised a judicial discretion to exclude statements obtained by methods deemed "contrary to the spirit of the rules".[40] This would suggest that trial judges were afforded two closely related grounds upon which to exercise a discretion to exclude. The first, derived from the late nineteenth century judicial practice of excluding confessional statements in spite of their being strictly admissible under the narrow voluntariness test. The second, from the Rules themselves which implied that a failure to comply with them was of itself a legitimate ground upon which the discretion to exclude could be invoked.[41]

However, it seems that during the course of the present century these two separate but associated grounds for the exclusion of 'voluntary' confessions were conflated into one which existed independently of the Rules. Thus, while the Rules, in either their original or amended form, did not precisely determine the criteria upon which the judicial discretion should be exercised,[42] a number of rulings made clear that the discretion to reject admissible evidence would be invoked, not on the basis of a breach of the Rules, but only if it were obtained by improper or unfair means or if its prejudicial effect outweighed its probative value.[43]

Indeed, only six years after the formulation of the Rules, the Court of Criminal Appeal, in *Voisin* (1918),[44] established that a failure to observe the Rules would not *ipso facto* render any statements obtained inadmissible or necessarily provoke a judge to exercise his discretion to exclude. The appellant had been requested to go to a police station. Detained in custody, he was asked questions in connection with the murder of a woman whose body had been found in a parcel with the words 'Bladie Belgiam' written upon it. The appellant had not been cautioned. He was asked to write the words 'Bloody Belgian' to which he wrote the words 'Bladie Belgiam'. The Court of Appeal ruled that:

> It cannot be said, as a matter of law, that the absence of a caution makes the statement inadmissible.... the appellant wrote these words quite voluntarily. The mere facts that they were police officers, or that the words were written at their request, or that he being detained ... do not make the writing inadmissible in evidence. They do not tend to ... explain the resemblance between this handwriting and that on the label or account for the same mis-spellings.... There was nothing in the nature of a 'trap' or the 'manufacture' of evidence ... the police, though they were detaining the appellant in custody for inquiries, had not then decided to charge him with this crime....
>
> It is desirable in the interests of the community that investigations into crimes should not be cramped.... Even if we disagreed with the mode in which the judge had ... exercised his discretion, which we do not, we should not be entitled to overrule his decision on appeal. This would be evidence admissible in law, unless it could be fairly inferred from other circumstances that it was not voluntary.[45]

In failing to criticise the behaviour of the police, the effect of this decision was to sanction custodial interrogations and, indeed, the practice of detaining persons for the purpose of conducting interrogations. It therefore revealed the Judges' Rules to be ineffectual as a limitation on police powers.

The case of *Cook* (1918),[46] also heard before the Court of Criminal Appeal, is a further illustration of the senior judges' attitude at the early part of the present century with respect to the meaning of 'voluntariness', to the non-observance of the Rules by the police and to the utility of police questioning to the interests of crime control. In this case it was argued for the appellant that once the trial judge had, at the request of counsel for the defendant, excluded the statement made under police questions, that judge should not, in summing up to the jury, have made comments adverse to the interests of the accused concerning the excluded statement. Giving the judgment of the Court Darling, J cited *Voisin* with approval and in dismissing the appeal added:

> It would be a lamentable thing if the police were not allowed to make inquiries, and if statements made by prisoners were excluded because of a shadowy notion that if the prisoners were left to themselves they would not have made them.[47]

It is not clear whether the statement the appellant had made to the police had been excluded in the exercise of the discretion of the trial judge or on the ground that it was made involuntarily. Nevertheless, Darling, J strongly implied that the statement had been wrongly rejected.[48]

For Neasey (1969), it was the tendency of the courts, towards the end of the nineteenth century, to express the voluntariness rule in restricted terms that was largely responsible for the development both of the pre-Judges' Rules discretion to exclude 'voluntary' statements and the Rules themselves.[49] Prior to the articulation of the Rules there had been a marked division of judicial opinion as to the admissibility of statements obtained under extra-judicial questioning, whether or not explicit threats or promises had been used. As the restricted conception of voluntariness came into prominence, so the judicial expedient of broadening the application of the voluntariness test declined. Following this development, however, the practice of using the judicial discretion to exclude 'voluntary' and therefore admissible evidence emerged to supplement the narrowly-drawn exclusionary rule. The aim was to meet the inability of the exclusionary rule, in the face of the investigatory practices employed by the 'new' police, to ensure confessions were indeed voluntary.[50] As Lord Sumner, in *Ibrahim* (1914), remarked:

> When judges excluded such evidence, it was rather explained by their observations on the duties of policemen than justified by their reliance on rules of law.[51]

Here Lord Sumner appears to accept that some judges considered the exclusionary rule to be expressed too narrowly to be capable of proscribing coercive methods employed by the police falling short of direct threats or promises. Nevertheless, it is clear that outside of the attenuated though nonetheless mandatory exclusionary rule outlined by Lord Sumner, and outside the residual discretion to exclude, there were no formal sanctions against improper custodial questioning or the use of coercive methods to procure confessions. A policeman who failed to observe the Rules did not commit an offence, either civil or criminal, punishable by the courts.[52] The quasi-legal status of the Rules as unenforceable 'advice' to the police, served — as a result of their ambiguous and contradictory provisions — both to legitimate the practice and obscure the origins of the police power to interrogate suspects in custody.

By their terms the Rules were intended to place restraints on police inquiries into crime once the accusatory stage of the prosecution process had arrived. Prior to this stage an officer could address questions to 'any person or persons whether suspected or not' from whom he believed useful information could be obtained.[53] The Rules implied that on the arrival of the accusatory stage, the police were to issue the usual caution and refrain from questioning suspects because it would be 'unfair' to interrogate a suspect after this point.[54] However, the Rules were ambiguous as to whether the entrance of the accusatory stage coincided with the suspect being arrested, being taken into formal custody, or his being charged.[55] Indeed, in contradiction to the suggestion that custodial interrogations offended against the common law implicitly incorporated in the Rules, Rules 2 and 3, when read together, carried the clear implication that police constables enjoyed a discretion to determine when the restrictions contemplated by the Rules should operate.[56]

The Rules effectively "left to the sense of fairness of the police officer"[57] the point at which individuals became accused persons to be cautioned against incriminating themselves and implied that custodial questioning was permissible provided it was preceded by the caution. This construction not only appears to conflict with the common law position as described by Avory, J in *Winkle* (1911),[58] it is also inconsistent with Rule 7, which states that a prisoner "must not be cross-examined" and that "no questions should be put to him".

The piecemeal nature of the Rules enabled the police to postpone the decision to charge where it was felt that to do otherwise would hinder their investigations.[59] This meant that the police could continue questioning suspects until they had "not merely sufficient evidence for making an arrest, but sufficient evidence for securing a conviction".[60] It also meant that even if judges were prepared to discipline the police by excluding evidence obtained in violation of the Rules, the police would continue to question suspects because the practice "would still offer substantial advantages to the police in the enforcement of the law".[61] This is supported by the consideration that should a full confession of guilt prove forthcoming from questioning conducted in contravention of the Rules, the police could attempt to persuade the author to plead guilty at his trial.[62] Not only would this preclude any judicial inquiry into possible breaches of the Rules, it would also avoid an assessment of the confession's 'voluntariness' and render the trial itself unnecessary, leaving prosecutions to proceed to conviction. As the Report of the 1929 Royal Commission pointed out:

> the effect of a plea of guilty is to relieve the Police of the task of proving the case, when their evidence may be weak or incomplete.[63]

Furthermore, were the accused to plead not guilty, a custodial confession to the police might provide 'leads' for the police to pursue in order to secure other evidence, even though the confession itself may be rejected by the court at trial. It is, therefore, difficult to counter the contention that it was 'unrealistic' to suppose that the police would refrain from questioning persons detained in custody merely because there was some chance that they would be prevented from making direct use of any confessions obtained by the sanction of exclusion.[64]

Historically, there had been a general assumption that arrests would not be made until criminal investigations were complete. Arrests were ordinarily made for the purpose of accusation or charge, so that invariably arrests coincided with charge and signalled the end of the investigatory and the beginning of the accusatory or judicial stage.[65] Charged to direct investigations, to manage prosecutions and having the authority to issue warrants for the apprehension of suspects, the justice of the peace had been the central figure in the pre-trial process.[66] The arrestee would be brought, without delay,[67] before the justice, typically by subordinate officers such as parish constables or watchmen, for examination in the inquisitorial manner directed by the Marian statutes.[68]

The rise of the 'new' professionalised police in the early part of the nineteenth century altered this pattern. At the outset the police were instituted as a preventive body and the function of establishing a *prima facie* case against a suspected person remained within the province of the justices. However, investigative activities became incompatible with the increasingly judicial status and function of the magistracy as police forces became established.

The Indictable Offences Act 1848 was designed to regulate the taking of statements from suspects during preliminary hearings before justices. It formally extended the privilege against compulsory self-incrimination — which had brought the judicial interrogation of prisoners to an end — from trials before the judges to preliminary examinations before magistrates.[69] The statute, however, did not bring the duties of the new police directly within its ambit. The procurement of extra-judicial statements from accused persons by the police was left to the judicially-evolved evidential requirement that such statements be given voluntarily.

In order to facilitate the reception in evidence of confessions alleged to have been voluntarily made, the police adopted the caution — developed by magistrates and made binding upon them by the 1848 Act[70] — as a means of satisfying the courts that the accused was informed that he was under no obligation to make a statement or to accuse himself.[71] Nonetheless, by about this time the police had become the initiators of criminal investigations. As such, the police could arrest suspects; detain them at police stations; accuse and charge them; determine the nature of the charge; decide when to charge; release or bail suspects; construct the case against the suspect; and prosecute the case to conviction.[72] In the context of the acquisition of extra-judicial confessions, judicial opposition to the role the police had acquired expressed itself in the assertion that as the judiciary and magistracy were prohibited from putting questions to accused persons, so too were lesser officers of the law.[73] As Channell, J pointed out to police officers:

> You are entitled to ask questions for your information, as to whether you will charge the man, but the moment you have decided to charge him and

practically get him into custody, then in as much as the judge even can't ask a question or a magistrate, it is ridiculous to suppose that a policeman can.[74]

This attitude was consistent with a concern that to permit persons to be interrogated in custody, without the presence of an independent observer, would be to undermine their privilege against self-incrimination. To a limited extent, the Judges' Rules incorporate this conception of the criminal process in their apparent recognition that the police might question persons in order to determine whether to charge, provided such persons were not in custody.[75] However, the Rules do not define what is meant by 'custody'.

As Lidstone and Early (1982) suggest, the Rules were posited on a "naive view of the investigation of crime", one which failed to "appreciate the effectiveness" of police interrogations.[76] Furthermore, it is a view that appears not to recognise that the logic of the adversarial prosecution process is such that the police see custodial interrogations as a legitimate means to effectively discharge their mandate of gathering evidence to prove the guilt of persons they suspect of involvement in crime.[77]

## A Royal Commission

The uncertainties of interpretation and practice were examined by the Royal Commission on Police Powers and Procedure.[78] The Commission was set up after the public alarm occasioned by the police interrogation of Miss Savidge.[79] It was appointed to:

> consider the general powers and duties of police in England and Wales in the investigation of crimes and offences ... to inquire into the practice followed in interrogating or taking statements from persons interviewed in the course of the investigation of crime; and to report whether ... such powers and duties are properly exercised and discharged, with due regard to the rights and liberties of the subject, the interests of justice, and the observance of the Judges' Rules both in the letter and the spirit; and to make any recommendations necessary.[80]

The Commission, which delivered its report in 1929, accumulated a "conspicuous conflict of evidence" suggesting police practice varied in respect of the questioning of persons in custody.[81] It observed that the "great majority" of police forces from which it received evidence claimed to follow the advice promulgated by Lord Brampton and to regard it as the "fundamental principle" governing their practice.[82] However, that evidence also suggested that some forces "limit the application of the principle to the charge for which the prisoner is in custody, and approved of the questioning of prisoners regarding any other offence".[83] Other forces claimed "a right to question prisoners on the charge for which they are in custody, although even these agreed that it should be done very sparingly".[84]

The Commission focused upon three procedural devices which enabled the police to question persons in violation of the common law and the Judges' Rules. As to the first, the 'delayed charge', the Commission thought that the practice of holding a person in custody after arrest and before he has been formally charged should be subject to definite limits and safeguards.[85] Secondly, the Commission was critical of the unauthorised practice under which the police detained persons in custody to deliberately differentiate 'detention on suspicion' from arrest, in order to evade the provisions of the Judges' Rules. It argued that the practice was "undesirable and unnecessary".[86] Similarly, respecting the police practice of detaining several suspects for questioning while their respective accounts were verified so as to eliminate the innocent, the Commission thought this to be forcing suspects "to prove their innocence under the threat of continued detention".[87] It therefore had "no hesitation" in concluding that the practice was "wrong both in law and principle and should not be employed".[88] In connection with the "clear evidence" it had received indicating that detention was regarded by the police as something less than arrest, allowing them to question freely without administering the caution, the Commission referred to a clarificatory memorandum submitted to it by the Home Office. The memorandum stipulated that:

> The word 'detention' is not a term of art, though it is used by some Police forces with a special restricted significance not recognised by other Forces. The technical term is imprisonment. Any form of restraint by a police officer ... is in law imprisonment.... Whether the imprisonment or 'detention' is initiated by words or action constituting technically an arrest is for this purpose immaterial, nor is it material for the purpose of Rule (3) of the Judges' Rules. *Any person who is in fact under restraint and knows he is under restraint should be treated as in custody within the meaning of that Rule.*[89]

Finally, regarding the practice of arresting individuals on a minor or holding charge pending further inquiries — a practice not sanctioned by the Judges' Rules yet one which the Director of Public Prosecutions, in giving evidence to the Commission, defended as being "first-rate"[90] — the

Commission argued that "deliberate recourse to this practice, which contains elements of subterfuge, is on principle to be deprecated".[91]

Satisfied that police practice lacked uniformity the Commission sought to:

> prescribe a clear working rule for the police based on the maxim, fundamental to our criminal law, that 'no one should be compelled to incriminate himself'.[92]

The Commission formed the view that persons in custody, because of their position relative to their custodians, were at a disadvantage and — in spite of the caution as to the right to silence, which had become no more than a hallowed shibboleth[93] — in practical rather than theoretical danger of being compelled to incriminate themselves. It, therefore, concluded that it was "desirable" to avoid any questioning at all of persons actually in custody.[94] Accordingly, the Commission called for:

> a rigid instruction to [be issued to] the police [making it clear] that no questioning of a person in custody, about any crime or offence with which he is or may be charged, should be permitted.[95]

Responding to the Commission's Report, the Home Office, in 1930, issued a circular, with the approval of the judiciary. It explained that:

> Rule (3) was never intended to encourage or authorise the questioning or cross-examination of a person in custody after he has been cautioned, on the subject of the crime for which he is in custody, and long before this rule was formulated, and since, it has been the practice for the Judge to not to allow any answer to a question so improperly put to be given in evidence.[96]

Despite the circular, the custodial questioning of suspects by the police continued.[97] Indeed, the circular itself provided tenuous examples of "exceptional circumstances" in which post-caution questioning might be justified.[98]

The circular purported to make clear that post-caution custodial questions were justifiable only when in accordance with Rule 7: "for the purpose of removing ambiguity". However, neither the Rules nor the circular unambiguously proscribed custodial questioning and, in the opinion of a former Metropolitan Police Magistrate, the "sanction of questions to remove ambiguities constitute[d] a most dangerous loophole for cross-examination of prisoners by the police".[99] Indeed, the Rules were so interpreted by the courts that it remained possible to evade the constraints they ostensibly provided by the simple police expedient of regarding those detained without being formally arrested or charged as 'helping with inquiries'. Such persons though *de facto* in custody continued to be vulnerable to questioning which breached the Rules.[100]

The continued equivocacy of the Rules led some commentators to insist that "Rule 3 of the Judges' Rules means precisely what it says and that the questioning of persons already in custody is permissible provided a caution is first administered".[101] Others, while accepting that a person should not be questioned upon the crime for which he was in custody, felt that "this was never intended to be applied to other crimes. If this was the case not only would it act to the detriment of the prisoner but to the community as a whole".[102] Another argued that it was "ludicrous to suggest that the police have no right to question a prisoner or person in custody about any crime or offence with which he is or may be charged. Police officers must question prisoners.... They would be failing in their duty ... if they did not ask a prisoner questions about other offences he may have committed".[103]

That judges tended to acquiesce in the face of continued police breaches of the Rules, to the extent that the Rules had virtually ceased to exist as a constraint on the police practice of questioning persons in custody, was commented upon by Williams (1960a) who noted that:

> detention for questioning, and questioning after arrest, are still practiced by some police forces without serious check. To add to the anomaly, it seems from reported cases that the judges have given up enforcing their own rules, for it is no longer the practice to exclude evidence obtained by questioning in custody.[104]

The judicial reluctance to exclude such evidence appears to have become entrenched after the Second World War and could be justified, following the precedent set by *Voisin* (1918),[105] on the basis that confessions considered to be 'voluntary'[106] were admissible in spite of their being obtained in breach of the Judges' Rules. As Lord Devlin (1960) commented:

> The essence of the thing is that a judge must be satisfied that some unfair or oppressive use has been made of police power. If he is so satisfied, he will reject the evidence ... if he is not so satisfied, he will admit the evidence even though there may have been some technical breach of the Rules.[107]

The judicial reasoning that saw the custodial questioning of persons as of itself an insufficient ground upon which to exclude ostensibly reliable evidence was also noted by Williams (1960a) who observed of statements obtained in breach of the Rules that "since about 1950 they have almost uniformly been admitted".[108] The case law pre-dating the Judges' Rules indicates that this reasoning had long enjoyed the support of a substantial number of judges. When seen against the background of that case law it becomes clear that from the outset the Rules were of marginal importance both in respect of the evidential reception of confessions and as a means of placing enforceable limits upon police practices.[109]

Although the discretion to exclude gave the courts latitude to soften the severity of the circumscribed voluntariness rule where the probative value of a confession appeared slight when weighed against its unfair or prejudicial effects,[110] that discretion was rarely invoked.[111] Furthermore, as non-compliance with the Rules was regarded as amounting to no more than 'technical' or 'excusable' breaches,[112] the protections they impliedly afforded suspects from being conscripted into assisting the police in securing convictions were seriously weakened.

In light of the social and crime control utility of custodial interrogations, together with the judicial unwillingness or inability to enforce their own rules, it may be concluded that the 1912 and 1918 Rules, could not have had anything more than a minimal impact upon the pre-trial treatment of suspects by the police. Indeed, the Rules, effectively, permitted the police to require detainees to establish the truth or falsity of the suspicions held against them.[113]

During the two decades following the Second World War, as it became clear that the courts considered *Voisin* (1918)[114] to represent the correct view of the law,[115] a number of learned commentators, in addressing the inconsistencies between the rhetoric of the law relating to the procurement of confessions and the practical realities of law enforcement, called not for the practice of the law to correspond more closely with its rhetoric but rather for the rhetoric of the law to openly acknowledge and incorporate the realities of prevailing police practices. Williams (1969a),[116] for example, observed a "wide divergence between the standards of behaviour laid down in the Judges' Rules (and other judicial statements) and the actual conduct of the police".[117] He argued that the caution police officers were required by the Rules to administer to suspects merely paid lip service to the right to silence and, in practice, failed to safeguard that right.[118] In any event, the rule granting individuals a right not to answer police questions was "a rule which from its nature can protect the guilty only".[119]

That neither the Judges' Rules nor the Home Office circular of 1930 were followed by the police or enforced by the courts was, Williams contended, simply because they were "incompatible with the successful performance of the function of the police".[120] He cited *Voisin* in support of his assertion that breaches of the Rules by the police were "socially justified", even if they resulted in "a number of innocent persons [being] subjected to the inconvenience of detention in the police station", for this was a "lesser evil" than the evil of allowing offenders to escape.[121] As the Rules presented "an unreasonable restriction upon the activities of the police in bringing criminals to book",[122] and as, in practice, the Rules had been "abandoned [with the] tacit consent"[123] of judges who "maintain in theory an idealist rule, while conniving at police practice",[124] the custodial questioning of individuals should be legalised.[125]

Indicating that he considered the imperatives of crime control to be paramount, Williams also contended that for persons detained in police custody "considerations of liberty, dignity and privacy must give way to some extent to the practical necessities of law enforcement".[126] For this reason any proposal to give a detained suspect a "legal right to have his lawyer present while he is making a statement", should be resisted.[127]

Although Williams accepted that the Judges' Rules operated imperfectly, he felt that to prohibit custodial interrogations would place an intolerable strain upon the self-restraint of the police and debilitate their morale.[128] Any modification of the rules relating to the detention and investigation of suspects should accommodate the needs and practices of the police with respect of their desire to interrogate suspected offenders in private.[129]

Williams also argued that although the police were "remarkably successful" in obtaining incriminating statements by means of interrogation and while "this very success naturally awakens dark suspicions", it did not necessarily follow that unfair methods were employed.[130] After all:

> When an offender has been caught in incriminating circumstances, he often judges it better to confess and plead guilty, hoping thereby to get a lighter sentence. Moreover (and this is a fact too little understood by those who express alarm when confessions are made to the police), a guilty person who finds himself detected often wishes to confess in order to obtain relief from the feeling of guilt.[131]

The assumption that, when interrogated by the police, the factually guilty are so tortured by self-reproach that they welcome the solace of confessing, discounts the incidence of persons who, though innocent of the offence for which they are suspected, nevertheless, make false confessions of guilt.[132] Williams was prepared, however, to acknowledge that occasionally "methods of debatable propriety" were employed by the police.[133] Indeed, in adverting to the then recent, controversial and highly publicised case of Timothy Evans,[134] Williams accepted that there were certain individuals of such mentality and temperament who would in an effort to end the "atmosphere of suspicion and hostility ... say and sign anything that seems to produce for the moment a more favourable feeling".[135]

In spite of his recognition of the dangers of false confessions from persons of a suggestible nature who, under police interrogation, might be improperly persuaded of their guilt,[136] Williams concluded that:

> the danger of a false confession ... can hardly be regarded as a general reason for refusing to receive evidence of confessions given to the police.... The veracity of the confession would normally be a matter for consideration by the court of trial.... We do not normally exclude evidence from the consideration of a court merely because of the bare possibility that it is untrue. Important as it is not to convict the innocent, we cannot draw up rules of procedure and evidence *merely* for the purpose of acquitting the innocent. Some slight risk of convicting the innocent in the rare and extraordinary cases must be accepted for the purpose of convicting the mass of those who are guilty.[137]

This comment implies that from a crime control perspective, wrongful convictions which result from uncorroborated confessions obtained in breach of the rules are an unhappy but inevitable concomitant of efficient police methods. Furthermore, if criminal conduct is to be repressed and if the criminal law is to be routinely enforced, such wrongful convictions must be stoically tolerated.[138]

Nonetheless, by the late 1950s it was generally felt that the law relating to the arrest, detention, interrogation and investigation of suspects by the police should be reviewed and clarified.[139] It was suggested that this would be an appropriate subject for the Royal Commission on the Police,[140] which was set up in 1960. However, the operation of the Judges' Rules was withdrawn from its terms of reference when the Home Secretary, R. M. Butler, announced that as the judges had previously dealt with the matter, the right course would be to ask them to reconsider the taking of statements from suspects.[141]

## The Revised Judges' Rules

On January, 24, 1964 the reformulated Judges' Rules[142] were promulgated "in an atmosphere of crisis and haste worthy of most desperate emergency legislation".[143] As Gooderson (1970) points out:

> This was not done ... through the medium of a judicial decision at all, but by an extra judicial announcement, made quietly and unobtrusively, without any express discussion or justification of the new policy, or even an indication that a new policy had evolved [so that] by and large it passed unnoticed that the position of the suspect *vis-à-vis* his interrogator ha[d] deteriorated markedly.[144]

Indeed, as with their predecessor, the new Rules were a product of Home Office consultations with the judiciary and were brought into force without first giving Parliament an opportunity to discuss them.[145]

The legal status of the Rules was not altered by their revision. Deprived of the force of law, they remained no more than "a guide to police officers conducting investigations", the breach of which rendered statements obtained "liable to be excluded from evidence in subsequent criminal proceedings".[146] The preamble to the Rules made clear, however, that like their predecessor, their observance was not a precondition to the evidential admission of confessions. The "fundamental condition" for the reception in evidence of any answer given to a question put by a police officer and of any statement made, remained compliance with the voluntariness rule. The slightly amended voluntariness requirement, which was to be "overriding and applicable in all cases", provided for the exclusion of any statement obtained "by fear of prejudice or hope of advantage, exercised or held out by a person in authority, or by oppression".[147] Therefore, statements obtained in breach of the new Rules, as with the old, became inadmissible not because of that breach but only if the trial judge found the statement to be 'involuntary', in the special sense of the term that evolved during the course of the nineteenth century.[148] Thus, the correctness of police interrogations continued to be dependent upon whether an attempt was made to tender in evidence any allegedly voluntary confessions that might have been secured.[149]

Although it was thought "absurd" that wrongful practices by the police should be deemed so only when the courts excluded statements obtained by their use,[150] the preamble to the new Rules made clear that:

The Judges control the conduct of trials and the admission of evidence against persons on trial before them: they do not control or in any way initiate or supervise police activities or conduct.... The new Rules do not purport, any more than the old Rules, to envisage or deal with the many varieties of conduct which might render answers and statements involuntary and therefore inadmissible.[151]

While some commentators expressed satisfaction with the new Rules, others argued that they left the dice "very much loaded in favour of the suspect".[152] One observer felt that the new Rules would "demand even higher standards of forbearance, introspection and foresight [on the part of the police] than the old". He also suggested that it would "be difficult to blame the police if they find these standards impossibly high".[153] However, in their explicit endorsement of custodial interrogations, the new Rules represent an official acceptance of the crime control practices that had been developed by the police.[154] For instance, the meaning of 'custody' had, under the old Rules, been the subject of a good deal of confusion. It was also productive of "frequent and improbable denials by the police that they had put any questions at all".[155] Under the new Rule I, such denials became unnecessary for the police were authorised to continue questioning "whether or not the person in question ha[d] been taken into custody so long as he ha[d] not been charged with an offence or informed that he may be prosecuted for it".

That the new Rule I — deviating from the position that had been set forth in the old Rule 7,[156] and the circular of 1930[157] — effectively sanctioned custodial interrogations, is borne out by its suggestion of a period of time between arrest and charge which might be legitimately exploited by the police for the purpose of putting questions. However, only four years before the new Rules came into force Lord Devlin (1960) had emphatically asserted that:

> The police have no power to detain anyone unless they charge him with a specified crime and arrest him accordingly.... any form of physical restraint is an arrest.... The police have no power whatever to detain anyone on suspicion or for the purpose of questioning him. They cannot even compel anyone whom they do not arrest to come to the police station.[158]

Not only would Rule I seem inconsistent with this statement, it appears irreconcilable with the common law requirement that an arrested person be immediately informed of the reasons for his arrest. As Lord Simon in the leading case of *Christie* v. *Leachinsky* (1947)[159] stated:

> If a policeman arrests without a warrant on reasonable suspicion ... he must in ordinary circumstances inform the person arrested of the true ground of arrest.... a citizen is entitled to know on what charge or on suspicion of what crime he is seized.... The matter is a matter of substance, and turns on the elementary proposition that in this country a person is, prima facie, entitled to his freedom and is only required to submit to restraints on his freedom if he knows in substance the reason why it is claimed that this restraint should be imposed.[160]

It would appear to follow, therefore, that a person arrested and informed of the reason for that arrest must also have been told (or might reasonably assume) that 'he may be prosecuted'. In such circumstances the questioning of the arrestee would seem to be wrongful. On the other hand, if the suspect had been detained without being informed of the grounds of his detention, the restraint upon his freedom, as Smith (1964) pointed out, would presumably be unlawful.[161]

**Conclusion**

The 1964 Judges' Rules, though silent in respect of the length of time permitted between arrest and charge,[162] served to accord further legitimacy to the police practice of detaining suspects for questioning in order to facilitate their construction of a sustainable case, before charge.[163] The revised Rules and the judicial decisions relating to them may, therefore, be seen as continuing a twentieth century trend under which the police were afforded greater latitude for pre-charge detention and interrogation. While they appeared to impose clear constraints upon the custodial questioning of suspects by the police, the Rules and the associated authorities actually worked to endorse the police practice of detaining persons for interrogation. They also worked to legitimate the status of the police as chief accountants in the interrogation process. The extent to which the police control of interrogations allowed them to convey functional images of suspects, of the investigative process and of themselves will be considered in the following chapters.

## Notes

1. See *Ibrahim* (1914) AC 599, p. 610. Also see *Warickshall* (1783) Leach. 263, pp. 263-4. See also *Thomas* (1836) 7 C. & P. 345, p. 346; *Court* (1836) 7 C. & P. 486, p. 487; *Holmes* (1843) 1 C. & K. 248; *Scott* (1856) D. & B. 47, p. 48; *Gillis* (1866) 11 Cox C.C. 69, p. 74; and *Baldry* (1852) 2 Den. 430, p. 445, *per* Campbell, LCJ; 3 Wigmore, 1970, p. 822.
2. Elliot, 1987, p. 192. See also 3 Wigmore, 1970, p. 246; Williams, 1983, pp. 224, 251; Mirfield, 1985, pp. 48, 61-5.
3. Elliott, 1987, *ibid.* See also Ratushny, 1971, pp. 474-6.
4. Jackson, 1986, pp. 225, 235. Ratushny (1971, p. 494) argued that the 'voluntariness rule inhibits the search for truth ... for a judge must ask not whether the statement is a reliable piece of evidence but whether it has been obtained in a certain manner.... though the answer to [this] ... might well provide some assistance in determining reliability'.
5. See, for example, *Berriman* (1854) 6 Cox C.C. 388; *Mick* (1863) 3 F. & F. 322; *Bodkin* (1863) 17 Cox C.C. 689; *Gavin* (1885) 15 Cox C.C. 656.
6. Abrahams, 1964a, p. 12.
7. Neasey, 1969, pp. 484-5.
8. *Ibrahim* (1914) AC 599, at p. 614, *per* Lord Sumner: 'The English law is still unsettled, strange as it may seem, since the point is one that constantly occurs in criminal cases'.
9. Lord Brampton, as Mr Justice Hawkins, sat as presiding judge in *Miller* (1895) 18 Cox C.C. 54 which may be contrasted with *Histed* (1898) 19 Cox C.C. 16 also heard before Hawkins, J. Extracts from Lord Brampton's 1882 address to the police are reproduced in the *Report of the Royal Commission on Police Powers and Procedure* (RCPPP), 1929, Cmd. 3297, pp. 147-8. See also *Vincent's Police Code*, 7th edn., 1931, pp. vii-xiv; Abrahams, 1964, pp. 13-5.
10. This was not authoritatively declared to be the common law position until the case of *Rice v Connelly* [1966] 3 WLR 17; 2 QB 414. However, see RCPPP, *Report*, 1929, para. 57, pp. 22-3; para. 98, p. 38.
11. Who there declared that '[w]hen a prisoner is in custody the police have no right to ask him questions' (*Gavin* (1885) 15 Cox C.C. 656, p. 657). See also *Male and Cooper* (1893) 17 Cox C.C. 689; *Histed* (1898) 19 Cox C.C. 16; *Knight and Thayre* (1905) 20 Cox C.C. 711.
12. *Best* (1909) 1 K.B. 692. See also *Brackenbury* (1893) 17 Cox C.C. 628; *Miller* (1895) 18 Cox C.C. 54; *Hurst* (1896) 18 Cox C.C. 374; *Rogers v Hawken* (1898) 19 Cox C.C. 122; *Booth and Jones* (1910) 74 JP 375; *Lewis v Harris* (1913) LTR 109.
13. See *Lewis v Harris* (1913) 110 LT 377; *Crowe and Myerscough* (1917) 81 JP 288; *Mathews* (1919) 14 Cr.App.R. 73.
14. See *Winkel* (1912) 76 JP 191; *Gardner and Hancox* (1915) 11 Cr.App.R. 267.
15. Devlin, 1960, p. 32. See also RCPPP, *Report*, 1929, para. 64, p. 25.

[16] The Chief Constable was prompted to seek this advice because, on the Birmingham Circuit, one judge had censured a member of his force for having cautioned a prisoner, whilst another judge had censured a constable for omitting to do so (see Abrahams, 1964a, p. 16; Devlin, 1960, p. 33). In reply to this request, Lord Alverstone wrote: 'There is, as far as I know, no difference of opinion whatever among any of the judges of the King's Bench Division upon the matter' (Abrahams, 1964a, pp. 16-17). This would suggest that Lord Brampton's earlier analysis of judicial practice merely reflected the attitude of the senior judiciary and not the consensus view of the wider judiciary.

[17] See *Voisin* (1918) 13 Cr.App.R. 89, p. 96, *per* Lawrence, J.

[18] The 1912 rules were stated in *Voisin*, (1918) *ibid.*, as follows: 1. When a police officer is endeavouring to discover the author of a crime there is no objection to his putting questions in respect thereof to any person or persons whether suspected or not from whom he thinks that useful information can be obtained. 2. Whenever a police officer has made up his mind to charge a person with a crime he should first caution such a person before asking any questions or any further questions as the case may be. 3. Persons in custody should not be questioned without the usual caution being first administered. 4. If the prisoner wishes to volunteer any statement the usual caution should be administered. It is desirable that the last two words ('against you') of such caution should be omitted, and that the caution should end with the words 'be given in evidence'.

[19] RCPPP, 1929, Minutes of Evidence, vol. 2, p. 6.

[20] The Court was created by the Criminal Appeal Act, 1907, s. 1. and superseded the Court for Crown Cases Reserved.

[21] In *Voisin* (1918) 13 Cr.App.R. 89, p. 90, Lawrence, J quoted the Rules to defence counsel, *arguendo*, and in *Cook* (1918) 34 TLR 515, p. 516, Darling, J cited them in delivering the judgment of the court.

[22] The additional rules were stated as follows: 5. The caution to be administered to a prisoner, when he is formally charged, should ... be in the following words: 'Do you wish to say anything in answer to the charge? You are not obliged to say anything but whatever you do say will be taken down in writing and may be given in evidence'. Care should be taken to avoid any suggestion that his answers can only be used in evidence against him, as this may prevent an innocent person making a statement which might assist to clear him of the charge. 6. A statement made by a prisoner before there is time to caution him is not rendered inadmissible in evidence merely by reason of no caution having been given, but in such a case he should be cautioned as soon as possible. 7. A prisoner making a voluntary statement must not be cross-examined, and no questions should be put to him about it except for the purpose of removing ambiguity in what he has actually said. For instance, if he has mentioned an hour without saying morning or evening, or has given a day of the week and day of the month which do not agree, or has not made it clear to what individual or what place he intended to refer in some part of his statement, he

may be questioned sufficiently to clear up the point. 8. When two or more persons are charged with the same offence, and statements are taken separately from the persons charged, the police should not read these statements to the other persons charged, but each of such persons should be furnished by the police with a copy of such statements and nothing should be said or done to invite a reply. If the persons charged desire to make a statement in reply, the usual caution should be administered. 9. Any statement made in accordance with the above rules should, whenever possible, be taken down in writing and signed by the person making it after it has been read to him and he has been invited to make any corrections he may wish.

[23] *Report*, 1929, Cmd. 3297.

[24] Home Office Circular No. 536053/23, June 24, 1930.

[25] Home Office Circular No. 238/1947.

[26] Home Office Circular No. 31/1964; see Abrahams, 1964, pp. 53-60; Fellman, 1966, p. 35.

[27] McCormick, 1946, p. 256. See also Neasey, 1969, p. 494.

[28] A Stipendiary Magistrate erroneously described them as *obiter dicta* when giving evidence to the RCPPP, see Minutes of Evidence, Q. 8180.

[29] An examination of the relevant departmental files, held at the Public Record Office, failed to illuminate the scope and nature of the deliberations of the judges of the Kings' Bench, the extent of Home Office involvement and revealed no evidence to suggest that Parliament had been consulted prior to, or had participated in, the formulation of the 1912 or 1918 Rules.

[30] See *Voisin* (1918) 13 Cr.App.R. 89, p. 96; *Dwyer* (1932) 23 Cr.App.R. 156; *Wattam* (1952) 36 Cr.App.R. 72; *Bass* [1953] 37 Cr.App.R. 51. See also Devlin (1960, p. 39): 'It must never be forgotten that the Judges' Rules were made for the guidance of the police and not for the circumspection of the judicial power'. Also see Brownlie, 1960, pp. 298-324; Fellman, 1966, p. 36; Neasey, 1969, p. 494; Gooderson, 1970, pp. 270-1; Leigh, 1975, p. 145. St. Johnston (1948, p. 93), however, contended that the Rules had 'with the passing of time come to have the force of law'.

[31] *Thompson* (1893) 2 Q.B. 12; *Ibrahim* (1914) A.C. 599; *Voisin* (1918) 13 Cr.App.R. 89; *Cook* (1918) 34 TLR 515; RCPPP, *Report*, 1929, pp. 65-67; Devlin, 1960, p. 32; *Callis* v *Gunn* [1964] 1 Q.B. 495, *per* Parker, LCJ, p. 501; *Ovenell* [1969] 1 QB 17; Teh, 1972, p. 491; *Greaves* (1980) 71 Cr.App.R. 232, *per* Donaldson, LJ, p. 236: 'it must be remembered that the whole purpose of the Judges' Rules ... is to ensure that statements are voluntary'.

[32] *Lewis* v *Harris* (1913) 30 LTR 109; *Voisin* (1918) 13 Cr.App.R. 89, *per* Lawrence, J, pp. 94-5; *Cook* (1918) 34 TLR 515.

[33] See *Ibrahim* (1914) AC 599, p. 614.

[34] *Ibid.* Compare McBarnet's (1981c, p. 110) suggestion that the Rules departed from a 'common law approach which had drawn the line between police powers and citizens rights firmly and clearly in favour of civil liberties'.

35 *Ibrahim* (1914) *ibid.*
36 *Miller* (1895) 18 Cox C.C. 54. See also *Berriman* (1854) 6 Cox C.C. 388.
37 *Brackenbury* (1893) 17 Cox C.C. 628; *Booth and Jones* (1910) 5 Cr.App.R. 177.
38 *Winkel* (1912) 76 JP 191; *Gardner and Hancox* (1915) 11 Cr.App.R. 267.
39 The concept of voluntariness had acquired a specifically legal and somewhat restricted meaning under the nineteenth century case law. During the twentieth century, before the enactment of the 1984 Police and Criminal Evidence Act, it permitted an increasingly 'extensive range of variation' (RCPPP, *Report*, 1929, para. 63, p. 25) and was 'interpreted in ways which stretch[ed] the meaning of the word to breaking point' (McBarnet, 1981c, p. 110).
40 *Voisin* (1918) *supra.* n. 30. See also *Histed* (1898) 19 Cox C.C. 16; *Knight and Thayre* (1905) 20 Cox C.C. 711, p. 713.
41 *Supra.*, n. 30. See also Devlin, 1960, pp. 35-40.
42 Though see *Ibrahim* (1914) AC 599, *per* Lord Sumner, p. 614; *Christie* [1914] AC 545, *per* Lord Moulton, pp. 559, 560, 564, 569; *Gardner and Hancox* (1915) 80 JP 135; *Voisin* (1918) 13 Cr.App.R. 89, p. 95, where Lawrence, J opined that a trial judge may exercise his discretion to exclude 'only if he thinks the statement was not a voluntary one ... or was an unguarded answer made in circumstances that rendered it unreliable, or unfair, for some reason to be allowed in evidence against the prisoner'; *Brown and Bruce* (1931) 23 Cr.App.R. 56; *Dwyer* (1932) 23 Cr.App.R. 156. Also see Fry, 1938, p. 445.
43 *Noor Mohamed* [1949] AC 182, p. 192; *Harris* v *DPP* [1952] AC 694, p. 707; *Kuruma* [1955] AC 197, p. 204; *Cook* [1959] 2 QB 340; *Callis* v *Gunn* (1963) 107 Sol.J. 831; *Ovenell* [1969] 1 QB 17, p. 26; *Elliott* [1977] Crim.L.R. 551; *Houghton* [1979] 68 Cr.App.R. 197, p. 206; *Sang* [1979] 2 All ER 1222, pp. 1229-1247. See also Pattenden, 1981, pp. 98-102.
44 *Voisin* (1918) 13 Cr.App.R. 89.
45 *Ibid.*, pp. 94-6. See also *Smith* [1961] 46 Cr.App.R. 51; *Massey* (1963) 107 Sol.J. 984; *Kennedy, Steele and Meakin* [1963] Crim.L.R. 108.
46 *Cook* (1918) 34 LTR 515.
47 *Ibid.*, p. 516.
48 *Ibid.*
49 Neasey, 1969, pp. 485, 489.
50 See *Berriman* (1854) 6 Cox C.C. 388; *Gavin* (1885) 15 Cox C.C. 656; *Male* (1893) 17 Cox C.C. 689; *Histed* (1898) 19 Cox C.C. 16, p. 17; *Knight and Thayre* (1905) 20 Cox C.C. 711, p. 713.
51 (1914) AC 599, p. 611.
52 Smith, 1960, p. 348; Teh, 1972, p. 491.
53 Rule 1. See also Devlin, 1960, pp. 27-8, 31; Brownlie, 1960, p. 306.
54 See *Straffen* [1952] 2 All ER 657, p. 658.
55 See Brownlie, 1960, p. 307; Teh, 1972, p. 493.
56 See *supra.*, n. 18.

[57] Mead, 1935, p. 499. See also Williams, G., 1960a, p. 327.
[58] *Winkle* (1911) 76 JP 191. Avory, J ruled that the police had no authority to conduct cross-examinations of persons detained in custody. See also *Mathews* (1919) 14 Cr.App.R. 23; *Grayson* (1921) 16 Cr.App.R. 7, p. 8, where the Lord Chief Justice denounced what amounted to 'an informal preliminary trial in private by the police' which was 'not in accordance with the principles of English justice' and not 'fair to prisoners'. Also see *Taylor* (1923) JP 87; *Brown and Bruce* (1931) 23 Cr.App.R. 56.
[59] See *Voisin* (1918) 13 Cr.App.R. 89, p. 95; RCPPP, *Report*, 1929, para. 151, p. 56; Williams, G., 1960a, p. 327; *Sergeant* [1963] Cr.App.R. 848; Teh, 1972, p. 494. See also Devlin, 1960, p. 33. See Gooderson, 1970, p. 272; Jackson, 1972, p. 102.
[60] Williams, G., 1960a, p. 327. See also St. Johnston (Chief Constable), 1948, p. 95, who spoke of the 'temptation ... for an officer who knows he has the right man, and who knows the evidence against him is not strong, to delay giving the caution in the hope that the suspect will incriminate himself still further'.
[61] Williams, G., 1960a, p. 328.
[62] See RCPPP, *Report*, 1929, pp. 104-5.
[63] *Ibid.*, para. 275, p. 104.
[64] *Ibid.*, p. 328. See also Brownlie, 1960, pp. 307-24; Smith, 1960, pp. 347-49; Williams, C., 1960, pp. 353-5; Fellman, 1966, p. 44; Leigh, 1975, p. 145; McBarnet, 1981c, pp. 109-11.
[65] Lidstone and Early, 1982, pp. 501-2.
[66] 1 Stephen, 1883, p. 497; Howard, 1931, pp. 48-9, 381-2.
[67] 1 Chitty, (1816, p. 59): 'When the officer has made his arrest, he is, as soon as possible, to bring the party to the gaol or to the justice ... and if he be guilty of unnecessary delay, it is a breach of duty'.
[68] 1 & 2, P. & M., c.13 (1554); 2 & 3, P. & M., c.10 (1555). See 1 Stephen, 1883, p. 225; Langbein, 1974, pp. 22-4; Beattie, 1986, p. 271.
[69] See 1 Stephen, 1883, p. 441.
[70] Indictable Offence Act 1848, s. 18.
[71] See 1 Chitty, 1816, p. 85. See also RCPPP, *Report*, 1929, para. 64, p. 26; pp. 142-3.
[72] See 1 Stephen, 1882, pp. 193-4; 72 *JP*, 1908, pp. 75-133; *Sol.J.*, 1928, p. 406; Howard, 1931, pp. 15-19.
[73] Lidstone and Early (1982, p. 501) argue that: 'When the new police were created they were invested with the authority of the State as well as that of the master but being poorly educated themselves and not skilled in interrogation threats or promises were commonly used to obtain confessions or admissions of guilt. It is then understandable that judges should seek to avoid the dangers of false confessions by the test of voluntariness'.
[74] Lidstone and Early (1982, p. 502) attribute this statement to Channell, J without making its source entirely clear. However, Channell, J is reported as

having made similar remarks in *Knight and Thayre* (1905) 20 Cox C.C. 711, p. 713; 69 JP 108; 21 TLR 310. For equivalent nineteenth century *dicta* see *Bodkin* (1863) 9 Cox C.C. 403; *Yeovile Murder Case* (1872) 41 JP 187; *Reason* (1872) 12 Cox C.C. 228, p. 229; *Gavin* (1885) 15 Cox C.C. 656, p. 657; *Thompson* (1893) 17 Cox C.C. 614; *Male* (1893) 17 Cox C.C. 689, p. 690; *Histed* (1898) 19 Cox C.C. 16, p. 17.

[75] Rule 1. See also Brownlie, 1960, p. 306.

[76] Lidstone and Early, 1982, p. 502. See also Devlin (1960, pp. 29, 67-68) who, in his assessment of the mid-twentieth century prosecution process, was of the view that suspects were invariably charged immediately upon their arrival in formal custody at a police station. Williams, G. (1961, p. 54) confirms that even by this late date, it was still widely assumed that the police assembled their evidence *before* making an arrest and, therefore, infrequently detained persons in order to elicit confessions of guilt.

[77] See RCPPP, *Report*, 1929, para. 151, p. 56, where it is recorded that the police defended this practice as being 'essential in the interests of justice'. See also Mead (1935, pp. 499-500), a former Metropolitan Police Magistrate, who expressed opposition to the caution on the ground that it gave suspects detained in police custody 'a momentary opportunity to reflect' which was to the disadvantage of the prosecution and impaired what he described as the duty of a police officer 'to prove the guilt of an accused person' when it was 'essentially in the interests of the public that he should succeed'. It is noteworthy that the earlier Royal Commission on the Duties of the Metropolitan Police (1906-8, Cd. 4156, p. 75) found it necessary in its report to remind police officers that, respecting individuals detained in custody, the police were required to discharge 'an executive and not a judicial function'. That is, to ascertain whether there was a *prima facie* case against the prisoner and not to determine the issue. See also RCPPP, *Report*, 1929, paras. 137-41, pp. 51-3, and compare Devlin, 1960, p. 28.

[78] 1929, Cmd. 3297.

[79] Miss Savidge had been arrested, with Sir Leo Money, by two Metropolitan police officers for 'behaving in a manner reasonably likely to offend against public decency'. The charge was dismissed by a magistrate. Questions on the matter were raised in the Commons, after which the Home Secretary referred the case to the Director of Public Prosecutions (DPP) with instructions to investigate whether the two officers could be proceeded against for perjury. As part of the DPP's investigations, it was felt necessary to 'ascertain' the characters and reputations of Sir Leo Money and Miss Savidge - who were potentially the principal witnesses for the prosecution - together with the circumstances of their association. (The DPP had considered it 'strange that a person of Sir Leo Money's position should be associating with a young woman in a different station of life'.) Subsequently, Miss Savidge, aged 22, was approached by police officers at her place of employ and invited to accompany

them to Scotland Yard. She had asked to go home first but as the police did not consider this to be a 'definite request' it was not conceded to. On arrival at Scotland Yard, she was taken for private interrogation, with no one else present except the police, and questioned in contravention of the Judges' Rules. The methods by which her presence was secured by the police and the events attending her interrogation - alleged to have been designed both to assist the two police officers resist a charge of perjury and to elicit information on which she could be discredited - resolved both Houses of Parliament to establish a tribunal to inquire into what was described as 'a definite matter of urgent public importance'. The tribunal reported in July, 1928 (Savidge Inquiry Report, Cmd. 3147). The RCPPP was expressly directed to consider the points raised by the tribunal's Minority Report, (pp. 17-33) written by Lees-Smith MP, which was not only critical of the treatment by the police of Miss Savidge but also of the 'mechanical precision with which the ... police witnesses corroborated every detail of each other's statements'.

80 RCPPP, *Report*, 1929, p. ii.
81 *Ibid.*, para. 161, p. 60.
82 *Ibid.*, para. 162, p. 60.
83 *Ibid.*
84 *Ibid.*
85 *Ibid.*, para. 143. p. 53.
86 *Ibid.*, para. 158, p. 59.
87 *Ibid.*, para. 154, p. 57.
88 *Ibid.*, para. 154, pp. 57-8.
89 *Ibid.*, para. 148, p. 55 (my emphasis).
90 *Ibid.*, para. 159, p. 59.
91 *Ibid.*, para. 160, p. 59.
92 *Ibid.*, para. 164, p. 61.
93 *Ibid.*, paras. 64-75, pp. 25-9. The Commission also found that its witnesses agreed that the caution had 'little or no effect' on the mind of an experienced criminal and that 'new offenders', particularly women, regarded it 'as unfriendly or discourteous interposition in an interview' (para. 70, pp. 27-8). Nevertheless, the Commission recommended that the caution be administered 'at the very outset of any questioning' (paras. 69, 72-5, pp. 27-39), as a safeguard against it being 'used or varied for tactical reasons' (para. 68, p. 27). For it found it 'difficult to appreciate the value or ethics of a caution which is deliberately withheld until the suspect has succeeded in incriminating himself' (para. 69, p. 27).
94 *Ibid.*, para. 165, p. 61. The Commission later qualified the suggestion of an absolute proscription against custodial questioning when (at para. 166, p. 62) it stated 'that a prisoner should not be questioned on matters connected with the charge for which he is in custody'. And see para. 174, p. 66, where it accepts that questions to clear up ambiguities are permissible.

[95] *Ibid.*, para. 169, p. 65.
[96] Home Office Circular No. 536053/23, June, 24, 1930. See Brownlie, 1960, p. 299.
[97] See, for example, *Brown and Bruce* (1931) 23 Cr.App.R. 56; *Wattam* (1952) 36 Cr.App.R. 72; *May* (1952) Cr.App.R. 91; *Bass* [1953] 1 QB 680; (1953) 36 Cr.App.R. 51; *Thomas and Cullen* (1961) Crim.L.R. 401; *Parman* (1963) 107 Sol.J. 984; *Sargeant* (1963) Cr.App.R. 848; *Massey* (1964) Crim.L.R. 43. See also Greaves, 1936, pp. 17-9; Brownlie, 1960, p. 320; Williams, G., 1960a, p. 329; Smith, 1960, pp. 348-56; Williams, C., 1960, pp. 353-55.
[98] *Supra.*, n. 96: A person arrested for burglary may, before he is formally charged, say 'I have hidden or thrown the property away', and after caution he would properly be asked 'where have you hidden or thrown it?' See Gooderson, 1970, p. 273.
[99] Mead, 1935, p. 499.
[100] Teh, 1972, pp. 494-500.
[101] Campbell (Colonel), 1959, p. 675.
[102] Packman (Inspector), 1959, p. 675.
[103] Payne (Detective Sergeant), 1959, p. 676.
[104] Williams, G., 1960a, p. 331. See Hiemstra (1963, p. 206) who contended that 'the judges themselves [had] emasculated the Judges' Rules'.
[105] (1918) 13 Cr.App.R. 89.
[106] The 1928-9 Royal Commission 'received a volume of responsible evidence' which it found 'impossible to ignore' suggesting a number of voluntary statements were "not 'voluntary' in the strict sense of the word". (RCPPP, *Report*, 1929, para. 268, p. 101.)
[107] Devlin, 1960, p. 38.
[108] Williams, G., 1960a, pp. 331-2; 1961, p. 52. See also Williams, C., 1983, p. 241.
[109] See Brownlie, 1960, pp. 323-4; Williams, C., 1960, p. 354; Leigh, 1975, p. 145.
[110] Devlin, 1960, pp. 35-6.
[111] Walsh, 1982, pp. 42-3; Zuckerman, 1989, p. 313.
[112] Devlin, 1960, pp. 37-9; Fellman, 1966, p. 48.
[113] See McBarnet, 1981b, p. 57; Lidstone and Early, 1982, pp. 448-9, 496-7.
[114] (1918) 13 Cr.App.R. 89.
[115] Namely, that infractions of the Judges' Rules would not *ipso facto* render statements obtained inadmissible. See Brownlie, 1960, pp. 306, 324; Smith, 1960, p. 347.
[116] Williams, G., 1960a, pp. 325-46; 1961, pp. 50-7.
[117] Williams, G., 1960a, p. 325. See Brownlie (1960, p. 324), also critical of the 'divergence between the policy of the law on questions in custody and police practice'. And see Smith (1960, p. 349) who denounced the 'superficial

impression' that had been created suggesting strict compliance with the Rules was 'compatible with effective law enforcement, when this is not the case'.

[118] Williams, G., 1960b, p. 50; 1961, p. 325. See also Hiemstra (1963, p. 205-6) who saw the caution as a potentially 'serious handicap in the detection of crime'. And argued that as it had become a 'dead letter' it should be abolished. Also see Hoffman (1964, pp. 24-5) who suggested the caution was an obstacle to the efficient investigation of crime because it discouraged the innocent from giving an explanation 'which would have satisfied the police'.

[119] Williams, G., 1963, p. 53.

[120] Williams, G., 1961, p. 50. See Jackson (1972, p. 137) who doubted 'whether the police could do their work efficiently if they did not develop practices for which there is no legal authority'.

[121] Williams, G., 1960a, p. 333; 1961, p. 52.

[122] Williams, G., 1961, p. 52. See also Smith (1960, p. 349) who believed that '[s]trict compliance with the Judges' Rules must be highly inconvenient for the police - and an undoubted handicap to them in their present task - and it is too much to expect them to enforce these very strict standards upon themselves'.

[123] Williams, G., 1961, p. 52.

[124] Williams, G., 1961, p. 55. See also Williams, C., 1960, pp. 354-6; Jackson, 1972, p. 104.

[125] Williams, G., 1960a, p. 341; 1961, p. 55. See Smith (1960, pp. 349, 351) who though seeing a 'flaw in the argument of those who favour unlimited interrogation', namely that it 'tends to assume the subject is guilty', nonetheless felt that if the police could not interrogate they 'would not be able to do their job properly'. Also see Hiemstra (1963, p. 205) arguing that it was 'obvious that police interrogation is completely indispensable in law enforcement. *It is necessary for the policeman to satisfy himself that he has sufficient grounds for arrest*, and is necessary to lead the police to accomplices' (my emphasis). And see St. Johnson, 1964, pp. 89, 96.

[126] Williams, G., 1961, p. 56.

[127] Williams, G., 1961, p. 56. In an earlier article Williams presented his opposition to legal advice in more measured terms. There, he accepted that the provision of legal assistance to detainees 'would certainly operate as a substantial safeguard against illegality'. However, in his view there was 'one fact that makes it impracticable. As soon as a lawyer is introduced ... he advises his client to answer no questions. Thus if a lawyer were admitted the whole proceeding would be stultified' (Williams, G., 1960a, p. 344). See also Smith, 1960, pp. 351-2; JUSTICE, Report, [1960] Crim.L.R 793, dissenting opinion of Foster QC., p. 819.

[128] Williams, G., 1960a, pp. 328, 340; 1960b, pp. 54-5.

[129] Williams, G., 1961, pp. 54, 56, 57. See also Smith, 1960, p. 349.

[130] Williams, G., 1960a, p. 334.

[131] *Ibid.* According to Wigmore the custodial interrogation of individuals suspected of crime was justified because it ensured that 'an innocent person is always helped by an early opportunity to tell his whole story.... However, and more important, [for the guilty suspect, the] nervous pressure of guilt is enormous; the load of the deed done is heavy; the fear of detection fills the consciousness; and when detection comes, the pressure is relieved; and a deep sense of relief makes confession a satisfaction. At that moment, he will tell all, and tell it truly. To forbid soliciting him, to seek to prevent this relief, is to fly in the face of human nature. It is natural, and should be law, to take his confession at that moment — the best one' (3 Wigmore, 1970, pp. 524-5). For similar comments see also Barry, 1966, pp. 259-260.

[132] See Gudjonsson, 1992, pp. 223-59.

[133] Williams, G., 1960a, pp. 335-6. See also Hiemstra, 1963, pp. 215-6.

[134] On the 30th of November, 1949, Timothy Evans, who was then 25 years of age, walked into a South Wales police station and told the duty constable that he had disposed of his wife's body down a drain outside his home at 10 Rillington Place, North London. The search of the drains revealed no sign of a body. On being informed of this Evans made a statement in which he alleged that his wife had died when his landlord, John Christie, had unsuccessfully tried to cause her to abort. On a subsequent search of the address the police found the bodies of his wife and baby daughter in a wash-house. Brought to London, Evans — who had been detained in the custody of the Welsh police for 48 hours — on being interrogated and charged, confessed to the murders. He was subsequently remanded to Brixton Prison where he made yet another confession. At his trial, which opened at the Old Bailey on the 11th of January, 1950, on the sole charge of the murder of his daughter, Evans' defence was that Christie, the chief prosecution witness, had committed the crime. The jury found Evans guilty; his appeal was rejected; he was hanged on the 9th of March, 1950. Three years later Christie, who had subsequently confessed to killing seven women including Evans' wife — he denied killing Evans' daughter — was convicted and sentenced to death. He was hanged on the 15th of July, 1953. The improbability of two murderers residing at the same address fuelled contentions that Evans had been the victim of a miscarriage of justice. Speculation that the prolonged interrogations of Evans breached the Judges' Rules; that the apparently full and voluntary confessions contained specific details of the murders because the police had, perhaps deliberately, conveyed them to him; that the police on being readily convinced of his guilt, failed to examine the available evidence adequately and indeed suppressed evidence that ran counter to their presumption of guilt, led to two official inquiries. The first inquiry, conducted by Henderson QC, and held in camera, reported in 1953 (Cmd. 8896). It concluded that the case against Evans was overwhelming. However, the demands for a further and public inquiry were met in 1965. Reporting in 1966, the Brabin Inquiry (Cmnd. 3101) found it more probable

than not that Evans had killed his wife (for which he was never tried) and had probably not killed his daughter. The conclusions of Brabin, J, regarding Evans' confessions and recantation failed to appease public disquiet. Sixteen years after his execution, on the 18th of October, 1966, on the recommendation of the then Home Secretary, Roy Jenkins, Evans was granted a free pardon. For accounts of this notorious case and the issues to which it gave rise, see Sargant, 1957, pp. 194-202; Kennedy, 1961; Jackson, 1972, pp. 112-3; Devlin, 1979, p. 73; Woffinden, 1987, pp. 17-50; Gudjonsson, 1992, pp. 235-9.

[135] Williams, G., 1960a, p. 336. Sargant (1957, p. 181), however, in his influential behaviourial study of the effects of combat and captivity had concluded that whenever 'the right pressure is applied in the right way and for long enough, ordinary prisoners have little chance of staving off collapse.... *Ordinary people ... are the way they are simply because they are sensitive to and influenced by what is going on around them....* Even greater nervous tension, because it is more persistent, can be aroused in a prison cell or police station by skilled interrogation than in a fox-hole by enemy snipers or machine gunners' (my emphasis). See also Barry, 1966, p. 257.

[136] Williams, G., 1960a, p. 336.

[137] *Ibid.* The Benthamite tone of Williams' contention that all confession statements secured by the police should be admissible to allow the courts to weigh all the relevant evidence, received wide support. See, for example, Hiemstra, 1963, p. 211.

[138] A view evidently endorsed by Barry, J (1966, p. 257).

[139] See Smith, 1959, p. 679; Williams, G., 1960a, p. 341; St. Johnson, 1966, p. 57; Jackson, 1972, pp. 103-5.

[140] The Commission (RCP) reported in May, 1962, Cmnd. 1728.

[141] RCP, *Report*, 1962, para. 5; Hoffman, 1964, p. 24; Marshall, 1964, pp. 97-8; Jackson, 1972, p. 105.

[142] Published in the form of a Home Office Circular (No. 31/1964), the new rules came into operation on the 27th of January, 1964. The Rules and their accompanying Administrative Directions are reproduced in [1964] 1 WLR 152; 1 All ER 237; Crim.L.R. 165.

[143] Hoffman, 1964, p. 23. See also Marshall, 1964, p. 98; 'Editorial Comment' [1964] Crim.L.R. 161, pp. 161-2; (1964) 128 *Sol.J.* 101; A Police Officer, 1964, p. 174; Smith, 1964, p. 182.

[144] Gooderson, 1970, p. 270. See also Thomas, 1964, p. 386; Smith, 1964, pp. 177, 180.

[145] Marshall, 1964, p. 98.

[146] H.O. Circular 31/1964, Appendix A.

[147] *Ibid.* The addition of the words 'or by oppression' to the voluntariness test propounded by Lord Sumner in *Ibrahim* [1914] AC 599, appears to have originated in dicta delivered by Parker, LCJ, in *Callis* v *Gunn* [1964] 1 QB 495, p. 501. Operating to clarify rather than to extend the scope of the

voluntariness test, the concept of oppression in the context of the new Judges' Rules was approved in *Priestly* (1965) 51 Cr.App.R. 1, *per* Sachs, J: 'the word 'oppression' ... imports something which tends to sap, and has sapped, that free will which must exist before a confession is voluntary'. See also *Prager* [1972] 1 All ER 1114, p. 1119; *Isequilla* [1975] 3 All ER 77, p. 82b; *DPP* v. *Ping Lin* [1975] 3 All ER, 175, p. 185e; *Hudson* (1981) 72 Cr.App.R. 163; *Rennie* [1982] 1 All ER 385.

148 Edmund Davis, LJ, in *Prager* [1972] 1 All ER 1114, rejected the contention that a breach of the rules was of itself a ground to reject confessions. He argued (at p. 1118j) that the acceptance of such a proposition 'would exalt the Judges' Rules into rules of law.... Their non-observance may, and at times does, lead to the exclusion of an alleged confession; but ultimately all turns on the judge's decision whether, breach or no breach, it has been shown to have been made voluntarily'. See also *Houghton* (1979) 69 Cr.App.R. 197.

149 'it was not contemplated that the rules would have any relevance to police interrogations which were not directed to obtaining statements meant to be put in evidence' (Hoffman, 1964, p. 26).

150 Commerton, 1964, p. 194.

151 This was underlined in *Sang* [1979] 2 All ER 1222, when Lord Diplock stated (at p. 1230d) that 'it is no part of a judge's function to exercise disciplinary powers over the police or prosecution as respects the way in which evidence to be used at the trial is obtained by them.... What a judge at the trial is concerned with is not how the evidence sought to be adduced by the prosecution has been obtained but with how it is used by the prosecution at the trial'.

152 St. Johnson, 1964, p. 92. See also Thomas, 1964, p. 386.

153 Marshall, 1964, p. 102. See also A Police Officer, 1964, p. 176.

154 See, (1964) 108 *Sol.J.* 106, p. 107; Abrahams, 1964b, p. 107; Hoffman, 1964, p. 26; Marshall, 1964, p. 98; Thomas, 1964, p. 383; Fellman, 1966, p. 44.

155 Hoffman, 1964, p. 25. Thomas (1964, p. 383) goes so far as to suggest that the old Rule 3 was itself 'responsible for the growth of the practice of 'inviting' suspected persons to attend a police station to answer questions'.

156 Which provided for custodial questioning only for the purpose of clearing up ambiguities. See *Massey* [1964] Crim.L.R. 43.

157 Home Office Circular No. 536053/23.

158 Devlin, 1960, p. 68. In this regard also see *Knight and Thayre* (1905) 20 Cox C.C. 711, and see the memorandum submitted by the Home Office to the 1928-9 Royal Commission, RCPPP, *Report*, para. 148.

159 [1947] AC 573.

160 *Ibid.*, pp. 587-8. Also see para. (*b*) of the preamble to the 1964 Rules.

161 Smith, 1964, p. 180. See also Zander, 1977, p. 353.

162 Rule II required the police to charge as soon as there was sufficient evidence.

163 Hoffman, 1964, p. 26; Thomas, 1964, pp. 383-4.

# PART III
# IMAGES OF THE POLICE-SUSPECT DYNAMIC

# 8 Pre-PACE Images: Detainees

**Introduction**

The legitimization of police interrogations under the Judges' Rules and associated judicial rulings may be understood as a concomitant of the general acceptance of the police as the cardinal agent of law enforcement. Modern professional police forces were established in nineteenth-century Britain in the face of widespread opposition emanating from a variety of sectional and class interests.[1] However, as Reiner (1986) points out, by the middle of the present century "the police were accepted throughout British society, to the extent of becoming symbols of national pride".[2] Reiner gains support for his view of the 1950s marking "the high point of police legitimation in Britain", from the national opinion survey conducted on behalf of the Royal Commission on the Police in 1960. The survey documented "an overwhelming vote of confidence in the police".[3]

That the police institution was able to attain this level of apparent consent and legitimacy was a direct result of the organisational policies espoused by the nineteenth century "architects of the benign and dignified police image", Peel, Rowan and Mayne.[4] Reiner identifies eight aspects to the organisational policies advanced by the founders of modern policing which played a crucial role in the movement to engineer consent for the police.[5]

Briefly, these policies comprised, firstly, the promotion of the image of police officers as full-time, disciplined members of a professional and bureaucratic organisation. The second major aspect in the formation and legitimation of the modern police lay in the adoption of the principle that it was incumbent upon officers having a duty to enforce the law to also obey and be governed by the 'rule of law'.[6] Thirdly, public support was to be secured by cultivating an image of the police as a civilian force guided by self-restraint, having moral and legal authority to enforce the law without the force of arms. The fourth policy consideration advanced by the architects of modern police forces as conducing legitimacy was the development of the doctrine of 'constabulary independence' as an aspect of the idea of the police being non-partisan servants of the public.[7] The service role was also explicitly fostered by the pioneers of the 'new' police in order to secure legitimacy for the institution. Further, preventive policing by uniformed officers was emphasised as a fundamental part of the legitimating policies. A seventh foundational element was, as Reiner puts it, "the successful appearance of effectiveness".[8] The final aspect of the formative policies identified as contributing to ultimate acceptance and legitimation of a full-time and professional law enforcement agency was the incorporation of "the main structurally rooted source of opposition to the police", the working class.[9]

Reiner (1985, 1986, 1992) argues that these aspects of the organisational strategy developed in the nineteenth century underpinned the gradual movement of the police towards increasing legitimacy. However, he asserts that this movement began to be undermined from the late 1950s when policing became exposed to increasing levels of public criticism and the politicised subject of a polarised law and order debate.[10] Consequently, the constructed and widely accepted image of the British police as an honest and impartial body suffered, causing the police to develop strategies designed to regain legitimacy.[11]

While the organisational policies expounded by the founders of the 'new' police, however poorly implemented in actuality, appear to have achieved widespread acceptance for traditional images of policing up until the 1950s, it is clear that these images continue to influence the way the police institution is perceived and the way its members view themselves. Furthermore, although the more visible powers and operational practices of the police have in recent years become a highly politicised issue, less empirical attention has been paid specifically to the role which constructed images of policing played in respect of the procedure and the practice attending police interrogations during the period when they were regulated by the Judges' Rules and their overriding requirement that statements made by suspects, when adduced as evidence at trial, should be voluntary.[12] This chapter will assess the extent to which specific and instrumental images of the police, police work and the policed may be discerned in this particular context and evaluate their potency and utility within the prosecution process that obtained prior to the changes introduced by the Police and Criminal Evidence Act, 1984 (PACE).

With respect to police interrogations conducted prior to the introduction of the PACE reforms, an assessment of the degree to which the constructed images of policing corresponded with the reality of police practice — or indeed the extent to which the formal rules were complied with — is hindered by the private and essentially invisible nature of police custodial activities. The authority the police enjoyed to exercise exclusive control over the conditions in which suspects were detained and questioned, and to exclude non-police actors from the interrogation process, shielded their activities from immediate external scrutiny.[13] Critically, this also meant that images of the police, their work, their competence, their interactions with suspects and the effectiveness of the controls to which they were subject, could only be obtained through the records they prepared. These records provided external viewers, such as solicitors, magistrates, barristers, juries and judges, with a single and ostensibly reliable source of information of the investigative process and then only when a prosecution had been instituted. The police, having unmediated access to suspects detained in custody, effectively controlled both the production and the presentation of the images — regarding themselves, their practices and those they interviewed — that formed a crucial element in the case assembled for prosecution.

On the basis of a sample consisting of 400 randomly selected committal papers — composed of statements and depositions prepared for the prosecution and conviction of defendants — relating to contested cases heard in the Crown Court prior to the introduction of the PACE reforms, the present chapter will consider a variety of images relating to the manner in which defendants, as suspects detained and questioned by the police, are portrayed in police accounts. These images will be discussed with reference to the outwardly faithful police depictions of the investigative and interrogative process of the pre-PACE adversarial system of criminal justice.

## Some Preliminary Points

Before turning to the variety of images identified in the survey of pre-PACE interrogation records, it is important to set out the manner in which the interrogations that comprise the pre-PACE sample were reported or recorded.

The revised Judge's Rules provided for accounts of custodial interrogations to be made in the form either of a statement written by the suspect, a written statement dictated to the police by the suspect, or a narrative record composed by the police.[14] It had been claimed of the revised Rules that if fully complied with they would so constrain the police that "many more [suspects would] find themselves writing their own statements whether they wish to or not".[15] However, as Table 1 demonstrates, in the cases that comprise the pre-PACE sample, no suspect is documented as having exercised his or her right to write a statement during their period of detention and interrogation.[16]

**Table 1  Mode of interview record, pre-PACE[17]**

| Mode of record | n | % |
| --- | --- | --- |
| Police witness statements | 394 | 98.5 |
| Contemporaneous notes | 4 | 1.0 |
| Dictated by detainee | 2 | 0.5 |
| Written by detainee | 0 | 0.0 |
|  | 400 | 100.0 |

The table shows that in most cases the information upon which the prosecution, the defence and ultimately the courts were to assess private custodial exchanges between the police and the accused, was derived almost exclusively from unverifiable police accounts of those exchanges as presented in the hand written witness statements of individual officers. This finding would appear to support the assertion that rather than write or dictate their own statements, most suspects preferred to leave the composition of the narrative record to the police.[18] However, the incidence of police witness statements in the pre-PACE sample might suggest that the police enjoyed considerable influence over suspects' decision-making during interrogations and a not inconsiderable influence over the images the courts would receive following interrogation.

Police accounts of what was said at interview were frequently found to have been prepared several months after the interrogations they purport to record had ended.[19] As McConville and Baldwin (1981) on the basis of their own pre-PACE study observed:

> The police rarely take a verbatim record during an interview, and the final record is at best an attenuated version of what was said, coloured, and distorted by the frailties of human memory.[20]

Indeed, in constructing their *ex post facto* accounts of custodial interviews, individual officers, as result of the decision in *Bass* (1953),[21] were not prohibited from collaborating with each other in order to tender self-corroborating narratives to the courts. In this case the Court of Appeal was presented with evidence indicating that subsequent to a custodial interview conducted in breach of the Judges' Rules, two officers had made almost identical notes recording a confession alleged to have been made voluntarily by the accused. Byrne, J found that:

> police officers nearly always deny that they have collaborated in the making of notes.... It seems to us that nothing could be more natural or proper when two persons have been present at an interview with a third person than that they should afterwards make sure that they have a correct version of what was said. Collaboration would appear to be a better explanation of almost identical notes than the possession of superhuman memory.[22]

Byrne, J would seem to have based his observations on the premise that police interrogators could be relied upon to record the totality of their exchanges with suspects. He does not appear to have considered the possibility that some officers might collaborate after an interview to fashion a *false* version of what was said.[23]

A second point to consider before turning to the selection pre-PACE images concerns the attendance of legal advisers during interrogation. In this respect, the present study supports the findings of early empirical research conducted by Zander (1972) and Baldwin and McConville (1979). The findings of the present study are set out in Table 2:

**Table 2 Adviser's attendance at interrogation, pre-PACE[24]**

| Adviser attends | n | % |
| --- | --- | --- |
| No | 356 | 96.2 |
| Yes (throughout interrogation) | 10 | 2.7 |
| Part of interrogation | 4 | 1.1 |
| Not known | 30 | — |
|  | 400 | 100.0 |

The table would suggest that prior to the introduction of PACE very few suspects received the benefit of legal advice during their period of detention and interrogation. Moreover, the findings presented in this and the earlier table would seem to point both to the dominance of police interests over that of detainees and to the ineffectiveness of the Judges' Rules.[25]

## Images of Detainees

The images of defendants identified in the survey as frequently appearing in police interrogation records may be brought within four broad though not mutually exclusive categories. The categories comprise those cases in which defendants, while detained as suspects, are depicted as being: (1) defiant and or confident; (2) unequivocally guilty; or (3) artful.

The categories or typologies may be seen on the one hand as of descriptive value, providing a means for mapping out the various kinds of individuals who are brought within the criminal process and who provide the police with the raw material to enable them to pursue their law enforcement function. On the other hand, they may be seen as vehicles affording information about the police and their work in the private sphere; their values and ideologies; and their capacity to present defendants in particular ways to powerful others in the criminal process. The categories also serve to highlight the issue of the relationship between the images conveyed in the police accounts and the realities which they purport to describe. This issue can be partly addressed in terms of a critical assessment of the plausibility of the images themselves, but is more thoroughly explored when the accounts or constructions are compared with the recorded realities of the PACE era.[26]

### *Defiant and or Confident Detainees*

The defiant and or confident defendant — as a suspect detained and interrogated by the police — was often shown to be self-assured, familiar with the mechanics of the criminal process and therefore unperturbed by being drawn into it. This image carries with it the implicit message that the detainee is 'factually guilty' but is aware that this is quite distinct from being found 'legally guilty' by a court of law. The impression conveyed is that the detainee is in some way responsible for the offence upon which he or she is being questioned. This impression stems both from the specific and instrumental ways in which such detainees are portrayed and from the confidence displayed by the police in their apparently well-founded and reasonable suspicions.

According to the case papers relating to Case AP/1051, D, while driving, had been stopped by two officers who identified themselves and explained that they suspected that stolen property was in the vehicle. D denied this. Upon examining the car, the officers found and seized certain items of property. D was arrested and taken into custody. During the formal custodial interview D claimed that he had purchased the property found in the car:

> PO: You mean to tell me you bought these from a man in a pub? Let me tell you now, I don't believe you.
> D: Please yourself. That's what I'm saying, now it's up to you to prove something different.
> PO: If that's your attitude, you will be detained here whilst we make enquiries....
> D: Please yourself....

At this point the interview was broken off. When resumed, D was asked who had stolen the property if he had not. To this he is reported to have replied:

> D: You've got to prove they're stolen, that's your job....
> PO: ... you are at least guilty of handling them.
> D: So get on and charge me....

Later, in spite of his initially combative and defiant attitude, D reportedly confessed. However, when asked to name his accomplices he is reported to have become uncooperative:

> PO: I doubt if the break was committed by you alone. Who else was with you?
> D: Don't be stupid ... don't think I'd go that low.
> ...
> PO: You will be charged with burglary....
> D: You do your job and leave me to worry about that.

This short extract is sufficient to enable the reader to assess the character of D, if not the case against him. The defiant attitude struck by D gives the impression that his initial claim to innocence — which he made no attempt to substantiate — was untrue. Although he was under no legal obligation to substantiate his story, he appears to exploit this by reminding the police that it was for them to establish that his story was not true. He therefore appears as a factually guilty person who seeks to 'brave it out' by defying the police to prove their case. The police for their part appear to be justified in detaining him in order to conduct further inquiries. However, D's unwillingness to implicate his accomplices indicates a concern to place an allegiance to his criminal associates above his moral duty to assist the police. Clearly, the unfavourable images of D which emerge from the police narrative account of his arrest and interrogation, present the court with a portrait of his character and culpability conducive to the prospect of conviction.

In Case BP/1097, D was arrested, detained and formally questioned on suspicion of being responsible for the burglary of a private house from which £15 was stolen:

PO: [The complainant] says that she was in the toilet when you called. When you knocked on the door she asked you to wait. When she left the toilet she heard the sound of the rustle of paper and when she got into the room, you were standing inside.... When you had gone ... she looked in her handbag ... and she found there was £15 cash missing.

D: That's not true. I didn't go into the room until after she had left the toilet and I didn't touch anything in the flat.

PO: Are you saying that this lady is telling lies?[27]

D: Well look at her, she's old, she don't know what she's doing, she might have lost the money.

PO: Well the money was in her purse before you came into the room and it was gone after you left.... I think you stole the money while she was in the toilet.[28]

D: You can't prove anything. I shall say I was never alone in the room and you try and prove different. That old lady will never get to court anyway.

In this case D is depicted in a similar manner to that of his counterpart in the previous case. Again, irrespective of the nature of any alternative forms of evidence that might connect D to the offence, the reader is left with an impression that the detainee is guilty. He is shown to have shifted his position from initially denying the offence, to one in which he appears to have formulated a strategic plan to challenge the police to attempt to prove their case in court. Moreover, he appears confident that the complainant would be either too infirm or perhaps unwilling to appear as a witness. The reader is invited to conclude that this confidence — seemingly based upon a cynical assessment of the capacity of the police to prove their case — is misplaced.

Other examples of defiant but ignorant suspects appearing to revel in the misguided belief that without their cooperation any case against them could not proceed to trial are found in Case AP/1197 and Case BP/1015. In the first of these cases the police had received a report of an attempted burglary. However, on arrival they found the perpetrators had left. Later that evening D was identified by a civilian witness as being one of the persons involved. D was arrested and detained in police custody where he was interviewed. Throughout the interview D reportedly maintained his innocence. However, at the close of the interview, the following exchange is reported to have taken place:

> PO: You were seen by a witness and identified ... as being one of four men concerned in stealing some copper cylinders from [the commercial premises].
> D: I haven't been anywhere. I was just walking along the road [when I was arrested].
> PO: You were in fact seen loading the copper into a van there. Whose is it?
> D: I don't know, its not mine.
> PO: I should like to know the identity of the other three men. Who are they?
> D: You've got the van, you can find out who owns it can't you? I'm not putting anybody else in.
> PO: Are you now admitting that you were involved?[29]
> D: I'm admitting fuck all, you prove it.

Here, while D is reported to have defiantly refused to admit guilt, he is shown to have inadvertently betrayed himself.

In Case BP/1015 the suspect had been approached by two officers, who informed him that he was being arrested in connection with a series of burglaries. He was then cautioned that he was not obliged to say anything but anything he elected to say might be put into writing and given in evidence. The suspect replied:

> D: I'm saying nothing.

He was conveyed to the police station where he is reported to have asked:

> D: What's this all about?

PO: You have been arrested following certain information received; we have reason to believe you are involved with [a named accomplice] committing burglaries last year.

D: You are going to have to prove it chum, I'm saying nothing.

Although it is reported that D was cautioned of his 'right to silence', his exercise of that right has the effect of implicitly confirming the suspicions of the police and of encouraging the reader to conclude that he is in some way involved. In this case the suspicions and the encouragement receive further credibility from the police witness statements which report that D was detained while his rooms were searched. There, it is reported, incriminating real evidence was recovered.

In Case PP/1090 the suspect, a car dealer, was arrested and questioned in connection with the theft of a number of motor cars. The police had also questioned his alleged accomplice (Z). Initially, D had maintained that he was innocent. Then, apparently with the realisation that the police had acquired evidence of his involvement, he appears to have adopted a relatively compliant attitude. However, he continued to resist the full force of the allegations communicated by the interviewer. The crucial exchange between D and the questioner is reported as follows:

PO: What about the accident you had ... in one of the cars?

D: Who told you that?

PO: [Z] told me. Besides that car others have been recovered in a damaged condition. Are you trying to tell me that damaged cars sell readily on the market, which would be the case if you believe [Z] and his brother are dealers?[30]

D: I'm not trying to tell you anything.

PO: You are trying to tell me that you didn't know these cars were stolen. You are trying to tell me that you thought [Z] and his brother were car dealers and although these cars were treated with no respect whatsoever, they could still be sold to members of the public. Is that correct?

D: That's my story and I'm going to stick to it.... I know it doesn't look too good for me but I'm not going to admit to stealing those cars....

PO: I have seen [Z] and as I have already told you, he's putting all the blame on you and you're saying its him. Isn't it a fact that you are both telling lies and you are all involved together?

D: Look, I admit to driving them, but as far as stealing them goes it will be my word against [his] and that's it.

In this exchange D is presented as being obdurate in manner. Despite the apparently considerable evidence in the possession of the police connecting him to the offence he resolves to stick to his story. While his story may be consistent with his innocence the implication remains that it is a fabrication and that he would be prepared to accept a lesser charge. The officer, for his part, is depicted as a concerned guardian of the public interest who has based his questions on his own thorough investigations; investigations that indisputably point to the guilt of the defendant.

The following case is perhaps a stronger example of a pre-PACE interview serving to convey a particular view of a suspect's character. The police account in this case is not limited to relating to others the suspect's voluntary responses to questions put in the course of police investigations. Here the dialogue appears to be concerned to show that D is an unsavoury character who impudently articulates the continuing threat law enforcement officers face as they go about their duties.

The suspect in Case AP/1163 was arrested on suspicion of being involved in a fight between two gangs in which an officer, who had attempted to make arrests, sustained injuries. During his formal custodial interview the suspect was told:

PO: You have been arrested on suspicion of being involved in the attack on PC [Wilson]....
D: He got what you all get one day when we blood you up.
PO: Are you saying that it is all right to go about knocking policemen about?[31]
D: If you harass my brothers and me then the war will start. All you Babylon will burn.
PO: I am not very impressed by this. I want to know what happened last night.

It was found that the image of the menacing, hostile, combative and sometimes violent suspect was commonly, though not exclusively, associated with young Afro-Caribbean males.[32] Such individuals were generally portrayed in stereotypical terms and depicted, through means of supposedly objective police accounts of social reality, as using a form of pidgin English (patois) ascribable to a particular and villainous section of the black community.[33]

A further example of this theme is found in Case PP/1014. The suspect, one of "a large contingent of West Indians",[34] was alleged to have attempted to prevent the police from making an arrest. He is reported to have become so violent that it became necessary to place him immediately in the police cells. Later, at the commencement of his formal interview, D was cautioned. His response, according to the police account, was to ask:

> D: What you talk. Why you dread arrest me?
> PO: You were arrested because you assaulted me while I was making a lawful arrest.
> D: Fuck sake, dread man, me no want to talk to you. You Babylon, you burn.
> PO: It's up to you whether you want to talk about it. Do you want to make a statement about this?
> D: Go away, leave me.
> PO: Very well, you will be charged with assaulting [me].
> D: Well you just go right ahead and charge me. It make no difference to me.

D was then charged. It is reported that when he refused to sign the charge sheet he turned to the officer he had allegedly assaulted and said:

> D: I will get you blood man, and I wreck this station.

The contrast between the fractious suspect and the courteous officer would be all too apparent to the reader, be that the prosecution, the defence, or the adjudicator.

The report of the dialogue between the suspect and the interviewing officer in Case AP/1122 also exhibits many of the features associated with self-assured, confident and practiced criminals. The formal custodial interrogation of D in this case followed an incident in which a number of 'West Indian' youths allegedly inveigled a cashier into opening her till and then made off in a car with a large amount of the cash therein. D had expressed a willingness to admit to being present but he continually refused to implicate others:

> PO: You admit being involved in the robbery then. Would you care to tell us who was with you?
> D: No way man, me you've got but you're going to have to work for the others. Just don't ask me.
> PO: Well, how about the car, whose it that, yours?
> D: I don't drive. I just went along for the fun. I made thirty sheets and now I got caught. Don't try and trick me for the other names.

PO: In view of what you have told us I am now telling you that you will shortly be charged with being involved in the robbery. Do you want to make a statement about what you have already said?
D: I'm saying nothing until I've seen our friend Mr [Q].
PO: Who is this Mr [Q]?
D: You got to know him man, he's our whitey solicitor. He always looks after me and my friends.
PO: In that case you had better speak to him first. Do you want to call him now?
D: No he'll be there to see me in the morning. My friends will tell him where I am.

At no point during the interrogation, as reported by the police, did D explicitly confess in answer to any direct question on his involvement in the offence. Rather, his damaging admissions were apparently volunteered in response to questions seeking information about the ownership of the alleged getaway car. To this it should be noted that the possibility of the police account being successfully challenged is limited, firstly, by the position accorded to police witnesses *vis-à-vis* defendants in the 'hierarchy of credibility'.[35] The other important basis which renders this police account relatively immune from challenge is the depiction of D as being arrogantly confident in the abilities of his solicitor. His somewhat indelicate (if not obtuse) references to his solicitor encourages the reader to take an unfavourable view of the suspect and of his adviser.

Case AP/1217 is a stark example of the characteristically truculent and defiant Afro-Caribbean male. Here D is seen to adopt a contemptuous attitude toward white institutions of authority. However, by virtue of his seemingly unguarded or absent-minded admissions, he emerges as an essentially dull-witted exponent of this attitude.

Arrested at his home on suspicion of being a member of a group responsible for committing a number of burglaries, D was taken into custody and formally questioned:

PO: What do you know about the tape recorder [recovered from your address]?
D: I hate you white rasses. Don't ask me to write anything.
PO: I'm not asking you to write anything, just tell us what you know.
D: You already know, we got it from the house. Why should I help you?
PO: What about all the other gear there? You might as well tell us the truth because you are going to the court anyway.

D: You tell the white pig judge what you like man, find the houses yourself. Now go away and leave me alone.

The dismissive attitude exhibited by D in this narrative account raises the clear inference that he is a burglar who has secreted the goods in question. It is not clear whether the property was recovered prior to trial, however, this exchange would also serve to explain any inability of the police to trace the goods.

Suspects interrogated by the police who exhibit contempt for the criminal justice process and display signs of a sociopathic disposition are, of course, not confined to any one single ethnic group. In Case PP/1029, for example, officers arrived at a public house in which a violent altercation had occurred. They approached D who "had blood all over both hands [and] blood on the trousers he was wearing". D was asked what he knew about the injuries sustained by the party to the fight who required hospital treatment. It is reported that he was cautioned before he replied:

D: A fucking Cockney, like the Paddies and Coons, I'll fix the lot of them.
PO: What did you do to him?
D: I bashed him with a glass. I'd do it to all the bastards. The Brums are all right but I can't stomach Cockneys, Paddies or Coons.

On being taken into police custody the suspect is reported to have added:

D: You punks are all the same, you won't do anything about the Irish blowing us up, but you'll lift me for doing the job for you. My arms aren't tied.

Part of the formal custodial interview is reported as follows:

PO: I have come to see you regarding the fight you were in at [the public house] tonight.
D: I know nothing about it, I ain't been in any fight.
PO: How do you account for the blood all over your coat?
D: Its from cuts on me.
PO: But you haven't got any cuts so let's have the truth.
D: Who was it, that Cockney bastard and his black cunt who put me in, you won't prove it as no one will stand up in court against me.
PO: Do you want to make a statement? If you do I will take it down or you can write it yourself.

D: I'm saying fuck all to you, he won't make it to court. I've taken note of you son.

Irrespective of the merits of his case, D is shown to have little, in terms of his personality or therefore his credit-worthiness, that might endear him to the courts. Nevertheless, the excerpt suffices as an illustration of the contrast found in the pre-PACE accounts between the defiant or uncooperative suspect and the composed police interviewer.

## *Unequivocally Guilty Detainees*

The unequivocally guilty detainee also appears with considerable frequency in the sample of interrogation records drawn from the pre-PACE era. These detainees appear as individuals having little or no desire to resist a compulsion to make full or partial confessions or to cooperate with the police. They seem intent on seeking the solace presumed to derive from "making a clean breast of it".[36] They appear to seek the cathartic effect said to follow an early avowal of guilt or, in some cases, seem to believe that an early confession might benefit them either by securing their early release from police custody or by attracting a lenient sentence from the court.[37] They are often presented as making damaging admissions either from a deep sense of remorse or as a result of introspective deliberations upon their own best interests.

Suspects within this class might admit to their part in an offence at the first available opportunity or when they are brought, under interrogation, to realise that the evidence against them is overwhelming. It is not uncommon for suspects in this model to offer a motive for their actions. Occasionally, however, they will be shown to be unwilling to incriminate others or alternatively to accept *full* responsibility themselves.

The police record of Case PP/1020 relates that the suspects, D1 and D2, had been arrested by officers of the Kingshire Police Force (KPO) for offences arising out of an alleged assault on an officer who attempted to arrest them on suspicion of driving a stolen car. Under interrogation by the Kingshire officers, D1 and D2 are shown to be compliant confessors:

KPO: You were arrested for taking a motor vehicle from [Cuddlestone] earlier tonight. What have you got to say about it?
D1: Yes all right we nicked it from near the Church.

174    *Interrogation and Confession*

> KPO: You were the driver of the vehicle?
> D1:   Yes.

At this point D1 was shown two passports, neither of which were in his name.

> KPO: Where did you get these from?
> D1:   They're a couple of mates I know.
> KPO: Did they give you these documents then?
> D1:   No.
> KPO: How did you come by them then?
> D1:   Went to the Registrars in [Boldham] and got copies of the birth certificates and used them to get the passports, then we could get to France.
> KPO: So you pretended you were [the persons to whom the passports were issued] and forged their signatures on all the necessary documents?
> D1:   Yes.

D1 was then questioned in respect of a number of items including a bank book also made out in the name of another person. He answered each question in turn, explaining that each of the items were taken as a result of thefts from private cars or homes. D2 was questioned separately by the same officer:

> KPO: You have been arrested for taking a car from [Cuddlestone] earlier tonight. I have spoken to [D1] and he has told me a lot. Now, what have you got to say?
> D2:   All right I may as well put my hands up.

D2 proceeded to volunteer a full confession, corroborating the confession of D1.

On the surface, the question put to D2 appears as an invitation to volunteer his own explanation. However, a close examination of the question reveals its true import. The question conveys specific messages to the accused. It communicates to D2 that D1 has effectively confessed and therefore has in all likelihood implicated him. It also implies that D2 can not realistically deny the offence.

According to the official record of the detainee's custodial interrogation in Case AP/1066 the following exchange was recorded:

Pre-PACE Images: Detainees 175

PO: Now look [D], on the night of 31 January and 1 February this year the service station [at a named address] was broken into and a calculator was stolen. I know you did it.
D: How did you know it was me?
PO: That's immaterial, did you commit this offence?
D: Yes I did. I'm sorry.

There is no evidence in the prosecution papers associated with this case to indicate that the officer had prior knowledge of who was responsible for the burglary. Conceivably, the claim was made in order to induce a confession. It is also possible that the source of the officer's apparent certitude was an informer, the identity of whom could not be revealed. Nevertheless, by his questioning of D, the officer would be aware that a confession would serve to confirm police suspicions and to facilitate a conviction. Furthermore, as the following extract from the same case illustrates, there remains the possibility that the detainee will surrender additional information which will enable the police to 'clear-up' other outstanding offences:

PO: There was another break just up the road about the same time ... the place was completely wrecked. Do you know anything about that?
D: Yes, I was low that week. I'm fed up of being on the dole.

The following account, excerpted from Case PP/1013, depicts the suspect as becoming a willing and extremely cooperative confessor after his initial strategies of evasiveness and of feigning ignorance had failed. The general impression gained is that the suspect, though ultimately compliant, is calculating, deceitful and underhand. This impression is reinforced by his use of criminal argot. The police, for their part, are seen to be well-informed, undeviating in the pursuit of 'the truth' and at all times concerned to ensure that any admissions made are given voluntarily.

D1 was suspected of being involved in the illegal sale of a car with a stolen MOT certificate:

PO: We are Regional Crime Squad and you are [D1].

...

D1: I don't know what you are on about.
PO: Do you know [D2]? He's been arrested for receiving stolen MOT's and I have good reason to believe you're involved.

176  *Interrogation and Confession*

    D1:    All right, fair enough. Gotta try ain't ya?

It is stated that the officer then referred to a quantity of cigarettes, alcohol and cash that had been found where D1 had been arrested. The officer asked, "what's all this then?"

    D1:    It's for a party.
    PO:    That's come from a pub break.
    D1:    All right, who's put me in, surely not [D2]?
    PO:    Which pub have you done?
    D1:    I don't know a friend called and left it for me.
    PO:    Its obvious you've done the break.
    D1:    I'll admit receiving.
    PO:    You didn't receive them.
    D1:    He must have used my coat.
    PO:    Who's that then?
    D1:    A friend.
    PO:    What's his name?
    D1:    No way. Look you've got me fair and square. I'll clear my sheet ... but you won't get any names.

Particularly, though not exclusively, with regard to those cases identified by the survey as falling within the 'unequivocally guilty' class, the police accounts of their custodial interactions with detainees are frequently presented in a manner that might suggest that a full trial into every aspect of each case is unwarranted or unnecessary. In other words, although confessions are not always necessary to sustain convictions,[38] the nature of apparently uncoerced and voluntary confessions, as detailed in the pre-PACE sample of cases, would seem to militate against an adversarial confrontation between the prosecution and defence at trial. In such circumstances it would be difficult for the defence to argue that the confession was either false or improperly obtained.[39] The next case, to some extent, illustrates this point.

Case AP/1038 concerned an incident which resulted in the hospitalisation of a two-year-old boy, the son of D. The case papers report that when D was initially questioned by officers, the following exchange was recorded:

    PO:    We are making enquiries as to the reason why your son, [S], was admitted to [the hospital].
    D:    Because I gave him tablets, that's why.

PO: [The officer 'immediately cautioned' D before asking:] Do you know what the tablets were?
D: Phenobarbitone.
PO: Where did you get them?
D: ... I was clearing out a cupboard at a friend's house and found them on the bottom shelf. I put them in my pocket so her children wouldn't get them.
PO: You thought they would be harmful to her children?
D: Yes.
PO: Thinking that they were dangerous and could even kill him, you gave the tablets to your baby?
D: Yes and I'd do it again.
PO: Why?
D: Because he was getting on my nerves.

She was later interviewed by a senior officer:

PO: I understand that you have already admitted to [the arresting officers] that you gave some Phenobarbitone tablets to your son, [S], is that correct?
D: Yes.
PO: You are aware that the tablets that you gave him could seriously harm him and in fact could have killed him as its a poison?
D: ['Crying'] Oh yes. I will tell you the truth, I did it to get back at my husband. It was the only way I could hurt him.

This case is merely one example from the pre-PACE accounts which would suggest that in the absence of a legal obligation on police interviewers to make contemporaneous records of interviews,[40] the police version of what was said may be viewed as virtually invulnerable. Moreover, while unverifiable police accounts of their exchanges with detainees may in effect subvert the trial process,[41] they may also serve, as Case BP/1015 demonstrates, to legitimate police decision making.

In this case D was arrested on suspicion of having committed a burglary. However, the police account of interrogation indicates that D was willing to confess only to the lesser offence of receiving stolen property:

PO: I have arrested you because certain matters have come to light and we have recovered property which is stolen.
D: What's that then?
PO: A stereo unit from your room. We have searched it with the proprietor, your boss.

178    *Interrogation and Confession*

> D:   Well, that's it then.
> PO:  Where did you get it from?
> D:   Do you really expect me to tell you?
> PO:  That's why I asked the question.
> D:   I haven't done any screwing, if that's what you mean.
> PO:  I suppose you bought it off a bloke in a pub?
> D:   That's about the truth. Look, I ain't a fool. You've got me. I ain't going to 'fanny' you. I knew it was 'nicked', I bought it for £15. It had to be 'nicked' at that price.
> PO:  My information is that you've been doing the breakings.
> D:   No.
> PO:  Well if you paid £15 for it, you must know who you bought it off?
> D:   I do but I ain't no 'grass'.[42]

D was then told that the police had information that he had committed the burglary and had disposed of the property with the aid of a named accomplice.

> D:   I punted a bit of gear out, yes. Look, I never did any burglaries.... [T]he honest truth is I never did any burglaries... I don't expect you to believe it, but it's the truth.

D was charged with receiving stolen goods. It may be that the officer's claim of having information that D had actually committed the burglaries — information that was never made explicit — was contrived or inaccurate. Irrespective of whether the officer possessed the information or whether this was a ploy designed to induce a confession to the greater offence of burglary, it appears to have been immediately discarded in the face of D's claim that he was not responsible for the crime. However, other cases from the study suggest that had the questioner reported himself as having maintained a sceptical air, the inference of guilt to emerge from the unverifiable yet putatively faithful police account, would have been sufficient to raise the prospect of a conviction for theft.

The self-confirming and self-legitimating capacity of pre-PACE interrogation records is seen in a slightly different context in the next case. D, in Case BP/1101, had been arrested with two others for being involved in breaking and entering a private house and stealing from that house a number of shot-guns together with certain electrical goods.

> PO: You understand why you are here. Is there anything you wish to say? Before you answer, I must tell you that we have recovered the property from [the garage belonging to one of the co-accused].
> D: You know it already. I can't tell you any more.
> PO: From what you are saying, I take it you are admitting breaking into and stealing the property?[43]
> D: Yes.
> PO: Because you are only a juvenile, one or both of your parents will have to be told where you are and someone will have to come to this station before you're charged or any further conversation can take place.
> D: My Mom should be in.
> PO: I will make the necessary arrangements.

The case papers report that when the officer left the interview room, in order to contact D's parents, the remaining officer recorded the following conversation:

> D: My Mother's not going to be too 'chuffed' considering the raid for them shot guns this morning.
> PO: Yes, I heard about that. What happened?
> D: It was about 7.30 this morning when the police came round. They searched everywhere for some shot-guns.
> PO: Yes, the information that they had was supposed to be very good. All I can say to you is that guns can be very dangerous. People are seriously injured and even killed every day because of guns.

Here the police account suggests that D was not subjected to any undue pressures and that the relevant provisions of the Judges' Rules governing the treatment of detainees were meticulously observed. However, it is clear that the first officer was aware that D was a juvenile *before* he apprised him of the evidence recovered and *before* the vital admission of guilt had been secured. The seemingly inconsequential dialogue between the second officer and D shows the latter to have initiated an exchange in which the officer acquaints D (and the external audience) with the strength of the suspicions that had preceded his arrest. It also depicts the officer delivering a chastening homily on the dangers of guns while conveying the idea that though police sources may occasionally misdirect them, they invariably arrest and proceeded against the right man. It is clear that the officers were aware of the pre-PACE rule prohibiting the custodial questioning of juveniles in the absence of a parent or guardian.[44] It is not known whether the officers were seeking to defend 'technical breaches'[45] of that rule.

That the police enjoyed virtually unimpeded control over pre-PACE interrogations is demonstrated in Case AP/1158. This case is also illustrative of the police capacity to deny non-police personnel access to detained suspects.

In this case the suspect, who had been visited at her home, was invited to accompany two officers to the police station to be interviewed in respect of an allegation, made by her former employer, to the effect that she, on diverse dates during the course of the preceding year, had stolen £3000.

PO: I have to ask you to come to [the police station] with us to be interviewed respecting this allegation made against you.
D: All right, but will I be long? There's the children to see to.
PO: Well your husband [HB] is here, he can look after them.
HB: I want to come with her.
PO: [To the husband.] Think of the children, you can come down to the police station later.

It is reported that during the course of the formal interview conducted at the police station, D eventually made certain damaging admissions. It is also reported that when HB arrived, D's earlier admissions were reinforced by the following exchange:

PO: ... I understand your husband is outside and he wants to see you.
D: Can I see him?
PO: Yes, I'll show him in. [After HB had entered the interview room.] Well are you going to tell him, or do you want me to tell him about the money?
HB: What's this?
D: I didn't pay it in.
HB: What are you talking about?
PO: She's referring to the [money]. She didn't pay it into [her former employer's] bank account.
HB: [To D.] Why?
D: Because the children needed clothes.
PO: Would you please leave now. There are certain formalities that have to be attended to....

Case BP/1088 is of interest not only as an illustration of the nature of police relations with suspects but also as an example of the personality-type who appear to gain relief from the act of confessing.[46] The excerpt suggests that the suspect's decision to confess is the result of firm but scrupulously fair questioning, the product of his being left to reflect upon his guilt or, alternatively, his assessment of the prospect of further detention. The officer, in contrast, is seen to be punctilious in his efforts to ensure that the detainee volunteers a statement.

> PO: Do you want to make a written statement about your part in the affair?
> D1: I don't know. I don't know what to do.
> PO: In that case you will be placed downstairs while [D2] is seen again and I shall see you later. [Moments later.] You have had long enough. Do you want to make a statement about it or not? You don't have to if you don't want to. If you do you can write it yourself or I will write it for you.
> D1: Yes, I'll make a statement. I'm glad it's all over really.

The statement was taken down at the dictation of the accused. With regard to the interrogation of D2, the police account of his interrogation has similar qualities to that respecting D1. The image here is one of a suspect who is brought to confront his guilt; a suspect who — after a permissible prod from the police[47] — is permitted time to reflect upon the seriousness of his crime.

> PO: I am DC [P] and this is PC [R]. We are making enquiries into an assault on an elderly woman.... I have reason to believe that you are responsible for that offence with [D1] and I must tell you that you are not obliged to say anything unless you wish to do so but anything you do say may be taken down in writing and may be given in evidence.
> D2: You seem to know all about it. Get on with it.
> PO: This was a very nasty assault... because that woman was 72 years' old. The consequences could have been more serious than they are.
> D2: Let me think for a minute. I want to sort things out.
> [Moments later.] It wasn't my idea, I was just there.

The study found many instances where suspects, when questioned in police custody, eventually resolve to offer remorseful confessions of guilt. In Case BP/1007 for example, the suspect was arrested and interrogated in respect of a complaint alleging that he had obtained a loan by falsely representing that he had succeeded in securing a lucrative building contract. When first questioned the suspect denied the offence. However, the police account shows that the formal interrogation was terminated after he made the following apologetic reply to a direct question of his guilt:

D: Yes, but I had promised [my girlfriend] a holiday. It meant a lot to me. I know I was foolish.... It was just temptation.... I have let the bank down badly. I know that the bank wouldn't have lent me the money if they had known what I was going to do with it. I am very sorry about it. I would like to say that I am very sorry about all those cheques I wrote out to people that haven't been paid because there was no money in my account. I knew that they wouldn't be paid because there was no money going in at all.... I went berserk really. I have got to be more sorry than anything else. I have been a nuisance to everyone the way I acted. I don't know why I did it.

One other case in a similar vein is Case PP/1025. The suspect was formally interviewed with regard to an allegation that he had obtained money by selling forged car insurance cover notes. It is apparent from the police account that his initial reticence very soon gave way as he began to give full details of his involvement. It is reported that the interview ended with these somewhat hackneyed and ritualistic expressions of remorse:

D: ... I've been foolish.... I admit I was silly.... I am sorry about this now. I regret the inconvenience caused to everyone concerned through my action in succumbing to temptation.

Case PP/1026 is offered as a final example of that class of suspect who appear in the pre-PACE narrative accounts to have little upon which to mount an effective defence. Having completed repairs to a family house, D in this case, was alleged to have returned, forced entry and to have stolen a wristwatch together with a quantity of cash. It was also alleged that he had deceived the householder to obtain payment for the repairs he had effected. When police officers approached D and told him that he answered the description of the alleged offender. D reportedly replied:

D: Fuck off, I don't know what you are talking about.

He was arrested and after being cautioned said:

D: The bastards, they've shit on me, they are all radgy [later when asked what 'radgy' meant he is reported to have replied: 'Nuts, you know, fucking bonkers'] and the son's a right wanker. He sits upstairs all day and wanks on dirty books.
PO: I'm not concerned about that. You are going with us to [the] police station. Would you mind proving who you are?

D produced his wallet and gave his name. At his formal interrogation sometime later, the questions put to D centred on the offence for which he was initially arrested.

> PO: How did you get the watch?
> D: He [the householder] threw [it at me].
> PO: Why?
> D: Because he wouldn't give me any more money. He did in the end though. He's shit scared, anything will frighten him, so I had the watch as well.
> PO: Why was he scared?
> D: Oh come on. I got to get me money haven't I?
> PO: You threatened him?
> D: [No reply.]

It is reported that the next series of questions put to D succeeded in eliciting voluntary and damaging admissions in respect of the materials he had used to conduct the repairs, though not in regard to the offence for which he had been arrested.

> PO: How much did you get [from the family]?
> D: I had twenty-seven pounds and seventy-two pounds....
> PO: Is that for the materials?
> D: No, they're all over the wall.
> PO: What the lot?
> D: You don't think I'd pay for them do you?
> PO: Where are they from?
> D: Look, if I came up to you and put louvre windows in, two new doors, new tiles on the roof and a few bricks, how much would you pay?
> PO: It would run out at about two hundred pounds.
> D: Well, if I said I would do it for one hundred pounds, you wouldn't ask any questions.

Asked, in the seasoned manner, if he would like to make a statement about the matter and whether he would like it written for him at his dictation D replied:

> D: No chance, we'll have it out in court. I'm a betting man, I'll take a chance. It's all a good laugh anyway. You can't get me for trying to con them. I didn't get the money, they're too mean. I'll tell you what, charge me, bail me, let me sit on the wall outside and I'll make a statement admitting everything and I'll tell you where I had the tiles from.

PO: We are not allowed to do that.
D: No statement then.

Clearly, the events attending this case, as represented in the police narrative, convey strong impressions inimical to a presumption of innocence. The police are seen as being patient, forbearing and incorruptible in their interactions with the accused. He on the other hand is seen to be volatile, abusive, disrespectful, untrustworthy and unprincipled. The unfavourable images of the suspect — coupled with the non-interrogation evidence, such as the statements made by the complainants — conspire to encourage the view that he is unequivocally guilty.

## Artful Detainees

This, the final broad category of frequently recurring images identified in the survey of pre-PACE accounts of interrogation, comprises a selection of cases in which detainees appear as individuals who may be characterised as artful or calculating. Typically, the culpability of such individuals is presented as being beyond doubt. However, the principal feature that unifies this class of detainee lies in the frequency with which they appear as persons who, either after being accused or after making damaging admissions, contrive to negotiate a deal with the police.

At this point it should be emphasised that irrespective of the category in which the cases which make up the pre-PACE sample have been placed, the images identified were, with rare exceptions, unfavourable to the accused. This should not be surprising particularly when two closely related points are considered. The first stems from the role the police play in the criminal justice process. That role is such that the investigation and prosecution brief conferred upon the police requires them not merely to inquire into the facts of a case but to construct a case for prosecution.[48] The second point arises from the consideration that the case papers which form the raw material for the present study were drawn exclusively from prosecutions that were determined in the Crown Court. Therefore, the cases would have been assembled in the firm expectation that each prosecution would culminate in a successful conviction.

Empirical studies of police interrogations conducted prior to the introduction of PACE have demonstrated that police officers were prepared to employ a wide range of psychological techniques against suspected offenders in order to induce compliance.[49] Apart from the use of threats, police officers have been observed to offer inducements, such as the granting of bail, in order to obtain admissions from suspects. The nature of the present study, based on the content analysis of official accounts of interrogation, prevents a direct assessment of such practices. The point is that if manipulative tactics were employed by the police this would not be immediately apparent from the interrogation records examined. Indeed, in respect of the practice that has been described as "bail bargaining",[50] for instance, the records suggest that the police *never* indulged in such practices and that when the subject of negotiated bail was raised it was *always* initiated by the accused. The following three cases are examples.

In Case PP/1039, D was arrested and later questioned in police custody with respect to a fight which resulted in one of the participants suffering injuries requiring medical attention. In the following D appears as an essentially self-interested individual who, having previous first-hand experience of criminal justice procedures, miscalculates that his written admission, if withheld, might provide a basis for negotiating bail. However, when confronted by the resolute refusal of the officer to entertain any notion of bailing him, D is shown to have capitulated and perhaps to have calculated that a plea of guilt might attract a sizeable reduction in the sentence he will receive from the court:

> PO: I have been to the Accident Hospital and [the victim] has been detained.
> D: Is he in a bad way?
> PO: He has a cut to the head and a few bruises to the ribs. It is not too serious.
> D: That's all right then.
> PO: Do you wish to make a written statement about the incident?
> D: Can I have bail tonight then?
> PO: No, you will appear before the Court [tomorrow], when you are free to apply.
> D: I won't make a statement then.
> PO: You will in due course be charged with wounding.
> D: I can only admit it.

The following extract from Case BP/1067 is similar. Here D, confronted by a courteous, dutiful and incorruptible interviewing officer, is also reported to have failed to negotiate bail in exchange for a written admission:

> PO: You are going to be charged with robberies.

186    *Interrogation and Confession*

> D: If I tell you will you give me bail?
> PO: I will tell you now that you have no chance of getting bail.
> D: Well I've got to try, I might as well tell you about it. I've done these jobs but I didn't thump anybody.
> PO: Do you wish to make a statement?
> D: Yes. You write it.

The theme is replicated in Case PP/1004. Here, D had been arrested and formally questioned in police custody in respect of the theft of a handbag. Invited to make a written statement, D is reported to have said:

> D: I will not make a statement until I have seen what is happening. You can see me some other time for that. Am I having bail?
> PO: I can enter into no deals about bail and I accept what you say. As far as I can see at the moment you will be having bail tomorrow morning and that is it.

Although the legal guilt of the defendants in these cases would be for the courts to determine, the narrative accounts of interview convey images that are wholly injurious to the character and creditworthiness of the accused. At the same time, however, the attitude and behaviour of police officers appears in these accounts as being above reproach. The following extracts are offered as further examples.

During his formal interrogation in police custody D, in case AP/1139, is reported to have persistently denied involvement in the offence for which he had been arrested. The interviewing officer reports himself as having delineated the evidence implicating D in these terms:

> PO: Let's look at the evidence. Immediately after leaving your brother's car, the man concerned [the complainant] reported to the police that he had been robbed. He says that he was threatened with a knife. You and your brother both possessed knives when you were arrested. In your actual possession was found a [credit] card, and another [credit] card was found in the back of the car. Both these [credit] cards are apparently the property of the man making the allegations. What have you to say about that?
> D: Look, Mr [D], we will pay him back the money.
> PO: It is not a question about paying back anything. This is a serious allegation, and you and your brother are likely to be charged with robbery. Do you understand?
> D: Well we never robbed anybody.

PO: We will see you again shortly.

In Case BP/1065 D was arrested and formally questioned on suspicion of violently robbing a woman of her handbag, of having caused her to suffer injuries in the process, and of stealing a quantity of cash from the handbag:

D: Who tell you it was me who is supposed to have done this robbery?
PO: From enquiries we have made I have good reason to believe you were involved.
D: I can prove where I was the evening the woman was robbed. I was playing basket-ball down [Woodland] Road.
PO: ... I haven't told you who was robbed, or what time this offence was committed, yet you know all about it.
D: So what, one of my mates could have told me couldn't they?... It's got nothing to do with me.... I was in the cafe in [Furnace] Road.
PO: What time did you leave this cafe, and who was with you when you left?
D: I left at half seven and I was on my own.
PO: When you left the cafe where did you go?

The police account documents that D then gave an account of his movements after leaving the cafe. The narrative record continues:

PO: You're telling me lies. You were seen by a number of people [in the street in which the offence occurred] just before the robbery.
D: What does the woman say happened? Before I say any more, I want to know what will happen to me.
PO: ... I can't make any promises to you ... from the evidence available, it appears you are responsible.
D: [Crying.] But robbery is serious isn't it? I'll get put away. What if I say I took the money and deny hitting her?
PO: So you admit taking her handbag and stealing the money?
D: Yeh, I took the bag but I never hit her, I've never hit a woman in my life.

...

PO: Whilst I believe you are now telling me most of the truth of the incident, I am satisfied that you did punch the woman in the stomach in order to steal her handbag and contents, and you will in due course be charged with this offence of robbery.
D: But I'm not admitting hitting her, then it wont look so bad for me will it?
PO: Do you want to make a written statement about this?

D:   I might as well.

The cases in which defendants appear as 'artful detainees' convey clear images to suggest they are scheming, venal or self-seeking individuals who are prepared to barter for some immediate gain. This may be contrasted with the images the accounts of interrogation contain of the police. Invariably, the pre-PACE accounts portray the police in a positive light. However, once the generally unverifiable nature of the pre-PACE accounts is acknowledged, the law enforcement picture they present becomes uncertain. That picture is largely composed of uniformly simplistic images constructed in order to assist prosecutorial objectives. Distilled from complex social dramas, these images serve to foster an impression of a rigid dichotomy between the morally reprehensible behaviour of suspects on the one hand and police propriety on the other.[51] Indeed, as McConville and Baldwin (1982) have argued, this dichotomy "forms the framework around which the interrogation record is constructed".[52]

Numerous instances of a behavioural divide between the police and the policed were found in the pre-PACE interrogation records, a selection of which will have been seen under the categories already discussed. It might reasonably be argued that one would expect those charged with upholding the law to possess characteristics which distinguish them from those who would offend against it. However, the point is that interrogations conducted prior to the introduction of PACE may have played a vital role "in the process of setting the suspect apart from the rest of conforming society and, importantly, of setting the police apart from the suspect".[53] Thus, while the primary objective of pre-PACE interrogations was to secure incriminating statements from suspects so as to establish guilt,[54] they may also have served to demonstrate or emphasise the morally reprehensible character of defendants and to create or reinforce images of police rectitude, impartiality, propriety and legitimacy.

**Conclusion**

It should again be emphasised that with the development of the Judges' Rules and throughout the pre-PACE era, the pre-trial process was such that police interrogators enjoyed, and indeed sought to preserve, virtually unqualified access to and unconditional control over persons detained in the privacy of the police station.[55] Not only were the police in a position to exercise unilateral control over the physical conditions under which individuals were held and questioned, they were also entitled to determine whether non-police personnel could attend[56] and therefore free to define the terrain of relevant issues over which their custodial interactions with detainees would range.

Thus, during the critical pre-trial period when an individual might be detained and questioned he would normally be exposed to a single, police, version of how the law interpreted his behaviour and to the police view of the weight of the evidence against him. Furthermore, it was the police who determined whether a charge would be preferred, the specific charge upon which a prosecution would proceed and whether the accused would receive bail or be remanded in custody pending his appearance before the magistrates.[57]

Moreover, the police also enjoyed exclusive control over the process under which key custodial exchanges between themselves and detainees were recorded and prepared for public presentation in court. While the vast majority of cases examined in the present study indicate that these records were not made contemporaneously to the events they recount, they were, nonetheless, widely viewed as reliable, faithful and comprehensive accounts of the totality of police involvement with and influence over detainees, rather than essentially partisan and partial reconstructions of past events.

These factors provided the police with considerable powers with which to emphasise the captive status of detainees, to amplify their own authority and to ensure that those placed at a structural disadvantage in the private space of the police station were subject to strong 'lawful' psychological pressures designed to induce compliance.[58] Clearly, the incidence and impact of such pressures would not usually be readily apparent from privately prepared and essentially unverifiable narrative accounts, constructed to discredit defendants and establish their guilt. If these accounts enabled the police to construct and present certain standardised and tendentious images of apparently guilty defendants, they might also serve to create and convey particular images of themselves and their role in the prosecution process. The capacity of the police to present themselves and their work in particular and instrumental ways through accounts of custodial interrogation will form the subject of the following chapter.

## Notes

[1] Thompson, 1975, p. 89; Davis, 1984, pp. 315, 328-35; Reiner, 1985, pp. 25-7, 39-42; 1992, p. 57.

[2] Reiner, 1986, p. 261. See also Bowden, 1978, p. 37.

[3] Royal Commission on the Police (RCP), *Final Report*, 1962, Cmnd. 1728, p. 102. The survey found that 83 per cent of the sample had 'great respect' for the police. Reiner argues that his view is not impaired by the many methodological and sampling limitations of the 1960 survey (Reiner, 1986, p. 261. The limitations are discussed in Whitaker, 1964, at pp. 15-17. See also Brogden, 1982, pp. 204-5). Reiner maintains that while the police 'had achieved a pinnacle of popularity' by the 1950s, since then the 'carefully constructed traditional image of benign and pacific policing' has gradually declined (Reiner, 1986, pp. 258-9).

[4] Reiner, 1986, p. 262; 1992, p. 61.

[5] Reiner, 1986, pp. 263-71; see also Reiner, 1985, pp. 48-61; 1992, pp. 61-72.

[6] Miller, 1977, p. 94; Bowden, 1978, p. 21; Jefferson and Grimshaw, 1984, pp. 157-161.

[7] See Jefferson and Grimshaw, 1984, pp. 14-15, 22-3, 42-51; Lustgarten, 1986, pp. 32-3, 53-67, 164-75.

[8] Reiner, 1986, p. 269. See also RCP, *Final Report*, 1962, Cmnd. 1728, pp. 101-4.

[9] Reiner, 1986, p. 269. Compare Brogden, 1982, pp. 180-81.

[10] See Reiner, 1985, pp. 49-51; 1986, pp. 259-275; 1992, pp. 57-8, 73-104. However, for evidence of widespread popular disquiet and lack of confidence in the police prior to the 1950s, see Howard, 1931, pp. 228-236, who discusses 'a series of disturbing episodes' involving police misconduct following the First World War which contributed to 'the demand for a thoroughgoing investigation of police methods'. There is also evidence to suggest that from their inception the new police and their methods have periodically been the subject of strong criticism (see, for example, Storch, 1975; Cohen, P., 1979).

[11] Reiner, 1986, pp. 271-73; 1992, pp. 73-104.

[12] Judges' Rules [1964] 1 WLR 152, see introductory note and paragraph (*e*) of the Rules which make clear that the voluntariness of a statement existed as a 'fundamental condition' to its admissibility. This would lead to the exclusion of statements obtained from suspects 'by fear of prejudice or hope of advantage, exercised or held out by a person in authority or by oppression'. See *Prager* [1972] 1 WLR 260. See also Devlin, 1960, p. 38; MacDermott, 1968, p. 10.

[13] The privacy in which the police were permitted to conduct interrogations is in itself a reflection of the acceptance of the police institution as valid in its mission and method. For a clear example of the police power to exclude non-police personnel from interrogations, see Softley, 1980, p.58.

[14] See Rule IV. See also Rule III (*b*) and Williams, 1979, p. 22.

[15] A Police Officer, 1964, p. 175.
[16] Pre-PACE research conducted by Softley (1980, p. 81) found that of 187 suspects interviewed at the police station, 52 (28 per cent) made a written statement to the police. In her pre-PACE study, Vennard (1984, p. 21) found that none of her sample of suspects wrote out their own statement. See also Smith and Gray, 1985, p. 477.
[17] For equivalent figures from the PACE component of the study see Chapter 12, p. 287.
[18] Williams, 1979, p. 7.
[19] Lord Devlin had argued that police officers made their notes 'at the time' of the interview or 'generally within at most an hour of [its] occurrence' (Devlin, 1960, p. 41). Williams, G. (1979, p. 12) however, found that 'judges habitually allow[ed] the police to use notes made appreciably after an interview'.
[20] McConville and Baldwin, 1981, p. 162. See also Mirfield, 1985, pp. 7-9.
[21] (1953) 37 Cr. App. R. 51.
[22] *Ibid.*, p. 59.
[23] See Kaye, 1991; Rozenberg, 1992; Dennis, 1993.
[24] For the number of cases in which detainees were interrogated in the presence of a legal adviser in the PACE aspect of the study, see chapter 12, p. 290.
[25] See Zander, 1972, pp. 346-8; Baldwin and McConville, 1979, pp. 145-52; Softley, 1980, pp. 68-9.
[26] See Chapter 12.
[27] In the course of the present and following chapters it will be seen that this form of 'question' is commonly employed by the police. With it the questioner attempts to 'interpret' the detainee's words, denials or posture so as to provide an incriminating account. Clearly, such questioning is inconsistent with the conventional image of the police as neutral or passive actors who simply *receive* voluntarily given answers to questions.
[28] This style of 'question' — also frequently employed during police interrogations — may be contrasted with that referred to in note 27. Here the police explicitly state their case theory in order to elicit an incriminating response.
[29] See note 27.
[30] *Ibid.*
[31] *Ibid.*
[32] On this, see, Cain, 1973, pp. 117-19.
[33] For a discussion of pre-PACE police attitudes to blacks, particularly young blacks, and the derogatory terms used by the police to describe them, see Holdaway, 1983, pp. 66-71. See also Cain, 1973, p. 117; Smith and Gray, 1983, p. 334.
[34] It was found that black suspects were invariably referred to as 'West Indian' or 'Jamaican' in the pre-PACE witness statements of police officers.
[35] Sanders, 1987, p. 238. See also Devlin, 1960, pp. 46-8.

192  *Interrogation and Confession*

[36] See Devlin, 1960, p. 50.
[37] See *Rennie* (1982) All ER 385, p. 388, *per* Lord Lane: 'Very few confessions are inspired solely by remorse. Often the motives of an accused are mixed and include a hope that an early admission may lead to an earlier release or a lighter sentence'.
[38] McConville and Baldwin, 1981, pp. 130-31, 138-40; 1982, pp. 166-9.
[39] Such confessions work to turn the trial process away from testing the case for the prosecution or from a full evaluation of conflicting versions of reality. Rather, the trial becomes merely a means with which to validate pre-trial avowals of guilt assumed to have been faithfully reported by the police(McConville and Baldwin, 1981, pp. 28-9).
[40] Prior to the 1984 Police and Criminal Evidence Act (PACE), officers rarely made contemporaneous records of their exchanges with suspects (Royal Commission on Criminal Procedure, *Report*, 1981, Cmnd. 8092, para. 4.5). PACE, Code C, para. 11.5, requires custodial interviews to be contemporaneously recorded by verbatim notes. By Code E, custodial interviews are normally to be recorded by audio tape. Where authority is given for an interviewing officer not to tape record an interview, it is to be recorded in writing and in accordance with Code C.
[41] Supra., n. 39
[42] The examination of pre-PACE interrogation records found it quite exceptional for the criminal argot attributed to detained suspects to be given such emphasis in police witness statements.
[43] See note 27.
[44] Judges' Rules [1964] 1 WLR 152; 1 All ER 237; Crim.L.R. 165, see accompanying Administrative Directions, number 4.
[45] Devlin, 1960, pp. 38-9.
[46] On this see Gudjonsson, 1992, pp. 28, 33-4, 68-72.
[47] I use the term 'permissible prod' with reference to the comment made to D beginning: 'This was a very nasty assault ...'. The point is that while the comment may have be designed to prompt D into cooperating with the police, it would appear not to constitute an inducement capable of offending against the voluntariness rule.
[48] See McConville and Baldwin, 1982, p. 170; McConville, *et al.*, 1991, pp. 36-98.
[49] See, for example, Softley, 1980; Irving, 1980; McConville and Baldwin, 1981, pp. 192-3.
[50] See Bottoms and McClean, 1976, pp. 199, 204; McConville and Baldwin, 1981, p. 192.
[51] See McConville and Baldwin, 1982, p. 172.
[52] *Ibid.*
[53] *Ibid.*, p. 171.
[54] *Ibid.*, p. 165.

[55] See Softley, 1980, p.58; Holdaway, 1983, pp. 23-35.
[56] In his pre-PACE observational study, Holdaway found that police officers were 'suspicious of this type of intrusion' (Holdaway, 1983, p. 28).
[57] Prior to the reforms introduced by PACE, police bail was successively governed by s. 38 of the Magistrates' Court Act, 1952 and s. 43 of the Magistrates' Court Act, 1980.
[58] See Driver, 1968, pp. 44-61; see also Garfinkel, 1956, pp. 420-4.

# 9 Pre-PACE Images: The Police

**Introduction**

Orthodox opinion in the pre-PACE era held that despite the difficulties associated with discharging the theoretically discrete roles of investigator, prosecutor and judge when fixed in a single agency, by and large the police functioned in the adversarial process as disinterested and dispassionate inquirers into the objective facts of a case and not merely as seekers of convictions.[1] The image of the police as neutral, quasi-judicial investigators,[2] for whom custodial interrogations operated as an efficient fact-gathering exercise, finds expression in the 1976 report of the Home Office Committee commissioned to examine the law and procedure relating to identification evidence.[3] The Committee was established following a number of miscarriages of justice in which mistaken identification evidence coupled with inadequate investigations — under which evidence that contradicted police case theories was either disregarded or treated as erroneous — had played a part. Its report states that:

> the police have a duty to make inquiries in a quasi-judicial spirit ... to be conducted as much with the object of ascertaining facts which exonerate as of ascertaining those which will convict.... It is because this quasi-judicial duty exists that it is not unreasonable to expect a suspect to make a voluntary statement to the police; no such expectation could reasonably be entertained if he were simply giving advance information to the enemy.[4]

Thus, according to the prevailing legal rhetoric, the police were not viewed as the enemy of suspects, instead they were seen as impartial, quasi-judicial recipients of voluntarily given admissions — whether exculpatory or inculpatory in nature — *collected* rather than *extracted* from persons detained in custody during the course of criminal investigations.

This view of the police role permitted police-constructed records of their interactions with detainees to be presented and accepted as incomparably reliable accounts undistorted either by the power differentials which, particularly in the custodial context, advantaged the police, or by police perceptions, values or interests.

In the previous chapter three typologies were identified. The typologies permitted an examination of the manner in which defendants, as suspects, appeared in pre-PACE accounts of detention and interrogation. In the present chapter the pre-PACE accounts are considered in order to ascertain how far the images the accounts contain of the police and of police investigations accord with widely accepted assumptions respecting the police role in the prosecution process. In meeting this object, the following typologies are employed to facilitate an assessment of the images identified: (1) the rule-bound officer; (2) the procedural officer; (3) the officer as logician; and (4) the officer as guide.

*The Rule-Bound Officer*

Of the many images found in the pre-PACE sample which bear on the police, their work and their interactions with detained suspects, one of the more insistent suggests that officers have a strong respect for the rights of detainees and are fastidious in their observance of the rules. The following case is an example.

In Case PP/1192, the image of the courteous, rule-observant police officer who is attentive to the detainee's rights, is coupled with the image of the well-briefed investigator for whom the conviction of the guilty is ancillary to his primary concern: solving crime. The suspect in this case was formally interviewed in police custody on suspicion of being involved in a burglary:

> PO: ... I wish to put some questions to you... You are not obliged to answer any of these questions....
> D: What questions?
> PO: Firstly, do you wish to have your solicitor present?
> D: What for? I have nothing to say.[5]

PO: The first question is, we now know that a quantity of jewellery is missing from the house you burgled and is not amongst the property recovered from you. Where is it?
D: I don't know anything about it.
PO: I am of the opinion that you have made more than one trip to this house and you have hidden the jewellery in wherever you were living and that is the reason why you have not given your address.
D: That could be right.
PO: Our only interest at this stage is to minimise loss to the owners of the property and to attempt to recover their possessions....
D: If I've got the property, it's in the flat.

The question beginning: "The first question is...." suggests the interrogator had earlier satisfied himself that D was involved in the burglary. Indeed, it would appear that investigations conducted prior to the interview had provided the police with evidence of his guilt and had furnished them with the strong suspicion that he had hidden the jewellery. It may be presumed, therefore, that the interrogation was conducted in order to confirm these suspicions, to secure admissions and to recover the stolen property. While the nature of the investigations undertaken is not made explicit, the clear implication is that they were sufficiently exhaustive as to provide the police with incontrovertible intelligence pointing to the offender. This impression is reinforced by the incriminatory responses reportedly made by D to the allegations put to him.

Together with the image of the rule-observant officer, the pre-PACE custodial records exhibited clear images of police interviewers apparently actuated by an uncompromising duty to ascertain 'the facts' or to get to 'the truth'. Case AP/1158[6] is but one example. During her custodial interrogation respecting the theft of £3000, D is reported to have made the following justificatory remark:

D: I had to bring up the children without help. There were bills to pay all the time as well as the mortgage.
PO: Are you saying you attempted to take money?
D: You don't understand, I had to.
PO: I can sympathise with you but I must know what has happened to this money.
D: What do you want me to say?
PO: I want the truth Mrs [D].

In this case, the external audience may conclude that the officer's declaration of sympathy is clearly and properly subordinated to his overriding duty to dispassionately investigate crime, to secure 'the truth' and to record it in an impartial manner for the prosecution of the prospective offender.

While the pre-PACE accounts generally depict the police as rule-observant and as disinterested recipients of voluntary statements, it was also apparent that in their mission to acquire 'the truth', police officers took exception to what they perceived as evasions or lies. They were also seen to take strong exception to silence. In short, officers appeared to communicate the idea that only 'truthful' voluntary statements would be uncritically received. This theme is evident in varying degrees in the following cases.

D in Case AP/1064 had been arrested, while waiting at the reception counter of a bank, on suspicion of stabbing and causing the death of X. According to the police account, D was forced into the street and there told of the reason for his arrest. At this D is reported to have said: "He isn't dead is he?" One of the three officers present is reported to have replied simply, "yes". It is reported that on being placed in a police vehicle D began to cry, saying: "I didn't want to kill him, I didn't think it would come to that". During the journey to the police station he repeated: "I didn't mean to kill him". Upon arrival at the station he was immediately placed in an interview room for questioning:

> PO: Now let's start from earlier this morning, can you recall the squabble you had in the living-room?
> D: Yes, [X] hit me in the face. We were both mad but it wasn't anything.
> PO: What happened then?
> D: I went down the passage to the kitchen, [X] was still in the living-room.
> PO: Where did you actually pick the knife up from?
> D: All I can remember is that it was in my hand, I don't know when I picked it up. I don't know which knife it was.
> PO: Where did you put it down?
> D: I don't know.
> PO: It's no good if you are not going to tell us the truth, you must be able to remember some things.

It may be that the police interrogated D immediately after his arrest in order to benefit from the distress he would doubtless experience in learning that his actions had caused the death of X and, therefore, to heighten the prospect of securing a confession. Certainly, assuming the police account of interview to be complete and accurate, although the police make their determination to get to 'the truth' quite clear, at no point did they offend against the rules relating to the taking of statements from suspects. The images transmitted in this exchange suggest, therefore, that the failure of D to provide the police with a full account of his role in the incident was due to his inability or unwillingness to come to terms with his criminal responsibility.

The picture painted in the pre-PACE accounts of police officers as uncritical recorders of 'truthful' statements, as rational, dispassionate and professional investigators who are not easily deterred by evasiveness or duped by implausible explanations, is seen in a number of cases. Case BP/1068 is but one. According to the witness statements of the officers concerned, D was formally interviewed in police custody on suspicion of being involved with two others in a number of shoplifting offences:

PO: We have just interviewed [Jane] and [Mary] and they admit committing a number of offences of theft at shops in [Eastfield] today.
D: I don't know what they did.
PO: When you were arrested you had in your car two pairs of pyjamas and 58 tea towels. [Jane] and [Mary] admit stealing this property from two shops in [Eastfield].
D: I just sat in the car. I have told you I don't know what they did.
PO: Do you admit that you were in the car when they brought the pyjamas and tea towels?
D: Yes.
PO: Then where did you think they had got this property from?
D: I don't ask.
PO: Surely you must have thought that something was funny when they put 58 loose tea towels in your car?
D: [No reply]
PO: If you live with [Jane] you obviously know that she has previous convictions for stealing from shops. All three of you are unemployed and yet you travel by car some 15 miles to [Eastfield], with petrol at about 70p. a gallon. Why did you go shopping in the city centre?
D: We come here a lot but I always wait in the car.
PO: Do you mean wait in the car to receive stolen property from [Jane] and [Mary]?
D: No.
PO: I understand that [Jane] was recently released from prison. I suggest to you that when they came back to your car with the pyjamas and tea towels you knew that they had stolen this property didn't you?

D: [No reply]
PO: Are you going to answer that question?
D: Don't be so impatient. I suppose you pick on me because I'm black.
PO: Mr [D], I have no interest whatsoever in the colour of your skin. What I'm interested in is the state of your mind when the property was brought to your car.
D: [No reply]
PO: Two women with criminal records, both of whom are unemployed, bring to your car two pairs of pyjamas and 58 tea towels. You surely are not asking me to believe that you thought that they had obtained this property legitimately?

Beyond the apparent concern of the questioner to ascertain the facts, it will be seen that D has been drawn into a dialogue in which he has a relatively passive role. The officer, on the other hand plays a leading, indeed directorial role. For example, it would appear that the statement beginning: "If you live with...." implicitly posits the expected answer to the appended question. Furthermore, the succeeding question, though clarificatory in form, is in effect leading in nature. Similarly, the next 'question' is no more than a statement with an accusation suffixed. That D is reported to have failed to respond to it works to lend credence both to the accusation and to the conclusions voiced by the officer who appears unperturbed by the suggestion of partiality.

The capacity of the narrative record to present or construct the police as impartial seekers of objective truth and to convey images of the police as experts in their field who, on the basis of usually undisclosed criminal intelligence, are able to distinguish honesty from mendacity, is seen in Case BP/1210. The police narrative account of this custodial exchange records that D1 had admitted to being involved in disposing of several stolen television sets but denied stealing them. He implicated others but maintained that his own involvement was limited to transporting the property after the theft had taken place on the directions of D2 who had retained the television sets.

PO: Where are the sets now then?
D1: You'd better ask [D2], he's done us for the money and the sets.
PO: So far as you are concerned you let a bloke like [D2], a man you have already said you don't know well, get rid of the sets for you?
D1: Yes that's it.
PO: That doesn't make sense to me [D1]. Do you really expect us to believe that?

D1: I don't care. [D2] is your man, I can't tell you where the sets have gone. You get [D2] and you'll get your sets.
PO: Do you wish to make a statement about this, its entirely up to you, you don't have to if you don't want to....
D1: Do you want me to plead guilty to stealing them?
PO: All I'm concerned about is the truth [D], its up to you entirely.
D1: I'd better leave it then.

Later, D2, separately detained and questioned in the police station, reportedly admitted that he, acting with one other, was responsible. The narrative account documents that following this admission of guilt the police turned to the identity of the accomplice:

PO: According to our information there was another man involved with you also.
D2: No, there was only the two of us.
PO: I understand that [P] was the third man.
D2: [After having 'remained silent for a moment'.] Oh, you know about him do you?
PO: It seems that way doesn't it? What's the point of leaving him out?
D2: All right, so he was with us but I don't want to mention him. You must know that he's already wanted by the police.
PO: There's no point in us continuing this interview if all you are going to tell us is a load of lies.

The following excerpt is offered as a final example from the pre-PACE sample of rule-observant police questioning. The case demonstrates, *ex facie*, that non-coercive, rational and persistent custodial questioning — even when faced with denials and evasions — is usually sufficient, without recourse to overtly manipulative ploys, to secure damaging 'voluntary' admissions.

D in Case BP/1062 was one of a number of individuals arrested in connection with a fight that had occurred in a public house. At his formal custodial interview he was accused of causing the complainant (TC), one of the parties to the dispute, to suffer injuries to his face:

D: What are you on about, I am the complainant. It was me that had the glass in the face.
PO: I know that but a man named [TC] also had a glass pushed into his face.
D: I'm not doing porridge for that.
PO: Did you put a glass in his face?

D: No, not me.
PO: [TC] says that the man who got into the ambulance with him and who had cuts to his face was the man who hit him in the face with a glass.
D: I didn't want to go in the ambulance with that lot.
PO: But you did get into the ambulance and you had cuts to your face didn't you?
D: Yes, and the guy who did me was in the ambulance with a blonde bird.
PO: [TC], who had the glass in his face, says that the man who did it got into the ambulance and you got into the ambulance.
D: It was an accident.
PO: What do you mean?
D: He came up to the bar and took a swing at me. I swung round and hit him with a pint glass.
PO: You will be charged with wounding this man.
D: If I put my hands up for this I'll get porridge.

## The Procedural Officer

The impression that pre-PACE interviews with suspects were typically conducted by police officers *after* they had first undertaken thorough — though usually unspecified — investigations, emerged as a distinct feature of the pre-PACE sample. This attribute is evident in many of the cases previously discussed. The following cases are also illustrative.

In Case PP/1034, D questioned by two officers. The nature of their inquiries were reportedly communicated to D in the following terms:

PO: I am Detective Sergeant [A] and this is Detective Constable [B]. Last October you reported to your insurance company that your car had been stolen and you had reported the theft to the police. All these things were untrue. Your car had been repossessed by your finance company and you obviously knew this.
D: Yes, that's true, but I did report it to the police. I telephoned [a named police station].
PO: We are from [that police station]. I have checked and there is no record that you have ever reported the theft of your car at that station or any other.
D: I telephoned but I had an appointment so I couldn't wait.
PO: On the day you told your car insurance company your car had been stolen you were visited by two men from the finance company who told you that they intended to repossess the car. Why have you never checked with the company to see if they had the car?

> D: I didn't bother but I tell you, as far as I am concerned I did nothing wrong.
> PO: The two men who called told you they were going to take the car, they say you picked up the keys from a shelf in your room and you became quite agitated, they then left and took the car. You then find your car missing, it was obvious who had taken it.
> D: I didn't get agitated. I told them I would make a payment at the end of the month.
> PO: You knew your car had been repossessed and if the money had been sent by the insurance company you would have kept it.
> D: Yes, I would but I didn't find out until January ... that the car had been repossessed.
> PO: If that were true why did you not report that to your insurance company, and go and see the finance company about the property you had left in the car?
> D: I didn't bother.
> PO: I am satisfied you made a false claim to your insurance company....

According to the narrative account of the exchange D was then shown the application form he had submitted to the insurance company:

> PO: On the form you also state that you have never been convicted of any driving offences. This is also not true. You have two convictions, one for speeding and one for driving without a licence or test certificate.
> D: I thought they didn't count after they were more than three years old. But anyway I can't see that I've done anything wrong.

It would appear from this extract that the police had conducted sufficiently extensive investigations prior to questioning D to enable them to contest or refute any misleading answers offered in response to their questions. D is seen to have been given an opportunity to account for his actions. However, his remarks, as recorded by the police, seem unsatisfactory. It would also appear that the questions asked were framed both to elicit admissions indicating D possessed the requisite criminal intent to commit the alleged offence and to damage his credibility. The introduction of his previous convictions, though potentially prejudicial to a fair trial, would seem to have been designed to meet this strategic end.

Case AP/1126 concerned the theft of a quantity of assorted cheeses valued at over £4000. D was employed as a van driver by the complainant company to deliver the cheeses. According to the police account, during the formal interview at the police station D held to his initial claim that the van had been stolen by persons unknown to him. The following extract suggests that the truth emerged as a direct result of the interviewing officer's proficient questioning and his reliance upon traditional, pre-interview, investigative methods:

> PO: ... would you tell us exactly how much cheese was on the van when you left [the depot]?
> 
> D: It was a full load, that would probably be just over two and a half tons, that's all.
> 
> PO: Now think carefully [D], are you sure that is true? My information is that the van was overloaded in fact it was carrying almost double the normal load.
> 
> D: Yes, that's right. I didn't tell the police that because of trouble about overloading.
> 
> PO: It's in your own interests to tell us the truth [D]. We obviously know more about this matter than you are prepared to tell us at the moment.
> 
> D: OK, I honestly haven't been able to sleep since this lot happened two weeks ago. I will tell you all about it but you understand I cannot tell you names.

In common with the many cases identified as falling within the present class of pre-PACE images, the nature of the criminal intelligence claimed to be possessed by the police is not fully articulated in the interrogation record. It is difficult, therefore, to determine the true extent of the officer's prior knowledge. Regardless, it is reported that D went on to tell the police where the stolen cheese could be found and what arrangements had been made for its disposal. He also furnished the police with a full confession respecting his part in the offence. The confession is documented in a police narrative account that reveals no noticeable breaches of the Judges' Rules. Consequently, it is highly unlikely that the confession would be excluded from trial.

## The Officer As Logician

The third category of frequently occurring images found in the pre-PACE sample has as its unifying theme representations of custodial encounters between police officers and detainees in which the former appear as discerning, proficient and rational inquirers. Such inquirers are seen to have an ability to 'record' voluntarily-made statements which point to criminal responsibility, simply by applying elementary logic. In contrast, those questioned by these inquirers generally emerge from the police accounts as inept or idiotic individuals whose crude or irrational prevarications are easily confounded by simple and reasoned questioning. The following extract from Case BP/1121 is presented as but one example from the sample. Here persistent, logical and apposite questions are seen to undermine the credibility of the detainee's explanation.

Following his arrest and detention at the police station, it is reported that D denied being involved in an incident which had resulted in the complainant sustaining serious injuries. Later, he admitted that a fight had occurred and that he had injured the complainant during it. However, he maintained that he had acted in self defence:

D: ... he took a swing at me.
PO: Did he connect?
D: No, I moved out of the way.
PO: Then what happened?
D: I hit him with a bottle.
PO: Did you pick up the bottle?
D: No, I had it in my hand all the time.
PO: Was it broken?
D: No.
PO: Did you break the bottle before you hit him?
D: No.
PO: What sort of bottle was it?
D: A small one.
PO: How many times did you hit him.
D: I don't know.
PO: Did the bottle break when you hit him?
D: Yes.
PO: Did you hit him more than once?
D: I don't know.
PO: It must have been more than once because he had cuts on his forehead and chin.
D: It was more than once.
PO: How many times then?
D: I don't know.
PO: He has cuts on his face, on his forehead and jaw, which required over sixty stitches, so it must have been more that once.
D: [No reply]
PO: When you hit him did the bottle break over his face?
D: Yes.

PO: Do you call this self-defence?
D: He was trying to punch and kick me, and you have to defend yourself.
PO: Not with a bottle.
D: [No reply]
PO: Isn't the truth that you ... deliberately attacked him?
D: No.

...

PO: Do you wish to make a written statement about this?
D: I make no statements.

It is evident that in spite of the forceful exertions of the questioner D refused to make an admission that explicitly contradicted his claim that he had acted in self defence. Nonetheless, he emerges from the custodial exchange with not only his story but also his character tarnished.

The following narrative account excerpted from Case AP/1031 is offered as one of a number of similar cases which appear to indicate that police officers who employ non-coercive questions founded upon deductive logic are, on that basis, ordinarily sufficiently well equipped to 'uncover' the culpability of those properly suspected of involvement in crime. In this case it is reported that D2 had been arrested and detained at the police station on suspicion of receiving stolen cash, the property of an individual who had been assaulted and robbed by D1 in the toilet of a public house:

PO: The lad that was robbed had about £10 cash stolen, only £4 of which has been recovered. Did you have any money?
D2: No, I did not.
PO: Did [D1] speak to anyone afterwards, except the police?
D2: No.
PO: So he couldn't have passed the rest of the money to anyone else. Is that right?
D2: I suppose not, no.
PO: Was there anyone else in the toilet when D1 went through the lads' pockets?
D2: No, only me....
PO: Well if [D1] didn't give the money to anyone else, he must have given it to you.
D2: No, he never done that. But he dropped £2 on the floor as he came out of the toilet.
PO: What happened to that afterwards?

D2: I don't know, I never had it.
PO: The police searched up there afterwards and the money wasn't there then, so where did it go?
D2: I don't know.
PO: I believe that when you wiped the lad's face with a towel, it was an act so that the police would not suspect that you were involved in the robbery. Is that true?
D2: No. It's not.

D2 later dictated a statement to his interrogators. In it he admitted receiving the stolen cash. Nevertheless, the dialogue cited above is of itself a compelling illustration of the virtues of traditional detective skills and common sense logic when utilised in the context of custodial interrogations. The following two extracts are further examples from the study which depict the triumph of common-sense logic over malfeasance.

In Case BP/1074 the formal interrogation of D followed his arrest and detention in police custody in regard to his alleged involvement in the theft of furniture belonging to the complainant, his former landlord.

PO: It seems funny to me that the day you left the house unexpectedly this property disappeared. You were the only one in the house when it went.
D: Look, I've told you, this [Welshman] was living there.
PO: No he wasn't. He had left before then.
D: Had he? I can't really remember, I was on drugs around then....
PO: Are you trying to tell us that you cannot remember what happened?
D: Yes.
PO: Does that mean you cannot say whether you took the furniture or not?
D: Yes, that's about right.
PO: Well, the stuff was taken from the house the day you left. You didn't tell [the landlord] that you were going. You were the only one living at the house apart from [the landlord]. The house was not broken into, therefore, it must have been done by someone in the house.

The police account of Case PP/1136 relates that D had been arrested and detained in police custody on suspicion of having stolen a stereo music centre. It is reported that D was charged with the offence following this exchange:

PO: Are you [R's] boyfriend?
D: Yes.
PO: Is it right that you lived at [a specified address] with her?

208  *Interrogation and Confession*

> D: I did for a few weeks but that don't mean I stole [X's] stereo.
> PO: How did you know it was [X's] stereo that was stolen?
> D: [No reply]
> PO: The only way you could have known that was if you had stolen it.

In common with many of the pre-PACE cases, these extracts contain images which suggest that elementary logic frequently plays a crucial part in exposing the criminality of those questioned by the police. Such images emerge from accounts which appear as faithful records of a process in which questioner and questioned interact on relatively equal terms, with the latter free to elect not to participate. Under this process all spurious or implausible explanations offered are rationally assessed and eliminated by the specialist inquirer who leaves external others to draw their own logical inferences. This theme may be observed in the following extract from Case BP/1177.

D1 and D2 were arrested and questioned at a police station on suspicion of attempting to sell a car knowing it to have been stolen. The arrestees contended that they had not known the car was stolen. They maintained that they were merely passengers; that the driver, a third party (D3), had led them to believe he owned the car; that he must have initiated the alleged sale; and that he had escaped, since he had gone to buy cigarettes just before their arrest:

> PO: Where is this man [D3]?
> D1: When we stopped the car [he] got out and went for some cigarettes.
> PO: That's rather odd, when you were arrested you had some cigarettes on you. Don't you think it's funny that he should leave the car and go and get some cigarettes?
> D1: No.
> PO: How long were you at [the site of what was alleged to be the intended sale]?
> D1: About ten minutes, I cant remember.
> PO: There are several shops close to [that site] which were open, [D3] could have got some cigarettes and joined you at the premises before the police arrived.
> D1: [No reply]
>
> ...
>
> PO: I have just interviewed your friend and he is very vague as to any details about the third person who was supposed to be in the car, and also he

declined to make a written statement about the matter. I would feel that if the story he told was the truth he would have nothing to lose by committing it to paper.
D1: It's up to him.
PO: He has given a different story as to how he met you today.
D1: He can say what he wants to.
PO: If you are both innocent respecting this vehicle, surely the story which you both tell would be identical?
D1: [No reply]

The material parts of the interview with D2 are reported in the case papers as follows:

PO: Do you wish to make a written statement about this matter?
D2: No. I don't make statements to the police until I've seen my solicitor.
PO: Do you wish me to contact your solicitor?
D2: No.
PO: Are you saying that you are quite innocent and you didn't know that this vehicle is stolen?
D2: Yes.
PO: Well, if you are innocent why don't you make a written statement giving your version of what is the truth in this matter?[7]
D2: I don't want to make a statement.
PO: Would it be true that if you made a written statement about what you know about this vehicle in so far as when you first saw the vehicle, who was with you, and what you did up until the time you were arrested, this could be compared with the statement which [D1] has made...?
D2: Yes.
PO: It would obviously be vastly different to the story you would give.
D2: He gives his story, I'll give mine later.

From this extract it would appear that rational argument failed to induce damaging admissions from the detainees. It may, however, be objected that the police account of their exchanges with the arrestees, allied with the refusal of D2 to make a written statement, would of itself form reasonable grounds for inferences unfavourable to the arrestees to be drawn.[8] The point here is that it would be wrong to assume that all police interrogations of the pre-PACE era centred around attempts to procure confession evidence. While this may have been the primary object in most cases,[9] prior to the introduction of PACE, police interrogations also served to present officers in a favourable light and to amplify or construct negative images of suspects.[10] The pre-PACE accounts of detention and interrogation carry a wide variety of images which firmly set the police apart from the policed. That the police might play an important role in the construction of such images is made clear in the following category.

## The Officer As Guide

The large majority of pre-PACE records were found to exhibit images which suggested the police merely received and meticulously chronicled the 'voluntarily' statements those they questioned made. In most cases, these statements appear as the un-coerced and uninfluenced effusions of the person questioned. Generally, such statements are reported to have been made without critical comment by the questioner. However, in a substantial minority of cases officers were found to have registered their opinion as to the weight of the evidence against the suspect, the plausibility of his or her explanation, or as to his or her character. Such evaluative comments may be distinguished from those discussed in the preceding category on the ground that they do not appear as the product of rational argumentation. Typically, they appear as expressions of justifiable impatience or irritation. Outwardly, such comments are addressed to the person questioned; however, their influence in this respect is not easily ascertained. Nevertheless, the manner in which they appear in the narrative accounts would suggest that the external audience is of foremost concern. The four cases that follow will illustrate the point.

Case AP/1089 concerned the interrogation of D, one of three persons arrested and accused by the police of being involved in a burglary.

PO: Right [D], you know what you've been arrested for and I have cautioned you. Have you anything to tell us?
D: I was there but I didn't go in
PO: What did you do?
D: Well, the other two had decided they were going screwing when we were in the pub. I didn't want to go.
PO: Well, why did you go? You knew what they were going to do.
D: Well, you know how it is, you can't say no.
PO: That's ridiculous, everyone had a choice and you have got a mind of your own. Let's start at the beginning, who drove the car?

In this extract the questioner is seen to register his negative estimation of the accused for the edification of the accused and presumably for that of external others. Here the officer communicates his conviction that at the time of the alleged offence the accused possessed the proscribed state of mind (the *mens rea*) which, together with the prohibited act (the *actus reus*), must normally be proved before a court having jurisdiction over criminal matters.[11] The officer also makes clear that in his expert opinion the criminal responsibility of the accused could not be negatived or mitigated by claims that his free-will had been impaired by 'peer pressure'.

In Case BP/1010, the police record documents that D was arrested on suspicion of having knowingly received a stolen television set.

PO: ... we've arrested [B] and he has admitted a burglary at a pub and a colour TV was stolen.
D: That one in my flat is [E's], it's not stolen.
PO: How long have you had it?
D: Ages, I'm not sure but it will be in the agreement.... I definitely didn't have it of [B].
PO: You have told us nothing but lies.... First you claimed you didn't know where [B] was but you have known all the time.
D: Well, he's a friend I couldn't tell you could I?

...

PO: ... You told me earlier you knew someone was committing burglaries and low and behold we arrest your former partner and he admits committing pub burglaries. So when we have information that you have a stolen TV, what are we to think?

...

PO: Why did you say the one in your house was [E's] when you bought it at the garage? You tell so many lies you don't know how to tell the truth.
D: I knew what you'd say as soon as I told you who I had it off.

The case papers relating to Case PP/1084 report that D, together with two other youths, was arrested on suspicion of stealing batteries valued at around five pounds from a service station kiosk. The police witness statements detail that one of the three youths had been seen to filch the batteries by a police officer. On being approached by the officer the youths made off. Later that day D was apprehended. At his formal interview, he maintained that while present at the time, he had not been involved in the alleged offence. D was asked why, if he was innocent, he had left the scene:

D: I know it looks bad but I was doing nothing wrong.
PO: ... why clear off ... if you've done nothing wrong?
D: Well, I got a bit scared. I know what you lot are like. I don't want to get involved with the law.
PO: ... you are talking a load of rubbish. You cleared off when you saw the policeman at the kiosk ... because you've been thieving and you had a guilty conscience didn't you?
D: No I didn't honestly, you've got to believe me.

Case PP/1006, the final case to be discussed within the present class of pre-PACE images relating to the police and their work, concerned an individual who, after having been under police surveillance, was arrested and accused of living on the earnings of a prostitute. The excerpt from the narrative record of formal interview centres on D's evidently futile attempt to convince the police of his ability to subsist on social security payments totalling twenty-two pounds a week:

PO: And you say you can live on that? How much rent do you pay?
D: £5 a week.
PO: What about gas and electricity, do you pay that?
D: Yes, its meters.
PO: What about food, who buys that?
D: I do, we don't eat much. Anyway, I don't let [her] buy anything when I'm around.
PO: And you both smoke, you both drink, and you can afford to play cards in the pub. All on £22 a week.
D: ['made no comment']
PO: ... you dress well, you go out drinking most nights. You and [Lolita] both smoke heavily and you play cards for money. You expect us to believe you can manage that on £22 a week?
D: I'm very careful, we don't go out every night anyway.
PO: What you are saying is you know [Lolita] was soliciting but you don't let her spend any of the money she gets because you provide everything for her on £22 a week....

Implicit in the scepticism seen to have been voiced by the questioner is a clear and unfavourable assessment of D's life-style, his credibility and his guilt. This in common with numerous similar cases, some of which have been discussed above, indicates that the custodial interrogations of the pre-PACE era provided the police with an essentially unverifiable and unchallengeable means with which to transmit to the courts their apparently disinterested opinions on the 'facts' discovered and statements received. The strong impression gained from the overwhelming majority of pre-PACE cases is that police officers are punctilious in their observance of the rules.[12] Indeed, the pre-PACE accounts of interview suggest that they scrupulously avoid any method which could be regarded as unfair or oppressive during their formal exchanges with suspects.[13]

## Conclusion

It has been seen that the interrogation process which prevailed prior to the introduction of PACE gave the police sovereignty over the conduct of interrogations and over accounts of interrogations. It has been suggested here that these accounts played a crucial role in legitimating the function and character of the police. Moreover, they served to communicate to external others distinct and functional images of the police themselves and of those interrogated by the police. How far the themes highlighted in this and the preceding chapter, respecting images of the police-suspect dynamic in the interrogation process of the pre-PACE era, have currency in reports or records of interrogations conducted under the PACE regime will be addressed in the following chapters.

## Notes

[1] Devlin, 1960, pp. 26-31, 62-66; 1979, pp. 71-3. Lord Devlin observed that as servants of the state charged to investigate *and* prosecute offenders, police officers were enjoined to be 'zealous and even ardent in the pursuit of crime'. This, he argued, meant that they could not be expected to be entirely dispassionate. However, he concluded that despite 'the general habit of the police never to admit to the slightest departure from correctness', they could, on the whole, be trusted to act fairly, reasonably and in accordance with the rules (Devlin, 1960, pp. 12-13, 22, 39-40, 43-6, 65-66; 1979, pp. 71-3, 81).

[2] Lord Devlin argued that under the pre-PACE adversarial system, the investigative and prosecution processes were disjoined. For him, the moment at which impartial, quasi-judicial investigations conducted by the police transformed to become prosecutions geared to secure the conviction of the guilty was marked by the administration of the caution. The caution, he

asserted, amounted to 'a declaration of war', for in delivering it the police 'announce that they are no longer representing themselves to the man they are a questioning as *the neutral inquirer* whom the good citizen ought to assist' (Devlin, 1960, p. 31, my emphasis). This rationale is explicit in both the original and revised Judges' Rules.

3 *Report to the Secretary of State for the Home Department of the Departmental Committee on Evidence of Identification in Criminal Cases*, 1976.

4 *Ibid.*, para. 5.98, pp. 130-1.

5 It should be noted that while D appears to have refused a solicitor on the ground that he had no intention of answering any questions, the police, nevertheless, were fully entitled to continue to subject him to interrogatories (*Rice* v. *Connolly* [1966] 2 QB 414).

6 Previously referred to in Chapter 8, at p. 180.

7 Clearly, this question is premised upon the widely held common sense assumption that only the guilty would wish not to cooperate with the police or to exercise their right to silence. As the Criminal Law Revision Committee (CLRC, Eleventh Report, Cmnd. 4991, 1972) put it 'it is only natural to expect an innocent person who is being interrogated to mention a fact which will exonerate him' (para. 37.) The Committee went so far as to suggest — without the support of empirical evidence — that hardened criminals tended to take advantage of the right to refuse to answer pre-trial questions and that this greatly hampered the police (*ibid.*, para. 30).

8 See Cross, 1970, pp. 70-2; CLRC, Eleventh Report, 1972, Cmnd. 4991, p. 16.

9 See McConville and Baldwin, 1982, p. 165.

10 *Ibid.*, pp. 170-4.

11 See, for example, *Harding* v. *Price* [1948] 1 KB 695, p. 700, *per* Goddard, LCJ.

12 An appearance that may be attributed to the manner in which the pre-PACE custodial exchanges were recorded. It has been contended that the non-contemporaneous narrative accounts followed 'an accepted formula' designed not only to foster the finding of legal guilt but also 'to establish that police officers ... behaved entirely in accordance with the Judges' Rules' (Lewis and Hughman, 1975, p. 111).

13 See Home Office circulars 31/64, para. 4; and 89/78, para. 2.

# 10 PACE Images: Detainees

## Introduction

The preceding two chapters considered particular ways in which police-suspect encounters during detention and interrogation appear in a sample of 400 pre-PACE cases relating to offences proceeded against in the Crown Court. In this and the following chapter, the discussion turns to images of custodial interactions between detained suspects and the police found in the sample of 283 post-PACE cases committed for trial in the same Crown Court. However, before assessing the images the PACE case papers contain of the police-suspect dynamic, it is necessary to conduct a brief review of the key socio-legal and political conditions that operated to shape the PACE legislation.

## Judges' Rules to PACE Codes

From its enactment in 1984, the Police and Criminal Evidence Act (PACE) has become a central feature of the British criminal justice landscape. It endures as an initial legislative attempt to rationalise the law relating to police powers and aspires to provide a comprehensive code delimiting the rights and duties of police officers as they bear upon the liberties of the citizen.

In respect of the PACE provisions which touch on the detention and interrogation of suspects, the source of the debate which informed them may be traced as far back as the period following the initial promulgation of the Judges' Rules at the beginning of the present century. From this period the police institution evolved to become an increasingly professionalised, politicised and vocal constituent in twentieth century law and order discourse. By the mid 1960s, with the revision of the Judge's Rules, the contours of the debate had become fixed.[1]

Notwithstanding the risk of oversimplification, it is helpful to divide the disparate participants to this debate into two broad schools or factions. The first school may be distinguished from the second on the ground that its members were generally of the view that procedural prescriptions relating to the investigation of crime, the reception of criminal evidence and the conviction of the guilty, unduly inhibited the police in the performance of their law enforcement duties. The rules, therefore, needed to be altered if the police were to succeed in their mission.[2]

In contrast, the second broad school of thought held that the police regularly violated their existing powers and that the courts were reluctant to discipline the police when clear breaches of the rules had occurred.[3] It was also argued that those detained and interrogated by the police were inadequately protected from abuse and were subject to conviction based on essentially unverifiable police reports of interrogation. For this school the privacy in which statements were taken from suspects by the police, coupled with the problem of establishing the authenticity and reliability of their content, were crucial matters of concern requiring urgent review.[4]

## Towards a Royal Commission

In 1972 the Criminal Law Revision Committee furnished the debate with a major, if controversial, Report.[5] The Committee had been asked by the Home Secretary in 1964 "to review the law of evidence in criminal cases" and, in particular, to consider "what provision should be made for modifying rules which have ceased to be appropriate in modern conditions".[6] Its Report concluded that the prevailing law of evidence was not only too restrictive but also illogical. It argued that irrational restrictions had led to the rejection of evidence which would "have been valuable for the ascertainment of the truth".[7] These restrictions were the product of an age when "the scales used to be loaded against the defence".[8] They no longer served any useful purpose for improved access to legal representation, greater rights of appeal against conviction and increasing levels of sophistication on the part of criminals had combined to "become a hinderance ... to justice".[9] The Committee therefore proposed that the laws of evidence be reformed so as to be "less tender to criminals generally".[10]

In respect of confession evidence and police interrogations, the Committee proposed that courts and juries be permitted to draw adverse inferences from a defendant's silence in the face of police questioning where the defendant seeks to rely on a fact not mentioned at the time of questioning.[11] Consequently, the caution, administered by police officers at the outset of an interrogation informing the suspect of the 'right to silence', should be replaced by a notice warning the suspect that of the danger of remaining silent.[12] The Committee also argued that in circumstances where adverse inferences might be drawn from silence this should be capable of acting as corroborating evidence.[13] Finally, the Committee called for a refinement of the common law rule which, in its "excessive strictness", rendered inadmissible all statements made in consequence of threats or inducements.[14] It recommended that the rule should "be limited to threats or inducements of a kind likely to produce an unreliable confession".[15]

The Committee's recommendations, and the Benthamite assumptions they express, reflected and supported the essentially crime control views of the then recently appointed Commissioner of Metropolitan Police, Sir Robert Mark, who had become an active spokesman for the proposition that the criminal justice system was being manipulated by criminals who, aided by unscrupulous lawyers, were evading conviction.[16] Nevertheless, after provoking vehement dissension, primarily directed to the proposed relaxation of the 'right to silence', the immediate implementation of the recommendations made by the Criminal Law Revision Committee was averted.[17]

In 1977, the debate over the adequacy of police powers, of evidential rules and of the protections afforded to suspected or accused persons was presented with a picture of the criminal justice process which ran counter to that tendered by the Criminal Law Revision Committee. The Fisher Report was the result of a two year inquiry into the Maxwell Confait case.[18] In 1972, three boys — aged fourteen, fifteen and eighteen — had been questioned by the police in connection with the death of Confait whose body was found in his blazing home. On the basis of the confessions the boys made to the police during interrogation, two were convicted of murder and all three of setting fire to the house in which the deceased lived. In October 1975 the boys were freed after the Home Secretary referred the case to the Court of Appeal which quashed the convictions when fresh evidence showed that the youths could not have committed the offences for which they were convicted.

The Fisher Report provided an authoritative vignette of the prevailing investigation and prosecution process and found that it exhibited weaknesses at several levels. The case demonstrated that it was possible "for a prosecution based wholly (or almost wholly) on uncorroborated confessions to proceed to trial without proper steps having been taken to seek evidence to support or contradict the evidence of the confessions".[19] With regard to the custodial interrogation of the boys, Sir Henry Fisher found that senior officers had contravened the Judges' Rules "without adverse comment from higher ranking police officers, from the officers of the Director of Public Prosecutions, from Treasury counsel, from defending counsel or from the judge at trial".[20] Indeed, not only did Fisher conclude that the requirement that persons in custody be told of their right to consult a solicitor[21] "had become a dead letter",[22] he also found that the Judges' Rules were "not known to police officers and members of the legal profession".[23] He therefore called for "the sanction for breach of the Judges' Rules ... to be certain and regularly applied", since "[a]t the moment it is neither".[24]

The Report's findings challenged the assertion that the criminal justice process had erected too many safeguards for suspected and accused persons to the benefit of the guilty.[25] The Report was, therefore, generally welcomed by members of the 'due process' school. Nevertheless, members of the 'crime control' school — including senior police officers who had been exhorting officers to expose misguided public opinion to the evidence that they alone, as experts in the field, could adduce[26] — continued to contend that investigations into crime were made more difficult by the unnecessary constraints the criminal justice system imposed upon its law enforcement officers.[27] Indeed, the successor to Sir Robert Mark, Sir David McNee, went so far as to confess that:

> many officers, early in their careers, learn the art of manipulating the law to their advantage, and, in the investigation of crime, begin to use methods which border on trickery and stealth.[28]

This he ascribed to laws and procedures which, he claimed, encouraged police officers "to rely on bluff and stealth — and on occasions force — in order to carry out their duties effectively".[29]

Thus, the criminal justice debate between the 'due process' school and the 'crime control' school,[30] may be understood as having been largely based upon "a growing concern among British policemen that their capacity to cope with routine crime was inadequate and that their powers needed strengthening both in terms of increasing equipment and personnel and, more importantly, changing legal procedure to increase probabilities of detection, conviction, and stiffer punishment".[31] This however conflicted with the "evidence of increasing abuse of existing powers by police and a growing number of allegations of brutality, discrimination, and malpractice".[32] Such evidence brought one legal commentator to conclude that the realities of the existing criminal justice system were such that it had "already given the police and the prosecution the very powers they [were] demanding".[33] Therefore, it was argued, "[t]he law does not need reform to remove hamstrings on the police: they exist largely in unrealised rhetoric".[34]

In the wake of a series of 'moral panics' associated with law and order, such contradictory conceptions of the criminal justice process, following a proposal advocated by Fisher,[35] led the Labour Government, in June 1977, to announce the setting up of a Royal Commission on Criminal Procedure (RCCP). The Commission was directed to examine: the powers and duties of the police in the investigation of crime; their affect upon the rights and duties of suspects; the prosecution process; and to make recommendations regarding criminal procedure and evidence; while "having regard both to the interests of the community in bringing offenders to justice and to the rights and liberties of persons suspected or accused of crime". Under the chairmanship of Sir Cyril Philips, the Commission received evidence from a wide range of interested bodies representing crime control and due process concerns. It also commissioned an unprecedented number of research studies into the pre-trial criminal process and published its final Report in January 1981.[36]

## Proposals of the RCCP

On the issue of the extra-judicial interrogation of detained persons and the admissibility of confessions received by the police, a majority of the Commission, while being "sympathetic to the position taken by the Criminal Law Revision Committee", favoured the retention of the privilege against compulsory self-incrimination (the right to silence) in both its pre-trial and trial forms.[37] The RCCP's Report relates that the Commissioners accepted that the 'voluntariness' rule contemplated that, for a suspected person, police interrogations were necessarily coercive, also that their freedom of choice might be impaired, as might their ability to exercise their right to silence, and that in consequence the reliability of statements made in police custody had to be rigorously tested.[38] However, the Commissioners found that the long-standing judicial test for determining the 'voluntariness' of a confession, and hence its reliability, did not concur with the psychological evidence which suggested that "custody in itself and questioning in custody develop forces upon many suspects which ... so affect their minds that their wills crumble and they speak when otherwise they would have remained silent".[39] The Commission concluded that since legal and psychological 'voluntariness' did not match, and since the concept of voluntariness embraced by paragraph (*e*) of the Judges' Rules was ineffective as a rule of conduct for the police, the rule should be abandoned.[40]

Not only did the Commission recommend the renunciation of the 'voluntariness' rule, it also proposed that the Judges' Rules themselves be abandoned. It argued that the conduct of police questioning should be regulated by a statutory code of practice to "replace the vagueness of the Judge's Rules [so as to] provide strengthened safeguards to the suspect and clear and workable guidelines for the police".[41] The primary purpose of the proposed code would be "to minimise the risk of unreliable statements".[42] While the code should include "an explicit condemnation and prohibition of the use of violence" and a recognition of Article 3 of the European Convention for the Protection of Human Rights and Fundamental Freedoms, the Commission felt that it should not, indeed could not, proscribe specific tactics employed by the police aimed at producing confessions.[43] Nevertheless, a breach of the code should not "lead to total immunity for the suspect from prosecution and conviction or to the automatic exclusion of evidence".[44] And since the exclusion of evidence was not a satisfactory way of securing compliance with the rules,[45] this would be achieved by a combination of contemporaneous controls, supervisory checks, disciplinary measures applied internally by the police and by criminal or civil actions through the courts.[46] However, since the primary objective of the code would be to ensure the reliability of the evidence obtained, evidence obtained in breach of it would not be accepted "uncritically and without comment by the criminal courts".[47] Additionally, while the Commission accepted that jurors and magistrates should be advised of the dangers of acting upon a statement obtained in breach of the code, it was opposed to the introduction of a formal corroboration requirement on the ground that injustices would flow if confessors could not be convicted solely on the basis of their confessions.[48]

Finally, in order to counter the problem of disputes over the accuracy of oral statements attributed to defendants, the Commission proposed the development of improved note-taking techniques.[49] Interviewing officers should make "contemporaneous verbatim notes" of custodial interviews so as to better resist challenges to the police record.[50]

*An Evaluation*

In its discussion of the detention and interrogation of suspects the RCCP premised its conclusions upon the assertion that "there can be no adequate substitute for police questioning in the investigation and, ultimately, in the prosecution of crime".[51] The Report states that this observation was based upon "knowledge of other countries" and the results of research it had commissioned.[52] However, empirical research conducted for the Commission by Baldwin and McConville,[53] demonstrates that only 7 per cent of their sample of cases would have been fatally weakened had the police failed to secure damaging statements from defendants.[54] This research is supported by other empirical research also conducted for the Commission. This research found that police investigators would have abandoned proceedings in only 8 per cent of the cases that formed the sample had the police failed to obtain incriminatory admissions during interrogation.[55] Furthermore, other research, again for the Commission, indicated that in other jurisdictions, particularly the United states, police interrogations played a relatively minor role in the prosecution process.[56] In spite of this evidence — and in spite of research which revealed that 75 per cent of suspects detained by the police were charged within six hours and that 95 per cent were charged within twenty-four hours[57] — the Commission recommended an extension to the period within which the police might detain and question uncharged suspects.[58]

In suggesting that the treatment of those detained in police custody be governed by a code of practice which would replace the Judges' Rules and provide "a clear and enforceable statement of the rights and safeguards for suspects",[59] the Commission failed to clearly specify the terms of the code. Rather, it elected to leave the formulation of the code to the Home Secretary and Parliament.[60] This, as one commentator observed, was "a major omission in view of the centrality of the proposed code in the structure of the Commission's suggestions for reform".[61]

For the Commission, the 'voluntariness' rule and the judicial discretion to exclude improperly obtained confession evidence could be abandoned since the code would better control police behaviour, safeguard the rights of suspects and protect against the use of unreliable statements.[62] Where the proposed code was breached the jury would be warned, without a formal corroboration rule, to look for independent support for the statement having been made.[63] In short, the Commission sought to transform the issue of the reliability of an adduced statement from one concerned with its admissibility under the traditional 'voluntariness' rule, to one concerned with the probative weight it should be accorded not by a judge but the jury. It was argued against this proposal that it would increase the risk of wrongful convictions based on evidence that is highly prejudicial and often decisive in the resolution of a prosecution.[64]

The Commission argued that abolition of the 'voluntariness' rule was justified on two grounds: the first, it was ineffective as a means of controlling the police and, secondly, legal and psychological voluntariness did not coincide.[65] To this it might be objected that a possible solution would be to attempt to broaden the legal definition of voluntariness and to strengthen its function as a means of deterring police misconduct. To suggest, as the Commission does, firstly, that in practice the 'disciplinary principle' has been rejected by English judges,[66] secondly, that it can only apply in the small proportion of cases that are contested[67] and, finally, that American research had exposed its ineffectiveness,[68] indicates an inadequate and partial treatment of the capacity of the exclusionary rule to act as an incentive to police compliance.

"The primary duty to ensure that the rules are obeyed should", as far as the Commission was concerned, "rest with the police service itself".[69] This assertion betrays the extent to which the Commission placed its faith in the impartiality and integrity of the police. It also betrays an unwillingness to consider the implications of the official inquiry that had acted as a catalyst in the setting up of the Commission[70] and had revealed a clear relationship between wrongful convictions and the ability of the police to flout rules designed to protect suspects from "unfair and oppressive" treatment.[71]

An illustration of the faith the Commission placed in its presumption of police probity is found in its consideration of 'verbals'.[72] As McConville and Baldwin (1982) point out, the Commission "merely translates the problem in to acceptable terms. The problem, as it sees it, is not that verbals might be intentionally *false* but that the recording of them might not be wholly *accurate*".[73] Indeed, in the view of the Commission the solution lay in improving the accuracy of police records of custodial interrogations through better note-taking and the piecemeal introduction of tape-recording. However, in directing the larger part of its discussion towards the development of measures to better ensure the accuracy and reliability of statements made to the police in the context of custodial interviews, the Commission failed to address itself to the continued scope its recommendations would afford the police to fabricate, alter or coerce statements from suspects during low visibility or off-the-record exchanges.[74] Proof of such statements would continue to be dependent upon the generally unverifiable assertions of officers who may have collaborated in the preparation of their account of the exchange.[75] The failure of the Commission to address this issue suggests it premised its proposals respecting the recording of statements upon a somewhat "naive view of the meaning of 'verbals', which diagnoses the problem as inaccuracy rather than the fabrication of statements".[76] It also implies an inadequate appreciation of the role played by the police in a criminal justice process that is based upon adversarial values. The rhetoric of the law suggests that this role is confined to "*discovering* whether there is evidence that will support a prosecution of the suspect or cause him to be eliminated from the enquiry".[77] In practice, however, that role requires the police to construct the strongest possible case against defendants for the purpose of securing convictions.[78] In the context of custodial interrogations this manifests itself in practices and procedures that are essentially inquisitorial in nature.[79]

It is clear that the problem of ascertaining what took place during exchanges between the police and defendants presents considerable difficulties for both the prosecution and the defence.[80] However, while PACE has broadly implemented the procedures for regulating and monitoring police interrogations proposed by the RCCP,[81] with the intended object of protecting suspects and police officers,[82] this leaves unanswered questions as to the value to be accorded to contemporaneous recordings, whether by notes or other electronic devices; the extent to which such devices may limit or obscure police malpractice; their impact upon police control over the construction of reality for external others; and the completeness and reliability of the records such devices produce.

*The Legislation*

The 1984 Police and Criminal Evidence Act (PACE) — together with the 1985 Prosecution of Offences Act[83] — effected major changes to the criminal justice process. It revised and replaced the patchwork of common law and statutory rules that had governed police investigations. In doing so it conferred additional powers on the police and, as a *quid pro quo*, introduced mechanisms designed to balance the extension of police powers with procedures to safeguard the rights of citizens and to ensure police accountability.

Giving general effect to the recommendations of the RCCP relating to the detention, treatment and questioning of suspects, the Act confers upon the Home Secretary a power, to be exercised with the approval of Parliament, to issue Codes of Practice.[84] Regarding the recording of police-suspect encounters, Code C provides that records of interviews should, so far as practicable, be made contemporaneously or as soon as possible after interview and should constitute a full verbatim record or at least an accurate summary.[85] The contemporaneous record of custodial interview should normally be made either by verbatim notes or by audio tape.[86]

The Act is heavily reliant on internal police discipline to ensure compliance with the Codes of Practice.[87] However, it also provides that confession evidence *must*, as a matter of law, be excluded from trial if it has been obtained by oppression or in circumstances that would otherwise render it unreliable.[88] The Act also gives judges a discretion to exclude any evidence if its admission "would have such an adverse effect on the fairness of the proceedings that the court ought not to admit it".[89]

It is clear that the Act and its accompanying Codes seek to give broad effect to the proposals of the Royal Commission on Criminal Procedure (1981). By its provisions the pre-PACE position, under which the police acted as the sole, unmonitored and inadequately regulated narrators of what had transpired during detention and interrogation, has been recast by the introduction of measures for internal supervision, contemporaneous recording and for the strengthening of suspect's rights.

However, uncertainties persist over the comprehensiveness, accuracy and reliability of interrogation records required by PACE particularly, though not exclusively, with respect to events that occur outside the formal custodial interview, where the transmission to the courts of statements alleged to have been made by defendants continue to be reliant upon the generally unauthenticated accounts of police officers.[90] Thus, despite the advances it has made on the pre-PACE position, the regime erected by PACE continues to present difficulties both for any determination of the existence, form and effect of inducements to which defendants, as suspects, may have been subject and for any firm conclusions as to the integrity, accuracy and reliability of the record. Nevertheless, the interrogation records generated as a result of the reforms introduced by PACE make possible an assessment of the various ways in which actors involved in the interrogation process appear in those records. The legislation also makes possible an examination of the nature of the police-suspect dynamic as it appears in those records. Finally, it enables comparisons to be made with images of the interrogation process derived from the pre-PACE era.

**Images of Detainees Under PACE**

The post-PACE aspect of the present study is based upon a sample comprising records of police interviews with detainees drawn from committal papers associated with 283 cases heard in the Crown Court following the implementation of the Act. A systematic examination of the sample permitted the classification of the various ways in which suspects and the police were represented. It also admitted an assessment of the apparent impact of PACE and facilitated an evaluation of the extent to which the images identified in the pre-PACE sample resonate in the PACE sample.

With respect to the great majority of defendants who, as suspected or accused persons, were detained and interrogated by the police under the PACE regime, the examination identified the following typologies. They are: (1) the unequivocally guilty; (2) the resolute; and (3) the evasive, artful and uncooperative.

*Unequivocally Guilty Detainees*

The 'unequivocally guilty' frequently appeared in the survey as a class of individuals who, on being detained and interrogated, were recorded as exhibiting a preparedness not only to cooperate with the police but to confess to the offence for which they were being questioned. The survey found that while such persons evinced a general inclination to confess at the earliest opportunity, there were a number of individuals who appeared to capitulate only on realising that their guilt was beyond dispute. As a class, therefore, the 'unequivocally guilty' in the PACE sample emerge as having similar qualities to their counterparts in the pre-PACE sample.

In Case UP/2009 two police officers, involved in a "drugs operation", observed D, who had parked her car outside a specified public house, to be engaged in a transaction with a "known drugs dealer". After the transaction, D was followed and, having parked her car, was approached by the police who searched her and recovered "a crystal-like substance". She was arrested and taken to the police station where a contemporaneously recorded interview was conducted:

> PO: Do you require a solicitor to be present at the interview?
> D: No because I'm pleading guilty.
> PO: Can you tell me what this is?
> D: Well, the officer said it was either cocaine or crack.
> PO: What do you believe it to be?
> D: I don't know, it's one of them.
> PO: Is it yours?
> D: Yes.
> PO: What were you going to do with it?
> D: I had it given to me to pass down to someone else on my way home.
> PO: Just to clarify, you obviously believe it to be either cocaine or crack, do you realise that it is illegal for you to possess?
> D: Yes.
> PO: Do you realise as well that it's also an offence to give it to someone else?
> D: Well, as I've told you, I was asked to pass it to someone on my way home.
> PO: Clarifying it ... you weren't going to take it yourself?
> D: No. I wasn't taking it myself.
>
> ...
>
> PO: The fact is [D], you are admitting you had got that on you to give to someone else.
> D: I'm admitting it was in my possession. I am pleading guilty to it.

It would appear from this exchange that D was concerned to have herself depicted as a lesser actor in the incident that resulted in her arrest. She is shown to be anxious to suffer the consequences of her conduct alone. She acknowledges her actions were unlawful but expresses a desire not to implicate any other party. Indeed, her attitude in interview might suggest a desire to secure early release from the psychological pressures associated with arrest, detention and interrogation.[91]

The detainees in the following two cases also appear in the interview records as compliant confessors. They seem quite prepared to furnish their questioner, and thus external others, with sufficient information about their part in the offence and their own cupidity as to render a determination of guilt by a court of law a virtual certainty.

The case papers for Case WP/2114 detail that on receiving a report that a burglary of a dwelling house was in progress, two officers went to the specified address. During their search of the surrounding area, a pedestrian (D), said to answer the description of the suspect, was approached by the officers and, after having attempted to escape, was arrested. The formal interrogation of D at the police station was recorded by contemporaneously made notes. The notes document that after D had been informed of the reason for his arrest and cautioned, the interviewing officer asked:

> PO: Am I correct in saying that you do not want a solicitor present at this interview?
> D: Yes.[92]
> PO: Did you go to [the site of the alleged burglary]?
> D: Yes.
> PO: Do you know who lives there?
> D: No.
> PO: Did you go inside?
> D: Yes.
> PO: How did you get in?
> D: Through the back window.
> PO: How did you open the window.
> D: I forced it.
> PO: Did the lock break?
> D: Yeah.
> PO: Why did you go into the house?
> D: I found myself in need of some money and ended up trying to steal some.
> PO: Did you steal anything inside the house?
> D: No
> PO: Why?
> D: Because I didn't see anything of value.
>
> ...
>
> PO: You realise it's against the law to break into people's houses with the intention of stealing?
> D: Yes I do realise this but I found myself without an alternative.
>
> ...
>
> PO: If there was something of value there would you have stolen it?
> D: Yes.[93]

PO:  Is there anything else you wish to say regarding this offence?
D:   I would like to apologise for upsetting the person's house I broke into. It's just that lately I've been having trouble making ends meet.

D emerges from the interview as 'unequivocally guilty'. However, he also appears as a contrite confessor who accepts his criminal responsibility without quibble.

In Case UP/2002, the interrogation of D1 followed an incident which resulted in fire damage to an unoccupied dwelling house. According to the witness statement of the arresting officer, on arriving at the home of the suspect, eight days after the incident, he asked:

PO:  Are you [D1]?
D1:  Yes. I've been waiting for you
PO:  Why is that?
D1:  The business about the fire.
PO:  Well, I have to arrest you on suspicion of arson.

After being cautioned D1 is reported to have said:

D1:  I'm not going to piss you about, I'll tell you exactly what happened. To think I'm in this shit for £30.

D1 was escorted to the police station where he was questioned in the absence of a legal adviser. The interrogation was recorded by means of contemporaneously made notes:

PO:  ... if you wish to have a solicitor present during this interview its a matter for yourself. Do you wish to have a solicitor present?
D1:  No.
PO:  I will inform you that [D3] and [D2] have been arrested for the same offence and have been both charged. First of all, do you admit being responsible for setting fire to the premises?
D1:  Yes.

D1 was then asked and answered questions relating to his friendship with D2 and D3 and his meeting them in a public house on the evening of the incident:

PO:  So when exactly did you discuss setting fire to the premises?

D1: As I was about to leave [the pub] with [D2], [D3] called me back and asked me if I would do a job for him.... He said he wanted his house burned down and when I asked why he said it was for insurance.... He said it would be worth £30 to me. I'd got no money so I agreed.... I told [D2] what [D3] had said and asked him if he wanted to help and have half the money. He agreed.

...

PO: Then what happened?
D1: We left the pub ... and got some petrol.
PO: Was that the petrol you used in the fire?
D1: Yeah.
PO: Who purchased the petrol?
D1: I did.

...

PO: What happened then?
D1: We went to [D3's] house ... and broke in.
PO: Did you know whether [D3] was at home at this time?
D1: Yes, he said he would be next door.

...

PO: Did you check to see if the gas and electric mains were switched off?
D1: No, I didn't think.
PO: How long were you in the house for?
D1: Five minutes at the most.
PO: Were you aware or concerned of the danger that could arise by setting fire to a dwelling house by means of petrol and the explosion you could have caused?
D1: I didn't think at the time.

For the remainder of the interview D1 was questioned as to his precise movements prior to, during and immediately after the incident. He appears to have cooperated fully with the police in that his answers served not only to further incriminate himself but also to implicate D2 and D3. He may be seen as a thoughtless, tractable and irresponsible figure whose actions were inspired by the prospect of financial gain. Nevertheless, this excerpt indicates that quite apart from admissions of guilt formally recorded in interviews carried out in the police station, unverifiable narrative accounts of exchanges said to have occurred outside the setting of a formal interview continue to have a role to play under the regime brought into operation by PACE.[94]

Case DP/2213, the final case to be discussed within the present category, recounts that D1 and D2 were arrested and detained at the police station on suspicion of stealing a wallet from the changing room of a sports centre. According to the contemporaneously made interview notes only D2 was formally interrogated. The notes relate that he was interviewed twice, on both occasions in the absence of a legal adviser.[95] The first interview, in which D2 seems cooperative in so far as he answers the questions put to him, is reported as having taken seventeen minutes. However, in the second interview, conducted an hour after the first and taking five minutes, D2 emerges as the offender who, having failed either to exculpate himself and to incriminate D1 or to delude his questioner, comes to be reconciled with his own criminal responsibility. Excerpts from the two interviews are reproduced here:

> PO: You have been arrested on suspicion of theft of a wallet and its contents yesterday. Are you prepared to answer my questions?
> D2: Yes.
> PO: Today you went [to the bank] and exchanged a $10 note for English currency. Where did you get that note from?
> D2: [D1].
> PO: When did he give you this note?
> D2: Last night.
> PO: Where were you when he gave it to you?
> D2: At [home]. I asked to borrow some money.
> PO: What did he say when he gave you this note?
> D2: He just said you can have this if you want. I asked where he got it from and he said don't worry. That's the answer he gives to everything.
> PO: So by him saying that you suspected it was stolen?
> D2: Yes, I suspected it was stolen when he gave it me. I thought it was a lot of money. I had no idea of its true value.
> PO: So although you suspected it was stolen you still took it off him?
> D2: Yes.
> ...
> PO: Yesterday afternoon, what did you do?

D2: ... We went to the gym. I got out at about three but [D1] stayed in. I was in the shower for about ten minutes then [D1] came out. I got dried and went out of the changing room. [D1] came out about two minutes later.
PO: Did you see anybody else in the changing room?
D2: A tall lad and an older man getting changed.
PO: [The complainant] had his wallet stolen yesterday from the changing rooms at the sports centre at about the time you were in there. Did you steal his wallet?
D2: No I didn't.
PO: Did [D1] steal his wallet?
D2: I don't know. He came out after me.
PO: Amongst the property in the wallet was a $10 note which I believe was the one you cashed this morning. Have you any comment?
D2: I've told you what we done. I got the $10 note off [D1] and cashed it. I don't know anything about a wallet.
PO: To sum up, you say you accepted the $10 note off [D1] believing it was stolen but you didn't actually steal the wallet or its contents?
D2: Yes. I accepted the note having my own suspicions that it was stolen but I didn't take the wallet.

At this point the first interview was terminated. It will be seen that the interviewing officer is concerned to elicit D2's freely-given answers to reasonable questions. D2 appears responsive to the officer's questions but is reluctant to concede involvement. His demeanour in the second interview, in contrast to the first, may be attributed to the realisation that his story had failed to convince his questioner:

PO: I have now had chance to speak to D1 and from what he tells me, I'll asked you once again, who stole that wallet?
D2: Me.
PO: Where did you steal it from?
D2: It was just there in the middle of a pile of clothes on a bench.
PO: Where were the pile of clothes?
D2: On a bench in the changing room.
PO: Where is the wallet now?
D2: ... in the river.

...

PO: What happened to the contents of the wallet?
D2: I took it out. Only the money. The rest was left in.
PO: So what money did you have out of it?

D2: Just a five pound note, a $10 note and some brown coloured notes but I didn't know what they was.

...

PO: Was D1 with you when you stole the wallet?
D2: He was still getting changed.
PO: Why did you steal it?
D2: I don't know.
PO: Is there anything else you wish to tell me?
D2: Just sorry for messing you about, that's all.

Notwithstanding his expression of remorse — regarding his part in what he seems to believe was a needlessly prolonged investigation, though not for the misdeed itself nor for his attempt to implicate D1 — D2 is shown to be guilty of the offence for which he was charged. He is also shown to be a mendacious, calculating and disloyal character.

*Resolute Detainees*

This class of detainee appears willing to cooperate with the police to the extent that its members generally answer the questions that are put to them. However, the following cases illustrate that such detainees may resolutely deny culpability in spite of the force of the questions asked by the police and the unfavourable connotations they often carry.

The following extract is from Case DP/2108. According to the witness statements of the arresting officers, they arrived at a specified block of flats to find D1 (the tenant of the flat they sought to search by authority of a warrant issued under the Misuse of Drugs Act, 1971) engaged in a conversation on the telephone situated in the foyer. It is reported that the police interrupted D1 and, after he had refused both to identify himself and to surrender the keys to the flat, arrested him and seized the keys. At this point D1 is reported to have "started to struggle violently". However, he was "eventually restrained and handcuffed". He was then conveyed to the police station where, in the presence of his legal adviser, a formal interview was recorded by contemporaneously made notes.

The record details that D1 was informed by the police that a number of items were recovered from the flat. He was then asked to identify the persons present in the flat when the warrant was executed. This he did. As will be seen, the questions then put to D1 were largely directed towards linking him with the items found in the flat:

> PO: When we entered your flat it was quite obvious ... that cocaine had been or was being smoked. What do you know about this?
> D1: I know nothing about this. I asked to be present when they were searching the flat but they refused.
> PO: Has anyone ever snorted cocaine in your flat?
> D1: I was hardly ever there so I wouldn't know....
>
> ...
>
> PO: ... there were some items on the large table which included a small tube containing white powder ... and two small bags which appeared to contain the same white powder.... Is this yours?
> D1: As I've said before, none of the stuff was mine.
> PO: If it is just bicarbonate of soda would it be yours?
> D1: ... I've just said none of the stuff is mine whether it be bicarbonate of soda or whatever.
> PO: Do you know whose it is?
> D1: I've got no idea.
>
> ...
>
> PO: There was also a plastic bottle which contained water, had a foil top and a plastic tube inserted through the side. This commonly is used to inhale smoke, especially when snorting cocaine. Is this yours?
> D1: I don't think to answer that. I've already said none of the stuff which is in there is mine.
> PO: ... would you accept that the people in your flat were using them to inhale or take controlled drugs?
> D1: Tell you the truth, I can't answer that because I weren't there.
>
> ...
>
> PO: In my opinion, cocaine has been smoked in that flat for some time and I believe that you have knowledge of this. Is that true?
> D1: No that's untrue.
>
> ...
>
> PO: Have you ever taken cocaine in any form?
> D1: I've never tried it.

234  *Interrogation and Confession*

    PO:    But you are aware it can be smoked?
    D1:    Yeah.
    PO:    It was being smoked in your flat, is not that right?
    D1:    Not with my knowledge.

...

    PO:    I believe you ... have been supplying cocaine. Is that right?
    D1:    It's wrong.
    PO:    Why did you obstruct us in every way possible when you were arrested?
    D1:    You obstructed me by cutting my phone call off. I asked you why you wanted to know my name. You wouldn't tell me. So I told you I wouldn't tell you my name unless I knew what it was in aid of. I asked if I was being arrested. I was told, not at the moment.... I was then asked to turn my pockets out, which I did. One officer grabbed for my keys. I refused to let it go and then I was set upon by one of the officers kneeing me in the groin.... I was kicked and punched in the face....

...

    PO:    You knew exactly what was going to happen; we were going to execute a search warrant at your flat ... and you struggled and would not release your keys in an attempt to prevent us from executing the warrant.... Is that not the case?
    D1:    How could it be the case when I wanted to be there when you searched the flat?
    PO:    You also knew there were three men you flat....
    D1:    Yes there were three other persons there.
    PO:    And you knew that if we had your keys we would have let ourselves in and found them smoking cocaine.
    D1:    You did have my keys. It weren't my concern if you caught them smoking cocaine.... I'm only concerned about myself.

It is clear from this extract that the persistence of the police questioner fails to elicit the incriminatory admissions sought after. D, on the other hand, is shown to be equally persistent in his claim that he was not involved in any wrongdoing. Indeed, the extract presents a picture of two protagonists competing to ensure their own version of the disputed events is ascendant in the interrogation record to be scrutinised by external others.

One striking feature of this and many other exchanges found in the PACE sample, is that of detainees who are recorded as having given their own explanation of the alleged offence. In the context of the present category, such explanations are often seen to run counter to police hypotheses. This may be contrasted with the bulk of the narrative accounts of interrogations in the pre-PACE sample. It has been seen that these accounts generally depict detainees as either cooperative malefactors who adopt an acquiescent stance in regard to police case theories or as individuals employing weak strategies in their attempts to evade criminal responsibility.

The apparent ability of suspects interrogated under PACE both to resist the assertions of their interrogator and to insist on their innocence is evident in the next case. Again this case is but one example of that class of detainee who resolutely deny guilt during interrogation.

The two witness statements made by officers in Case WP/2008 relate that "a large crowd of drunken young men" were seen "spilling out" of a public house. The officers' statements report that a member of the crowd threw a glass smashing a window of the public house. The officers, both wearing uniform, attempted to arrest the individual they identified as being responsible. The suspect resisted the officers, one of whom had caught hold of him by his shirt. In the struggle the shirt "came from his body" into the hands of the officer. With the assistance of the "encircling mob", the suspect managed to free himself. It is reported that during the ensuing melee the now shirtless suspect kicked one of the officers and ran off. D, who was found near to the scene, was arrested, taken to the police station and there questioned in the presence of his legal adviser. The interview was recorded by contemporaneously made hand-written notes:

PO: In your own words would you tell us what happened when you left the public house and why you were detained by the officer?
D: ... I was going round the corner, there was a group of lads crossing the road ... then there was a scuffle and two police officers come. One of them grabbed hold of me and there was a struggle. We both went down on the floor ... the boots just started coming in while we were both on the floor.... I broke free, ran toward the bus stop and then the officer come and arrested me. I was handcuffed and brought here. That's it.

...

PO: Where's your shirt?
D: I don't know. In the road.

...

PO: Do you know why the officer detained you?
D: No.
PO: ... for throwing a bottle through the window of the public house. Did you cause that damage?
D: No.

...

PO: Why did you struggle with the officer?
D: What did he grab me for? I was approached from behind ... it's natural, you'd struggle anyway.
PO: But you knew it was a police officer didn't you?
D: Not at first....

...

PO: When did you lose your shirt?
D: When the kicks started coming in. I struggled to get loose, the officer had hold of my shirt and it just come off.
PO: Were you the only person without a shirt?
D: Don't know. Didn't stop to look.

...

PO: You were seen by a number of witnesses without your shirt ... kicking the officer around the head. What have you to say to that?
D: I never kicked the officer in the head.

...

PO: The second officer ... the one who arrested you... confirms what went on. Is he lying when he says it was you who assaulted his colleague?
D: There was a large number of youths, any one of them could have assaulted the police officer.
PO: A number of them did and you were also seen assaulting the officer with them. Do you have anything to say to that?
D: They're mistaken.
PO: You were the only one without a shirt and you were seen by the witnesses kicking the officer.
D: Sorry, those witnesses must be mistaken.

...

PO: I can assure you [D], they did see what went on. Are you going to tell us the truth in respect of this incident?
D: I've told you the truth.

Despite further questions of a similar nature, D maintained that the witnesses were mistaken and that he had not participated in the incident but was a victim. Irrespective of whether he was telling 'the truth', it is apparent that D proved to be resistant both to the attempts made to manipulate him into challenging the integrity or authority of the arresting officer and to the efforts made by the questioner to extract damaging admissions from him.

The image of the suspect who, while under interrogation, persistently denies committing the offence for which he has been detained is again evident in Case DP/2177. In this case a quantity of cannabis resin was recovered by officers, who were engaged in a surveillance operation, from a vehicle carrying four persons after the occupants had been observed leaving a public house. The following is an excerpt from the contemporaneously recorded interrogation of the driver which was attended by his legal adviser.

PO: As a result of you being stopped tonight your vehicle was searched and found in the ashtray ... were these two large pieces of resin. Is it yours?
D: No.
PO: There were three other people in the van with you.... Does it belong to them?
D: I don't know who it belongs to.
PO: What do you recognise it to be?
D: I don't recognise it to be anything.

D was then asked to account for his movements before journeying into the district in which he was arrested that night. After he had answered the questioner stated:

PO: Why travel twenty-five miles or so to a reputable drug dealing public house ... to go for a drink when you could have stayed [where you were]?
D: Bit boring.

...

PO: It appears to us that you collected your friends ... and went to the pub ... with the sole intention of buying the cannabis because your reasons for going are weak to say the least. Would you comment on that?
D: I can't really comment. Why weak?
PO: I believe you were the subject of a stop and search a few months ago?
D: True.
PO: What was found on you?
D: A very small quantity of cannabis.
PO: Cannabis resin?
D: Yes.
PO: So what is that?
D: I don't recognise it....
PO: So cannabis has changed its appearance has it?
D: No. I only got caught with a small amount. Nothing like that.
PO: There's no problem with the quantity. What do you believe it to be?
D: I don't know. Cannabis is usually black.
PO: The reason you are avoiding the question is you know that that amount is a dealing amount and you are up to your neck in it.
D: No, it's nothing at all like that.
PO: This cannabis resin must belong to you or your friends, surely you can see that?
D: Fair comment.
PO: So whose is it?
D: Ask the other three.
PO: ... I am specifically asking you because; one, its your vehicle; two, you were driving; three, you were seen to drive off from the pub with a coloured man.
D: It is my vehicle. I do drive it. What if it had been a Chinese man?
PO: We know from experience that coloured men in [this vicinity] are notorious for dealing drugs. Do you agree?
D: I don't know.... It's nothing to do with me.
PO: You do realise the serious nature of this offence?
D: Yes.
PO: Perhaps that's why you are so evasive....

Soon after this point, with D continuing to deny being involved, the interview was concluded. Nevertheless, it would seem that he failed to adequately dispel the suspicion under which he was held. The record of interview suggests that suspicion was well-founded. Despite this, the police are seen to struggle in their attempts to elicit a full confession.

Case UP/2026 is the final case excerpted in the present category as an example of a detainee who, detained and formally questioned under the

PACE regime, resolutely denies involvement in the offence in spite of seemingly clear evidence to the contrary. In this case a neighbour, suspecting two men of committing a burglary, telephoned the police. The police arrived at the private address to discover D1 leaving the dwelling house by a window. D1 was arrested and later interviewed at the police station where he confessed to the offence and implicated D2. Presently, D2, who had been found outside the premises when the police arrived — in what the arresting officers suggest was a state of inebriation — was also conveyed to the police station and there questioned as to his involvement. The interview was recorded contemporaneously and in the absence of a legal adviser.

PO: ... I wish to question you about the burglary .... [The caution.] Do you understand?
D2: Yes.
PO: Do you know [D1]?
D2: Yes.

...

PO: Did you come to [the town centre] with him today?
D2: No. I met him.
PO: Did you have a drink with him in [a specified public house]?
D2: There were a few of us in the pub.
PO: Did you leave the pub with [D1]?
D2: Yes. Four of us there was. Outside the pub there's a patio thing ... with a bench. [D1] said he wanted to go and see a friend who lives nearby. I was sitting on the bench having a drink with [named others], we finished the drink, [the others] went. [D1] hadn't come back so I walked across the road, round the side of a block of flats and on the floor there was two bottles of whisky and [D1] was inside.... I thought he was inside his mate's flat.... I turned round to go to the front of the flat and I bumped into a copper.

...

PO: Whose was the whisky?
D2: I don't know. It was outside on the floor.
PO: You didn't see how it got there?
D2: No.
PO: Did you know that [D1] had broken into the flat and was in the process of stealing?

D2: No. I thought he was in his mate's flat.
PO: What would you have done with the whisky had the police not come?
D2: Drunk it.

At this point the interview was brought to an end; some ninety minutes later it was resumed.

PO: It would appear that what you told me is not quite correct. I understand having spoken to [D1] that he handed the items to you out of the window. Is that true?
D2: No.
PO: He told you he was going to burgle a place didn't he?
D2: No.
PO: And you followed him over to the flat didn't you?
D2: Yes. I was with [the others] sitting on a bench. When that was finished, [D1] hadn't come back so I walked over there.
PO: And [D1] handed the items to you didn't he.
D2: He handed nothing to me. I walked round the corner ... the whisky was on the floor and I picked it up.
PO: A witness saw the items being handed over from someone in the flat to someone outside the flat. The one outside was you.... Isn't that what happened?
D2: No.

The study found that of those detainees who fell into the present class, few were interrogated in the absence of a legal adviser. This case is offered as one example of those unrepresented suspects who stoutly deny being involved in the alleged offence in spite of the seemingly strong evidence that connects them to it. Irrespective of whether such denials were sincere, the study found it uncommon for unrepresented suspect to display such perseverance in the face of hostile questioning designed to secure incriminatory admissions.

*Evasive, Artful and Otherwise Uncooperative Detainees*

Aside from those detainees who appeared to fall within the classes previously discussed, the study identified a third category involving a significant proportion of detainees. Broadly, as the following examples will illustrate, these detainees were recorded as adopting, with varying degrees of sophistication, either an evasive, artful or generally uncooperative stance during interrogation. Here, it is important to note that the 1994 Criminal Justice and Public Order Act (CJPOA) effected significant changes to the law governing the manner in which a suspect's pre-trial or trial exercise of the 'right to silence' may be dealt with at trial.[96] It repeals the statutory prohibition against the prosecution commenting on that silence.[97] It also permits a court to draw 'proper' inferences from a suspect's failure to mention facts when questioned.[98] However, it is to be emphasised that all cases in the PACE sample were determined before the relevant provisions of the 1994 Act came into force.[99]

The discussion now turns to the first of a selection of cases from the PACE sample as falling in the present category. In Case UP/2027 it is reported that D had aroused the suspicions of two police officers when he was found to be breathing heavily and perspiring in the vicinity of a recently perpetrated robbery. According to the witness statement of the officers, D was arrested after they confronted him in the street and asked:

PO: Where have you just come from?
D: From the snooker club.
PO: Where?
D: [Samson Street]
PO: You fit the general description of a man who has just committed a robbery [in that area] and has been chased in this general direction. I am arresting you on suspicion of committing this offence.
D: I've been at the snooker club.

The formal interrogation of D, held at the police station was attended by his legal adviser and recorded by contemporaneously made notes. The notes record that following the administration of the caution, D was asked:

PO: What have you got to say about the incident?
D: I don't know anything in regards to any robbery and I don't want to answer any particular questions to police officers.

Following this remark and in spite of the number of wide-ranging questions put to him by the police, D obdurately refused to answer.

PO: Are you a married or single man?
D: No comment.
PO: You live at [Ritual Street]?
D: No comment.

PO: How long have you lived at that address?
D: No comment.
PO: Have you got any children?
D: No comment.
PO: Can you account for your movements this morning?
D: No comment.

...

PO: Is [Ritual Street] your fixed address?
D: No comment.
PO: Would you like a cigarette?
D: No comment.
PO: Were you responsible for this offence of robbery?
D: No comment.
PO: By making no comment you are not denying or admitting the offence.
D: No comment.

...

PO: Why are you making no comment?
D: No comment.
PO: Is it on the advice of your solicitor?
D: No comment.
PO: By me asking the questions I'm giving you the opportunity to account for your movements.... By you answering it would be possible for us to prove or disprove your involvement. Would you agree?
D: No comment.

...

PO: ... from your answers I can assume that your are not denying the offence.
D: No comment.
PO: Do you agree that when you were arrested you said you had come from the snooker club?
D: No comment.
PO: How would you describe the weather today?
D: No comment.

...

PO: I'm giving you every opportunity to answer questions. Why do you choose not to?

D: No comment.
PO: By making no comment it indicates to me that you are responsible for this offence.
D: No comment.
PO: Would you agree your actions are not those of an innocent man?
D: No comment.

The interview is recorded as having continued in this manner until it was finally abandoned. Whilst being subject to a variety of questions ranging from the ostensibly innocuous to the directly accusatory, all of which specifically designed to gain a response, D is shown to possess considerable fortitude in maintaining a 'no comment' stance for the duration of the interview.

The scope the contemporaneously recorded interrogation provides for those not present at the interview to draw inferences unfavourable to the interests of the accused who declines to answer the reasonable questions put to him by those commissioned to investigate crime is also evident in the following case. However, as was seen in the case above, such records also provide for the documentation of some of the various 'legal' strategies that might be employed in an attempt to undermine a suspect's exercise of the 'right to silence'.

In Case DP/2061 officers were directed to commercial premises where intruders were reported to be engaged in burglarious activities. It is reported by the officers that whilst searching the surrounding area D was seen to be running. The officers called for him to stop and lie on the floor. D complied. He was then arrested and taken into custody. The first formal interview was attended by a legal advisor, the second was not. Both were recorded by contemporaneously made notes:

PO: ... since your arrest ... we have made enquiries with witnesses to the incident. Before I reveal what they have said I am giving you the opportunity to explain your actions. Have you any explanation?
D: Sorry, I don't wish to say anything.
PO: Witnesses have related to us that you ... were seen [acting suspiciously]. And you were chased [before] being apprehended by myself. Is that correct?
D: Sorry, I don't wish to say anything.
PO: Can you explain the screwdriver and saw blade which were on your person at the time of your arrest? What were they for?
D: Sorry, I don't wish to say anything.

...

> PO: Is that as far as we are going to get? Are you going to explain anything about the incident at all?
> D: Sorry, I don't wish to say anything.
> PO: Will you read these notes and tell me if you wish to add or alter anything?

The twenty-minute interview was abandoned after D had read and signed the notes. Some fourteen hours later the second interview was convened.

> PO: Right [D], you know who I am. This is detective sergeant [P], he is also from the CID.... I know you've been interviewed during the night about why you've been arrested ... you chose not to answer any questions, is that right?
> D: Sorry, I don't wish to say anything.
> PO: I would like to point out that the reason we want to interview you is to see if you can offer any reasonable explanation about the incident last night. Do you understand that?
> D: Sorry, I don't wish to say anything.
> PO: If you haven't done anything wrong and you can offer an explanation ... it would prevent you from appearing in court. If you haven't done anything wrong and can prove that to us, now is the time to tell us. Do you appreciate that?
> D: Sorry, I don't have anything to say.

It will be noted that D adopts uncooperative stance both in the presence and in the absence of his legal adviser. The study found that detainees infrequently exercised their right to silence in this manner. When it is considered that strong social and psychological pressures to answer questions operate upon suspects,[100] particularly in the 'inherently coercive' atmosphere of a police station,[101] this feature of the study should not be surprising.

The final case excerpted under the present head illustrates that when a suspect is evasive, artful or uncooperative, this may frustrate police attempts to induce incriminatory replies to the precise questions asked but may not preclude the instituting of proceedings. This case would suggest that should a detainee employ such strategies, he or she should be reminded that the effect on those who will ultimately determine the issue may not be entirely favourable.

According to the arresting officers' witness statements in Case WP/2153, D1, who had been followed into a set of public toilets by the officers, was seen to be looking under the partitions of the cubicles. The occupant of one of the cubicles (D2) was regarded by the officers as suspicious. As he left the cubicle, carrying toilet paper with writing upon it, one of the officers approached him and reportedly said:

PO: You have been in the toilet for the past three quarters of an hour and your actions have been observed, therefore, I am arresting you on suspicion of attempting to procure an act of gross indecency.
D2: I knew it was the police.... Why do you persecute us?

While D2 was being detained, one of the officers knocked on the door of the cubicle occupied by D1:

PO: This is the police, open this door immediately.
D1: What's going on...?
PO: I shall be forced to kick this door open if you don't open it now.
D1: OK. OK.

D1 and D2 were taken into custody and questioned. During his interrogation D1 confessed to contravening the Sexual Offences Act, 1956.[102] However, he denied having known or communicated with D2. Later, in the absence of a legal advisor, D2 was interviewed. It will be seen from the following extract that the strategy adopted by D2 during his interrogation was one which may be characterised as being based upon qualified cooperation:

PO: Do you understand why you were arrested?
D2: Not particularly.
PO: You were arrested on attempting to procure an act of gross indecency.
D2: Can you explain what an act of gross indecency is?
PO: Acts of masturbation in a public place, oral sex, buggery etc. Now do you understand?
D2: Yes.
PO: Why did you go to the toilets?
D2: I went to the toilets, one, in the full knowledge that it was known to be a cottage.
PO: What is a cottage?
D2: A cottage is a place ... for gay men to find affection.
PO: Are you gay?

D2: Yes. I am gay.
PO: Continue with your previous answer.
D2: Two, to have a shit and, three, to see what was happening in terms of gay culture in the [area]. Four, to make notes about my past experiences when I was very young in that toilet and others that have been pulled down.
PO: Did you go there to find a man to have sex with?
D2: Not necessarily. It was only a possibility because that was an occurrence of that particular toilet.
PO: So if the opportunity arose you would have participated in sexual activity with another man?
D2: No, not with anyone I did not like. Not in such a dangerous situation and definitely not because I've got a boyfriend and there is also the risk of infection of sexually transmitted diseases which I wouldn't like to pass on to anyone.
PO: You said, 'not necessarily for sex it was only a possibility'. So presuming it was someone you liked would you then have had sex or possibly gone somewhere with that person?
D2: That's a leading question and I'm not answering it.
PO: Can you give a direct answer as to your intentions?
D2: My intentions are to document behaviour and events in the toilets that I was arrested in for use as creative material for either a book or as a part of a documentary of small town England and its insular behaviour.
PO: Is it possible that if the opportunity arose in the toilets you would have had sex with a man?
D2: No.
PO: You said earlier, 'not necessarily' that means to me possibly yes possibly no. So it was possible wasn't it?
D2: Anything is possible.

D2 appears in the interrogation record as a rational and articulate individual, one who is fully conscious of the object of the questions put to him and alert to police interrogation techniques. However, from the perspective of the prosecution, he also appears to cooperate with the police only to the extent that he is willing to expound upon answers that have little prospect of directly implicating him in the offence for which he has been arrested. Therefore, although he seems to face the repeated attempts to obtain incriminatory admissions from him with some considerable composure and tenacity, this may be construed as evasiveness and, therefore, as evidence of guilt.

## Conclusion

This chapter began with a summary of the process through which custodial interrogations by the police, formerly the subject of judge-made rules, came to be regulated by statute. It gave a brief account of the relevant provisions of PACE before considering a selection of cases generated in the period following the introduction of the 1984 Act and its Codes of Practice. The cases were assessed in order to isolate some of the images they contain with respect to suspects who were detained and interrogated by the police and whose cases were determined in the Crown Court. The images gleaned from these records will, in chapter twelve, be considered with reference to those found in the pre-PACE sample. However, first it is necessary to evaluate the images contained in the PACE sample respecting both the police and their methods.

## Notes

[1] As has been seen in Chapter 8 above, the 1964 Judges' Rules were introduced against a historical backdrop of considerable concern regarding the conduct of custodial interrogations, their effective regulation and the reality of police practice.

[2] See Chapter 8, above. See also McNee, 1979, p. 85; Greenawalt, 1974, pp. 236, 238, 248. And see Mark, 1978, p. 55, where he argues that should the police 'apply the existing laws and procedures according to the letter. The effect would be disastrous. Only the weak, the spontaneous and intellectually underprivileged would continue to be amenable to the law'.

[3] Again see Chapter 8, above. See also Cox, 1975, p. 164; McBarnet, 1978, pp. 458-60.

[4] For an official acknowledgement of these concerns see the final report of the *Royal Commission on the Police*, 1962, Cmnd. 1728, para. 369. For an earlier judicial expression of concern see *Thompson* [1893] 2 QB 12, p. 18, *per* Cave J.

[5] Eleventh Report, *Evidence (General)*, Cmnd. 4991 (CLRC).

[6] *Ibid.*, p. 5.

[7] *Ibid.*, p. 10.

[8] *Ibid.*, para. 21, pp. 10-12.

[9] *Ibid.*, where the report speaks of a 'large and increasing class of sophisticated criminals' who skilfully exploit their rights in order to avoid conviction.

[10] *Ibid.* Indeed, the Committee felt that the laws of evidence had led to the assumption that defendants had 'a sacred right to the benefit of anything in the

law which may give them a chance of acquittal, even a technicality, however strong the case is against them' (*Ibid.*, p. 15).

[11] *Ibid.*, para. 29, pp. 16-17; and see pp. 17-34, 68-9.
[12] *Ibid.*, pp. 24-6.
[13] *Ibid.*, para. 40, p. 23.
[14] *Ibid.*, pp. 41-44.
[15] *Ibid.*, p. 43.
[16] See *The Sunday Times*, 2 July, 1972, pp. 14, 16; *The Times*, 6 October, 1973, supplement, p. 2; *The Times*, 7 November, 1973, p. 5; 'Minority Verdict', Dimbleby Lecture given by Mark, (1973) 90 *The Listener*, pp. 613-18, reprinted in Mark, 1977, pp. 55-77. See also Reiner, 1980.
[17] See generally, Devlin, in *The Sunday Times*, 2 July, 1972, p. 16; Simon, 1972, *The Times*, 5 October, p. 17; MacKenna, 1972, pp. 605-21; Cross, 1973, pp. 329-40; *The Times*, leader, 16 February, 1973, p. 19; Miller, 1973, pp. 343-355; Zuckerman, 1973; Zander, 1974, pp. 954-55; Devlin, 1979, pp. 441-2. Although the Commission, somewhat hesitantly, suggested that experiments with tape-recorders in police interrogations should be conducted (*supra.*, n. 5, pp. 28-33), its report was criticised for failing to recommend measures explicitly directed towards defects in existing recording procedures (see Gerstein, 1979, p. 91). The 'right to silence' in both its pre-trial and trial forms in England and Wales has been modified, along the lines suggested in the CLRC's report, by ss. 34 to 38 of the Criminal Justice and Public Order Act 1994.
[18] *Report of an Inquiry by the Hon. Henry Fisher into the circumstances leading to the trial of three persons on charges arising out of the death of Maxwell Confait and the fire at 27 Doggett Road, London SE6*, 1977 (Fisher Report).
[19] *Ibid.*, p. 19. The police gave evidence to Fisher admitting that once the confessions had been obtained from the boys 'enquiries continued only to strengthen the evidence against them' (*Ibid.*, p. 23). McBarnet (1978, p. 456) argues that such convictions were possible not because of any 'accident or freak occurrence' but because of the structural forces that operate 'in a system based on adversarial investigation and advocacy'.
[20] Fisher Report, *supra.*, n. 18, p. 162. And see pp. 11, 17-18.
[21] See principle (*e*) of the preamble to the Judges' Rules and Administrative Direction No. 7.
[22] Fisher Report, *supra.*, n. 18, p. 162. Empirical research conducted prior to and soon after the Fisher Report confirmed that suspects were habitually denied access to legal advisers by the police. See Zander, 1972; Baldwin and McConville, 1979; Zander, 1979.
[23] Fisher Report, *supra.*, n. 18, p. 13.
[24] *Ibid.*, p. 17. For subsequent cases evincing similar features to that of Confait and illustrating that police 'bad habits die hard' see Baxter and Koffman, 1983, pp. 19-21; Thomas, 1987, pp. 219-20.

[25] See, for example, Mark, 1977, pp. 55-73.
[26] See, for example, Mark, 1966, p. 319; Mark, 1978, Foreword, in Critchley, *A History of Police in England and Wales*, p. xiii.
[27] See Mark, 1977, p. 63. See also Kettle, 1980, pp. 23-27; Chibnall, 1979, pp. 135-49.
[28] McNee, 1979, p. 78.
[29] *Ibid*. It would seem that for McNee, such contributions from the police to the ongoing law and order debate, even when clearly designed to influence both public and Parliamentary opinion, did not conflict with the 'political neutrality ... and impartiality' he professed to be 'central to the British policing system' (McNee, 1979, *The Guardian*, 25 September, p. 25). His predecessor was more explicit: 'We who alone see the reality and the recorded crime should not be reluctant to speak about it. We who are the anvil on which society beats out the problems and abrasions of social inequality, racial prejudice, weak laws and ineffective legislation should not be inhibited from expressing our views, whether critical or constructive' (Mark, 1977, p. 118, and see pp. 41-3). See also McNee, 1983, pp. 180-2; Manning, 1977, p. 167; and see *supra*., n. 27.
[30] Also described as a debate between 'Libertarians' and 'Utilitarians' (see Gernstein, 1979, pp. 95-114).
[31] Reiner, 1983, p. 144.
[32] *Ibid*.
[33] McBarnet, 1981b, p. 155.
[34] *Ibid*.
[35] Fisher Report, *supra*., n. 18, pp. 6-7.
[36] Royal Commission on Criminal Procedure, *Report* (1981) Cmnd. 8092 (RCCP, *Report*).
[37] *Ibid*., paras. 4.52-3, 4.63-6. All but one of the Commissioners, however, supported the view adopted in the Eleventh Report of the Criminal Law Revision Committee (*supra*., n.5. para. 104) to the effect that the right of the defendant, under the 1898 Criminal Evidence Act, to make an unsworn statement at his trial was a 'useless anachronism' (RCCP, *Report*, para. 4.67).
[38] RCCP, *Report*, para. 4.68.
[39] *Ibid*., para. 4.73.
[40] *Ibid*., and para. 4.109.
[41] *Ibid*., para. 4.109; and see paras. 4.109-114.
[42] *Ibid*., para. 4.110; and see para. 4.133.
[43] *Ibid*., paras. 4.132-3.
[44] *Ibid*., para. 4.133.
[45] *Ibid*., para. 4.132.
[46] *Ibid*., paras. 4.117-30.
[47] *Ibid*., para. 4.133.
[48] *Ibid*., para. 4.74.
[49] *Ibid*., paras. 4.12-15.

50 *Ibid.*, para. 4.12. The Commission considered the widespread employment of tape-recording to be 'impracticable' because of the estimated cost and 'overwhelming operational difficulties' (para. 4.20; see also paras. 4.21-4). It did, however, recommend its gradual introduction (para. 4.25). Furthermore, while it felt that considerations of cost also militated against the immediate introduction of videotaped interviews, the Commission did not want to discourage the police from using it 'when they felt that the circumstances warrant it' (para. 4.31).

51 RCCP, *Report*, para. 4.1.
52 *Ibid.*
53 Baldwin and McConville, 1980, RCCP, Research Study No. 5.
54 *Ibid.*, pp. 27-33. See also McConville and Baldwin, 1980, pp. 993-95; McConville and Baldwin, 1982b, pp. 165-175
55 Softley, 1980, p. 94, and see p. 87.
56 Morris, 1980, pp. 10, 13.
57 RCCP, *Report*, para. 3.96.
58 *Ibid.*, para. 3.104.
59 *Ibid.*, para. 4.75.
60 *Ibid.*, paras. 4.111, 4.15-16.
61 Inman, 1981, p. 471.
62 RCCP, *Report*, paras. 4.73, 4.131, 4.118.
63 *Ibid.*, paras. 4.133, 4.74.
64 Inman, 1981, p. 472. In support of this contention Inman cites the research of Baldwin and McConville (1980, RCCP, Research Study No. 5), who found a high correlation in their sample between confessions made to the police and conviction rates. See also Devlin, 1960, p. 48; Morris, 1980, p. 12.
65 RCCP, *Report*, paras. 4.69, 4.73.
66 *Ibid.*, para. 4.124, citing the judgment of Lord Diplock in *Sang* [1979] 2 All ER 1222, p. 1230.
67 *Ibid.*, para. 4.125.
68 Inman shows that the Commission misapplied the American research which was primarily concerned with the exclusion of improperly obtained real evidence and not the exclusion of confession evidence. She demonstrates that 'far from supporting the Commission's view [that research] supports the *opposite* conclusion' (Inman, 1981, p. 475, my emphasis).
69 RCCP, 1981, *The Balance of Criminal Justice*, Summary of the Report, p. 11.
70 Fisher Report (1977) *supra.* n. 18.
71 *Ibid.*, para. 2.13.
72 That is, the police fabrication or alteration of admissions attributed to suspects. See RCCP, *Report*, para. 4.2.
73 McConville and Baldwin, 1982a, p. 296.
74 Although such exchanges may occur outside as well as within the police station (see, for example, Williams, G., 1979, pp. 10, 12-15; McConville and Morrel,

1983, pp. 158-62), the Commission appears to have contented itself with the finding that in respect of Crown Court trials, 'there were few cases where the prosecution was greatly assisted by evidence of conversations held outside the police station' (para. 4.3), and the consideration that since the majority of defendants pleaded guilty, comparatively small amounts of court time was spent with challenges to the accuracy or authenticity of police interrogation evidence (para. 4.7).

[75] *Bass* [1953] 1 QB 680. See also Williams, G., 1979, pp. 12-13, where he argues that in these circumstances the police account is 'virtually impregnable' especially where the defendant has a criminal record. And see McConville and Baldwin, 1981, pp. 165-6; McConville, *et al.*, 1991, pp. 57-60.

[76] McBarnet, 1981c, p. 113.

[77] RCCP, *Report*, para. 1.7 (my emphasis).

[78] See Fisher Report (1977) *supra.* n. 18, para. 2.30; Devlin, 1979a, pp. 71-2; McBarnet, 1978, p. 456; McConville and Baldwin, 1981, pp. 124-5, 189-93.

[79] See Devlin, 1979b, p. 442; and Devlin, 1979a, p. 78.

[80] See Morton, 1975, pp. 830-1; McConville and Baldwin, 1981, p. 166; Vennard, 1984, pp. 21-2.

[81] For an account of the reception the report of the RCCP received from interested and concerned parties to the 'law and order' debate and for a discussion of the place of its recommendations (a number of which were amended or lost) in the legislative process, through the 1982 and 1983 Bill stages, to form the basis of the 1984 Act, see Reiner, 1985, pp. 167-69; Freeman, 1985, pp. vii, 5-6; Zander, 1985, pp. xv-xvii; Leigh, 1986, pp. 91-117.

[82] See RCCP, *Report*, paras. 3.94, 4.31.

[83] The 1985 Act established the Crown Prosecution Service to advise on cases referred to it by the police; to assume control over criminal proceedings instituted by the police; and to discontinue those proceedings when it deems such action to be appropriate.

[84] PACE, ss. 66-7. Section 66 also governs the issuance of Codes relating to the search of persons, vehicles and premises; the seizure of property found by the police on persons or premises; and the identification of suspects. Code E, issued in pursuance of s. 60, provides for the tape-recording of custodial interviews.

[85] Code C, paras. 11.5, 11.7

[86] See Code C, paras. 11.5, 11.8, 11.10, 11.11, 11.13 and Code E, para. 3.

[87] See PACE, s. 67 (10).

[88] PACE, s. 76 (2). Section 67 (11) of the Act makes the Codes of Practice admissible in evidence and obliges the court to take the relevant Code into account where pertinent to any question to be determined by the court.

[89] PACE, s. 78 and see s. 82 (3) which preserves the discretionary power of the court to exclude any evidence.

[90] See McConville and Morrell, 1983, pp. 161-2; Dixon, *et al.*, 1990, p. 133; Wolchover and Heaton-Armstrong, 1991, pp. 242-4.

[91] See Irving and Hilgendorf, 1880, pp. 28-36; Walkley, 1987, pp. 22, 26; Gudjonsson, 1992, pp. 25-7.

[92] There is no evidence within the documents relating to this case to suggest that D was expressly asked if he desired a legal adviser. Furthermore, the question and its reply provides some evidence for supposing that an informal and unrecorded exchanged between the police and D had taken place prior to the commencement of the formal interview. See PACE, Code C, paras. 11.2, 6.6 and Annex C.

[93] As the police removed certain property, including jewellery, a camera, a video and other electrical goods from the house, it may be assumed that D, who claimed he 'didn't see anything of value' intended to steal cash or other comparatively small items which he could easily exchange for cash. Thus, despite the serious nature of the offence, D may be regarded as a petty offender. Indeed, it would seem that the police questioner considered him as such.

[94] See PACE, Code C, paras. 11.1, 11.2A, 11.5 and 11.13; Code E, para. 4.3B. The problem of how a meaningful waiver of the right to legal advice may be authenticated is also highlighted by this case. In this particular instance, it may be contended that the manner in which D1 was asked if he wish to have a solicitor present implied that he would have to arrange this for himself and be required to meet the costs incurred.

[95] Indeed, the interrogation record indicates that at no point was D2 advised of his right to legal advice. See PACE, Code C, paras. 11.2, 6.6 and Annex C.

[96] CJPOA 1994, ss. 34-38.

[97] Prior to the 1994 Act, the prosecution was prevented from commenting on a defendant's failure to give evidence by s. 1 (b) of the Criminal Evidence Act 1898.

[98] CJPOA 1994, s. 34. See also s. 35, allowing 'proper' inferences to be drawn from a defendant's failure to give evidence; s. 36, allowing 'proper' inferences to be drawn from a suspect's failure to account for objects, substances or marks; and s. 37, allowing 'proper' inferences to be drawn from a suspect's failure to account for presence at a particular place.

[99] The 'right to silence' provisions became effective on April 10, 1995.

[100] See Driver, 1968, pp. 42-61; Irving, 1980, p. 103; Softley, 1980, pp. 73-4; RCCP, *Report*, 1981, paras. 4.46, 4.73.

[101] See Commerton, 1964, p. 179. See also Biderman, 1960, pp. 120-47; *Miranda v. Arizona* (1966) 348 US 436, pp. 456-8, 467-8, 478-9; Griffiths and Ayres (1967) 300-19; Irving, 1980, p. 153; Inman, 1981 p. 476.

[102] Section 32 of which provides that: 'It is an offence for a man persistently to solicit or importune in a public place for immoral purposes'.

# 11 PACE Images: The Police

**Introduction**

The preceding chapter, in its assessment of interview records generated since the implementation of the PACE reforms, advanced a number of typologies and, within those typologies, discussed a selection of images relating to defendants during the period when they were detained as suspects and interrogated by the police. Drawing on the sample of 283 post-PACE interview records, the present chapter will assess the images the records contain relating to the police and to police investigative practices. It must, however, be acknowledged that of themselves these records — quite apart from questions as to their internal exactness, fidelity and reliability — cannot provide a comprehensive picture either of police interrogations or of police investigations since those cases that did not proceed to trial in the Crown Court were excluded from the study.[1]

Although restricted to those cases which resulted in Crown Court trial, the study will provide a valuable insight into the functions of custodial interrogation, the nature of police-suspect relations as represented in interview records and the investigative techniques employed by police investigators. The significant point is that this insight is derived from the very material which frequently plays a key role in cases assembled for prosecution and determined by the courts.[2]

**Images of the Police and Police Questioning Under PACE**

McConville and Baldwin (1981) found that in addition to securing confessions, police interrogations served a variety of collateral purposes. These range from recovering stolen property, clearing police books of unsolved crimes and clarifying knowledge possessed by the police. They include obtaining evidence against alleged accomplices, exonerating the innocent, reinforcing partial or subjective perceptions and, finally, communicating stereotyped images that work to establish a firm normative dichotomy between law enforcers on the one hand and law breakers on the other.[3]

The extent to which such findings may be shown to have validity in the post-PACE prosecution process is circumscribed by the consideration that the overriding impression gained from the present study is that police interrogations are, on the whole, directed towards gaining evidence to be used against suspects at trial. Certainly, it is generally understood that for the police the primary purpose for conducting custodial interrogations with persons suspected of involvement in crime is to secure admissions or confessions.[4]

During the course of the present study it became clear that in their efforts to obtain confessions, admissions or other evidence that might be used against suspects, police officers frequently made use of a variety of persuasive and manipulative tactics. Applied with varying degrees of sophistication, these tactics generally centred upon the manipulation of information allegedly or actually possessed by the police; pointing out the advantages for the suspect in cooperating or confessing; manipulating the self-esteem of the suspect; and adopting a confrontational approach towards the suspect.[5] As other researchers have pointed out, such tactics — which place reliance upon styles of questioning that "overtly manipulate the suspect's decision making"[6] — may be productive of reliable as well unreliable confessions.[7]

The interview records examined during the present research suggest the following question-forms were commonly used by investigating officers:[8]

> *Establishment questions*; these aim to establish a non-hostile relationship with the suspect to put him or her at ease, or off guard, and to "create an atmosphere in which cooperation is more likely".[9]
>
> *General information-seeking questions*; this form of question is normally non-confrontational in character and is "designed to elicit the suspect's own story".[10]
>
> *Offence-focused information questions*; such questions focus directly on a particular offence and are designed to elicit direct answers from the suspect. An example might be: 'OK, you know why you've been arrested don't you, what do you have to say about [the incident]?'[11]
>
> *Leading questions*; these are fashioned to persuade the suspect to give particular answers by foreclosing other possible answers ('The

truth is you left the shop knowing the goods were in your bag and with no intention of paying for them. Isn't that right?').[12]

*Statement questions*; these have been described as 'statements which masquerade as questions' and are used to confront the suspect with a statement of fact which he or she is invited to confirm or contradict.[13]

*Questions seeking the view or opinion of the suspect*; these questions purport to solicit the suspect's own view or opinion. However, they are generally directive or leading in nature in that they invite the suspect to accept a proposition contained in the question posed ('The fire must have been started deliberately, don't you agree?').

*Questions attributing a view or opinion to the suspect*; in effect these questions seek to force the suspect to adopt a police opinion. The police questioner, therefore, may reinterpret or paraphrase a statement made by the suspect in an effort to gain the suspect's assent to its reformulation. Alternatively the questioner may make a statement or offer an opinion carrying legal or evidential implications which the suspect is persuaded to accept, ('Are you asking us to believe...').[14]

*Questions seeking an explanation for apparently incriminating evidence*; such questions are used by the police to confront the suspect with evidence which appears to incriminate them and, without adverting to any specific offence, ask for an explanation, ('You were arrested after having been found running away from an abandoned car which has been reported stolen. What have you to say for yourself?').[15]

*Questions imputing involvement based on evidence*; through this form of question the police directly accuse the suspect of an offence on the basis of evidence which is disclosed to the suspect ('Look, the statement made by [X], the property recovered and the finger prints found, all point to your involvement don't they?').

*Accusatory questions*; here the police directly accuse the suspect of involvement in the offence in a manner similar to the 'imputing involvement' question-form. However, in this form the accusation may not be supported by evidence or the evidence may not be disclosed to the suspect ('You're lying. We know a lot more about this than you think. So let's have the truth. You and [X] did this together didn't you?').

*Legal closure questions*; these are questions that are phrased in legally significant terms in an attempt to force the suspect to adopt them in his or her replies.

A quantitative analysis of the frequency with which leading questions and legal closure questions appeared in the pre-PACE and the post-PACE sample will be presented in the following chapter. At this stage, however, it is noted that the use of the more manipulative question-styles appeared to be particularly evident in cases where detainees did not readily comply with the police agenda or admit to the offence for which they were detained and questioned. Conversely, the use of simple information-seeking or neutral questions appeared to have been confined to those suspects who seemed willing to cooperate with the police.

It is worth noting that researchers have drawn attention to other factors that influence the decision making of detained suspects and the approach employed by the police in their questioning of them. Such situational and contextual factors include: the age and sex of the detained suspect; their criminal history; their previous contacts with the police; the nature of the alleged offence; the nature and strength of suspicions harboured against the suspect; police perceptions of the seriousness of the alleged offence; the cogency of the evidence available to the police when questioning the suspect (whether that evidence be 'real evidence', the product of civilian or police witness statements, or in documentary form); the offence type; the presence of a legal adviser in the interview; and the length of detention.[16]

Though clearly relevant, an exhaustive evaluation of the role played by each of the potentially identifiable variables is beyond the scope of the present research since the sample did not yield sufficient information to enable a consistent and reliable estimation of, for example, the strength of the available evidence, the police view of the seriousness of the alleged offence or whether the suspect had previous contacts with the police. However, those factors which proved to be consistently traceable, such as the use of leading questions and the presence or absence of a legal adviser, are discussed in the next chapter.

That said, the post-PACE sample permitted the formulation of three typologies or models which together incorporate the overwhelming majority of interrogation records studied. The typologies (which are not proposed as alternatives since, to some extent, they overlap with each other) categorise the approach taken by police investigators during interrogations as: (1) to receive voluntary confessions; (2) to confront detainees with apparently incriminating evidence; and (3) to test or confirm police case theories. Although the categories provide for an evaluation of the various tactics routinely employed by the police in their interactions with detainees, they also serve as tools with which to assess the images the PACE sample contain of policing, the police role in the investigative process and police attitudes to that role as voiced by the police themselves.

*Interrogations for the reception of voluntary confessions*

The first category of images derived from the PACE sample embraces that comparatively small number of exchanges in which the police appear to exert little or no influence over the detainees they question. Such cases appear in sharp contrast to the large majority of cases examined, in that investigating officers seem to adopt a relatively passive role during interrogation, to rely chiefly upon the use of offence focused information questions and to leave the detainee free to tender his own uncoerced account. The following two cases are offered as examples:

The witness statement of the arresting officer in Case RN/2222 reports that while on patrol in the early hours of the morning he saw D standing in the doorway of a retail shop. D was approached and asked:

PO: What are you doing?
D: Walking to [Princethorpe].
PO: By standing in a doorway?
D: I suppose not.
PO: Have you anything in your pockets you shouldn't?
D: No, go on search me.

On searching D, the officer recovered and took possession of a kitchen knife. It is reported that he then asked:

PO: What have you got this for?
D: Self defence. Why?
PO: Would you use it if you were set upon?
D: Yes, no problem. I've been beaten up twice before.
PO: Have you any ID?
D: No.
PO: In that case I am arresting you for carrying an offensive weapon.

D was conveyed to the police station where he was interviewed by the arresting officer while a second officer recorded the interview by way of contemporaneous notes. The ten-minute interview is recorded as follows:

PO: You have been arrested earlier this morning carrying an offensive weapon and a plastic carrier bag. I wish to ask you some questions regarding your arrest. Do you wish to have a solicitor present whilst I do so?
D: No.
PO: Can you tell us why you were in a doorway in [Main Street] at 4 a.m. this morning with a knife and a carrier bag?
D: I was going to wait till the police vehicle passed. I was then going to attempt to steal food or money, which ever was available, for me and the girl I'm living with.
PO: Why?
D: Because we spent all our money over Christmas. She relies on me for her money.
PO: Where were you going to get the food or money from?
D: Any shop, nowhere in particular.
PO: What was the knife for?
D: If there was any boxes there I could get into them with the knife and the bag to carry the stuff away.

...

PO: Have you stolen anything this morning?
D: No, nothing at all. I was arrested before I got the chance.
PO: Have you committed any other offences you want to tell us about?
D: No I haven't committed any offences. I've tried to keep out of trouble but times are bad.
PO: Does the girl you live with know what you were going to do?
D: No.
PO: Are you sure you haven't broken into anywhere or stolen anything this morning?
D: No.

After D had signed the interview notes to indicate that he agreed they were accurate, the interview was terminated. The picture painted in this account of detention and interrogation suggests a legitimate arrest, following from a legitimate stop and search, founded upon reasonable suspicions. However, the account also suggests that the main purpose in the police decision to conduct a formal interview was to elicit a confession.[17] Since the suspect is seen to emerge from the contemporaneously recorded interview as a willing confessor, the actions of the police appear wholly justified.

In their witness statements, the arresting officers in Case W/P2146 state that whilst on patrol they observed a stationary car to be enveloped in "a plume of smoke and flame". As they approached the car they saw D1 walking away from the flames towards another stationary vehicle. The passenger seat of that vehicle being occupied by D2. Despite being told to stay where they were by the approaching officers, D1 and D2 ran off. However, on searching the area, the officers found the suspects hiding in an adjacent field. The suspects were arrested on suspicion of having stolen the car. At the police station the formal contemporaneously recorded interview conducted with D1 was attended by his solicitor:

PO: I understand that you stole the Jaguar from the [Golf Club] car park this morning. Is that correct?
D1: Yes.
PO: Can you tell me how you went about stealing it?
D1: I picked up a set of keys in the course of my work. I went for a drink with [D2] at the [Hare and Hound]. After that I went to [the Golf Club]. Not to steal a car but for a drink.
PO: You went to [the Golf Club] with [D2]?
D1: Yes.
PO: Carry on.
D1: When I got to the [Golf Club] I saw the Jaguar parked up on the car park and like a fool I went over and checked and saw if the keys fitted it. They did so I asked [D2] if he would follow me in the van while I went for a drive. I was driving up and down for a bit. I decided that the best thing to do would be to park the car and go but then I started panicking in case the car was fingerprinted.... Then stupidly I decided the best thing to do would be to burn it out. That's the picture when you come. [D2] had nothing to do with it; the burning or the taking. I'm sorry for the trouble or damage and everything.
PO: What did you use to set fire to the car?
D1: There was some matches in the car.
PO: Did [D2] give you the matches to burn the car?
D1: No.
PO: He knew you were stealing the car from the [Golf Club]. Is that correct?
D1: Only when I actually took it, yes.
PO: So by driving your vehicle whilst you took the Jaguar he assisted you in the theft?
D1: I don't know if that's assisting or what.
PO: Did he encourage you by driving your car? What do you say to that?

D1: No.
PO: Would you have taken the Jaguar if [D2] hadn't driven your vehicle?
D1: Yes.
PO: So you were determined to take the Jaguar come what may?
D1: If somebody had tried to stop me I wouldn't have taken it.
PO: Can you describe how you set fire to the Jaguar?
D1: I tipped a bit of petrol on it which was in the back of my van. I put petrol on and set it on fire. I put a match to it and set it on fire.
PO: Did [D2] do or say anything to try and stop you setting the car on fire?
D1: No, he was sitting in the van.

...

PO: Is there anything else you want to say about stealing the Jaguar and setting it on fire?
D1: I'm just sorry that I set it on fire and stole it in the first place. It was a stupid thing to do. I didn't plan to burn the car, I just panicked. It was stupid of me. I'm sorry.
PO: Is there anything else about other cars you want to tell me?
D1: No. I haven't touched a car in four years and then it was just the one.

Beyond the appearance of a successfully concluded case, there are three salient features in the thirty-minute interview. The first is the remark made by the questioner at the start of the interview record. This remark might suggest that a pre-interview exchange between the police and the accused, and perhaps the solicitor, had taken place. Alternatively, it may be that the remark was no more than a bare assertion of presumed guilt based upon information gleaned from the arresting officers. Indeed, the study found that police questioners frequently commenced formal interviews with such statements; the apparent object being to establish at the outset the parameters of their dialogue with detainees who, as in this case, are then invited to supply the fine details of their misconduct from within the tacitly defined framework.

The second relates to the attempts made by the questioner to elicit information from D1 that would implicate D2. It will been seen that these attempts — in contrast to the questions directed towards ascertaining the criminal responsibility of D1 — make use of mainly leading questions. The third salient image stems from the impression that D1 was permitted to give a largely unaided and voluntary account of his criminal activity. However, he does so by observing the convention or formula followed by the great majority of such confessors. By this convention the confessor should make an early avowal of guilt; he should also intimate that his actions were irrational and aberrational and not premeditated; finally, the confessor should voice apposite expressions of remorse. In observing this convention the confessor may preclude or minimise the intensification of any psychological pressures that might ensue should the police elect to adopt an aggressive stance in interview. It is clear, however, that the convention or formula may be utilised by innocent as well as guilty confessors.

*Interrogations in which D is confronted with apparently incriminating evidence*

Those cases from the PACE sample identified as falling into this class may be divided into two groups. The first, those in which the detainee is confronted with what appears to be cogent evidence pointing to guilt. The second, those in which the disputed evidence appears to be less than decisive. Case CP/2024 and Case PN/2202 are representative of the former, while Case TP/2221 and Case NN/2049 are examples of the latter.

The witness statements made by the officers concerned in Case CP/2024 detail that in the early hours of the morning they arrived at D's home and, after having conducted a search of the premises, arrested him on suspicion of being involved in the robbery of a betting shop. His girlfriend (GF), who was present when the police arrived, is reported to have 'accompanied' the officers to the police station where she was later interviewed. During his period in custody at the police station, D was formally interviewed on four separate occasions. It is reported that at the beginning of each of these contemporaneously recorded interviews he was properly cautioned. There is, however, no record in any of the relevant documents of his being notified of his right to free legal advice. In the following extracts it will be seen that the police, through means of persistent questioning based on what appears to be reliable information gleaned from their pre-charge investigations, methodically pursue their quarry, close off his options and bring him to 'tell the truth'. It will also be seen that the police are greatly assisted in their efforts by a signed statement made by GF while she was at the police station:

PO: You have been arrested this morning on suspicion of robbery which occurred [on a specified date and at a specified address]. That was three weeks ago. What do you know about it?

| | |
|---|---|
| D: | Nothing. I don't even know where the place is. I only know two shops down there.... |
| PO: | How do you know these shops? |
| D: | Coz [GF's] mother lives just across the road. |
| PO: | Is [GF] your woman? |
| D: | Yeah. |
| PO: | When was the last time you were in [Pickleston]? |
| D: | About a month and a half ago. What day did this robbery happen anyway? |
| PO: | Friday. |

The interview record documents that D was then asked, and answered, a series of questions relating to his movements prior to and after he had collected his wages from his place of work on the date in question. It continues:

| | |
|---|---|
| PO: | Do you bet? |
| D: | No. I ain't got no money to waste. |
| PO: | Do you know where the bookies in [Pickleston] is? |
| D: | No and that's the honest truth. |
| PO: | ... this robbery was committed at [a specified time and date], now according to your version of events you would have been at home then wouldn't you? |
| D: | Yes. I'd have been watching the television. |
| PO: | Apart from [GF] would anyone else be at your house then? |
| D: | I don't know. People come and people go. |

D then answered questions relating to his and to GF's income and expenditure. The interviewing officer then said "I am going to finish the interview now because I want to see how the enquiries are going elsewhere. I will speak to you later". The record indicates that after an hour had elapsed the second formal interview was initiated:

| | |
|---|---|
| PO: | [GF], your girlfriend? |
| D: | Yes. |
| PO: | How long? |
| D: | 3 years. |
| PO: | Do you get on well? |
| D: | Yeah we get on. |
| PO: | You not having any rows at the moment? |
| D: | No. |
| PO: | Have you ever given her large sums of money? |

D: No.
PO: In the last month?
D: No.
PO: £200?
D: No.
PO: Did you come back one night two weeks ago and give her £200?
D: No.
PO: You are absolutely sure?
D: I can't give her £200 I'm in debt with me car; kids need clothes.
PO: So the answer is definitely no?
D: Definitely no.
PO: She wouldn't tell lies about you?
D: No.
PO: She's being spoken to in this police station. She has stated that two weeks ago you gave her £200. With that money she bought clothes and a suit for herself.
D: Suit?
PO: Clothes. Now at the start of this interview I asked you if you were getting on well, you replied yes and would she lie about you, you said no.
D: Right.
PO: So are you saying that [GF] is lying?
D: If she's saying I gave her £200 two weeks ago, where did I get it?
PO: That's our point [D], you got the money from the bookie robbery.
D: 'made no reply'.

...

PO: OK, we'll show you the statement of [GF] next interview. Is there any more you want to say?
D: No.

The interview was terminated soon after this point. The third interview commenced some sixty minutes later:

PO: OK, you have had time to think, did you give your woman £200?
D: No I didn't give her money.
PO: ... I believe she would remember whether she has been given money, especially £200.
D: She should.
PO: So why should she say that?
D: I don't know. I didn't give her £200.
PO: Well why did she say you did?

D: I don't know.

It is recorded that at this juncture one officer left the room and returned with GF:

PO: [To GF.] Have you just made this statement?
GF: Yeah.
PO: In this statement which is yours, do you say that that man there (indicates [D]) gave you £200?
GF: Yeah.
D: When did I give you £200?
GF: I told them the truth.

After GF had left the interview room:

PO: You've just seen your girlfriend, [GF].... She's made a three page statement, she states you gave her £200 [at] about the time of the robbery. We believe this to be part of the proceeds of the robbery. In interview she also states that she bought some clothes with it. You were one of the persons responsible for the robbery weren't you?
D: I wasn't in [Pickleston].

...

PO: OK, I'm going to end this interview now. Before you go back to the cell I'll ask you to think very carefully about all we have said and remember we have given you every opportunity to tell the truth, haven't we?
D: Yes.

Fifty minutes later the fourth and final recorded interview began:

PO: Again you've been given an opportunity to think about all that has been said. Can you remember [the date in question]?
D: Yes.

D was again asked to give an account of his movements. After having done so, the officer pointed out that it departed from that given by GF:

PO: ... [GF] remembers the day because ... you did something you've never done before and that was you dropped a wad of notes in front of her ... it

was £200 that's why she remembers. Yet you deny both the money and the movements. Why is that?
D: I couldn't tell you.
PO: Is that because her story puts you out of the house without an alibi at the time of the robbery and the £200 was either part or all of the proceeds?
D: No reply.
PO: She even goes into detail about how she received the money from you ... it must be the truth.
D: No reply.
PO: You are not answering some of the questions, now is that because we are starting to get to the truth?
D: No reply.
PO: Look [D], our information is you were involved in this Bookies job. We haven't just picked your name out of a hat. The fact that [GF] received some money from the job was all part of our information. Something which we have known long before today. You've persistently denied what [GF] has been saying although you agree she had no reason to lie. She has done what she thinks best for her man. Now what is the truth?
D: OK then, I'll tell you....

D went on to claim that on the day of the robbery while driving through Pickleston he was flagged down by a group of men who paid him £250 to drop them off and to say nothing. The remainder of the recorded interview was concerned with details of events he described. D, who maintained that he had not been involved in the robbery itself, was charged with dishonestly receiving part of the stolen money.

The impression gained from the case papers is one of a well-planned investigation which justly placed emphasis upon the custodial interrogation of a person strongly suspected of involvement in criminal activity. On its face, the interview record also suggests that, in spite of D's continued denials, the repeated questioning of him and the confidence exhibited by the police in their suspicions, proved wholly justified. However, there is one feature in case that requires closer consideration. This, as has already been mentioned, is the apparent failure of the police to inform D of his right to free legal advice.[18] The absence of an adviser in any of the recorded interviews with D leaves the officers open to the charge that they actively denied him access to that advice. This presents a potential, if only slight, threat to the reception in evidence of the admissions made.[19]

A second point concerns the questioning of GF. Since the actual statement attributed to GF is not contained in the relevant case papers, it can be assumed that it did not form part of the case presented against D.

This is perhaps surprising in light of the pivotal role played by the statement in the questioning of D. It may be that its omission could be defended on the ground that with D's admissions, GF's statement became evidentially superfluous to the prosecution's case. Nevertheless, without the statement itself or information as to the circumstances in which it was made, a thorough assessment of the investigative practices of the police and their impact upon the present case is made more difficult.

The papers regarding Case PN/2202 relate that the complainant reported to the police that during the early hours of the day in question four hooded individuals, one of whom the complainant felt able to describe, had gained entry to his house, threatened him with a knife, tied him up and made off with £5000 cash together with items of jewellery. Later that day two detective constables went to D1's address and there arrested him. He was conveyed to the police station where he was formally interviewed by the detectives on three occasions, each being recorded by contemporaneous notes. The first of these interviews was not attended by a legal adviser:

PO: ... You were arrested earlier for an offence of robbery which happened at [a specified address on a specified day]. Were you involved in this robbery?
D1: No.
PO: Tell me where you were [that] evening.
D1: I was in [the White Horse pub].
PO: Who were you there with and what time did you leave?
D1: I was alone. I left there at about eleven.

...

PO: You answer the description of one of the [persons] who went to [the complainant's address] and threatened the occupants of the house with a knife and stole a lot of money. I propose to organise an identification parade. Before I do so I must ask you if you agree to stand on an identification parade?
D1: Yes I do.

Soon after this the interview was discontinued. The next recorded interview, which was attended by a legal adviser, took place the following day:

PO: Do you have any complaints about the identity parade?
D1: No.

PO: You were identified by the complainant. Do you have anything to say?
D1: Yeah. It was a mistaken identity.

...

PO: He is certain you are the one, together with three friends, who broke into his house, armed with a knife and stole over £5000 pounds in cash and jewellery. How can he be mistaken?
D1: I don't know.
PO: He had a clear view of your face didn't he?
D1: What, at the parade?
PO: He had a clear view of your face at the house.
D1: I wasn't at the house.
PO: He said, 'I recognise you'.
D1: He's wrong.
PO: And you said, 'Get face down'.
D1: I didn't.
PO: Who had the knife?
D1: I don't know I wasn't there.

From this point and for the remainder of the fifty-five-minute interview, the officer asked D1 questions as to his usual clothing; his employment; his leisure time; his income and expenditure; and as to his friends and associates. D1 is recorded as having answered each question. The interview was concluded with the questioner making the following statement:

PO: I have no further questions. I want you to think about what's happened and perhaps you'll tell the truth at a later interview. We have other enquiries to make and a number of people to arrest. We will conduct a further interview after a break for refreshments. You have seen this officer write down the questions and answers. I will invite you to read the record and, if you agree it's a true and accurate record, to sign the notes.

The notes were duly signed by D1. Some three hours later D1 was again formally interviewed, again in the presence of his legal adviser. The contemporaneously made notes of this interview indicate that it commenced with the questioner asking, and D1 replying to, further questions on his background, his relatives, his clothing, his associates and his movements on the day in issue. It continues:

PO: Who saw you go to bed?
D1: Nobody. Everybody was asleep.
PO: What time did you get up?
D1: About twelve.
PO: Did anyone see you before that?
D1: I couldn't tell you, I was asleep.
PO: So you could have come in at 9 a.m. and no one would have seen you?
D1: 9 a.m. everybody's awake.
PO: 8 a.m. then. No one could have seen you come in probably?
D1: Yeah, they probably wouldn't have.

...

PO: The man who picked you out on the ID parade is in no doubt whatsoever that you were the leader of the four who robbed him. You were the one who had the knife. Have you anything to say?
D1: It's not true.
PO: You know him.
D1: I don't know him.
PO: You know his face.
D1: I've seen him a couple of times.
PO: And he's seen you a couple of times, and knows your face.
D1: He probably has.
PO: When your mask slipped down in the bedroom he immediately recognised you and said, 'I know who you are'.
D1: It's not true.
PO: You told him to, 'look away and shut up'. Yes?
D1: It's not true, I wasn't there.
PO: You slapped him across the face a couple of times. Yes?
D1: As I said I wasn't there.
PO: You grabbed his nightshirt whilst he was on the bed and held the knife up against his face and you wanted to know where the money was. Your exact words were, 'if you don't tell me where the money is I'll stick this in you'. Do you remember that?
D1: That's not true.
PO: You pulled the wire of the light out of the socket and the wire of the telephone out of the socket. You tied him up on the bed, face down. Yes?
D1: That's not true. As I said I wasn't there.
PO: When he was in a terrified state he told you where the money and jewellery was and you took it. Do you remember that?
D1: Not true. I wasn't there.
PO: And you, the one with the knife, cut him with it.
D1: That's not true.

...

PO: You don't remember any of this?
D1: I wasn't there so how can I remember any of it.
PO: I'm not surprised. If I was in your shoes now I wouldn't admit to doing a thing like this either. So I can understand why you're lying. Is that clear?
D1: I'm not lying.
PO: There is no doubt in [the complainant's] mind whatsoever and I want you to remember that you had the opportunity to tell the truth and express your remorse for this wicked and disgraceful crime and you haven't done so. Do you understand that?
D1: I'm telling you the truth.
PO: I have no further questions at this stage....

At this juncture, this the final recorded interview with D1 was concluded. The interviews, when read in light of the associated case papers, suggest that the police, as a result of their pre-charge investigations, had fully acquainted themselves with the details of the case. The statements taken from the complainant, his family and neighbours, together with the results of the identification parade appear as the basis for the evidently strong suspicions of guilt held by the police. In the interviews that followed the identification parade these suspicions are not only articulated as confident assertions of fact, they also appear to have justified converting the interrogation from one concerned with eliciting voluntarily-given explanations from D1, into one geared to pressurising him into making damaging (and of course 'truthful') admissions.

A number of ploys are employed by the questioner in an attempt to intensify the psychological pressure on D1. The most pronounced being, firstly, the attribution to the detainee of comments alleged by the complainant to have been uttered by his assailant and, secondly, the imputation that a brutal callousness lay behind the failure of the detainee to confess. It would seem that the use of these ploys did not trouble the legal adviser sufficiently to provoke him into intervening on behalf of his client.[20]

As previously stated, the study identified a second group within the present class of images relating to those detainees who were confronted with apparently incriminatory evidence. These differ from those discussed above in the respect that the evidence upon which the detainees were arrested, or that about which they were questioned, appeared to be less cogent. The following two cases are examples.

According to the witness statements of two police constables in Case TP/2221, D1 and D2, were seen walking in the vicinity of recently activated shop alarms. This is reported to have aroused the officers' suspicions. They proceeded to arrest D1 and D2. The following is from the contemporaneously made record of interview with D1:

PO: Can you tell me what you were doing on [Main Street]?
D1: I was on my way to one of my friend's relatives.
PO: What friend would that be?
D1: [D2].

...

PO: Where were you actually stopped in [Main Street]?
D1: Outside the [supermarket].
PO: And you were with [D2] then?
D1: Yes.
PO: Where had you been?
D1: We'd been to the park.
PO: What had you been to the park for?
D1: No comments.
PO: Where had you been prior to going to the park?
D1: The [Bat and Wicket] pub.
PO: Had you been there all evening?
D1: Most of the evening.
PO: And what time did you leave the [Bat and Wicket]?
D1: Closing time I think.

...

PO: So you walked from the [Bat and Wicket] to the park?
D1: Yes.
PO: How long do you think you were in the park?
D1: I wouldn't like to say, maybe an hour to an hour and a half.
PO: And you don't want to say what you were doing in the park?
D1: No.
PO: Did you meet anyone else in the park?
D1: No.

...

PO: When you were arrested you had some sort of mud or dirt on your clothing didn't you?
D1: I'm not sure, it was dark.
PO: Well you did. Can you give any explanation as to how that got on to your clothing?
D1: More than likely from the park; it's all grass and mud in the park.
PO: What were you doing in the park then?
D1: No comment.
PO: Why are you saying 'no comment' to what you were doing in the park?
D1: Because when I was in the park it's nothing to do with you. You want to know what I was doing in [Main Street].
PO: I'm asking you to give an explanation as to how the mud got on to your clothing.
D1: No comment.
PO: Did you at any stage go behind the shops on [Main Street]?
D1: No.
PO: You're quite definite about that?
D1: Yes.
PO: At no stage did you go behind any of the shops?
D1: No.

...

PO: You have some cuts on your hand. Would you like to give an explanation as to how you got those?
D1: It's one cut, it's on my knuckle and it isn't a cut, its a graze. You can see that yourself.
PO: Well it's a puncture wound, shall we put it that way? Can you tell us how you got that?
D1: It must have come from the park.
PO: From the park. You have also got one on your ring finger.
D1: None of them are cuts, that comes from this ([D1] 'then indicated that he suffered from eczema').

...

PO: And you at no stage went behind any of the shops [in Main Street]?
D1: No.
PO: And you are not responsible for breaking into any of the premises?
D1: No.

...

PO: Is there anything you wish to add or clarify?
D1: Just that I didn't break into any shop.

The formal interview was concluded at this point. The record of this five-minute interview, which was attended by a solicitor, suggests the questioner, who was unconnected with the actual arrest of D1, was not fully apprised of the issues relevant to D1's detention. This may explain the appearance of a disjointed venture, one lacking any easily discernible direction or purpose.

The interview presents a picture of an interviewing officer making heavy weather of the questions put to D1. It might be argued in defence of the officer's approach that the questions were intended to serve several ends. The seemingly laboured and hopeful approach adopted by the questioner may have been designed to help him to compare D1's account with that given by the arresting officers and with that yet to be given by D2. It may have assisted in evaluating the strength of the evidence already in the possession of the police and in assessing the detainee's attitude to that evidence. The approach may have been adopted to afford D1 an opportunity to eliminate himself from the inquiry or to allow the questioner to glean information that might be verified by the police. Finally, the approach may have been taken in order to elicit information that would enable the questioner to seize on any contradictions D1 might make or, quite simply, to facilitate the acquisition of a confession. Irrespective, the case papers convey the impression of a hastily prepared and largely speculative interview — one which followed, and was shaped by, an arrest that evidently failed to furnish the questioner with sufficiently precise information to enable him to connect the suspect in any persuasive way with the alleged offence. Put alternatively, the questioning appears to have been directed towards producing evidence to validate the arrest, rather than being based upon evidence which justified the initial arrest.

Many of the features exhibited in Case TP/2221 may be observed in the following extracts from Case NN/2049. In this case the two detainees had been arrested on suspicion of stealing a van. The contemporaneously made notes of interview with D1 details that the interview began with the detainee being formally cautioned of his 'right to silence'. It continues:

PO: Do you understand why you have been arrested?
D1: Yeah.
PO: Do you wish a solicitor present during the interview?

D1: No.
PO: Can you tell me who you were with last night?
D1: [D2].
PO: Can you tell me where you were?
D1: At [D2's] house.
PO: How long where you at [D2's] house?
D1: From 10.30 to 11.15 p.m.
PO: Where did you go at 11.15 p.m.?
D1: We were walking around.
PO: Doing what?
D1: Talking, you know, general things.
PO: Can you tell me where you were walking?
D1: Around [Stalkington] and then towards the college.
PO: Do you know the area well?
D1: No.
PO: Why were you going to the college?
D1: To meet two girls.
PO: Who are they?
D1: One was named [Tina]. I don't know the other's name.
PO: What were you going to do then?
D1: Walk around, talk.

...

PO: Did you meet them?
D1: No, because you arrested us.
PO: At around midnight last night the vehicle I mentioned was stolen from outside an address in [Crown Lane]. A witness called the police stating two youths were breaking into a green van and have driven off in it towards [Usher Road]. Some eight minutes later a uniformed officer was on patrol in his police vehicle when he saw a green van on [Usher Road]. This officer can positively state that he saw the driver, a large built male with short hair wearing a blue shirt. [D1], I can only say that looking at you now, I would describe you as a large built youth with short hair wearing a blue T-shirt. Would you agree with that description yourself?
D1: Yeah.
PO: So I'll put it to you that the officer is quite correct and that he saw you driving that stolen vehicle last night.
D1: The officer's wrong then.
PO: You have agreed with me that the description is a fair one?
D1: Yes.
PO: The stolen vehicle was abandoned a very short distance from where you were arrested. It seems such a remarkable coincidence that you and your

friend, who had been seen by the officer in the stolen vehicle, were just round the corner from where it was abandoned. Would you agree?
D1: No.
PO: Perhaps then you could give me a feasible story?
D1: I can't see that it's a coincidence at all.
PO: Why?
D1: 'Cause a car gets stolen round the corner? No.
PO: ... I believe the officer's quite correct and that you are telling lies about last night's events.
D1: You're lying as well in saying I took it.

...

PO: [D1], I'll ask you once more and I want you to answer this last question truthfully if you can. Did you have any involvement with the stolen vehicle last night?
D1: No.
PO: I have no further questions at this stage....

At this point the thirty-seven-minute interview was concluded. The forty-minute custodial interview with D2, conducted by the same interviewing officer, also in the absence of a legal adviser, is reported in its contemporaneously made record to have followed a substantially similar course:

PO: This stolen vehicle was abandoned a short distance from where you were arrested. It seems very strange that the officer who saw you in the car should find you a short distance from where the car was abandoned.
D2: No, because I'm not likely to walk to two police cars if I had just been chased by police in a stolen motor vehicle. I would have made my way in the opposite direction.

...

PO: I think that you are lying. I think your excuses are feeble and I believe that you and [D1] stole the motor vehicle, went for a ride, were chased by the police and then abandoned the vehicle. That's the correct version of last night's events isn't it?
D2: To your account yes but not to mine.
PO: I have no further questions....

Although the custodial interrogation of the detainees appears to have been conducted with the justification that they were reasonably suspected of involvement in the crime, it would seem that the questioner had little information upon which to proceed. Firstly, contrary to what the questioner had implied, the case papers make clear that the witness who reported the incident to the police had not in fact seen two youths perpetrating the crime. Rather, the witness states that while lying in bed she *heard* what she believed were two or possibly more youths breaking into the van. She contacted the police when, on looking out of her bedroom window, she saw that the van had disappeared. Secondly, the arresting officer's account is of doubtful pertinence or force since it is not clear whether, or to what extent, it actually implicates the detainees. As the case papers make no direct reference to the arresting officers account, it cannot be determined whether it was embellished or fabricated by the questioner in order to draw the detainees into making a confession. While it is impossible on the basis of the interview record alone to test the strength of the suspicions held against the detainees, the reader may be left with the impression that the questioner failed in his attempt to present these suspicions, and the identification evidence on which they were based, as being beyond reproach. This impression is compounded by the image of a questioner casting insufficiently focused questions about the respective interviews in the hope of securing damaging admissions.

*Interrogations in order to test or confirm police case theories*

The cases that comprise the final category of insistent images relating to the apparent aim of the police in custodial interview and to the approach taken by officers during interview, suggest that in order to secure evidence for prosecution, police questioners might not only confront detainees with ostensibly incriminatory evidence, or seek to weaken the resolve of resistive detainees. The point here is that they might also conduct interrogations to confirm police-held case theories through the acquisition of admissions or to challenge detainees to contest the evidence accumulated against them. Case MP/2017 is merely one example.

In this case two youths were arrested and formally interviewed at the police station after it had been reported that a woman had sustained an injury to her arm from a pellet that had been fired from an air rifle:

PO: A woman was hit with a pellet in the back garden of her house. Now, first of all, I'll ask you straight out, are you responsible for causing that wound to that woman?
D1: No.
PO: You wasn't? Are you aware as to how that wound occurred?
D1: Yea.
PO: You are? all right then there's no rush. If you can tell me in your own words first of all what happened?
D1: Me and [D2] were err, shooting the pellet gun in my mom's back garden.
PO: And whereabouts does your mom live?
D1: [Address given] and err, first we started shooting bottles and err, I got worried about smashing my mom's windows, so we err, started putting them on the fence.
PO: You said there was you and [D2], who's [D2]?
D1: [D2] is a good friend.
PO: He's a friend of yours. Carry on.
D1: And we err, decided to change around and start shooting down the bottom of the garden, and err, we put the bottles on top of the fence and started shooting them.
PO: At the bottom of your garden?
D1: Yea. And we were aiming at that and a err, we were shooting a few times and err, [D2] took a shot and then a lot of the family come out.
PO: A lot of whose family?
D1: The woman's family, the one who was hit.

...

PO: Can you tell me exactly what happened?
D1: Err, well, we'd been in the garden and we went back in had a bit of dinner and we came back out again and err, we had a few shots at err, a couple of bottles and err, an old vase and we, you know, just messing about in round the garden and we put the bottle on top of the fence and err, I had a few shots. Then D2 had a couple and err, and err, you know, we realised we'd hit the woman.
PO: Well I don't know because I wasn't there, you were. I want you to tell me what happened when, as you say, this woman got hit. How did you know she got hit?
D1: Well, err, he fired the gun.
PO: [D2] fired the gun?
D1: Yea, and err, the woman sort of run into the house and then came back out with about four or five of the family.
PO: You saw her run into the house?
D1: Yea. That's when we, you know, packed up.

PO: Because [D1] I think that you know very well [D2] took aim to try and hit that woman with a pellet.
D1: No. He didn't take aim, he didn't take aim at all.
PO: What was he aiming at when this woman got hit?
D1: He was aiming at a little plastic bottle.
PO: And where was that positioned?
D1: On top of the fence.
PO: So how did you know she'd been hit, you say she went running into the house?
D1: Because she run, you know, and they all came out screaming and shouting.
PO: All within a few seconds was that?
D1: Yea....

...

PO: From where [D2] was standing with the gun, firing it at this bottle, where would it have gone if it had just missed, directly into this girl?
D1: Yea.
PO: Yes.
D1: Yea.
PO: ... Well didn't he see her there?
D1: He must of.
PO: Course he must of, cos I believe that he mentioned something to you and unintentionally (sic) shot that pellet at that girl, didn't he? Didn't he [D1]? So tell me about it.
D1: He just said he was going to scare her.
PO: Yes.
D1: And he didn't mean to hit her, as far as I know he just said he was going to scare her.
PO: And he aimed it at her?
D1: Well, he aimed it at the garden.
PO: Directly, he looked as though he was aiming it at her, obviously you can't say because you didn't fire it but he said, 'watch this' and aimed at her and fired. Is that right?
D1: Yea.

...

PO: Is there anything else?
D1: No. I'm just sorry the shot hit the person.

The sixteen-minute interview, conducted in the absence of a legal adviser, was brought to an end at this point. A superficial appraisal of the record would suggest that the interviewer was indeed concerned to have D1 give an account of the incident "in [his] own words". However, a closer examination highlights the capacity of police interviewers to manipulate the agenda and, in consequence, the responses the detainee may legitimately supply. As this case demonstrates, this may be achieved without contravening, in any way that is manifest in the record, the provisions of PACE.

The following extract from the record of the interview with D2, also conducted in the absence of a legal adviser, provides a further illustration of this theme. In this case the police control over the content of the interview, and the level of psychological tension in the interview, is enhanced by referring to comments made by D1 during his interrogation. It will be seen that while the seriousness of the crime is also emphasised — to further amplify the psychological constraints on D2 — the substance of D1's comments are denied to the detainee:

> PO: Now I understand that lunch time today you'd been at the house of who, your friend?
> D2: My friend [D1].
> PO: And where does he live?
> D2: [Address given].
> PO: And is it right that, err, what were you doing at that address?
> D2: We were just firing my gun in his garden and like a little accident occurred.
>
> ...
>
> PO: Can you tell, tell me about this incident, what actually happened?
> D2: I just aimed it. I didn't mean to, like, hit the woman but I just aimed it and it hit her but I didn't even know it hit her until the guy came round the corner and said that I'd just hit his mom with the gun. I didn't even know.
> PO: I don't think that's quite right [D2], as I've said to you we've already spoken to [D1].
> D2: Yea.
> PO: And he has told us what happened.
> D2: Yea.
> PO: And he has told us what you said. Now I don't want to tell you what he told us and I don't really think he's got any reason to tell lies because

I'm sure the same as you realised, that you are both in serious trouble with this. It's not just a game.
D2: Yea.
PO: It's a serious incident that's happened. This woman has been hit with a pellet.
D2: Yea.
PO: And she's in hospital, do you understand that?
D2: Yea.
PO: And I, all I want you to do is to tell me the truth.
D2: Yea.
PO: You say you aimed it at her?
D2: Yea. But it was an accident.
PO: Well if you aimed it, it wasn't an accident was it? Now is it right that you aimed it and you tried to hit her?
D2: Yea.
PO: You did?
D2: Yea.
PO: What happened?
D2: Well what happened when?
PO: Well, you're saying to me you're in [D1's] garden.
D2: It was in the garden and we just like aimed it and fired it.
PO: Aimed it at the woman [?] ... you aimed it at her and you just carried on aiming and hit her [?].[21]
D2: Yea.
PO: Could you see where you'd hit her?
D2: No.
PO: How did you realise you'd hit her after you'd fired it?
D2: When the guy came out.
PO: I mean, you could see you aimed it, you fired it.
D2: And then the people, like the family, come out.
PO: Is there any more you want to say about this?
D2: All I'm saying, I'm sorry, I didn't mean to do it.
PO: Well you can't say that because you did mean to do it.
D2: Well I did mean to do it....

It would appear from the two interviews that it was quickly established which of the suspects had shot the complainant. This would suggest that while some importance is properly given to the details of the incident, the prime concern for the police was to secure an admission of guilt. Put shortly, it would seem that the questioner had resolved from the outset that D2 had acted with the proscribed criminal intent: that he deliberately injured the complainant. However, rather than permit the detainees to give their own unforced explanations, the questioner is seen to dictate the course the interviews and to do so in ways which might cast doubt on the reliability of the admissions made.

## Conclusion

The evidence presented in this chapter would seem to suggest that the introduction of contemporaneous recording systems has reduced the scope for police officers to amplify or indeed construct images which set those suspected of criminal activity apart from 'conforming society'.[22] However, the PACE sample of cases also suggests an increase in the use of a range of manipulative tactics by the police to secure compliance and or incriminatory material from detainees. This raises the general question of how far the PACE provisions for the contemporaneous recording of formal custodial interrogations have worked to shed light on the previously concealed reality of police-suspect encounters. This and related questions are addressed in the following chapter.

## Notes

[1] As the records studied are concerned only with cases determined in the Crown Court, those which were determined at summary trial or those which did not proceed to trial are excluded.

[2] See McConville, et al., 1991, pp. 57, 65-76

[3] McConville and Baldwin, 1981, pp. 102-3, 141-4, 153-8. See also Irving, 1980, pp. 114-16; McConville and Baldwin, 1982b, pp. 165-75; McConville, et al., 1991, p. 75; McConville and Hodgson, 1993, pp. 111-14.

[4] See Irving, 1980, ibid; Morris, 1980, p. 10; Softley, 1980, pp. 86-8; McConville and Baldwin, 1981, p. 110-14; Dixon, 1991, p. 244; McConville, et al., 1991, pp. 57, 67, 76-7; Evans, 1993, pp. 1-2, 47-8; McConville, 1993, pp. 29-33, 39-45; Stevenson and Moston, 1994, pp. 151-7.

[5] See, for example, O'Hara, 1956; Inbau and Reid, 1962; Aubry and Caputo, 1965; Royal and Schutt, 1976. See also Firth, 1976; Walkley, 1977. For an evaluation of the tactics discussed or espoused in these works, see Irving and Hilgendorf, 1980, pp. 18-26; Irving, 1980, pp. 138-51; Morris, 1980, pp. 18-19; Irving and McKenzie, 1989a, pp. 17-25; Irving and McKenzie, 1989b, pp. 167-73; McConville, et al., 1991, pp 68-76; Evans, 1993, pp. 4-6, 31-8; McConville and Hodgson, 1993, pp. 119-53.

[6] McConville, et al., 1991, p. 69.

[7] Inman, 1981, pp. 476-9; Gudjonsson and Clark, 1986, pp. 83-104; Gudjonsson and MacKeith, 1988, pp. 191-4; McConville, *et al.*, 1991, pp. 66-9.

[8] The question-forms highlighted here draw on those identified by McConville, *et al.*, 1991, pp. 69-70 and McConville and Hodgson, 1993, pp. 137-40 whose analysis builds upon the work of Gudjonsson and MacKeith, 1988, pp. 187-94.

[9] McConville and Hodgson, 1993, p. 137. The authors offer the following as examples: 'How many family do you have?'; 'How long have you lived on the caravan site?'

[10] McConville, *et al.*, 1991, p. 70. See also McConville and Hodgson, 1993, p. 137.

[11] See McConville and Hodgson, 1993, p. 137.

[12] See Marquis, *et al.*, 1972, pp. 167-186; Lipton, 1977, pp. 90-95; Powers, *et al.*, 1979, pp. 399-347; Cahill and Mingay, 1986, pp .212-224; McConville, *et al.*, 1991, p. 69; McConville and Hodgson, 1993, p. 137.

[13] See McConville, *et al.*, 1991, p. 69. See also McConville and Hodgson, 1993, p. 138.

[14] See McConville and Hodgson, 1993, p. 138.

[15] *Ibid.*

[16] For an overview and assessment of the operation of such factors, see Evans, 1993, pp. 11-24. See also Gudjonsson and MacKeith, 1988, pp. 187-94.

[17] McConville (1993, p. 31) argues that: 'The general practice of the police following arrest, is to detain the arrestee in order to obtain evidence by questioning'.

[18] While PACE places an onus on detainees to request a solicitor, the Act requires detainees to be informed that they may at any time consult and communicate privately with a solicitor and that independent legal advice is available free of charge from the duty solicitor. Furthermore, interviewing officers are required 'immediately prior to the commencement or re-commencement of any interview' to remind detainees of their 'entitlement to free legal advice' and to ensure that all such reminders are noted in the interview record'(see PACE, s. 58 and Code C, paras. 6, 11.2 and 15.3).

[19] See Sanders, *et al.*, 1989; Sanders and Bridges, 1990.

[20] It should be noted that there are many grounds which might explain the legal adviser's apparent passivity, including a lack of confidence or experience (see Baldwin, 1992, pp. 28-9, 49-51; McConville and Hodgson, 1993, pp. 15-37, 169-71.

[21] Significantly, the contemporaneous notes of interview do not make clear whether the officer's words amounted to questions or bare assertions.

[22] See McConville and Baldwin, 1982b, pp. 170-4; Pepinsky, 1970, pp. 379-92.

# 12 Images of the Police-Suspect Dynamic

The study of 400 pre-PACE committal papers relating to contested cases determined in the Crown Court, identified a clear leitmotif in the picture of police-suspect relations presented in the narrative accounts of detention interrogation prepared by police officers. This appears in the form of a pronounced behavioural dichotomy between those detained and interrogated by the police and the police themselves. Broadly, the pre-PACE accounts present a picture of police officers as models of integrity, probity and proficiency. The general picture of police officers as rule-observant and effective questioners contrasts with the picture the pre-PACE accounts contain of suspects whose 'illegal' acts and reprehensible qualities are either self-evident or are revealed under the reasonable, logical and non-coercive questions put to them. Thus, while detained suspects are reported to have used expletives and criminal argot, and are shown to be willing to make admissions in exchange for some immediate gain (such as bail), police officers, who invariably appear to be animated by high moral values, are seen as not prepared to engage in deals, as not using bad language, as solicitous to the welfare and rights of suspects and, moreover, as not extorting admissions from suspects.

The authenticity, reliability and plausibility of the pre-PACE accounts and, perforce, the images they convey of police-suspect interactions, are called into question by the substantial body of anecdotal and material evidence — some provided by police officers themselves — which shows that prior to PACE some police officers were quite prepared to employ oppressive interrogative techniques and to distort or indeed fabricate confession evidence in order to secure convictions against those believed to be guilty.[1] This evidence, together with the data and images considered in Chapters 8 and 9, permits the inference that the authority, powers and discretions delegated to officers in the period before the implementation of

PACE, enabled the police to further their own instrumental ends in the formally adversarial criminal justice process; that is, the construction of cases which worked to enhance the persuasiveness of the case for the prosecution and weaken the position of defendants.[2]

The images presented in the pre-PACE accounts were produced privately. They appear as essentially unverifiable constructs. They often play a crucial role in the case assembled against the accused. They also play a part in subverting the rhetoric of criminal justice which presupposes the innocence of the accused.[3] However, it was the police, and the police alone, who were empowered to produce and transmit such images. This serves to obscure two fundamentally important issues. The first, the extent to which the images are pragmatic, functional and subjective reconstructions shaped by the legal demands of evidential sufficiency. Secondly, the extent to which the images worked to confer legitimacy upon the power of the police to interrogate suspects and to adduce incriminatory statements alleged to have been made by persons detained and isolated in police custody.

Thus, while pre-PACE images of the police-suspect dynamic may be seen to be consistent with the pre-eminence of police interests, they may also be seen as products of the role the police are required to play in the adversarial process. In practice that role effectively obliges them not only to elicit damaging admissions from suspected persons who might prefer to exercise their legal right to remain silent also to *report* that which is destructive to the credibility of the accused rather than to *record* all exchanges between questioner and questioned in their entirety.[4] Put shortly, the representations of social reality enshrined in the pre-PACE accounts are more than mere products of police perceptions, they are, by definition, partial, selective and tendentious constructs.

An attempt has been made, through PACE and its attendant Codes of Practice for the contemporaneous recording of interviews, to eliminate the scope for the manufacture and coercion of confession evidence by the police and to protect officers from unfounded allegations by defendants that they either did not make the admissions ascribed to them or that the admissions were coerced from them.[5] In this regard Table 3, which sets out the method used to record formal custodial exchanges between police officers and individual detainees, contrasts favourably with its pre-PACE comparator:

**Table 3  Mode of interview record, pre-PACE and under PACE**

| Mode of record | pre-PACE | n | % | PACE | n | % |
|---|---|---|---|---|---|---|
| Police witness statements | | 394 | 98.5 | | 8 | 2.9 |
| Contemporaneous notes | | 4 | 1.8 | | 242 | 86.1 |
| Dictated by detainee | | 2 | 0.5 | | 0 | 0.0 |
| Tape-recorded | | - | - | | 31 | 11.0 |
| Not known | | - | - | | 2 | - |
| | | 400 | 100.0 | | 283 | 100.0 |

From this table it can be seen that the vast majority of custodial interviews from the PACE sample were recorded contemporaneously either by notes or audio tape. This welcome product of the PACE reforms must, however, be considered in light of research which demonstrates that "official records of interrogations, even if 'verified' by contemporaneous notes and attested to by third parties such as solicitors, constitute only a partial representation of what transpired".[6]

Here, a distinction should be drawn between contemporaneously recorded interviews and police summaries of recorded interviews. The point is that while contemporaneous records may or may not provide complete accounts of what actually took place, the reliability of police summaries is open to the stronger criticism that many officers lack the skills needed to compile accurate and balanced synopses of interviews.[7]

The nature and scope of the current study, confined as it is to a comparative analysis of first-hand (rather than summarised) accounts of formal interrogation, prohibits a definitive assessment of the completeness of the records examined. However, other researchers have shown that crucial exchanges between police officers and detainees may not appear in the official record.[8] Clandestine or 'informal' interrogations may occur within or outside the police station and prior to or following formal interrogation.[9] This would suggest that official (whether custody or interview) records may not provide as close or comprehensive a picture of the detention and interrogation process as some commentators have suggested.[10] Moreover, the official record may serve to give an appearance of strict compliance with the rules while concealing any use that may have been made of manipulative or oppressive tactics.[11]

The present study indicates that following the implementation of PACE, police-suspect encounters, when duly recorded, are indeed more open to external scrutiny than those of the pre-PACE era and reflect what actually took place more closely. It also reveals that crude dichotomies between the policed and the police — strongly evident in the pre-PACE sample — have become less distinct. This is exemplified in the reported and recorded use of expletives. In the pre-PACE sample, it was almost always either the defiant, discourteous or morally corrupt detainee, rather than the reasonable, rule-observant and morally upright police officer, who used expletives. This theme was not so clearly evident in the PACE sample. The apparent pre-PACE/post-PACE divide may be represented in the number of individual detainees who were reported or recorded as having used two or more expletives during interview:

**Table 4  Use of expletives by detainee, pre-PACE and under PACE**

| Expletives used by detainees | pre-PACE n | % | PACE n | % |
|---|---|---|---|---|
| Yes | 57 | 14.3 | 12 | 4.4 |
| No | 342 | 85.7 | 262 | 95.6 |
| Not known | 1 | - | 9 | - |
|  | 400 | 100.0 | 283 | 100.0 |

As Table 4 indicates, detainees interrogated under the PACE regime were recorded as being less reliant upon expletives than their pre-PACE counterparts. However, with the apparent decrease in the use of expletives by detainees, the study also found a decline in their use of criminal argot and, as Table 5 details, a marked increase in the use of criminal argot by police officers:

**Table 5  Use of criminal argot by the police, pre-PACE and under PACE**

| Criminal argot used by police | pre-PACE | n | % | PACE | n | % |
|---|---|---|---|---|---|---|
| Yes |  | 26 | 6.5 |  | 51 | 18.6 |
| No |  | 373 | 93.5 |  | 223 | 81.4 |
| Not known |  | 1 | - |  | 9 | - |
|  |  | 400 | 100.0 |  | 283 | 100.0 |

It might be concluded from these findings that detainees have become increasingly conscious of the manner in which they express themselves and alert to how they might appear in the interrogation record. Alternatively, the findings might be taken as suggesting that the latitude previously enjoyed by the police to sanitise the official record respecting their formal exchanges with detainees has been circumscribed by the requirement for custodial interviews to be recorded contemporaneously. This would further suggest that pre-PACE images of police-suspect exchanges have more to do with police perceptions and attitudes than with objective reality.

The overwhelming impression gained from the pre-PACE reports and the post-PACE records of detention and interrogation is that PACE-regulated interviews, and the images they contain, present an obstacle to the previously unimpeded police project of furnishing the courts with strong, unambiguous accounts conducive to prosecution and generally damaging to the interests of individual detainees. Quite simply, images in the pre-PACE sample which offer a picture of 'good cops' being confronted by 'bad suspects' were found to be a less significant feature of the PACE sample. For instance, post-PACE suspects appeared more willing than pre-PACE suspects either to cooperate with the police or to challenge the version of events put to them by officers without resort to coarse or abusive language. For their part, officers in the PACE sample were frequently seen to struggle in their efforts to establish or maintain the air of authority, confidence and competence exhibited by their pre-PACE colleagues.

## Legal Advice

The study indicates that one potential obstacle to the 'police project' lies in the PACE provision for free legal advice to all suspects who request it.[12] In the pre-PACE era access to legal advice was permitted provided that "no unreasonable delay or hindrance" was caused to the police in the performance of their duties.[13] Empirical studies conducted during this period suggest that this provision was used by the police to prevent almost 80 per cent of those detained and interrogated by the police from receiving legal advice.[14] As was seen in chapter eight, these studies gain a measure of support from the present study which found that as many as 96.2 per cent of detainees (n = 356) formally interrogated by the police in the period prior to PACE received no legal advice during interrogation.

One possible explanation for the low number of detained suspects in the pre-PACE sample who were accompanied by a legal adviser during interrogation (n = 10; 2.9%) is that few suspects actually asked to consult with a solicitor whilst in police custody.[15] This, however, must be qualified by the consideration that the police have a significant role to play in the take-up of legal advice by detainees. As one researcher put it:

> There can be no doubt that many, if not most, police officers only pay 'lip service' to the existence of the right to see a solicitor.[16]

While it must be accepted that practice may vary between police stations and across police forces, research conducted in different forces following the introduction of PACE indicates a considerable increase in the number of detainees who request and receive legal advice. Both Brown (1989) and Sanders, *et al.*, (1989), for example, found that request rates had risen to around 25 per cent and advice rates to about 20 per cent. The current study of the interrogation process under PACE complements this research. The number of detainees who were formally interrogated in the presence of a legal adviser is set out in Table 6:

**Table 6  Adviser's attendance at interrogation, under PACE**

| Adviser attends | n | % |
| --- | --- | --- |
| No | 178 | 63.1 |
| Yes (throughout interrogation) | 90 | 31.9 |
| Part of interrogation | 14 | 5.0 |
| Not known | 1 | - |
|  | 283 | 100.0 |

Again, as these figures are derived from a sample of official records, rather than by direct observation, the calibre, extent and nature of the legal advice received by detainees cannot be adequately determined.[17] Nor can it be ascertained definitely whether (or what) tactics were employed against those who did not receive legal advice to dissuade them from seeking it. That the official record may not be a reliable source of information in this respect is demonstrated by Sanders and Bridges (1990) who found that in some 41.4 per cent of the cases they observed a number of 'ploys', ranging from the "incomplete or incomprehensible reading of rights" to misleading suspects about their rights, were used to discourage detainees from seeking legal advice.[18] The official record, therefore, may not operate as a means with which to constrain police impropriety. Indeed, as it is unlikely that police impropriety would appear in the official record, it may instead serve to "*mislead* rather than to inform".[19]

Nevertheless, the present study found that while there was an increase in the number of detained suspects who received legal assistance during interrogation, there remained a large body of detainees who did not. This permits the inference that although some detainees may have received legal advice prior to their formal interview or may have simply elected to waive their right to legal advice, others may have been dissuaded from exercising that right so as to heighten the persuasive influence of police interviewers during their interactions with detainees and to reinforce their capacity to isolate detainees from the outside world.[20]

## Questionable Questioning

Many of the cases from the pre-PACE sample give the impression that damaging admissions often follow as fortuitous by-products of largely neutral and seemingly innocuous questioning. This contrasts with the general picture to emerge from the PACE sample. The post-PACE cases suggest that psychologically manipulative techniques are regularly employed by police questioners in order to elicit incriminating admissions from suspects.[21] The number of occasions in which a series of the most repeated manipulative forms of question (leading questions[22] and legal closure questions[23]) were used in the respective samples is set out in the following tables:

**Table 7  Police use of leading questions, pre-PACE and under PACE**

| Leading questions | pre-PACE | n | % | PACE | n | % |
|---|---|---|---|---|---|---|
| Yes | | 87 | 21.9 | | 210 | 76.1 |
| No | | 311 | 78.1 | | 66 | 23.9 |
| Not known | | 2 | - | | 7 | - |
| | | 400 | 100.0 | | 283 | 100.0 |

**Table 8 Police use of legal closure questions, pre-PACE and under PACE**

| Legal closure questions | pre-PACE | n | % | PACE | n | % |
|---|---|---|---|---|---|---|
| Yes | | 45 | 11.3 | | 148 | 54.2 |
| No | | 353 | 88.7 | | 125 | 45.8 |
| Not known | | 2 | - | | 10 | - |
| | | 400 | 100.0 | | 283 | 100.0 |

The tables evidence a significant increase in the use of leading and legal closure question forms. This would seem to indicate that pre-PACE suspects were more willing to cooperate with police questioners and volunteer answers to police questions than their post-PACE counterparts. The frequent recourse police officers in the PACE sample were observed to have had to manipulative question forms would also suggest that custodial interrogations are often driven more by presuppositions of guilt and rather less by concerns to receive any genuinely non-induced or unprompted explanations detainees may care to offer to the police.[24]

However, the increase across the samples in the use of manipulative techniques may be more apparent than real. This is because the PACE sample may have brought to light a previously hidden pre-PACE practice which, as a result of the requirement for contemporaneous recording, is preserved in the PACE records. Nevertheless, the point remains that while contemporaneous records may permit a more comprehensive representation of the interrogation process — and of police methods within that process — than their forerunner, they may not be any more complete or reliable.

**Conclusion**

The data examined in the course of the present study strongly suggests that PACE has had little effect upon police behaviour. Although contemporaneous recordings provide more immediate, if only partial, 'snapshots' of police-suspect encounters — and while the records examined appear to support the contention that the police have abandoned many of their more egregious practices during formal interrogations[25] — it is not clear whether or to what extent the official record serves to mask police malpractice rather than to reduce or eradicate it. And while the PACE provision for legal advisers to attend interrogations at the request of individual detainees appears to have ensured that many more suspects are accompanied by a legal adviser during interrogation, this may not present a major obstacle to police officers.[26] This is because legal advisers may be marginalised by the police during interrogations. Many may be inclined to adopt a non-interventionist or non-adversarial stance. Others, unwilling to assist their clients even when the police adopt an aggressive stance during interrogations, may feel that rigorous questioning is a legitimate part of the investigative process and, therefore, may cooperate with the police in the belief that their clients should be encouraged to answer all 'reasonable' questions put to them by the police.[27]

Furthermore, the Act does not appear to have had a marked affect upon the number of suspects who make either damaging admissions or full confessions. Out of the pre-PACE sample of 400 cases, 342 (88.1%) of the detainees who were formally interrogated by the police made either partial or full confessions of guilt. The number from the research sample of 283 post-PACE cases is 248 (87%).[28] Whilst there is some research evidence to suggest that the introduction of PACE has led to a fall in the number of suspects who make admissions,[29] the findings of the present study would seem to support those of McConville (1993) who found that from a sample of 534 cases, 305 (58.2%) detainees either made or repeated confessions during formal interrogation.[30] Evans (1993) found that as many as 76.8 per cent (n = 126) of his sample made confessions to the police during detention and interrogation.[31] Thus, while it may not be possible to state conclusively that confession rates have not been affected by PACE, the available empirical evidence in support of a decline in confession rates remains, as Moston and Stephenson (1993) contend, minimal.[32]

The continued success of the police in securing confessions may suggest that very few genuinely innocent suspects are detained and interrogated by them. However, another explanation may be found in the strong statistical correlation identified by Evans (1993) between the use of persuasive tactics by the police and admissions or confessions.[33] The important point here is that irrespective of their legality or justness, such tactics may generate false as well as truthful confessions.[34]

The current study also suggests that the control enjoyed by the police over the interrogation process in the pre-PACE era has not been significantly impaired by the PACE reforms. For example, under PACE the police retain the authority to exclude non-police personnel form custodial interrogations.[35] They also retain the capacity to circumvent the contemporaneous recording requirements imposed upon them by the Act by conducting 'informal' or off-the-record interviews.[36] Nevertheless, confessions secured in this manner may be received in evidence by the courts.[37] Thus, the legitimacy of formal interrogations conducted under the PACE regime is assisted by the scope the Act leaves for 'informal' (but legal) interviews. This consideration would suggest that continuing concerns over the authenticity and reliability of interrogation records have some justification.[38]

The accounts of interrogation contained in the pre-PACE sample give a largely sanitised and invariably police-drawn picture of police-suspect encounters. In that picture, suspects were almost always depicted negatively while the police generally emerged in a positive light. This partial, police-constructed, representation of social reality has the effect of emphasizing the investigative character of policing and of downplaying its adversarial, confrontational and manipulative aspects. The PACE regime, in providing for formal interrogations to be recorded contemporaneously, has undoubtedly reduced the capacity of the police to distort reality and, therefore, has enhanced the authenticity and reliability of the official record. Nevertheless, the prospect of securing absolute authenticity and reliability is compromised by the failure of the Act either to proscribe or effectively monitor police-suspect exchanges that take place off-the-record.[39] As a result the police retain the ability to construct images of themselves as "upholders of societal norms"[40] and as disinterested principals in the fight against crime — images which help to distinguish the police from the amoral and criminogenic defendant population.

## Notes

[1] See, for example, Devlin, 1960, p. 39; Royal Commission on the Police, 1962, *Final Report*, Cmnd. 1728, para. 369; *Sheffield Police Appeal Inquiry*, 1963, Cmnd. 2176: concerning the appeals of two police officers against their dismissal from the Sheffield City Police Force. The dismissals followed an incident in which six persons, suspected of committing break-ins, were arrested, taken into custody and subjected to a series of prolonged interrogations. During interrogation a number of the suspects were 'seriously assaulted' by officers who used a truncheon and "an instrument which was called a 'rhino tail'" (described as 'a short flexible piece of gut-like material'). The charges against the suspects were dropped after, at the committal hearing, one of them stripped to the waist and revealed the weals and bruising he had sustained to the magistrates, as a result a police internal inquiry was initiated.

However, a private action was also brought against the two detectives who pleaded guilty to charges under s. 20 of the Offences Against the Person Act, 1861. At their appeal against dismissal from the Force, the appellants contended that 'the assaults were committed pursuant to the instructions and under the supervision of senior officers', that they were under 'undue pressure to obtain speedy results', that they received 'wrong and biased advice to plead guilty' and that they were victims of 'unfair discrimination in punishment' as between themselves and other guilty officers. In dismissing the appeals the tribunal severely criticised both the Force as a whole and senior officers who had conspired to concoct false versions of the incident in an effort to meet or mitigate the allegations against the appellants. For further discussion on the issue of police malpractice and the extraction or manufacture of confession evidence, see Morton, 1972, p. 806; 1975, pp. 830-31; Williams, 1979, pp. 7-15; McNee, 1979, p. 78; 1983, p. 180; Holdaway, 1983, pp. 32-5, 102-19, 124-9, 148-52; Smith and Gray, 1983, p. 218; McConville, *et al.*, 1991, pp. 83-4; Maguire and Norris, 1992, pp. 14-15; Morton, 1993, pp. 121-7, 251-77; Bridges, 1994, p. 32.

[2] See Devlin, 1979b, pp. 441-2; Williams, G., 1979, pp. 9, 13, 15; Baldwin and Kinsey, 1982, p. 265; McConville and Baldwin, 1981, pp. 189-90; McConville, *et al.*, 1991, pp. 11-13, 36, 65-75, 135-7.

[3] That is to say, while the rhetoric of the law suggests a person is presumed innocent until the contrary is proved in a court of law, interrogations are generally predicated on a belief in the suspect's guilt and conducted to 'confirm' that guilt before trial.

[4] See McConville and Baldwin, 1981, p. 190; Sanders, 1987, pp. 232-5; Maguire and Norris, 1994, p. 73.

[5] See *Keenan* [1989] 3 All ER 58, p. 604; *Canale* [1990] 2 All ER 187, p. 190.

[6] McConville, *et al.*, 1991, p. 58. See also Dixon, *et al.*, 1989, pp. 200-1; Sanders, *et al.*, 1989, pp. 140-4; Sanders and Bridges, 1990, p. 506; Maguire and Norris, 1992, pp. 46-7; Moston and Stephenson, 1992, pp. 35-6.

[7] See Baldwin and Bedward, 1991; Baldwin, 1992a.

[8] Maguire, 1988, p. 31; Sanders, *et al.*, 1989, pp. 140-4; Dixon, *et al.*, 1989, pp. 200-1; Sanders and Bridges, 1990, pp. 504-6; McConville, 1992, pp. 532-48; 1993, pp. 71-2; Evans, 1993, pp. 28-9.

[9] See McConville and Morrell, 1983, pp. 161-2; Sanders and Bridges, 1990, p. 505; Dixon, *et al.*, 1990, p. 133; Baldwin and Bedward, 1991, p. 671; Wolchover and Heaton-Armstrong, 1991, p. 242; McConville, 1992, pp. 532-48.

[10] See, for example, Irving and McKenzie (1988, p. 102) who, in respect of off-the-record interrogations within the police station, claim that custody officers — charged under PACE with the welfare of detainees and with the recording in the custody record of all matters relating to individual detainees — 'were not prepared to allow any contact between suspect and investigating officer, save in

the formal interrogation situation'. However, see also Irving and McKenzie, 1989a, p. 183; Maguire, 1988, p. 33; MacKay, 1990, p. 79.

[11] See McConville, et al., 1991, pp. 58-60, 78.

[12] PACE, s. 58.

[13] Judges' Rules, 1964, para. (c) and accompanying Administrative Direction, para. (a). Under PACE, Code C, the police are obliged to inform suspects of their right to free legal advice both orally and by written notice (para. 3.1-2). Section 58 (4) of the Act provides that upon a suspect's request, access to legal advice must be permitted 'as soon as is practicable'. Though access may be delayed for up to thirty-six hours in the case of a serious arrestable offence, it may not be denied outright. If the police improperly deny access, any confession evidence obtained may be excluded under PACE, s. 76 or s. 78.

[14] See Zander, 1972, pp. 346-8; Baldwin and McConville, 1979, pp. 145-52; Softley, 1980, pp. 68-9.

[15] See MacKay, 1990, pp. 75-6.

[16] Ibid., p. 75.

[17] See, however, McConville and Hodgson (1993, pp. 15-37) who found wide variations in the qualifications, experience and abilities possessed by legal advisers. See also Baldwin, 1992b.

[18] Sanders and Bridges, 1990, pp. 489-504. Significantly, the April 1995 revision of Code C provides that no police officer shall at any time do or say anything with the intention of dissuading a person in detention from obtaining legal advice (para. 6.4).

[19] See McConville, et al., 1991, pp. 48-55.

[20] See Walkley, 1987, p. 20; Sanders and Bridges, 1990, pp. 498-507; McConville, et al., 1991, pp. 52-5.

[21] For a discussion, see Gudjonsson, 1992, pp. 31-8; Moston and Stephenson, 1993a, pp. 105-11.

[22] See Cahill and Mingay, 1986; Gudjonsson, 1992, pp. 12-14.

[23] See McConville, et al., 1991, p. 70.

[24] It should be noted, however, that other researchers have suggested that police officers are now adopting non-coercive styles of questioning. On this, see Williamson, 1992, p. 296; Moston and Stephenson, 1993a, p. 105; Baldwin, 1993, pp. 325-6.

[25] McConville, et al., 1994, p. 116.

[26] See Dixon, 1991b, p. 44.

[27] See Baldwin, 1985, pp. 32-3, 85, 88-90; 1993, pp. 48-52; McConville and Hodgson, 1993, pp. 155-71; McConville, et al., 1994, pp. 109-115, 126-7.

[28] The appearance of a high confession rate (as compared with other recent research) should be qualified by the consideration that the pre-PACE and PACE samples are composed entirely of contested cases determined in the Crown Court. They therefore exclude detainees who may have confessed/made

damaging admissions but were not charged or prosecuted to trial for a serious offence.

[29] Irving and McKenzie, 1989a, p. 234; Moston, *et al.*, 1992, pp. 23-40; Gudjonsson, 1992, pp. 51-4; Moston and Stephenson, 1993b, pp. 33-42.

[30] McConville, 1993, pp. 60-1.

[31] Evans, 1993, pp. 22-4, 29.

[32] Moston and Stephenson, 1993a, p. 103.

[33] Evans, 1993, pp. 31-8.

[34] Gudjonsson, 1992, pp. 24, 222, 230-32.

[35] See PACE, Code C, paras. 6.9, 6.10, 6.12 and the accompanying Note for Guidance, 6D.

[36] Sanders and Bridges, 1990, pp. 504-6; McConville, 1993, pp. 71-2; Moston and Stephenson, 1993a, pp. 111-3.

[37] In *Williams* (1992) *The Times*, February 6, the Court of Appeal upheld the conviction of the appellant who, after having received a post-charge 'social visit' in police cells from investigating officers, made a confession during a subsequent formal interview. The appellant's claim that he had been persuaded to confess during the hour-long visit was rejected by the Court as was his contention that the trial judge should have excluded the confession.

[38] See, for example, McConville, 1992, pp. 532-48.

[39] See *ibid.*, pp. 536-45.

[40] Pepinski, 1970, p. 388.

# 13 Continuity and Change

## Introduction

In order to situate interrogations and their chief object, confessions, in a wide social, historical and political context, this study traced the origins and early development of key features of the criminal justice process as they evolved to shape its modern contours. In so doing the study highlighted some of the tensions that are intrinsic to a criminal process that has sought to incorporate within its formally adversarial structures values associated with crime control and rhetoric associated with due process.

The present chapter begins by offering a brief thematic overview of the historical evidence discussed in the earlier chapters. It then considers the place and role of the police in the criminal process having particular regard to the legal regulation of custodial interrogations prior to and following the introduction of the Police and Criminal Evidence Act, 1984 (PACE).

## The Centrality of Confessions: Legitimating Projects

The abolition of the ordeal in 1215 by edict of the Roman church precipitated the establishment of the criminal jury as the paradigmatic form of adjudication in serious cases. Procedures for public accusation and prosecution had been standardised by the Crown during the latter half of the twelfth century. By the beginning of the thirteenth century presenting juries had evolved beyond their role as communal informers and accusors. Following the crime control crisis brought on by the demise of the ordeal, presenting juries began to be used to determine cases. Though prompted by the 1215 edict, the English trial jury sprang from the developing social and crime control programme instituted by the Crown to assert its authority over all alleged felonies at the expense of its jurisdictional rivals and to assert its growing preference for human rather than divine structures for judgment and sanction.

The verdict of jurors sworn to tell the truth of the matter at issue could not be legitimately had, however, without the consent of the accused. The Crown, therefore, required that *peine forte et dure* be used against those who withheld their consent. Formally this coercive device was limited to securing compliance from those who, suspected of serious crime, refused to submit to petit jury trial. However, *peine forte et dure* may have been used to extract confessions. Certainly, as an entirely pre-trial measure *peine forte et dure* was used to coerce information detrimental to the interests of accused persons in order to facilitate and legitimate the petit jury mode of trial.[1] Trial by jury emerged not as a due process right (as it is conventionally viewed)[2] but as a means to further the social and crime control interests of the Crown and 'consent' to trial by jury was constructed through coercion in order to legitimise the law.

Early juries were presumed to have prior knowledge of the matter in question. By the late Middle Ages — as a result of the social and economic forces that had disrupted the demographic composition and social structure of Medieval England — the criminal jury had become dependent upon evidence placed before it by royal officials.[3] Chiefly, it was the justices of the peace who fulfilled this vital evidence-gathering role. From the late thirteenth century justices had been empowered to investigate accusations and to determine minor infractions against the peace.[4] However, with the separation of function between presenting and trial juries and with the collapse of the self-informing quality formerly possessed by those juries, justices were made responsible for investigating offences, for initiating prosecutions in more serious cases and for the production of evidence favourable to the case for the Crown.

This development meant that the burden of persuading jurors of a defendant's guilt gradually shifted to the Crown and away from civilians who became ineligible for jury service if they had prior knowledge of the issue. It also meant that the efficient management of the progressively bureaucratised criminal process would necessarily place greater reliance on confessions made in open court in the form of guilty pleas and on confessions made in the extra-judicial context. The reliance placed upon confessions by the 'pre-modern' criminal process was to become, over succeeding centuries, an entrenched and defining feature in its evolution. Moreover, in spite of the concessions wrested from the Crown during the seventeenth century, the structural reliance historically placed on confessional statements remains as a fundamental aspect of contemporary criminal justice procedures.

The compulsory *ex officio* oath procedures of the High Commission and Star Chamber Courts served to complement the investigative and prosecutorial activities of the justices. The social and crime control project pursued by these courts was, in turn, supplemented by the royal prerogative authorizing the infliction of physical torture on recalcitrant suspected and accused persons. Geared to the coercion of incriminatory material, each of these methods of pre-trial examination — whether by justices under the sixteenth-century Marian statutes, by the inquisitorial *ex officio* oath process or by practice of official torture — usually took place in private. This feature, when set in contrast with the prevailing legal rhetoric of public accusation and public trial, suggests that it was recognised that covert and quintessentially coercive pre-trial procedures were of doubtful legitimacy for the procurement of reliable confessions of guilt. This point is supported by the consideration that once an extra-judicial confession had been obtained its author would be expected to 'freely' repeat it in open court. The point here being that under these pre-trial procedures, public legitimacy could be secured through private means and private coercion could be legitimated by public acts of confirmation.

The seventeenth century saw a popular reaction both to the virtual absence of express due process protections against unwarranted inquisitions and to the extensive social and crime control policies pursued by royal government. As a result official torture fell into disuse; the High Commission, Star Chamber and similar courts associated with the inquisitorial oath were abolished; the due process principle, enshrined in the maxim *nemo tenetur prodere seipsum*, providing that no person should be compelled to incriminate themselves, began to be established; and judges were gradually reconstructed as non-partisan, relatively passive umpires attentive to the interests of defendants.

During the late seventeenth and early eighteenth centuries, with the official acceptance of the privilege against compulsory self-incrimination, two fundamental and closely related due process precepts were also explicitly recognised. The first, that the burden of proving the guilt of an accused person was to rest upon the prosecution, reflected the consideration that in the formal setting of the court defendants should not be compelled to incriminate themselves. Moreover, those against whom criminal proceedings were brought were not to be placed under any obligation to establish their innocence. The prosecution was to carry the burden of producing admissible evidence capable of sustaining its case. And, in persuading the jury beyond reasonable doubt of the accused's guilt, it was required to discharge its burden without the aid of the accused.

The second due process precept, the presumption of innocence, is no more than a concomitant of the first. It also recognises that defendants should not be obliged to assist the prosecution in its attempt to prove its case. Individuals accused of crime are, therefore, entitled to remain silent at his trial. Indeed, the practice was such that prior to the 1898 Criminal Evidence Act the accused was prohibited from giving evidence on oath at trial.[5] Although the prohibition may have operated to preserve the legitimacy of the oath as a truth-telling agent, it also worked to reinforce the principle that until such time as any prosecution brought on behalf of the state had succeeded in convincing the community, as represented by the trial jury, of the guilt of those it accused and had done so on the basis of admissible evidence, defendants were to be presumed innocent.

The privilege against compulsory self-incrimination, the burden of proof and the presumption of innocence afforded a degree of due process protection to individuals from inquisitorial methods of trial. They also advantaged the prosecution since their observance conduced and legitimated good and firm convictions.[6] However, these protective principles of criminal evidence and, moreover, adversarial trial itself could be circumvented where persons accused of crime were alleged to have furnished the authorities with full extra-judicial confessions of guilt. In these circumstances a prosecution, unless successfully contested, could legitimately proceed to conviction without either the voluntariness or the reliability of the alleged confession being assessed in open-court adjudication.

Prior to the statutory reforms introduced by PACE the principal procedural constraint upon the evidence-gathering practices of either the justices, before their preferment to judicial office, or their subordinates, the police, was the judge-made evidential requirement that all extra-judicial confessions attributed to defendants be shown — to the satisfaction of the trial judge rather than the jury — to have been voluntarily made. Failure to so satisfy the judge would, according to the terms of the voluntariness test, result in the exclusion of the alleged confession. The exclusionary rule, therefore, existed as an express precondition to the admission in evidence of confessional statements alleged by the prosecution to have been made in the pre-trial setting.

The construction placed upon the exclusionary rule by some eighteenth- and nineteenth-century judges suggests that the 'voluntariness rule' constituted a clear articulation and extension of the privilege against self-incrimination beyond the trial to the pre-trial stages of the criminal process. Although it was not to be fully formulated until nearly a hundred years after the emergence of the *nemo tenetur prodere seipsum* doctrine, the exclusionary rule was seen as being intimately linked with the privilege against self-incrimination. Both worked to afford suspects qualified protection from conviction on the basis of coerced confessions. Throughout the nineteenth and early twentieth centuries the exclusionary rule was interpreted as having this specific function by, for the greater part, first instance judges in their individualised, case-by-case attempts not only to ensure the 'voluntariness', and thereby the reliability, of the confessions they received but also to discipline the unauthorised extra-judicial questioning of detained suspects by lesser law enforcement officers.

However, the mid-nineteenth century was to witness the beginnings of a number of judicial attempts to restrict such applications of the exclusionary rule. This period in the operation of the rule was marked by concerted efforts mounted by the senior judiciary to ensure that the 'reliability principle' predominated over the 'disciplinary principle' as the primary and official rationale underlying the voluntariness test.[7]

By this time, in the face of the acute social and economic changes set in train by the onset and development of industrial capitalism, the 'new' police had been established. Also by this time the 'new' police had begun to overcome the marked ideological, cross-class and sometimes violent hostility that had been provoked by the creation of a full time, salaried, military-style force for domestic order. It was in this period that the police effectively assumed the central role in the prosecution process formerly performed by the justices.[8] This role allowed the police, without express authorization, to detain and interrogate suspects in the private space of the police station; to deny detainees access to third parties; to subject detainees to psychological (and sometimes physical) pressures in order to secure confessions; to make essentially unverifiable records of the interrogation process; to utilise, reinforce and indeed construct positive images of themselves and negative images of suspects; to assemble evidence for prosecution; to initiate the vast majority of prosecutions;[9] and (until the creation of the Crown Prosecution Service under the 1985 Prosecution of Offences Act) to actively steer those prosecutions through the judicial process.

Again, prior to the implementation of the PACE reforms, the primary procedural restriction on the autonomy enjoyed by the police to subject detained suspects to private and unsupervised interrogatories, and to furnish the courts with confessions ascribed to detainees, was the evidential requirement for 'voluntary' confessional statements. However, should the police contend that the accused made such a statement after he had been duly informed that he was not obliged to answer any questions put to him (that is, that the pre-trial expression of the privilege against self-incrimination: the 'right to silence' was knowingly waived),[10] and support this contention with an essentially unchallengeable account of the interrogation,[11] the necessarily *ex post facto* voluntariness test might — subject to the rarely exercised judicial discretion to exclude admissible evidence[12] — be satisfied.

Inconsistent judicial rulings as to the scope of the voluntariness rule, and as to the admissibility of statements obtained from suspects by police officers during custodial interrogations,[13] led the police to seek judicial clarification and advice. In 1912 the advice was enshrined in four 'rules' promulgated by a coterie of senior judges acting in concert with the Home Office. In 1918 the Judges' Rules were extended and, with their revision in 1964, remained in force as guidance to the police until they were replaced in 1986 by Codes of Practice issued under PACE.

Formally, the Rules were designed to alert police officers to the overriding evidential requirement of voluntariness. However, their primary effect was to confirm the pre-eminence of the police in the investigative and prosecution process and to further underpin the reliance placed by the criminal process upon confession evidence.[14]

The Rules were intended as much for the guidance of judges as they were for the police since they served to fashion a judicial consensus out of what had been sharply divergent judicial attitudes both to custodial questioning by the police and to the admissibility of confessions obtained by the police. However, in spite of this consideration, not only did the Judges' Rules effectively licence the pre-charge detention and questioning of suspects by the police, they also worked to gradually silence that strand of judicial opinion distrustful of police power *vis-à-vis* the right of accused or suspected persons against self-incrimination. The Judges' Rules were initially drafted as a result of concerns expressed by the police. They were designed to facilitate the acquisition of confessional statements by the police. Later, by dint of police working practices coupled with demands voiced on behalf of the police, the Rules came to legitimate the police power to interrogate suspects in custody and to supply the courts with defendants against whom confessions, admissions or other damaging material had been 'recorded' by the police.[15] The Rules also legitimated the police as the sole reporters of exchanges between themselves and those detained by the police, giving the police full and absolute sovereignty over the contents of the records made, thus enabling the police to convey to the courts specific images both of those detained and interrogated and of the police themselves.

Ostensibly, the Judges' Rules were never intended to encourage or authorize the questioning or cross-examination of persons detained by the police,[16] rather the express intention was to permit questioning in custody only to clear up ambiguities in statements voluntarily made by detainees, after caution, in respect of the offence for which they had been arrested.[17] Although this interpretation accorded with the principle that persons arrested by the police were to be taken before a magistrate without delay and were not to be detained for the purpose of conducting investigations,[18] it manifestly did not accord with police practice.

In an attempt to account for the capacity of police working practices to determine the breadth of police powers and for the corresponding failure of the executive or the courts to apply existing law, Lord Devlin (1960) stated that:

> It is part of the natural growth of an institution that, having been brought into existence for a purpose, it shapes and contains itself within rules for carrying out the purpose.... Each organ of inquiry into crime has begun informally and with freedom to behave as it liked; each has gone on to make its own practice and then its practice has been formulated in rules.... There is a constant drift, always in the same direction, from unfettered administrative action to regulated judicial proceeding. Any one who wishes to understand the part that the police now play in England in the investigation of crime, needs to have observed and understood that drift.... If asked whether the police can do such-and-such a thing with impunity, the answer may be, 'Possibly, but in practice they do not do it'. That means either that the practice is maturing or that a fully grown practice is not yet quite ripe....[19]

The historical evidence demonstrates that such remarks — which are essentially ahistorical and apolitical in nature since they suggest policing institutions evolve naturally from an unregulated to a regulated form — fail to appreciate the reality of the adversarial criminal process within which the police operate and fail to recognise the value placed by that process on incriminatory material elicited from suspects whilst detained in police custody. Above all, such remarks fail to acknowledge that the kind and quantum of regulation to which an institution such as the police is subject may, in great part, be a function of the police and their success in warding off greater regulation or other forms of accountability.

During the period following their establishment in the nineteenth century the 'new' police were able to establish and preserve a considerable measure of autonomy and independence in respect of the exercise of their ill-defined and often unspecified powers. However, the case law demonstrates that on the subject of confession evidence obtained through custodial interrogations, the police were not, at the outset, given unqualified freedom to behave as they liked. Nevertheless, it may be accepted that during the period following the Second World War and prior to PACE the working practices evolved by the police in defiance of the early judicial authorities[20] were, with the tacit consent of the executive and the courts, legitimated. In this way the ability of the police to supply the criminal process with material damaging to detainees interrogated in police custody was safeguarded.

For the police, the practice of detaining and interrogating suspects before charge is a highly desirable administrative aid since through it confessions, guilty pleas and convictions are virtually assured.[21] Indeed, from around the second half of the century, with implicit support of judges who exhibited an inclination to treat confessions attributed to detainees as being voluntary,[22] not only did the practice become increasingly routine, it was one which was accommodated in the revised version of the Judges' Rules.[23]

That the practice of detaining and questioning suspects for the purpose of securing incriminating evidence was prevalent prior to the introduction of the PACE reforms, was largely police-driven and was legitimated through crime control ideologies is confirmed by the decision of the Court of Appeal in *Mohammed-Holgate* v. *Duke* (1983).[24] It was conceded by the Court in this case that the issue was "surprisingly, and perhaps significantly, bare of direct authority".[25] Nevertheless, the Court confidently asserted that the police practice of interrogating persons under arrest for the purpose of obtaining admissions was "wholly familiar" and "perfectly common".[26] Indeed, it was "a long-established and widespread practice".[27]

For Latey J, the practice raised issues germane to the competing interests of crime control and due process.[28] However, as the power had "for a long period been so exercised without apparently any question or challenge", he did not, "think it right ... to say that it [was] being wrongly exercised".[29] Lord Diplock, in the House of Lords, also saw a long history in the police practice of using the period of detention in order to question suspects and to procure evidence. He also maintained that it was a practice that had been given "implicit recognition" in the Judges' Rules.[30]

Thus, in the view of the highest courts, and in apparent ignorance of the controversies of the nineteenth and early twentieth centuries,[31] it was perfectly proper for the police to arrest, detain and question suspects in police custody and to do so when the police themselves had decided that such action was more likely to secure incriminating evidence. For as the Court of Appeal made clear:

> the obtaining of a statement by means of the greater stress and pressure involved in the deprivation of liberty would in no way by itself make that statement a statement which was improperly obtained or a statement which would be rejected at a criminal trial.[32]

The observations made by the judges in *Mohammed-Holgate* v. *Duke* are significant for they serve to elucidate the post-war attitude of an increasingly corporatised judiciary not only to the success of the police in securing unmediated access to those held in their custody but also to the utility of the incriminating material the police attributed to defendants and tendered in evidence. The virtually unfettered autonomy enjoyed by the police to detain and interrogate suspects before charge, to deny detainees access to solicitors and to prepare authoritative accounts of the investigative process for the courts rested upon the legitimating assumption that police officers could be relied upon to furnish the courts with accurate, reliable and complete records of their custodial interactions with detainees. The examination of cases drawn from the pre-PACE era, however, suggests that the police control of custodial interrogations and of the mechanisms through which interrogations were monitored, afforded police officers considerable scope to exploit this assumption.

Prior to PACE the police were accorded broad and unsupervised latitude to play a partisan role in their investigations, with strong incentives not only to coerce confessions which would facilitate convictions but also to draw upon and construct imagery broadly favourable to their own interests and damaging to the interests of those believed to be criminally responsible. Unencumbered by the presence of 'outsiders' the pre-PACE interrogation process enabled the police to elicit information conducive to the preparation of cases *against* — rather than about — suspected persons in a manner akin to the repudiated inquisitional procedures notoriously employed by Tudor and Stuart governments or, alternatively, to those commonly associated with contemporary civil jurisdictions.[33] As Lord Devlin (1979) pointed out:

> we rely upon the police to do the job that the procurator fiscal or the juge d'instruction does abroad. And, to that extent, we have made the police inquisitors.[34]

Lord Devlin also explained that:

> It is unnatural to fight quasi-judicially.... When a police officer charges a man it is because he believes him to be guilty, not just because he thinks there is a case for trial.[35]

Lidstone and Early (1982) go further in their contention that:

> When a police officer arrests a man he does so because he believes he is guilty and the interrogation is an attempt to produce evidence of that guilt.[36]

Thus, in the context of a criminal process which is predicated upon the model of adversarial trial yet which displays inquisitorial features in its pre-trial stages, it would be erroneous to assume that the police adopt a non-partisan approach to their functions. This is because the imperatives of prosecution and adversarial adjudication require the police to present evidence which points to the guilt of the person standing trial rather than to establish 'the truth'.[37] Custodial interrogations, conducted on police territory and on police terms, provide the police with a method with which to implicate suspects in this process. Quite simply, for the most part the police interrogate in order to support the case for prosecution rather than to elicit information which would militate against prosecution.

This characteristic feature of the police function is reflected in the presumption of guilt frequently exhibited by officers in both the pre-PACE and PACE samples examined in this study. It is also reflected in the manipulative techniques which were seen to have been employed by the police in order to obtain admissions. Finally, it is found in the largely negative images conveyed in the samples respecting those who were detained, interrogated and prosecuted. Such images stand out in stark contrast to the generally self-promoting and self-legitimating images the samples contain of the police. The message of the study is not, however, confined to the products of private interrogations but has implications for the nature of law itself and its legitimating forms.

In protecting the confession as an admissible and *prima facie* reliable specie of evidence, the law, as broadly conceived, has had recourse to a variety of legitimating forms. These have been utilised as the social organisation of criminal justice has changed at different historical moments and, typically, when there has been a crisis of legitimacy over prevailing arrangements.

The PACE legislation may be seen as marking the revival of statutory control and the restoration of regulation consistent with the rule of law. This contrasts with the non-statutory Judges' Rules which as a legitimating form operated at different levels. At one level they were expressed in terms of rules which in legal discourse convey the idea of authority, uniformity and compliance. At another level, however, they were not rules of law at all but merely codes of guidance. The use of 'rules' in this ambiguous sense enabled the construction of the suspect as a free and voluntary agent who makes knowing and intelligent decisions, albeit in a disempowered setting. Thus, according to the sub-text of the Judges' Rules, it was entirely a matter for the informed and uninhibited suspect whether he or she would answer reasonable police questions or have a legal adviser in attendance during questioning.

PACE recognises that suspects may be exposed to unfair or unreasonable pressures.[38] It therefore makes the freedom enjoyed by the police to detain suspects in custody and to question them in order to obtain incriminating admissions,[39] subject to the mandatory duty of the court to exclude any confession that was or may have been obtained by oppression or as a result of conduct likely to render the confession unreliable.[40] PACE assists the courts in this duty by requiring custodial interviews to be recorded contemporaneously.[41] As a consequence, the set-piece interrogation has been transformed from an event which is *reported* to one which is *recorded*. Alongside this aspect of change however is another feature of continuity: the continued vitality of non-contemporaneously recorded interrogations as admissible evidence.[42] There are, therefore, two systems presently in existence. Under the first, legitimacy is secured through the construction of statutory control. However, this has been achieved alongside the second and less publicly known reality of admissible non-contemporaneously recorded interrogations. These contradictory features present problems not only for the legitimacy of law but also for the police who are given conflicting signals as to how they might legitimately go about their law enforcement duties.

## Conclusion

Law secures its legitimacy through a number of embedded and enduring claims: law is relatively autonomous; it is founded in reason rather than coercion, though it might, as a last resort, secure compliance through force; it represents the general will of society as a whole rather than that of particular interests; it is universal in its scope and impartial in its application. Such claims embrace a number of subordinate claims, for example, that those responsible for operationalising and enforcing the law are themselves subject to legal regulation and are allocated discretion only in restricted and defined circumstances.

Collectively, these claims lend support to the notion of law as legitimate; indeed they are viewed as essential preconditions to legitimate law. However, the validity of such claims is called into question by a legal system that has permitted and encouraged the procurement of extra-judicial confessions by means of, or in circumstances which might be construed as involving, coercion. Throughout the history of the criminal process, reliance upon confessions has resulted in an on-going struggle for the legitimacy of law and legal procedures. In respect of confession evidence, this struggle has taken a number of different forms. In large part, these have centred on the means by which confessions might be legitimately acquired and utilised as evidence of guilt.

The dependence upon confessions has been one of the continuities in the history of English criminal justice. In one form or another, from admissions obtained by torture, through compulsory interrogation or cross-examination, to the utilisation of putatively voluntary statements, the English criminal justice system has continuously sought to use confessions as part of prosecution evidence. Elements of change, however, may be discerned in the various methods under which confessions may be lawfully obtained. Thus, while convictions founded on confessions made in the public setting of open court attract legitimacy through judicialisation and transparency, doubts over confessions alleged by official actors to have been made in the private domain have necessitated the development and maintenance of legitimating structures. As part of the legitimation project the privilege against compulsory self-incrimination was formally extended from the trial to the pre-trial and private spheres of the criminal process. The requirement for 'voluntary' confessions, the provisions of the Judges' Rules and those of their successor, PACE, are more recent aspects of the legitimating project. Each, with varying degrees of success, have the object of defending the reliance placed on confessions by the criminal process and each seek to compensate for the absence of public supervision over the private and pre-trial application of state power on citizens.

Once the coercion of confessions through official torture had lost its legitimacy, new structures were created to preserve the status and role of confessions. The powers given to justices to conduct extra-judicial examinations derived some measure of legitimacy from their subordination to statutory control. However, the fact that justices might utilise their coercive powers to engage in direct confrontation with the suspect worked to threaten the legitimacy of inquisitorial examinations at a time when such examinations were increasingly seen as being incompatible with the quasi-judicial status accorded to justices. As other state actors (the police) took up the investigation and prosecution functions left by the judicialisation of justices, new legitimating forms were imported to sustain the notion of state power being operationalised only through and in accordance with due process of law.

As the police assumed the power to conduct interrogations in private, the legitimacy of confessions as evidence was called into question because there was no legal warrant to support police practices in this respect. Later, with the creation of minimal and non-statutory constraints on their evidence-gathering powers, the police were able to produce self-legitimating narratives to support their investigative activities and the role of confessions in the criminal process. By fostering positive representations of themselves and their practices alongside negative images of suspects, the legitimacy of interrogations was reinforced. However, increasing evidence of police malpractice has worked to undermine this edifice of legitimacy. The recording provisions of PACE may be seen as going some way to restore confidence in the completeness, accuracy and reliability of interview records. However, this study suggests that it would be wrong to treat the picture which emerges from PACE-regulated interviews with anything but the utmost care. For as the Royal Commission on Criminal Justice (1993) observed:

It may never be possible to ensure that all transactions are recorded, particularly if individual police officers are determined, for their own reasons, that particular transactions should not be.[43]

Thus, suggestions that the video recording of interviews would provide a more comprehensive record of what took place than audio-records and so offer greater protection to suspects and police officers, are also to be treated with caution.[44] Video recordings may present a more convincing picture of the conditions immediately attending the making of extra-judicial confessions, nevertheless, that picture may not be any more complete or reliable.

## Notes

[1] Groot, 1988, pp. 10-15, 20; Green, 1988, p. 326.
[2] See Devlin, 1966, p. 126.
[3] Green, 1988, pp. 13-17.
[4] Putnam, 1924, pp. 1-5.
[5] See Noble, 1970, pp. 250-66.
[6] See Kaufman, 1979, p. 1; Zuckerman, 1989, pp. 128-9.
[7] For a discussion of the 'reliability principle' and the 'disciplinary principle' as grounds for the exclusion of confession evidence, see Ashworth, 1977, pp. 723-35.
[8] Hay and Snyder, 1989, pp. 4, 16, 39-47.
[9] For an estimate of the proportion of prosecutions initiated by the police in the period under consideration see Devlin, 1960, pp. 20-1; Sigler, 1974, p. 643.
[10] Under the police "the caution has become a technique for the validation, as evidence, of statements, not only against the suggestions of 'fear or favour', but against any suggestion that the statement was obtained by any process that might be called unfair" (Abrahams, 1964a, p. 10).
[11] In *Bass* (1953) 37 Cr.App.R. 51, the Court of Appeal formally validated the practice of police officers collaborating, post-interview, to produce agreed and therefore virtually unchallengeable accounts of custodial interviews.
[12] See McConville and Baldwin, 1981, p. 180; Zuckerman, 1989, p. 313.
[13] In this regard, compare the judicial articulation of the voluntariness rule in *Ibrahim* [1914] AC 599, pp. 609-14, with the comments made by Darling, J in *Cook* (1918) 34 TLR 515, p. 516.
[14] This much was acknowledged in the 1929 *Report of the Royal Commission on Police Powers and Procedure*, Cmd. 3297, p. 100.
[15] McConville and Baldwin (1981, pp. 106-114) found a close correspondence between police interrogations, confession evidence and convictions.
[16] Home Office Circular 536053/23, 1930.

[17] See Rule 7.
[18] See Maitland, 1885, p. 123. See also the Magistrates' Court Act 1952, s. 38; Devlin, 1960, pp. 68, 71; Leigh, 1975, p. 34.
[19] Devlin, 1960, pp. 9-10.
[20] See for example *Gavin* (1885) 15 Cox C.C. 656; *Male and Cooper* (1893) 17 Cox C.C. 689; *Knight and Thayre* (1905) 20 Cox C.C. 711; *Winkel* (1912) 76 JP 191; *Mathews* (1919) 14 Cr.App.R. 23.
[21] McConville and Baldwin, 1981, pp. 126, 132.
[22] Williams, G., 1960a, pp. 331-2.
[23] See Rule 1 of the 1964 Rules.
[24] [1983] 3 All ER 526, Court of Appeal; [1984] 1 All ER 1054, House of Lords.
[25] *Mohammed-Holgate* v. *Duke* [1983] 3 All ER 526, Court of Appeal, *per* Latey, J, p. 533.
[26] *Ibid., per* Arnold, P, p. 531.
[27] *Ibid.*, per Latey, J, p. 533, citing the Report of the *Royal Commission on Criminal Procedure* (1981, Cmnd. 8092, para. 3.66, p. 41) in support.
[28] *Ibid.*, p. 534.
[29] *Ibid.*
[30] *Holgate-Mohammed* v. *Duke* [1984] 1 All ER 1054, House of Lords, p. 1059. Lord Diplock also cited the 1981 Report of the Royal Commission (*supra.*, n. 27) in support of his contention.
[31] A substantial body of case law from this period: 'Repeatedly and emphatically ... ruled that the police do not have the authority, even after caution, to question or cross-examine an accused person who has been taken into custody' (Fellman, 1966, p. 37).
[32] *Mohammed-Holgate* v. *Duke* [1983] 3 All ER 526, Court of Appeal, *per* Arnold, P, p. 533.
[33] See, for example, Damaska, 1973, pp. 506-89; 1975, pp. 480-544; Lustgarten, 1986, pp. 2-4.
[34] Devlin, 1979b, p. 442.
[35] Devlin, 1979a, p. 72.
[36] Lidstone and Early, 1982, p. 507. See also McConville and Baldwin, 1981, p. 190.
[37] McConville and Baldwin, 1981, *ibid.*
[38] See Royal Commission on Criminal Justice, *Report*, 1993, Cm. 2263, p. 25.
[39] PACE, s. 37(2).
[40] The duty to exclude a confession for oppression or unreliability under PACE, s. 76(2) is supplemented by s. 78 which gives trial judges a discretion to exclude evidence that has been obtained unfairly.
[41] See PACE, Code C, para. 11.5; Code E, paras. 2.1, 3.1, 3.3, 3.4 and 3.5.
[42] See PACE, Code C, para. 11.1 and 11.5(c).
[43] *Supra.*, n. 40, p.26.
[44] See McConville, 1992, pp. 532-48.

# Bibliography

A Barrister (1967), 'Questioning: A Comment', *Criminal Law Review*, 91.
A Police Officer (1964), 'The Judges' Rules and the Police', *Criminal Law Review*, 173.
Abrahams, G. (1964a), *Police Questioning and the Judges' Rules*, London: Oyez.
Abrahams, G. (1964b), 'The Judges' Rules', 108, *Solicitor's Journal*, 106.
Allen, A.K. (1953), *The Queen's Peace*, London: Stevens.
Allen, C.K. (1953), 'Unsworn Statements by Accused Persons', 69, *Law Quarterly Review*, 22.
Andrews, J.A. (1963), 'Involuntary Confessions and Illegally Obtained Evidence in Criminal Cases - 1', *Criminal Law Review*, 15.
Andrews, J.A. (1963), 'Involuntary Confessions and Illegally Obtained Evidence in Criminal Cases - 2', *Criminal Law Review*, 77.
Anon. (1964), 'An Historical Argument for the Right to Counsel During Police Interrogation', 73, *Yale Law Journal*, 1000.
Ascoli, D. (1979), *The Queen's Peace: The origins and development of the Metropolitan Police 1829-1979*, London: Hamilton.
Ashworth, A.J. (1977), 'Excluding evidence as Protecting Rights', *Criminal Law Review*, 723.
Aubry, A. and Caputo, R. (1965), *Criminal Interrogation*, (2nd edn., 1970), Springfield, Ill.: Thomas.
Baker, J.H. (1977), 'Criminal Courts and Procedure at Common Law', in Cockburn J.S. (ed), *Crime in England 1550-1800*, London: Methuen.
Baker, J.H. (1979), *An Introduction to English Legal History*, (2nd edn.), London: Butterworths.
Baker, J.H. (1990), *An Introduction to English Legal History*, (3rd edn.), London: Butterworths.
Baker, T. (1966), *The Normans*, London: Cassell.
Baldwin, J. (1992a), *Preparing the Record of Taped Interviews*, Royal Commission on Criminal Justice, Research Study No. 2., London: HMSO.
Baldwin, J. (1992b), *The Role of Legal Representatives at the Police Station*, Royal Commission on Criminal Justice, Research Study No. 3., London: HMSO.
Baldwin, J. (1993), 'Police Interview Techniques: Establishing Truth or Proof?', 33(3), *British Journal of Criminology*, 325.

Baldwin, J. and Bedward, J. (1991), 'Summarising Tape Recordings of Police Interviews', *Criminal Law Review,* 671.

Baldwin, J. and McConville, M. (1977), *Negotiated Justice: Pressures to Plead Guilty,* London: Robinson.

Baldwin, J. and McConville, M. (1979), 'Police Interrogation and the Right to see a Solicitor', *Criminal Law Review,* 145.

Baldwin, J. and McConville, M. (1980), *Confessions in Crown Court Trials,* Royal Commission on Criminal Procedure, Research Study No.5. London: HMSO.

Baldwin, J. and Moloney, T. (1992), *Supervision of Police Investigation in Serious Criminal Cases,* Royal Commission on Criminal Justice, Research Study No. 4., London: HMSO.

Baldwin, R. and Kinsey, R. (1982), *Police Powers and Politics,* London: Quartet.

Barnes, T.G. (1977), 'Due Process and Slow Process in the Late Elizabethan - Early Stuart Star Chamber', 6, *American Journal of Legal History,* 221.

Barry, Sir J.V. (1965), 'Police Interrogation' 5, *Sydney Law Review,* 254.

Bartlett, R. (1988), *Trial by Fire and Water: the Medieval Judicial Ordeal,* Oxford: Clarendon.

Baxter, J. and Koffman, L. (1983), 'The Confait Inheritance - Forgotten Lessons?', 14, *Cambrian Law Review,* 11.

Beard, C.A. (1904), *The Office of Justice of the Peace in England,* New York: Columbia University Press.

Beattie, J.M. (1986), *Crime and the Courts in England 1600-1800,* Oxford: Clarendon.

Bellamy, J. (1973), *Crime and Public Order in England in the Later Middle Ages,* London: Routledge and Keegan Paul.

Bellamy, J. (1984), *Criminal Law and Society in Late Medieval and Tudor England,* Gloucester: Sutton.

Bennun, M.E. (1973), 'Defendants Who Fail to Give Evidence', 36, *Modern Law Review,* 554.

Bentham, J. (1825), *A Treatise on Judicial Evidence,* 2 vols., extracted from the manuscripts of Jeremy Bentham by Dumount, M. London: Baldwin, Cradock and Joy.

Bentham, J. (1827), *Rationale of Judicial Evidence,* published under the superintendence of John Bowring in *The Works of Jeremy Bentham,* 12 vols., 1843 (vol.7, 1962 edn.), New York: Russell & Russell.

Benyon, J. and Bourne, C. (eds) (1986), *The Police,* Oxford: Pergamon.

Berger, M. (1980), *Taking the Fifth,* Lexington, Mass.: Heath.

Bidderman, A.D. (1960), 'Social-Psychological Needs and 'Involuntary' Behaviour as Illustrated by Compliance in Interrogation', 23, *Sociometry,* 120.

Blackstone, W.S. (1765-1769), *Commentaries on the Laws of England,* 4 vols., Oxford: Clarendon.

Blumberg A.S. (1967), *Criminal Justice*, (1974 edn.), Chicago: Quadrangle.
Bottoms, A.K. and McClean, J.D. (1976), *Defendants in the Criminal Process*, London: Routledge and Kegan Paul.
Bowden, T. (1978), *Beyond the Limits of the Law: a comparative study of the police in crisis politics*, Harmondsworth: Penguin.
Bridges, L. (1994), 'Normalising Justice: The Royal Commission on Criminal Justice', in Field, S. and Thomas, P.A. (eds), *Justice and Efficiency? The Royal Commission on Criminal Justice*, 21 (1), *Journal of Law and Society* (Special Issue).
Brogden, M. (1982) *The Police: Autonomy and Consent*, London: Academic Press.
Brogden, M. (1987) 'The emergence of the police: the colonial dimension', 27 (1), *British Journal of Criminology*, 4.
Brogden, M., Jefferson, T., Walklate, S. (1988) *Introducing Policework*, London: Unwin Hyman.
Brown, D. (1989), *Detention at the Police Station Under the PACE Act*, London: HMSO.
Brownlie, I. (1960), 'Police Questioning, Custody and Caution', *Criminal Law Review*, 298.
Brownlie, I. (1967), 'Police Powers - IV. Questioning: A General View', *Criminal Law Review*, 75.
Bunyan, T. (1977), *The History and Practice of the Political Police in Britain*, London: Quartet.
Burn, R. (1823), *The Justice of the Peace and Parish Officer*, (23rd edn.), with 'Supplement' by Chetwynd, G. London: Cadell.
Cahill, D. and Mingay, D. (1986), 'Leading questions and the police interview', 2 (3), *Policing*, 212.
Cain, M. (1973), *Society and the Policeman's Role*, London: Routledge.
Campbell, A.K.A. (1959), 'Letters to the Editor', *Criminal Law Review*, 673.
Chambliss, W.J. (ed) (1969), *Crime and the Legal Process*, New York: McGraw-Hill.
Cheyney, E.P. (1913), 'The Court of Star Chamber', 18 (4), *American Historical Review*, 727.
Chibnall, S. (1979), 'The Metropolitan Police and the News Media', in Holdaway, S. (ed), *The British Police*, London: Arnold.
Chitty, J. (1816), *Practical Treatise on the Criminal Law*, 4 vols., London: Valpy.
Christian, L. (1983), *Policing By Coercion*, London: GLC Police Committee and Pluto Press.
Clapp, A.C. (1956), 'Privilege Against Self-Incrimination', 10 (3), *Rutgers Law Review*, 541.
Cockburn, J.S. (1977), 'The Nature and Incidence of Crime in England 1559-1625: A Preliminary Survey', in Cockburn, J.S. (ed), *Crime in England 1550-1800*, London: Methuen.

Cockburn, J.S. (1978), 'Trial by the Book? Fact and Theory in the Criminal Process, 1558-1625', in Baker, J.H. (ed), *Legal Records and the Historian*, London: Royal Historical Society.

Cockburn, J.S. and Green, T.A. (eds) (1988), *Twelve Good Men and True: The Criminal Trial Jury in England, 1200-1800*, Princeton, NJ: Princeton University Press.

Cohen, M. (1981), 'Challenging Police Evidence of Interviews and the Second Limb of Section 1 (f) (ii) - Another View', *Criminal Law Review*, 523.

Cohen, P. (1979), 'Policing the Working Class City', in Fine, B., Kinsey, R., Lea, J., Piccioto, S. and Young, J. (eds), *Capitalism and the Rule of Law*, London: Hutchinson.

Cohen, S.A. (1979), *Due Process of Law*, Toronto, Canada: Carswell.

Commerton, E.A. (1964), 'Confessions in the Criminal Law', 15 (2), *Northern Ireland Legal Quarterly*, 166.

Cornish, W.R. (1968), *The Jury*, London: Allen Lane, Penguin.

Cornish, W.R. (1978a), 'Defects in Prosecuting - Professional views in 1845', in Glazebrook, P.R. (ed), *Reshaping the Criminal Law*, London: Stevens.

Cornish, W.R. (1978b), 'Criminal Justice and Punishment', in Cornish, W.R., Hart, J., Manchester, A.H. and Stevenson, J. *Crime and Law in Nineteenth Century Britain*, Dublin: Irish University Press.

Cornish, W.R. and Clark, G.de N. (1989), *Law and Society in England 1750-1950*, London: Sweet & Maxwell.

Cox, B. (1975), *Civil Liberties in Britain*, Harmondsworth: Penguin.

Criminal Law Revision Committee, Eleventh Report, *Evidence (General)*, Cmnd. 4991 (1972) London: HMSO.

Critchley, T.A. (1966), *A History of Police in England and Wales*, London: Constable.

Cross, A.R.N. (1970), 'The Right to Silence and the Presumption of Innocence - Sacred Cows or Safeguards of Liberty?', 11, *Journal of the Society of Public Teachers of Law*, 66.

Cross, Sir R. (1973), 'A Very Wicked Animal Defends the 11th Report of the Criminal Law Revision Committee', *Criminal Law Review*, 329.

Damaska, M. (1973), 'Evidentiary Barriers to Conviction and Two Models of Criminal Procedure: A Comparative Study', 121, *University of Pennsylvania Law Review*, 506.

Damaska, M. (1975), 'Structures of Authority and Comparative Criminal Procedure', 84, *Yale Law Journal*, 480.

Davis, J. (1984), 'A Poor Man's System of Justice: The London Police Courts in the Second Half of the Nineteenth Century', 27 (2), *Historical Journal*, 309.

de Gama, K. (1988), 'Police Powers and Public Prosecutions: Winning By Appearing To Lose?', 16, *International Journal of the Sociology of Law*, 339.

Deeley, P. (1971), *Beyond Breaking Point: A Study of Techniques of Interrogation*, London: Baker.

Dennis, I. (1993), 'Miscarriages of Justice and the Law of Confessions: Evidentiary Issues and Solutions', *Public Law*, 291.
Deosaran, R. (1985), *Trial by Jury: Social and Psychological Dynamics*, Trinidad: University of West Indies Press.
Devlin, P. (1956), *Trial by Jury*, London: Stevens.
Devlin, P. (1960), *The Criminal Prosecution in England*, Oxford: Oxford University Press.
Devlin, P. (1966), 'The Police in a Changing Society', 57 (2), *Journal of Criminal Law, Criminology and Police Science*, 123.
Devlin, P. (1979a), *The Judge*, Oxford: Oxford University Press.
Devlin, P. (1979b), 'The Practice of Judging', 101, *Listener*, 441.
Dixon, D. (1991a), 'Common Sense, Legal Advice and the Right of Silence', *Public Law*, 233.
Dixon, D. (1991b), 'Politics, Research and Symbolism in Criminal Justice: The Right of Silence and the Police and Criminal Evidence Act', 20, *Anglo-American Law Review*, 27.
Dixon, D., Bottomley, A.K., Coleman, C.A., Gill, M. and Wall, D. (1989), 'Reality and Rules in the Construction and Regulation of Police Suspicion', 17 *Journal of the Sociology of Law*, 185.
Dixon, D., Bottomley, A.K., Coleman, C.A., Gill, M. and Wall, D. (1990), 'Safeguarding the rights of suspects in police custody', 1 (2), *Policing and Society*, 115.
Douglas, D.C. (1964), *William the Conqueror: The Norman Impact Upon England*, London: Eyre & Spottiswoode.
Driver, E.D. (1968), 'Confessions and the Social Psychology of Coercion', 82, *Harvard Law Review*, 42.
Easton, S. (1991), *The Right to Silence*, Aldershot: Avebury.
Elliott, D.W. (1987), *Elliott and Phipson Manual of the Law of Evidence*, (12th edn.), London: Sweet & Maxwell.
Elton, G.R. (ed) (1960), *The Tudor Constitution: Documents and Commentary*, (2nd edn., 1982) Cambridge: Cambridge University Press.
Emlyn, S. (1730), *A Complete Collection of State Trials and Proceedings for High Treason and Other Crimes and Misdemeanours*, London: Walthoe.
Emsley, C. (1983), *Policing and its Context, 1750-1870*, London: Macmillan.
Emsley, C. (1987), *Crime and Society in England, 1750-1900*, London: Longman.
Emsley, C. (1991), *The English Police: A Political and Social History*, Hemel Hempstead: Harvester Wheatsheaf.
Evans, R. (1993), *The Conduct of Police Interviews with Juveniles*, Royal Commission on Criminal Justice, Research Study No. 8., London: HMSO.
Fellman, D. (1966), *The Defendant's Rights Under English Law*, London: University of Wisconsin Press.
Firth, A. (1976), 'Interrogation', *Police Review* (No. 4324), 1507.

Foster, H. (1979), 'Trial by Jury: the Thirteenth-Century Crisis in Criminal Procedure', 13 (2), *University of British Columbia Law Review*, 280.

Foucault, M. (1977), *Discipline and Punish: The Birth of the Prison*, London: Allen Lane.

Freestone, D. and Richardson, J.C. (1980), 'The Making of English Criminal Law: (7) Sir John Jervis and his Acts', *Criminal Law Review*, 5.

Fry T.P. (1938), 'Admissibility of Statements made by Accused Persons', 11, *Australian Law Journal*, 425.

Garfinkel, H. (1956), 'Conditions of Successful Degradation Ceremonies', 61 (5), *American Journal of Sociology*, 420.

Gatrell, V.A.C. (1990), 'Crime, authority and the policeman-state', in Thompson, F.L.M. (ed), *The Cambridge Social History of Britain 1750-1950, Vol. 3: Social agencies and institutions*, Cambridge: Cambridge University Press.

Gernstein, R.S. (1979), 'The Self-Incrimination Debate in Great Britain', 27, *American Journal of Comparative Law*, 81.

Gilbert, G. (1760), *The Law of Evidence by a Late Learned Judge*, (2nd edn.), London: Owen.

Glasbeek, H. and Prentice, D. (1968), 'The Criminal Suspect's Illusory Right of Silence in the British Commonwealth', 53, *Cornell Law Quarterly*, 473.

Glazebrook, P. (1977), 'The Making of English Law: (3) The Reign of Mary Tudor', *Criminal Law Review*, 582.

Goldstein, A.S. (1960), 'The State and the Accused: Balance of Advantage in Criminal Procedure', 69, *Yale Law Journal*, 1149.

Goldstein, A.S. (1974), 'Reflections on Two Models: Inquisitional Themes in American Criminal Procedure', 26, *Stanford Law Review*, 1009.

Gooderson, R.N. (1970), 'The Interrogation of Suspects' 48, *Canadian Bar Review*, 270.

Gordon, P. (1983), *White Law: Racism in the Police, Courts and Prisons*, London: Pluto.

Grano, J.D. (1979), 'Voluntariness, Free Will and the Law of Confessions', 65, *Virginia Law Review*, 859.

Greaves, H.R.G (1936), *Reactionary England*, London: Acorn.

Green, T.A. (1985), *Verdict According to Conscience: Perspectives on the English Jury Trial 1200-1800*, London: University of Chicago Press.

Green, T.A. (1988), 'A Retrospective in the Criminal Trial Jury, 1200-1800', in Cockburn, J.S. and Green, T.A. (eds).

Greenwalt, K. (1974), 'Perspectives On the Right to Silence', in Hood, R. (ed), *Crime, Criminology and Public Policy*, London: Hienemann.

Greer, S. (1994), 'The Right to Silence, Defence Disclosure, and Confession Evidence', in Field, S. and Thomas, P.A. (eds).

Griew, E. (1961), 'Imputations on the Character of the Prosecutor or the Witness for the Prosecution - A Restatement', *Criminal Law Review*, 142, 213.

Griffiths, J. (1970), 'Ideology in Criminal Procedure or A Third 'Model' of the Criminal Process', 79 (3), *Yale Law Journal*, 359.
Griffiths, J. and Ayres, R.E. (1967), 'A postscript to the Miranda project: Interrogation of draft protesters', 77 (2), *Yale Law Journal*, 300.
Groot, R.M. (1988), 'The Early-Thirteenth-Century Criminal Jury', in Cockburn, J.S. and Green, T.A. (eds).
Gudjonsson, G. and Clark, N. (1988), 'Suggestibility in police interrogation: a social, psychological model', 1, *Social Behaviour*, 83.
Gudjonsson, G. and MacKeith, J. (1988), 'Retracted Confessions: legal, psychological and psychiatric aspects', 28 (3), *Medicine, Science and the Law*, 187.
Gudjonsson, G.H. (1992), *The Psychology of Interrogations, Confessions and Testimony*, Chichester: Wiley.
Guy, J.A. (1985), *The Court of Star Chamber and its Records to the Reign of Elizabeth I*, London: HMSO.
Hale, M. (1678), *Pleas of the Crown*, London: Tonson.
Hale, M. (1739), *The History of the Common Law of England*, (1971 edn.), Gray, C. (ed), Chicago: University of Chicago Press.
Harding, A. (1966), *A Social History of English Law*, Harmondsworth: Penguin.
Harding, A. (1973), *The Law Courts of Medieval England*, London: Allen & Unwin.
Hart, J. (1978), 'Police', in Cornish *et al.*, *Crime and Law in Nineteenth Century Britain*, Dublin: Irish University Press.
Hay, D. (1975), 'Property, authority and the criminal law', in Hay, D., Linebaugh, P. and Thompson, E.P. *Albion's Fatal Tree: Crime and Society in Eighteenth-Century England*, London: Allen Lane.
Hay, D. (1983), 'Controlling the English prosecutor', 21 (2), *Osgoode Hall Law Journal*, 165.
Hay, D. (1988), 'The Class Composition of the Palladium of Liberty: Trial Jurors in the Eighteenth Century', in Cockburn and Green (eds), *Twelve Good Men and True: The Criminal Trial Jury in England, 1200-1800*, Princeton, NJ: Princeton University Press.
Hay, D. and Snyder, F. (1989), 'Using the Criminal Law, 1750-1850: Policing, Private Prosecution, and the State', in Hay, D. and Snyder, F. (eds), *Policing and Prosecution in Britain 1750-1850*, Oxford: Clarendon.
Hay, D. and Snyder, F. (eds) (1989), *Policing and Prosecution in Britain 1750-1850*, Oxford: Clarendon.
Heydon J.D. (1976), 'Confessions and Silence', *Sydney Law Review*, 375.
Hiemstra, V.G. (1963), 'Abolition of the Right Not to be Questioned', 80, *South African Law Journal*, 187.
Hoffman (1964), 'The Judges' Rules' 7, *Lawyer*, 23.
Holdaway, S. (1983), *Inside the British Police: A Force at Work*, Oxford: Basil Blackwell.

Holdaway, S. (ed) (1979), *The British Police*, London: Arnold.
Holdsworth, W.S. (1903-1966), *A History of English Law*, 16 vols., London : Methuen/Sweet & Maxwell.
Horowitz, G. (1958), 'The Privilege against Self-Incrimination: How Did It Originate', 31, *Temple Law Quarterly*, 121.
Howard, A. (ed) (1965), *Criminal Justice in Our Time*, Virginia: University of Virginia Press.
Howard, P. (1931), *Criminal Justice in England*, New York: Macmillan.
Hurnard, N.D. (1941), 'The Jury of Presentment and the Assize of Clarendon', 56, *English Historical Review*, 374.
Ignatieff, M. (1979), 'Police and People: The Birth of Mr Peel's 'Blue Locusts', *New Society*, 443.
Inbau, F. and Reid, J. (1962), *Criminal Interrogation and Confessions*, (2nd edn.), 1967, Baltimore: Williams & Wilkiins.
Inman, M. (1981), 'The Admissibility of Confessions', *Criminal Law Review*, 469.
Irving, B. (1980), *Police Interrogation: A Case Study of Current Practice*, Royal Commission on Criminal Procedure, Research Study No. 2., London: HMSO.
Irving, B. and Hilgendorf, L. (1980), *Police Interrogation: The Psychological Approach*, Royal Commission on Criminal Procedure, Research Study No. 1., London: HMSO.
Irving, B. and McKenzie, I. (1987), 'Police Interrogation; the effects of PACE', 3 (1), *Policing*, 4.
Irving, B. and McKenzie, I. (1988), *Regulating Custodial Interviews*, London: Police Foundation.
Irving, B. and McKenzie, I. (1989a), *Police Interrogation: The Effects of the Police and Criminal Evidence Act 1984*, London: Police Foundation.
Irving, B. and McKenzie, I. (1989b), 'Interrogating in a legal framework', in Morgan, R. and Smith, D.J. (eds), *Coming to terms with policing*, London: Routledge.
Jackson, J. (1993), '(2) The Evidence Recommendations', *Criminal Law Review*, 817.
Jackson, J.D. (1979), 'Confessions and the Doctrine of Oppression', *New Law Journal*, 264.
Jackson, J.D. (1986), 'In Defence of a Voluntariness Doctrine for Confessions: *The Queen* v. *Johnston* Revisited', 21 (1), *Irish Jurist*, 208.
Jackson, R.M. (1972), *Enforcing the Law*, Middlesex: Penguin.
Jardine, D. (1837), *A Reading on the Use of Torture in the Criminal Law of England*, London: Baldwin & Cradock.
Jefferson, T. (1988), 'Race, Crime and Policing: Empirical, Theoretical and Methodological Issues', 16, *International Journal of the Sociology of Law*, 521.
Jefferson, T. and Grimshaw, R. (1984), *Controlling the Constable: Police Accountability in England and Wales*, London: Muller, Cobden Trust.

Jenks, E. (1912), *A Short History of English Law: From the Earliest Times to the End of the Year 1911*, London: Methuen.
Joy, H.H. (1842), *On the Admissibility of Confessions and Challenge of Jurors in Criminal Cases in England and Ireland*, Dublin: Stevens & Norton, and Maxwell.
JUSTICE (1960), 'Preliminary Investigations of Criminal Offences', *Criminal Law Review*, 793.
Kamisar, Y. (1965), 'Equal Justice in the Gatehouses and Mansions of American Criminal Procedure', in Howard, A. (ed).
Kamisar, Y. (1980), *Police Interrogation and Confessions*, Michigan: Arbor, University of Michigan Press.
Kaufman, F. (1979), *The Admissibility of Confessions*, (3rd edn.), Toronto: Carswell.
Kauper R.G. (1932), 'Judicial Examination of the Accused - A Remedy for the Third Degree', 30, *Michigan Law Review*, 1224.
Kaye, T. (1991) *'Unsafe and Unsatisfactory'? The Report of the Independent Inquiry into the Working Practices of the West Midlands Police Serious Crime Squad*, London: Civil Liberties Trust.
Keeton, G.W. (1966), *The Norman Conquest and the Common Law*, London: Benn.
Kennedy, L. (1961), *Ten Rillington Place*, London: Gollancz.
Kenyon, J.P. (ed) (1986), *The Stuart Constitution 1603-1688: Documents and Commentary*, (2nd edn.) Cambridge: Cambridge University Press.
Kettle, M. (1980), 'The Politics of Policing and the Policing of Politics' in Hain, P. (ed), *Policing the Police (2)*, London: Calder.
King, M. (1981), *The Framework of Criminal Justice*, London: Croom Helm.
King, P. (1984), 'Decision-Makers and Decision-Making in the English Criminal Law, 1750-1800', 27 (1), *Historical Journal*, 25.
Kiralfy, A.K.R. (1962), *Potter's Historical Introduction to English Law and its Institutions*, (4th edn.), London: Sweet & Maxwell.
Lambert, J.R. (1970), *Crime, Police, and Race Relations*, London: Oxford University Press.
Langbein, J.H. (1973), 'The Origins of Public Prosecutions at Common Law', 17, *American Journal of Legal History*, 313.
Langbein, J.H. (1974), *Prosecuting Crime in the Renaissance: England, Germany, France*, Cambridge, Mass.: Harvard University Press.
Langbein, J.H. (1977), *Torture and the Law of Proof*, Chicago: University of Chicago Press.
Langbein, J.H. (1978), 'The Criminal Trial before Lawyers', 45 (2), *University of Chicago Law Review*, 263.
Langbein, J.H. (1979), 'Understanding the Short History of Plea Bargaining', 13 *Law and Society Review*, 261.
Langbein, J.H. (1982), 'Albion's Fatal Flaws', 98, *Past and Present*, 96.

Langbein, J.H. (1983), 'Shaping the Eighteenth-Century Criminal Trial, A View from the Ryder Sources', 50 (1), *University of Chicago Law Review*, 1.

Lawson, P.G. (1988), 'Lawless Juries? The Composition and Behaviour of Hertfordshire Juries, 1573-1624', in Cockburn, J.S. and Green, T.A. (eds), *Twelve Good Men and True: The Criminal Trial Jury in England, 1200-1800*, Princeton, NJ: Princeton University Press.

Leadam, I.S. and Baldwin, J.F. (eds) (1918), *Select Cases Before the King's Council, 1243-1482*, Selden Society, vol.35. Cambridge, Mass.: Harvard University Press.

Lee, W.L.M. (1901), *A History of Police in England*, London: Methuen.

Leigh, L.H. (1975), *Police Powers in England and Wales*, London: Butterworths.

Leigh, L.H. (1986), 'Some Observations on the Parliamentary History of the Police and Criminal Evidence Act 1984', in Harlow, C. (ed), *Public Law and Politics*, London: Sweet & Maxwell.

Leng, R. (1993), *The right to silence in police interrogation: a study of some of the issues underlying the debate*, Royal Commission on Criminal Justice, Research Study No. 10., London: HMSO.

Leo, R.A. (1994), 'Police Interrogation and Social Control', 3 (1), *Social and Legal Studies*, 93.

Levy, L.W. (1968), *Origins of the Fifth Amendment: the Right Against Self-Incrimination*, New York: Oxford University Press.

Lewis, D. and Hughman, P. (1975), *Just How Just*, London: Secker & Warburg.

Lidstone, K. (1981), 'Investigative Powers and the Rights of the Citizen', *Criminal Law Review*, 454.

Lidstone, K. and Early T. (1982), 'Questioning Freedom: Detention for Questioning in France, Scotland and England', 31, *International and Comparative Law Quarterly*, 488.

Lipton, J. (1977), 'On the psychology of eyewitness testimony', 62 (1), *Journal of Applied Psychology*, 90.

Lowell, A.L. (1897-8), 'The Judicial Use of Torture', (parts I and II, 11), *Harvard Law Review*, 220 and 290.

Loyn, H.R. (1962), *Anglo-Saxon England and the Norman Conquest*, New York: Longman.

Lustgarten, L. (1986), *The Governance of the Police*, London: Sweet & Maxwell.

MacDermott, Lord. (1957), *Protection from Power Under English Law*, London: Stevens.

MacDermott, Lord. (1968), 'The Interrogation of Suspects in Custody', 21, *Current Legal Problems*, 1.

MacDonald, T.D. and Hart, A.H. (1947), 'The Admissibility of Confessions in Criminal Cases', 25, *Canadian Bar Review*, 823.

MacKay, P. (1990), 'Changes in Custody Practice Since the Introduction of the Police & Criminal Evidence Act 1984', 14 (2), *The Criminologist*, 63.

MacKenna, Sir B. (1970), 'Police Interrogation' 120, *New Law Journal*, 665.

MacKenna, Sir B. (1972), 'Criminal Law Revision Committee's Eleventh Report: Some Comments', *Criminal Law Review*, 605.
Macnair, M.R.T. (1990), 'The Early Development of the Privilege against Self-Incrimination', 10, *Oxford Journal of Legal Studies*, 66.
Maguire, M. (1988), 'The Effects of the PACE Provisions in Detention and Questioning', 28, *British Journal of Criminology*, 19.
Maguire, M. and Norris, C. (1992), *The Conduct and Supervision of Criminal Investigations*, Royal Commission on Criminal Justice, Research Study No. 5., London: HMSO.
Maguire, M. and Norris, C. (1994), 'Police Investigations: Practice and Malpractice', in Field, S. and Thomas, P.A. (eds), *Justice and Efficiency? The Royal Commission on Criminal Justice*, Oxford: Blackwell.
Maguire, M.H. (1936), 'Attack of the Common Lawyers on the Oath *ex officio* as Administered in the Ecclesiastical Courts of England', in Wittke (ed), *Essays in History and Political Theory in Honour of Charles Howard McIlwain*, Cambridge, Mass.: Harvard University Press.
Maitland, F.W. (1885), *Justice and Police*, London: Macmillan.
Maitland, F.W. (1908), *The Constitutional History of England*, (1963 reprint), Cambridge: Cambridge University Press.
Manning, P.K. (1977), *Police Work: The Social Organisation of Policing*, Cambridge, Mass.: MIT.
Mark, R. (1966), 'A Matter of Conviction', *Criminal Law Review*, 311.
Mark, R. (1973), *Minority Verdict*, the 1973 Dimbleby Lecture, London: BBC.
Mark, R. (1977), *Policing a Perplexed Society*, London: Allen & Unwin.
Mark, R. (1978), *In the Office of Constable*, London: Collins.
Marquis, K., Marshall, J. and Oskamp, S. (1972), 'Testimonial validity as a function of question form, atmosphere, and item difficulty', 2 (2), *Journal of Applied Psychology*, 167.
Marshall, G. (1964), 'Comment', *Public Law*, 97.
McBarnet, D.J. (1976), 'Pre-trial Procedures and the Construction of Conviction', in Carlen, P. (ed), *Sociological Review Monograph: The Sociology of Law*, Keele University.
McBarnet, D.J. (1978), 'The Fisher Report on the Confait Case: Four Issues', 41, *Modern Law Review*, 455.
McBarnet, D.J. (1981a), 'Balance and clarity: has the Royal Commission achieved them?', *Criminal Law Review*, 445.
McBarnet, D.J. (1981b), *Conviction: Law, the State and the Construction of Justice*, London: Macmillan.
McBarnet, D.J. (1981c), 'The Royal Commission and the Judges' Rules', 8 (1), *British Journal of Law and Society*, 109.
McConville, M. (1984), 'Prosecuting Criminal Cases in England and Wales: Reflections of an Inquisitorial Adversary', 6 (1), *Liverpool Law Review*, 15.

McConville, M. (1992), 'Videotaping interrogations: Police behaviour on and off camera', *Criminal Law Review*, 532.

McConville, M. (1993), *Corroboration and Confessions. The impact of a rule requiring that no conviction can be sustained on the basis of confession evidence alone*, Royal Commission on Criminal Justice, Research Study No. 13., London: HMSO.

McConville, M. and Baldwin, J. (1980), 'Confessions: The Dubious Fruits of Police Interrogation', 130 (2), *New Law Journal*, 993.

McConville, M. and Baldwin, J. (1981), *Courts, Prosecution and Conviction*, Oxford: Clarendon.

McConville, M. and Baldwin, J. (1982a), 'Recent Developments in English Criminal Justice and the Royal Commission on Criminal Procedure', 10, *International Journal of the Sociology of Law*, 287.

McConville, M. and Baldwin, J. (1982b), 'The Role of Interrogation in Crime Discovery and Conviction', 22 (1), *British Journal of Criminology*, 165.

McConville, M. and Hodgson, J. (1993), *Custodial Advice and the Right to Silence*, Royal Commission on Criminal Justice, Research Study No. 16., London: HMSO.

McConville, M. and Morrel, P. (1983), 'Recording the Interrogation: Have the Police got it Taped?', *Criminal Law Review*, 158.

McConville, M., Hodgson, J., Bridges, L and Pavlovic, A. (1994), *Standing Accused: The Organisation of Criminal Defence Lawyers in Britain*, Oxford: Clarendon.

McConville, M., Sanders, A. and Leng, R. (1991), *The Case For the Prosecution*, London: Routledge.

McCormick, C.T. (1938), 'The Scope of Privilege in the Law of Evidence', 16 (4), *Texas Law Review*, 447.

McCormick, C.T. (1946), 'Some Problems and Developments in the Admissibility of Confessions', 24 (3), *Texas Law Review*, 239.

McEwan, J. (1992), *Evidence and the Adversarial Process: The Modern Law*, Oxford: Blackwell.

McLain, B.W. (1988), 'Juror Attitudes toward Local Disorder: The Evidence of the 1328 Trailbaston Proceedings', in Cockburn, J.S and Green, T.A. (eds), *Twelve Good Men and True: The Criminal Trial Jury in England, 1200-1800*, Princeton, NJ: Princeton University Press.

McNaughton, J. (1960), 'The privilege against self-incrimination - its constitutional affectation, raison d'etra and miscellaneous implications', 51, *Journal of Criminal Law, Criminology and Police Science*, 138.

McNee, D. (1979), 'Policing in Modern Britain', in Stott and Miller (eds), *Crime and the Responsible Community*, London: Hodder & Stoughton.

McNee, D. (1983), *McNee's Law*, London: Collins.

Mead, F. (1935), 'Cautions', 99, *Justice of the Peace and Local Government Review*, 499.

Menlowe, M. (1988), 'Bentham, self-incrimination and the law of evidence,' 104, *Law Quarterly Review*, 286.
Miller, C.J. (1973), 'Silence and Confessions - What are they worth?', *Criminal Law Review*, 343.
Miller, W.R. (1977), *Cops and Bobbies: Police Authority in New York and London, 1830-1870*, Chicago: Chicago University Press.
Milton, F. (1967), *The English Magistracy*, London: Oxford University Press.
Mirfield, P. (1981), 'Confessions - the 'Person in Authority' Requirement', *Criminal Law Review*, 92.
Mirfield, P. (1985), *Confessions*, London: Sweet & Maxwell.
Moir, E. (1969), *The Justice of the Peace*, Harmondsworth: Penguin.
Monkkonen, E.H. (1981), *Police in Urban America, 1860-1920*, Cambridge: Cambridge University Press.
Moreland, R. (1956), 'Historical Background and Implications of the Privilege Against Self-Incrimination', 54 *Kentucky Law Journal*, 267.
Morgan, E. (1949), 'The privilege against self-incrimination', 34 (1), *Minnesota Law Review*, 1.
Morgan, J. (1990), *The Police Function and the Investigation of Crime*, Aldershot: Avebury.
Morgan, R. and Smith, D.J. (eds) (1989), *Coming to terms with policing*, London: Routledge.
Morris, P. (1980), *Police Interrogation: Review of Literature*, Royal Commission on Criminal Procedure, Research Study No. 3., London: HMSO.
Morton, J. (1972), 'The Rights of the Suspect', 122, *New Law Journal*, 805.
Morton, J. (1975), 'To Combat Verbals', 125, *New Law Journal*, 830.
Morton, J. (1993), *Bent Coppers: A Survey of Police Corruption*, London: Little, Brown.
Moston, S. and Stephenson, G.M. (1993a), 'The Changing Face of Police Interrogation', 3, *Journal of Community & Applied Social Psychology*, 101.
Moston, S. and Stephenson, G.M. (1993b), *The Questioning and Interviewing of Suspects Outside the Police Station*, Royal Commission on Criminal Justice, Research Study No. 22,. London: HMSO.
Moston, S., Stephenson, G.M. and Williamson, T.M. (1992), 'The Effects of Case Characteristics on Suspect Behaviour During Police Questioning', 32, *British Journal of Criminology*, 23.
Mummery, D.R. (1981), 'Due Process and Inquisition', 97, *Law Quarterly Review*, 287.
Neasey, F.M. (1969), 'The Rights of the Accused and the Interests of the Community', 43, *Australian Law Journal*, 482.
Neasey, F.M. (1977), 'The Right to Remain Silent', 51, *Australian Law Journal*, 360.
Noble, R. (1970), 'The Struggle to Make the Accused Competent in England and Canada', 8 (2), *Osgoode Hall Law Journal*, 249.

O'Connor, P. and Cooney, T. (1980), 'Criminal Due Process, the Pre-Trial Stage and Self-Incrimination', 15, *Irish Jurist*, 219.

O'Donoghue, F. (1966), 'Imputations on the Character of Prosecution Witnesses', 29, *Modern Law Review*, 492.

O'Hara, C.E. (1956), *Fundamentals of Criminal Investigation*, (2nd edn.), 1970, Springfield, Ill.: Thomas.

O'Regan, R. (1965), 'Adverse Inferences from Failure of an Accused Person to Testify', *Criminal Law Review*, 711.

Oaks, D. (1970), 'Studying the Exclusionary Rule in Search and Seizure', 37, *University of Chicago Law Review*, 665.

Odgers, S. (1985), 'Police Interrogation and the Right to Silence', 59, *Australian Law Review*, 78.

Osborne, B. (1960), *Justices of the Peace 1361-1848*, Dorset: Sedghill.

Packer, H. (1964), 'Two Models of the Criminal Process', 113 (1), *University of Pennsylvania Law Review*, 1.

Packer, H. (1968), *The Limits of the Criminal Sanction*, Stanford: Stanford University Press.

Packman, I.V. (1959), 'Letters to the Editor', *Criminal Law Review*, 675.

Parker, G. (1984), 'The prisoner in the box - the making of the Criminal Evidence Act, 1898', in J.A. Guy and H.G. Beale (eds), *Law and Social Change in British History*, London: Royal Historical Society.

Pattenden, R. (1981), 'The Purpose of Cross-Examination Under Section 1 (f) of the Criminal Evidence Act 1898', *Criminal Law Review*, 707.

Pattenden, R. (1982), *The Judge, Discretion and the Criminal Trial*, Oxford: Oxford University Press.

Pattenden, R. (1991), 'Should Confessions be Corroborated' 107, *Law Quarterly Review*, 317.

Payne, G.C. (1959), 'Letters to the Editor', *Criminal Law Review*, 675.

Pepinski, H.E. (1970), 'A Theory of Police Reaction to Miranda v. Arizona', 16, *Crime and Delinquency*, 379.

Peters, E. (1985), *Torture*, Oxford: Blackwell.

Phillips, D. (1977), *Crime and Authority in Victorian England*, London: Croom Helm.

Phillips, D. (1989), 'Good Men to Associate and Bad Men to Conspire: Associations for the Prosecution of Felons in England, 1750-1850', in Hay, D. and Snyder, F. (eds).

Phillips, H.E.I. (1939), 'The Last Years of the Star Chamber, 1630-41', 21, *Transactions of the Royal Historical Society*, (4th Series), 103.

Phillips, H.E.I. (1941), 'The Court of Star Chamber, 1603-1641, with Special Reference to the Period 1625-41', 18 (52), *Bulletin of the Institute of Historical Research*, 35.

Pitt-Lewis, G. (1896), 'A Bill for the Protection of Innocent Prisoners', 39 (231), *Nineteenth Century*, 812.

Pittman, R.C. (1939), 'The Colonial and Constitutional History of the Privilege against Self-Incrimination in America', 21, *Virginia Law Review*, 763.

Ploscowe, M. (1935), 'The Development of Present-Day Criminal Procedures in Europe and America', 48, *Harvard Law Review*, 433.

Plucknett, T.F.T. (1956), A Concise History of the Common Law, (5th edn.), London: Butterworth.

Pollock F.M. and Maitland, F.W. (1898), *The History of English Law Before the Time of Edward I*, 2 vols., (2nd edn., 1911), Cambridge: Cambridge University Press.

Post, J.B. (1985), 'The Admissibility of Defence Counsel in English Criminal Procedure', in Kiralfy, A., Slatter, M. and Virgoe, R. (eds), *Custom, Courts and Counsel*, London: Cass.

Postema, G. (1977), ' The Principle of Utility and the law of procedure: Bentham's theory of adjudication', 11, *Georgia Law Review*, 1393.

Pound, R. (1934), 'Legal Interrogation of Persons Accused or Suspected of Crime', 24, *Journal of Criminal Law and Criminology*, 1014.

Powell, E. (1989), *Kingship, Law, and Society: Criminal Justice in the Reign of Henry V*, Oxford: Clarendon.

Powers, P., Andriks, J. and Loftus, E. (1979), 'Eyewitness Accounts of Females and Males', 64 (3), *Journal of Applied Psychology*, 399.

Pue, W.W. (1983), 'The Criminal Twilight Zone: Pre-Trial Procedures in the 1840s', 21 (1), *Alberta Law Review*, 335.

Punch, M. (ed) (1983), *Control in the Police Organisation*, Cambridge Mass.: MIT.

Putnam, B.H. (ed) (1924), *Early Treatises on the practice of the Justices of the Peace in the Fifteenth and Sixteenth Centuries*, 7, Oxford Studies in Social and Legal History, Oxford: Oxford University Press.

Ratushny E. (1971), 'Unravelling Confessions', 13, *Criminal Law Quarterly*, 453.

Ratushny, E. (1979), *Self-Incrimination in the Canadian Criminal Process*, Toronto: Carswell.

Reiner, R. (1980), Fuzzy Thoughts: The Police and Law-and-Order Politics', 28 (2), *Sociological Review*, 377.

Reiner, R. (1983), 'The Politicization of the Police in Britain', in Punch, M. (ed), *Control in the Police Organisation*, Cambridge Mass.: MIT.

Reiner, R. (1985), *The Politics of the Police*, Brighton: Wheatsheaf.

Reiner, R. (1986), 'The Modern Bobby', (4), *Policing*, 258.

Reiner, R. (1991), *The Politics of the Police*, (2nd edn.), Brighton: Wheatsheaf.

*Report of an Inquiry by the Hon. Henry Fisher into the circumstances leading to the trial of three persons on charges arising out of the death of Maxwell Confait and the Fire at 27 Doggett Road, London SE6*, 1977, London: HMSO.

*Report of an Inquiry by the Hon. Mr Justice Brabin into the case of Timothy John Evans*, Cmmd. 3101, 1966, London: HMSO.

*Report of the Royal Commission on Police Powers and Procedure*, Cmd. 3297, 1929, London: HMSO.

*Report of the Royal Commission upon the Duties of the Metropolitan Police*, Cd. 4156, 1908, London: HMSO.

*Report to the Secretary of State for the Home Department of the Departmental Committee on Evidence on Identification in Criminal Cases*, 1976, London: HMSO.

*Report, by J Sott Henderson QC, of an Inquiry into Certain Matters arising out of the Deaths of Mrs Beryl Evans and of Geraldine Evans and out of the Conviction of Timothy John Evans of the Murder of Geraldine Evans*, Cmd. 8896, 1953, London: HMSO.

Roberts, S.K. (1988), 'Juries and the Middling Sort: Recruitment and Performance at Devon Quarter Sessions, 1649-4670', in Cockburn, J.S. and Green, T.A. (eds).

Rothblatt, H. and Rothblatt, E. (1960), 'Police Interrogation: The Right to Counsel and to Prompt Arraignment' 28, *Brooklyn Law Review*, 24.

Royal Commission on Criminal Justice, (1993), *Report*, Cm. 2263, London: HMSO.

Royal Commission on Criminal Procedure, (1981), *Report*, Cmnd. 8092, London: HMSO.

Royal Commission on Criminal Procedure, (1981), *The Balance of Criminal Justice*, London: HMSO.

Royal Commission on Criminal Procedure, (1981), *The Investigation and Prosecution of Criminal Offences in England and Wales: The Law and Procedure*, Cmnd. 8092-1, London: HMSO.

Royal Commission on the Police, (1962), *Final Report*, Cmnd. 1728, London: HMSO.

Royal, R. and Schutt, S. (1976), *The Gentle Art of Interviewing and Interrogation: Professional Manual and Guide*, Englwood Cliffs, NJ: Prentice Hall.

Sanders, A. (1987), 'Constructing the Case for the Prosecution', 14 (2), *Journal of Law and Society*, 229.

Sanders, A. (1988), 'The Limits to Diversion From Prosecution', 28 (4), *British Journal of Criminology*, 513.

Sanders, A. and Bridges, L. (1990), 'Access to Legal Advice and Police Malpractice', *Criminal Law Review*, 494.

Sanders, A., Bridges, L., Mulvaney, A. and Crozier, G. (1989), *Advice and Assistance at Police Stations and the 24 Hour Duty Solicitor Scheme*, London: Lord Chancellor's Department.

Sargant, W. (1957), *Battle for the Mind*, London: Heinemann.

Schaefer, W. (1966), 'Police Interrogation and the Privilege Against Self-Incrimination', 61 (4), *North Western University Law Review*, 506.

Scraton, P. (1985), *The State of the Police*, London: Pluto.

*Sheffield Police Appeal Inquiry* (1963), Cmnd. 2176. London: HMSO.

Sigler, J.A. (1974), 'Public Prosecutions in England and Wales', *Criminal Law Review*, 642.

Silver, A. (1967), 'The Demand for Order in Civil Society: A Review of Some Themes in the History of Urban Crime, Police and Riot', in Bordua, D.J. (ed), *The Police: Six Sociological Essays*, New York: Wiley.

Skyrine, T. (1979), *The Changing Image of the Magistracy*, London: Macmillan.

Smith, D.J. and Gray, J. (1983), *Police and the People in London IV: The Police in Action*, London: Policy Studies Institute, No. 621.

Smith, J.C. (1959), 'Letters to the Editor', *Criminal Law Review*, 677.

Smith, J.C. (1960), 'Questioning by the Police: Some Further Points - 2', *Criminal Law Review*, 347.

Smith, J.C. (1964), 'The New Judges' Rules - A Lawyer's View', *Criminal Law Review*, 176.

Softley, P. (1980), *Police Interrogation: An Observational Study in Four Police Stations*, Royal Commission on Criminal Procedure, Research Study No. 4., London: HMSO.

St.Johnston, T.E. (1948), 'The Legal Limitation of the Interrogation of Suspects and Prisoners in England and Wales', 39, *American Journal of Police Science*, 89.

St.Johnston, T.E. (1966), 'The Judges' Rules and Police Interrogation in England and Wales', 57, *Journal of Criminal Law and Police Science*, 85.

Staunford, W. (1607), *Pleas of the Crown*, London: Honyman.

Stead, P.J. (1985), *The Police of Britain*, London: Macmillan.

Steer, D. (1980), *Uncovering Crime: The Police Role*, Royal Commission on Criminal Procedure, Research Study No. 7., London: HMSO.

Stephen, H. (1896), 'A Bill to Promote the Conviction of Innocent Prisoners', 30, *Nineteenth Century*, 566.

Stephen, H. (1898), *Prisoners on Oath*, London: Heinemann.

Stephen, J.F. (1877), 'Suggestions as to the Reform of the Criminal Law', 2 (10), *Nineteenth Century*, 737.

Stephen, J.F. (1883), *A History of the Criminal Law of England*, 3 vols., London: Macmillan.

Stephen, J.F. (1886), 'Prisoners as Witnesses', 20 (116), *Nineteenth Century*, 453.

Stephenson, C. and Marcham, F.G. (eds) (1937), *Sources of English Constitutional History*, New York: Harper & Row.

Stephenson, G.M. (1990), 'Should collaborative testimony be permitted in courts of law?', *Criminal Law Review*, 302.

Stephenson, G.M. and Moston, S.J. (1994), 'Police Interrogation', 1, *Psychology, Crime & Law*, 151

Stone, J. (1935), 'Cross-Examination by the Prosecution at Common Law and under the Criminal Evidence Act, 1898', 51, *Law Quarterly Review*, 443.

Stone, J. (1942), 'Further problems in the interpretation of the Criminal Evidence Act, 1898, s.1, proviso (f)', 58, *Law Quarterly Review*, 369.

Storch, R.D. (1975), 'The Plague of Blue Locusts: Police Reform and Popular Resistance in Northern England 1840-1857, 20 (1), *International Review of Social History*, 61.

Storch, R.D. (1976), 'The Policeman as Domestic Missionary: Urban Discipline and Popular Culture in Northern England 1850-1880', 9 (4), *Journal of Social History*, 481.

Summerson, H. (1983), 'The Early Development of the Pein Forte et Dure', in Ives, E. and Manchester, A. (eds), *Law, Litigants and the Legal Profession*, London: Royal Historical Society.

Taylor, P. (1864), *A Treatise on the Law of Evidence*, (4th edn.), London: Maxwell.

Teh, G.L. (1972), 'An Examination of the Judges' Rules in Australia', 46, *Australian Law Journal*, 489.

Teh, G.L. (1973), 'The Criminal Suspect's Right to Silence: A Hallowed Shibboleth', 4, *University of Tasmania Law Review*, 113.

Thayer, J.B. (1898), *A Preliminary Treatise on Evidence at the Common Law*, Boston: Little, Brown.

Thomas, D.A. (1964), 'The Revised Judges' Rules', 4 (4), *British Journal of Criminology*, 383.

Thomas, T. (1987), 'The Confait Confessions', 3 (3), *Policing*, 214.

Thompson, D. (1967), 'Questioning: A Comment', *Criminal Law Review*, 94.

Thompson, E.P. (1975), *Wigs and Hunters: The Origin of the Black Act*, London: Alan Lane.

*Tribunal of Inquiry in Regard to the Interrogation by the Police of Miss Savidge* (1928) Cmnd. 3147.

Usher, R.G. (1913), *The Rise and Fall of the High Commission*, Oxford: Clarendon.

Van Caenegem, R.C. (1973), *The Birth of the English Common Law*, (2nd edn., 1988), Cambridge: Cambridge University Press.

Veall, D. (1970), *The Popular Movement for Law Reform, 1640-1660*, Oxford: Clarendon.

Vennard, J. (1984), 'Disputes Within Trials Over the Admissibility and Accuracy of Incriminating Statements', *Criminal Law Review*, 15.

Vincent, H. (1931), *Vincent's Police Code and General Manual of the Criminal Law*, (17th edn.), London: Butterworth.

Walkley, J. (1987), *Police Interrogation, a handbook for investigators*, London: Police Review.

Weinberger, B. (1991), 'Are the Police Professionals? An Historical Account of the Police Institution', in Emsley, C. and Weinberger, B. (eds), *Policing in Western Europe*, London; Greenwood.

Wells, C.I. (1911), 'Origin of the petty jury', 27, *Law Quarterly Review*, 347.

Whitaker, B. (1964), *The Police*, London: Eyre Methuen.

Whitaker, B. (1979), *The Police in Society*, London: Eyre Methuen.

Wigmore, J.H. (1891), 'Nemo Tenetur Prodere Seipsum', 5, *Harvard Law Review*, 71.

Wigmore, J.H. (1902), 'The Privilege Against Self-Incrimination; Its History', 15, *Harvard Law Review*, 610.
Wigmore, J.H. (1940-1979), *A Treatise on the Anglo-American System of Evidence in Trials at Common Law*, 10 Vols., (vol. 3, revised by Chadbourn, J.H. (1970); vol. 8, revised by McNaughton, J.T. (1961)), Boston: Little, Brown.
Williams, C. (1960), 'Questioning by the Police: Some Further Points - 2', *Criminal Law Review*, 352.
Williams, C. (1983), 'Judicial Discretion in Relation to Confessions', 3, *Oxford Journal of Legal Studies*, 222.
Williams, E. (1914), 'The Modern View of Confessions', 30, *Law Quarterly Review*, 292.
Williams, G. (1955), 'Evidence Obtained by Illegal Means', *Criminal Law Review*, 339.
Williams, G. (1960a), 'Questioning by the Police: Some Practical Considerations', *Criminal Law Review*, 325.
Williams, G. (1960b), 'The Privilege Against Self-Incrimination Under Foreign Law: England', 51, *Journal of Criminal Law, Criminology and Police Science*, 166.
Williams, G. (1961), 'Police Interrogation in England' 52, *Journal of Criminal Law Criminology and Police Science*, 50.
Williams, G. (1963), *The Proof of Guilt*, (3rd edn.), London: Stevens.
Williams, G. (1979), 'The Authentication of Statements to the Police', *Criminal Law Review*, 6.
Williams, G. (ed) (1951), *The Reform of the Law*, London: Victor Gollancz.
Williamson, T.M. (1992), 'Investigative Interviewing', 8(4), *Policing*, 286.
Woffinden, B. (1987), *Miscarriages of Justice*, London: Hodder & Stoughton.
Wolchover, D. (1981), 'Cross-Examination of the Accused on his Record when a Confession is Denied or Retracted', *Criminal Law Review*, 312.
Wolchover, D. and Heaton-Armstrong, A. (1991), 'The Questioning Code Revamped', *Criminal Law Review*, 232.
Zander, M. (1972), 'Access to a solicitor in the police station', *Criminal Law Review*, 342.
Zander, M. (1974), 'The CLRC Evidence Report - A Survey of Reactions', 71, *Law Society's Gazette*, 954.
Zander, M. (1977), 'The Criminal Process - a subject ripe for a major inquiry', *Criminal Law Review*, 249.
Zander, M. (1979), 'The investigation of crime: a study of cases tried at the Old Bailey', *Criminal Law Review*, 203.
Zellick, G. (1984), 'The Purpose Behind an Arrest', *Criminal Law Review*, 94.
Zuckerman, A.A.S. (1973), 'Criminal Law Revision Committee 11th Report, Right of Silence', 36, *Modern Law Review*, 509.
Zuckerman, A.A.S. (1989), *The Principles of Criminal Evidence*, Oxford: Clarendon.

# Index

Act of Supremacy 1558  27
*actus reus*  211
Administration of Justice (Miscellaneous Provisions) Act 1933
  21n, 59n
Alverstone, Lord  127
ancient modes of proof  11, 13, 19
*Articuli Cleri* statute  25, 32
Assize of Clarendon 1166  13-4, 43,
  45
Assize of Northamption 1176  13-4,
  43, 45

Bacon, Sir Francis  32
bail bargaining  185
bail statute  49-50 *see also* Marian
  statutes
*Baldry* (1852)  71, 83, 85, 91, 114
Baldwin, J.  162, 163, 188, 221, 222,
  253
Baldwin, J.F.  25
Barnes, T.G.  35
*Bass* (1953)  163
Beard, C.A.  43, 47, 48
behavioural divide  188, 283, 286
Bellamy, J.  44, 46, 48
*Berriman* (1854)  88
*Best* (1909)  127
'Birmingham Six'  1
*Bodkin* (1863)  110
*Booth and Jones* (1910)  108
*Brackenbury* (1893)  111, 114
Brampton, Lord  125, 126, 127, 128,
  134

Bridges, L.  288

'Bridgewater Four'  1
Brown, D.  288
burden of proof  298-10
Butler, R. M.  140

*Cass* (1784)  69
Charles I  33
*Cheverton* (1862)  89
*Christie* v. *Leachinsky* (1947)  143
Coke, Sir Edward  28, 30
committal papers  4, 161
committal statute  50-3 *see also*
  Marian statutes
common law courts  23-4, 26, 31-2
compurgation oath  13, 24
conciliar courts  26, 32, 36
Confait, Maxwell
  case  217
confessions
  corroboration, and  1, 28, 140,
    217, 220, 222,
  exclusion of *see* exclusionary
    rule
  extra-judicial  5-6, 51, 64, 68,
    76, 116-18, 125-6, 128, 133,
    301, 308, 310
  false  86, 140, 176, 293
  meaning of  6n
  status of  1-2, 4-6, 11, 18-20, 24,
    31-2, 53, 55, 300-1, 308
*Cook* (1918)  130

County and Borough Police Act 1856  83
crime control
  considerations of  4, 43-4, 46, 49, 54, 98-9, 109-10, 130, 138, 140, 216, 304
Criminal Appeal Act 1907  119n, 145n
criminal argot  175, 283, 286
Criminal Evidence Act 1898  40n, 75, 249n, 252n, 300
Criminal Justice Act 1948  21n, 59n
Criminal Justice and Public Order Act 1994  241, 248n, 252n
Criminal Law Revision Committee 1972  214n, 216-17
custodial interrogations *see* interrogations; police interrogations
custody  106-8, 125, 127, 128, 132, 134-7, 142

defendants
  testimonial incompetency of  40n, 64-5, 74-5, 300
Devlin, Lord  1, 137, 142, 303, 306
disciplinary principle  76, 90, 106, 108, 110, 222, 301
due process
  considerations of  43-4, 46, 54, 98-99, 107, 109-10, 216, 304

early juries  3, 12, 14-20, 298 *see also* petit jury trial; presenting jury; trial by jury
  self-informing nature of  41-2, 48, 52, 298
Early, T.  134
ecclesiastical courts  25, 26, 27, 29, 32, 35
Edward III  25, 42
Edward VI  27

Elizabeth I  27, 29
Elliot, D.W.  125
Evans, R.  291
Evans, Timothy  140
  case  153-4n
*ex officio* oath  12, 24-5, 27-29, 32-35, 45, 299 *see also* inquisitorial oath
examining justices  43-52 *see also* justices of the peace
exclusionary rule
  common law  66-77, 86-88, 91, 105, 108-3, 116-7, 125, 128-31, 222, 300-301 *see also* voluntariness requirement
  statutory  2, 7n, 224, 251n, 307, 311n
expletives  283, 286
extra-judicial confessions *see* confessions
extra-judicial interrogations *see* interrogations; police interrogations

factual guilt  140, 164 *see also* legal guilt
Felton, John
  case  28-9
Fisher Report 1977  217-19
Fisher, Sir Henry  218
Fortescue, Sir John  28
Foster, H.  14
Fourth Lateran Council  14, 24
Fry, T.P.  117

*Gavin* (1885)  111, 114, 127
Gilbert, G.  67
Gooderson, R.M.  141
grand jury *see* presenting jury; early juries
'Guilford Four'  1

Henry II  12, 13
Henry III  15
Henry VII  46
Henry VIII  27, 46
hierarchy of credibility  171
High Commission Court  27-8, 29, 33, 35, 53, 55, 299
*Histed* (1898)  114
Holdsworth, W.S.  50
Home Office Committee Report on identification evidence 1976  195

*Ibrahim* (1914)  113, 131
Indictable Offences Act 1848  77n, 84-7, 89-90, 94-98, 107, 133
*Inquisitio*  12, 18, 23, 24, 26
inquisitorial oath  12, 25-7, 32-3, 36 55, 301 *see also* ex officio oath
inquisitorial procedures  3, 23-36, 42, 46-7, 54, 63, 65, 299-300, 306, 309
interrogations
 extra-judicial  1-3, 45, 52, 55, 63, 84, 87-100, 107-8, 110, 219
 judicial  24, 31, 35-36, 65-6, 133
 police *see* police interrogations
 custodial *see* police interrogations

Jardine, D.  17, 28
*Johnston* (1864)  91, 105, 117
Judges' Rules  4, 7n, 127-43, 145-6n, 159-61, 163-4, 189, 188, 204, 215, 218, 220-1, 304-305, 307, 309
judicial interrogations *see* interrogations; police interrogations
jury of presentment *see* early juries; presenting jury

justices of the peace  3, 36, 41-54, 84, 133, 300 *see also* magistrates

Kaufman, F.  75
*Knight and Thayre* (1905)  114

*Lambe* (1791)  70, 92
Langbein, J.H.  17-18, 49
Leadam, I.S.  25
leading questions  254-5, 260, 289-90
legal closure questions  256, 289-90
legal guilt  164, 186 *see also* factual guilt
Levy, L.W.  26, 53, 64, 65, 66
Lidstone, K.  134
Lilburn, John
 case  33-5
*Lloyd* (1934)  74

MacDermott, Lord  17
Magistrates' Court Act 1980  193n
Magistrates' Court Act 1952  193n
magistrates  63, 85, 87, 92, 96, 109, 133 *see also* justices of the peace
'Maguire Seven'  1
Maitland, F.W.  13, 14
*Male and Cooper* (1893)  112
Marian statutes  49-54, 70, 83, 92, 133 *see also* bail statute; committal statute
Mark, Sir Robert  217, 218
Mary I  27, 49
Mayne, R.  159
McConville, M.  162, 163, 188, 221, 222, 253, 291
McCormick, C.T.  128
McNee, Sir David  218
*mens rea*  211
Metropolitan Police Act 1829  83
*Mick* (1863)  90
*Miller* (1895)  107

Mirfield, P. 68, 71, 75
miscarriages of justice 1, 6, 195
*Mohammed-Holgate* v. *Duke* (1983) 304
Moreland, R. 66
Morgan, E. 32
Moston, S. 291

Neasey, F.M. 130
negotiated bail *see* bail bargaining
*nemo teneture produre seipsum* 32, 118, 299, 301 *see also* privilege against compulsory self-incrimination; right to silence
'new' police 54, 63, 83-4, 89, 113, 125, 131, 133, 160, 301, 304
Norman Conquest 11-13, 41

oaths *see* compurgation oath; *ex officio* oath; inquisitorial oath
Offences Against the Person Act 1861 293n
ordeal 11, 13, 14, 15, 16, 19, 24, 297

Peel, Sir Robert 159
*peine forte et dure* 17-18, 298
petit jury trial 11, 14-20, 35, 41, 50, 52, 298 *see also* early juries; trial by jury
  consent to 15-9, 298
*Pettit* (1850) 85
Philips, Sir Cyril 219
Police and Criminal Evidence Act 1984 1, 128, 160, 215, 223, 297
  Codes of Practice 1, 4, 224, 247, 284
  history 215-23
police interrogations
  forms of questioning in 254-6
  legal advice in 139, 163-4, 265

281n, 287-9, 291
private nature of 161, 188-9, 284, 301
psychological pressures in 189, 226, 244, 261, 269, 289-91, 301, 305, 307
purposes of 188, 253-4, 258, 304, 306, 309
recording of 4, 5, 7n, 161-3, 177, 189, 192n, 220-5, 248n, 250n, 280, 284-7, 290, 292, 303, 305, 307, 309-10
techniques in 184-5, 254, 280, 283, 289-90, 306
police-suspect dynamic 2, 4, 5, 6, 213, 215, 225, 284
post-PACE images of detainees 225-47, 283-92
post-PACE images of police interrogations 256-80, 283-92 *see also* police interrogations
pre-PACE images of detainees 164-88, 283-92
pre-PACE images of police interrogations 196-213, 283-92 *see also* police interrogations
prerogative courts 23, 26, 29, 31-33, 35-6, 46, 53, 54, 63
presenting jury 3, 14-18, 24, 41, 44-6, 48, 52, 54, 297 *see also* early juries; petit jury trial; trial by jury
presumption of innocence 85, 184, 284, 300
*prison forte et dure* 17
Prisoners' Counsel Act 1836 75
privilege against compulsory self-incrimination 23-4, 35, 36, 52, 55, 63, 65, 66, 67, 71, 75, 88, 109-13, 117-19 133, 134, 219, 299, 301, 302, 309 *see also*

*nemo nemo teneture produre seipsum*; right to silence
*Pro-Camera Stellata* statute 29
Prosecution of Offences Act 1985 223, 301

Ratushny, E. 17
*Reason* (1872) 106
Reiner, R. 159-60
reliability principle 106, 301
research methods 5-6
right to silence 118, 138-9, 168, 217, 219, 241, 243, 244, 284
    inference from exercise of 216-17, 241, 252n
    caution as to 72, 75-6, 84-87, 89-90, 94-98, 105-7, 109, 110, 112-114 125, 127-129, 131-39, 167, 168, 217, 303
    pre-trial 36, 85, 105, 110, 118, 219, 241
    trial 36, 51-2, 85, 110, 219, 241
    *see also nemo teneture produre seipsum*; privilege against compulsory self-incrimination
*Rogers* v. *Hawkin* (1898) 107, 113
Rowan, C. 159
Royal Commission on Criminal Justice 1993 6n, 309-10
Royal Commission on Criminal Procedure 1981 219-24
Royal Commission on Police Powers and Procedure 1929 127, 132, 134, 310n
Royal Commission on the Police 1962 142, 161, 249n
royal prerogative 27, 29, 299 *see also* torture
*Rudd's Case* (1775) 68

Sanders, A. 288

Savidge, Miss 134
    inquiry into police interrogation of 149-50n
Sexual Offences Act 1956 245
Sheffield Police Appeal Inquiry 1963 292-3n
Smith, J.C. 143
Smith, Sir Thomas 28
*Spilsbury* (1835) 74
Star Chamber Court 29-31, 33, 34, 45, 53, 55, 299
Statute of Westminster 1275 16
Statute of Westminster 1285 42
Staunford, W. 18
Stephen, J.F. 54
Stephenson, G.M. 291
Summerson, H. 17

Taylor, P. 106
Thayer, J.B. 15
*Thompson* (1783) 69
*Thompson* (1893) 111
*Thornton* (1824) 80n
*Tonge's Case* (1662) 66
torture 3, 17-18, 23, 26-30, 35-6, 52, 55, 66-7, 299, 308-9
'Tottenham Three' 1
Treason Act 1696 64
trial by jury 12, 15, 17, 19, 24-5, 43, 46, 49, 298 *see also* early juries; petit jury trial
    consent to 15-9, 298
*Twelve Bishops' Trial* (1641) 35

Veall, D. 31
verbals 222-3
*Voisin* (1918) 129, 137, 138
voluntariness requirement 3-4, 55, 63-4, 67-77, 86-100, 105-119, 125, 128-3, 138, 141, 160, 219-22, 300-2, 309 *see also* exclusionary rule

*Warickshall* (1783) 69, 106, 117
*White's Case* (1741) 68
Wigmore, J.H. 25, 65, 68, 70-75, 86, 118
William I 24
*Williams* (1992) 295n

Williams, G. 137-140
*Wilson* (1817) 73
*Winkle* (1911) 132
*Yeovil Murder Case* (1877) 106

Zander, M. 163